MCSE: Windows Server 2003 Design Study Guide

Exam 70-298

OBJECTIVE	CHAPTER
CREATING THE CONCEPTUAL DESIGN FOR NETWORK INFRASTRUCTURE SECURITY BY GATHERING AND ANALYZING BUSINESS AND TECHNICAL REQUIREMENTS	
Analyze business requirements for designing security. Considerations include existing policies and procedures, sensitivity of data, cost, legal requirements, end-user impact, interoperability, maintainability, scalability, and risk. Objective	1
Analyze existing security policies and procedures; Analyze the organizational requirements for securing data; Analyze the security requirements of different types of data; Analyze risks to security within the current IT administration structure and security practices	1
Design a framework for designing and implementing security. The framework should include prevention, detection, isolation, and recovery.	2
Predict threats to your network from internal and external sources; Design a process for responding to incidents; Design segmented networks; Design a process for recovering services	2
Analyze technical constraints when designing security.	1
Identify capabilities of the existing infrastructure; Identify technology limitations; Analyze interoperability constraints.	1
CREATING THE LOGICAL DESIGN FOR NETWORK INFRASTRUCTURE SECURITY	
Design a public key infrastructure (PKI) that uses Certificate Services.	6
Design a certification authority (CA) hierarchy implementation. Types include geographical, organizational, and trusted; Design enrollment and distribution processes; Establish renewal, revocation and auditing processes; Design security for CA servers	6
Design a logical authentication strategy.	4, 6
Design certificate distribution; Design forest and domain trust models; Design security that meets interoperability requirements; Establish account and password requirements for security	4, 6

SYBEX

SYBEX

NOTE   Exam objectives are subject to change at any time without prior notice and at Microsoft's sole discretion. Please visit Microsoft's web site (www.microsoft.com/learning) for the most current listing of exam objectives.

SYBEX

MCSE:
Windows Server 2003
Network Security Design
Study Guide

MCSE:
Windows® Server 2003
Network Security Design
Study Guide

Brian Reisman

Mitch Ruebush

San Francisco • London

SYBEX

Associate Publisher: Neil Edde
Acquisitions Editor: Maureen Adams
Developmental Editor: Jeff Kellum
Production Editor: Elizabeth Campbell
Technical Editors: Kevin Lundy, Warren Wyrostek
Copyeditor: Judy Flynn
Compositor and Graphic Illustrator: Happenstance Type-O-Rama
CD Coordinator: Dan Mummert
CD Technician: Kevin Ly
Proofreaders: Laurie O'Connell, Nancy Riddiough
Indexer: Lynnzee Elze
Book Designers: Bill Gibson and Judy Fung
Cover Designer: Archer Design
Cover Photographer: Photodisc and Victor Arre

Library of Congress Card Number: 2003115675

ISBN: 0-7821-4329-6

Screen reproductions produced with FullShot 99. FullShot 99 © 1991-1999 Inbit Incorporated. All rights reserved.

FullShot is a trademark of Inbit Incorporated.

The CD interface was created using Macromedia Director, COPYRIGHT 1994, 1997-1999 Macromedia Inc. For more information on Macromedia and Macromedia Director, visit http://www.macromedia.com.

Microsoft ® Internet Explorer © 1996 Microsoft Corporation. All rights reserved. Microsoft, the Microsoft Internet Explorer logo, Windows, Windows NT, and the Windows logo are either registered trademarks or trademarks of Microsoft Corporation in the United States and/or other countries.

SYBEX is an independent entity from Microsoft Corporation, and not affiliated with Microsoft Corporation in any manner. This publication may be used in assisting students to prepare for a Microsoft Certified Professional Exam. Neither Microsoft Corporation, its designated review company, nor SYBEX warrants that use of this publication will ensure passing the relevant exam. Microsoft is either a registered trademark or trademark of Microsoft Corporation in the United States and/or other countries.

TRADEMARKS: SYBEX has attempted throughout this book to distinguish proprietary trademarks from descriptive terms by following the capitalization style used by the manufacturer.

The author and publisher have made their best efforts to prepare this book, and the content is based upon final release software whenever possible. Portions of the manuscript may be based upon pre-release versions supplied by software manufacturer(s). The author and the publisher make no representation or warranties of any kind with regard to the completeness or accuracy of the contents herein and accept no liability of any kind including but not limited to performance, merchantability, fitness for any particular purpose, or any losses or damages of any kind caused or alleged to be caused directly or indirectly from this book.

Manufactured in the United States of America

10 9 8 7 6 5 4 3 2 1

SYBEX

To Our Valued Readers:

Thank you for looking to Sybex for your Microsoft Windows 2003 certification exam prep needs. We at Sybex are proud of the reputation we've established for providing certification candidates with the practical knowledge and skills needed to succeed in the highly competitive IT marketplace. Sybex is proud to have helped thousands of Microsoft certification candidates prepare for their exams over the years, and we are excited about the opportunity to continue to provide computer and networking professionals with the skills they'll need to succeed in the highly competitive IT industry.

With its release of Windows Server 2003, and the revised MCSA and MCSE tracks, Microsoft has raised the bar for IT certifications yet again. The new programs better reflect the skill set demanded of IT administrators in today's marketplace and offers candidates a clearer structure for acquiring the skills necessary to advance their careers.

The authors and editors have worked hard to ensure that the Study Guide you hold in your hand is comprehensive, in-depth, and pedagogically sound. We're confident that this book will exceed the demanding standards of the certification marketplace and help you, the Microsoft certification candidate, succeed in your endeavors.

As always, your feedback is important to us. Please send comments, questions, or suggestions to support@sybex.com. At Sybex we're continually striving to meet the needs of individuals preparing for IT certification exams.

Good luck in pursuit of your Microsoft certification!

Neil Edde
Associate Publisher—Certification
Sybex, Inc.

To my Family, supporting me as always: Tami, Thatcher, and Collin whom I cannot live without. I would also like to dedicate this work to my father for never giving up in his fight with cancer.
—Brian

To my loving wife, Jennifer, and my son and daughter, Elliott and Avery, whom I adore. I love you and I am sure you are delighted to have me back.
—Mitch

Acknowledgments

I would like to extend my enormous appreciation for everyone who worked on this book: our Acquisitions Editor: Maureen Adams for putting this whole thing together, our Production Editor: Elizabeth Campbell for keeping the project running and being so understanding with all of my "distractions" during the process, our Editor: Judy Flynn who made our sentences coherent, the folks who put together the CD test engine: Dan Mummert and Kevin Ly, and last and certainly not least our Developmental Editor: Jeff Kellum who has become more than an editor in my eyes, rather a friend. He's tough when he needs to be and supportive all of the time. I don't think I could have made it through all of this without him always there... Thanks Jeff!

I would, of course, like to thank my friends and family for putting up with(out) me during the majority of the process: Tami, my wife, and the bravest woman I know, Thatcher, the sweetest 5 year-old in the world, and his little brother Collin who just sat up this morning for the first time. I'd also like to thank my Mom and Dad, Alice and Joel Reisman, who were very understanding of all of the times I couldn't make it over to visit, My in-laws, Jim and Kay Fuglie, for just being wonderful people and grandparents and always there to help.

—Brian Reisman

We would like to acknowledge all the people without whose hard work and patience this book would not have been possible. The staff at Sybex, including Judy Flynn, Maureen Adams, Elizabeth Campbell, Jeff Kellum as our Editors. We would also like to thank our technical editors, Kevin Lundy and Warren Wyrostek, who reviewed the chapters and provided valuable feedback to make it a better book. We would also like to thank Dan Mummert and Kevin Ly for their work on valuable CD resource provided with this book.

I would like to thank my family: my wife Jenn, who has been very supportive but says I should never write a book again. My three year old son Elliott, who just really wants to play, and my 7 month old daughter, Avery, who wanted to participate and helped me write some of the book (these parts were later edited out). I love you all.

—Mitch Ruebush

Contents at a Glance

Contents

Table of Design Scenarios

Introduction

Microsoft's Microsoft Certified Systems Administrator (MCSA) and Microsoft Certified Systems Engineer (MCSE) tracks for Windows Server 2003 are the premier certifications for computer industry professionals. Covering the core technologies around which Microsoft's future will be built, this program provides powerful credentials for career advancement.

This book has been developed to give you the critical skills and knowledge you need to prepare for one of the core design requirements of the MCSE certification in the Windows Server 2003 track: Designing Security for a Microsoft Windows Server 2003 Network (70-297).

The Microsoft Certified Professional Program

Since the inception of its certification program, Microsoft has certified almost 1.5 million people. As the computer network industry increases in both size and complexity, this number is sure to grow—and the need for proven ability will also increase. Companies rely on certifications to verify the skills of prospective employees and contractors.

Microsoft has developed its Microsoft Certified Professional (MCP) program to give you credentials that verify your ability to work with Microsoft products effectively and professionally. Obtaining your MCP certification requires that you pass any one Microsoft certification exam. Several levels of certification are available based on specific suites of exams. Depending on your areas of interest or experience, you can obtain any of the following MCP credentials:

Microsoft Certified Desktop Support Technician (MCDST) This is the most recent offering by Microsoft. The program targets individuals with very little computer experience. The only prerequisite Microsoft recommends is that you have experience using applications that are included with Windows XP, including Microsoft Internet Explorer and Outlook Express. You must pass a total of two exams to obtain your MCDST.

Microsoft Certified Systems Administrator (MCSA) on Windows Server 2003 The MCSA certification is the newest administrator certification track from Microsoft. This certification targets system and network administrators with roughly 6 to 12 months of desktop and network administration experience. The MCSA can be considered the entry-level networking certification. You must take and pass a total of four exams to obtain your MCSA. Or, if you are an MCSA on Windows 2000, you can take one Upgrade exam to obtain your MCSA on Windows Server 2003.

Microsoft Certified Systems Engineer (MCSE) on Windows Server 2003 This certification track is designed for network and system administrators, network and system analysts, and technical consultants who work with Microsoft Windows XP and Server 2003 software. You must take and pass seven exams to obtain your MCSE. Or, if you are an MCSE on Windows 2000, you can take two Upgrade exams to obtain your MCSE on Windows Server 2003.

Microsoft Certified Application Developer (MCAD) This track is designed for application developers and technical consultants who primarily use Microsoft development tools. Currently, you can take exams on Visual Basic .NET or Visual C# .NET. You must take and pass three exams to obtain your MCSD.

MCSE versus MCSA

In an effort to provide those just starting off in the IT world a chance to prove their skills, Microsoft introduced its Microsoft Certified Systems Administrator (MCSA) program.

Targeted at those with less than a year's experience, the MCSA program focuses primarily on the administration portion of an IT professional's duties. Therefore, there are certain Windows exams that satisfy both MCSA and MCSE requirements, namely exams 70-270, 70-290, and 70-291.

Of course, it should be any MCSA's goal to eventually obtain his or her MCSE. However, don't assume that, because the MCSA has to take three exams that also satisfy an MCSE requirement, the two programs are similar. An MCSE must also know how to design a network. Beyond these three exams, the remaining MCSE exams require the candidate to have much more hands-on experience.

Microsoft Certified Solution Developer (MCSD)   This track is designed for software engineers and developers and technical consultants who primarily use Microsoft development tools. As of this printing, you can get your MCSD in either Visual Studio 6 or Visual Studio .NET. In Visual Studio 6, you need to take and pass three exams. In Visual Studio .NET, you need to take and pass five exams to obtain your MCSD.

Microsoft Certified Database Administrator (MCDBA)   This track is designed for database administrators, developers, and analysts who work with Microsoft SQL Server. As of this printing, you can take exams on either SQL Server 7 or SQL Server 2000. You must take and pass four exams to achieve MCDBA status.

Microsoft Certified Trainer (MCT)   The MCT track is designed for any IT professional who develops and teaches Microsoft-approved courses. To become an MCT, you must first obtain your MCSE, MCSD, or MCDBA, then you must take a class at one of the Certified Technical Training Centers. You will also be required to prove your instructional ability. You can do this in various ways: by taking a skills-building or train-the-trainer class, by achieving certification as a trainer from any of several vendors, or by becoming a Certified Technical Trainer through CompTIA. Last of all, you will need to complete an MCT application.

Microsoft recently announced two new certification tracks for Windows 2000: MCSA: Security and MCSE: Messaging. In addition to the core operating system requirements, candidates must take two security specialization core exams, one of which can be CompTIA's Security+ exam. MCSE: Security candidates must also take a security specialization design exam. As of this printing, no announcement had been made on the track for Windows Server 2003. Check out Microsoft's website at www.microsoft.com/traincert.com for more information.

How Do You Become Certified on Windows Server 2003?

Attaining an MCSA or MCSE certification has always been a challenge. In the past, students have been able to acquire detailed exam information—even most of the exam questions—from online "brain dumps" and third-party "cram" books or software products. For the new exams, this is simply not the case.

Microsoft has taken strong steps to protect the security and integrity of its certification tracks. Now prospective candidates must complete a course of study that develops detailed knowledge about a wide range of topics. It supplies them with the true skills needed, derived from working with Windows XP, Windows Server 2003, and related software products.

The Windows Server 2003 certification programs are heavily weighted toward hands-on skills and experience. Microsoft has stated that "nearly half of the core required exams' content demands that the candidate have troubleshooting skills acquired through hands-on experience and working knowledge."

Fortunately, if you are willing to dedicate the time and effort to learn Windows XP and Server 2003, you can prepare yourself well for the exams by using the proper tools. By working through this book, you can successfully meet the exam requirements to pass the Designing Security for a Microsoft Windows Server 2003 Network exam.

This book is part of a complete series of MCSE Study Guides, published by Sybex Inc., that together cover the core MCSE requirements, Please visit the Sybex website at www.sybex.com for complete program and product details.

MCSE Exam Requirements

Candidates for MCSE certification on Windows Server 2003 must pass seven exams, including one client operating system exam, four networking operating system exams, one design exam, and an elective.

 For a more detailed description of the Microsoft certification programs, visit Microsoft's Training and Certification website at www.microsoft.com/traincert.

You must take one of the following client operating system exams:

- Installing, Configuring, and Administering Microsoft Windows 2000 Professional (70-210)
- Installing, Configuring, and Administering Microsoft Windows XP Professional (70-270)

plus the following networking operating system exams:

- Managing and Maintaining a Microsoft Windows Server 2003 Environment (70-290)
- Implementing, Managing, and Maintaining a Microsoft Windows Server 2003 Network Infrastructure (70-291)
- Planning and Maintaining a Microsoft Windows Server 2003 Network Infrastructure (70-293)

- Planning, Implementing, and Maintaining a Microsoft Windows Server 2003 Active Directory Infrastructure (70-294)

plus one of the following design exams:

- Designing a Microsoft Windows Server 2003 Active Directory and Network Infrastructure (70-297)
- Designing Security for a Microsoft Windows Server 2003 Network

plus one of a number of electives, including:

- Implementing and Supporting Microsoft Systems Management Server 2.0 (70-086)
- Installing, Configuring, and Administering Microsoft Internet Security and Acceleration (ISA) Server 2000, Enterprise Edition (70-227)
- Installing, Configuring, and Administering Microsoft SQL Server 2000 Enterprise Edition (70-228)
- Designing and Implementing Databases with Microsoft SQL Server 2000 Enterprise Edition (70-229)
- Implementing and Managing Microsoft Exchange Server 2003 (70-284)
- Implementing and Administering Security in a Microsoft Windows Server 2003 Network (70-299)
- The design exam not taken as a requirement

    Also, if you are an MCSE on Windows 2000, you can take two Upgrade exams:

- Managing and Maintaining a Microsoft Windows Server 2003 Environment for an MCSA Certified on Windows 2000 (70-297)
- Planning, Implementing, and Maintaining a Microsoft Windows Server 2003 Environment for an MCSE Certified on Windows 2000 (70-294)

    In addition, if you are an MCSE in Windows NT, you do not have to take the client requirement, but you do have to take the networking operating system, design, and an elective exam.

Windows 2000 and Windows 2003 Certification

Microsoft recently announced that it will distinguish between Windows 2000 and Windows Server 2003 certifications. Those who have their MCSA or MCSE certification in Windows 2000 will be referred to as "certified on Windows 2000." Those who obtained their MCSA or MCSE in Windows Server 2003 will be referred to as "certified on Windows Server 2003."

Microsoft also introduced a more clear distinction between the MCSA and MCSE certifications by more sharply focusing each certification. In the new Windows 2003 track, the objectives covered by the MCSA exams relate primarily to administrative tasks. The exams that relate specifically to the MCSE, however, deal mostly with design-level concepts. So, MCSA job tasks are considered to be more hands-on, while the MCSE job tasks involve more strategic concerns of design and planning.

The Designing Security for a Microsoft Windows Server 2003 Network Exam

The Designing Security for a Microsoft Windows Server 2003 Network exam covers concepts and skills related to designing a secure Windows Server 2003 network. It emphasizes the following elements:

- Creating the conceptual design for network infrastructure security by gathering and analyzing business and technical requirements
- Creating the logical design for network infrastructure security
- Creating the physical design for network infrastructure security
- Designing an access control strategy for data
- Creating the physical design for client infrastructure security

This exam involves understanding the design decisions behind the security options in Windows Server 2003. You will need to understand what is important to the company in the Case Study and determine the best process, technology, and implementation of the technology to help solve the company's security issues. This exam is focused on what technology to use and where it should be used on the network. It is not focused on how to administer or specifically implement a security technology. Focusing on what the technology is, what problems it solves, and what else might be required to implement it is most helpful. Careful study of this book, along with hands-on experience, will help you prepare for this exam.

Microsoft provides exam objectives to give you a general overview of possible areas of coverage on the Microsoft exams. Keep in mind, however, that exam objectives are subject to change at any time without prior notice and at Microsoft's sole discretion. Please visit Microsoft's Training and Certification website (www.microsoft.com/traincert) for the most current listing of exam objectives.

Types of Exam Questions

In an effort to both refine the testing process and protect the quality of its certifications, Microsoft has focused its exams on real experience and hands-on proficiency. There is a greater emphasis on your past working environments and responsibilities and less emphasis on how well you can memorize. In fact, Microsoft says a certification candidate should have at least a year's worth of hands-on experience.

Microsoft will regularly add and remove questions from the exams. This is called *item seeding*. It is part of the effort to make it more difficult for individuals to merely memorize exam questions that were passed along by previous test-takers.

Microsoft will accomplish its goal of protecting the exams' integrity by regularly adding and removing exam questions, limiting the number of questions that any individual sees in a beta exam, and adding new exam elements.

Exam questions may be in a variety of formats: Depending on which exam you take, you'll see multiple-choice questions as well as select-and-place and prioritize-a-list questions. Simulations and Case Study–based formats are included as well. Let's take a look at the types of exam questions and examine the adaptive testing technique so you'll be prepared for all of the possibilities.

For more information on the various exam question types, go to www.microsoft.com/traincert/mcpexams/policies/innovations.asp.

Case Study–Based Questions

Case Study–based questions first appeared in the MCSD program and are prominent in the design-focused exams, including Designing Security for a Microsoft Windows Server 2003 Network. These questions present a scenario with a range of requirements. Based on the information provided, you answer a series of multiple-choice and select-and-place questions. The interface for Case Study–based questions has a number of buttons, each of which contains information about the scenario.

Multiple-Choice Questions

Multiple-choice questions come in two main forms. One is a straightforward question followed by several possible answers, of which one or more is correct. The other type of multiple-choice question is more complex and based on a specific scenario. The scenario may focus on several areas or objectives.

Select-and-Place Questions

Select-and-place exam questions involve graphical elements that you must manipulate to successfully answer the question. For example, you might see a diagram of a computer network, as shown in the following graphic taken from the select-and-place demo downloaded from Microsoft's website.

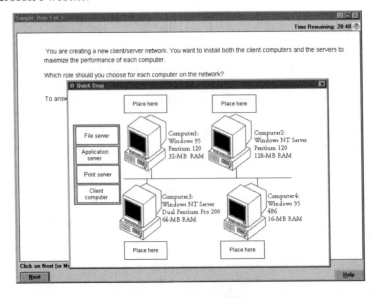

A typical diagram will show computers and other components next to boxes that contain the text "Place here." The labels for the boxes represent various computer roles on a network, such as a print server and a file server. Based on information given for each computer, you are asked to select each label and place it in the correct box. You need to place *all* of the labels correctly. No credit is given for the question if you correctly label only some of the boxes.

In another select-and-place problem you might be asked to put a series of steps in order by dragging items from boxes on the left to boxes on the right and placing them in the correct order. One other type requires that you drag an item from the left and place it under an item in a column on the right.

Simulations

Simulations are the kinds of questions that most closely represent actual situations and test the skills you use while working with Microsoft software interfaces. These exam questions include a mock interface on which you are asked to perform certain actions according to a given scenario. The simulated interfaces look nearly identical to what you see in the actual product, as shown in this example.

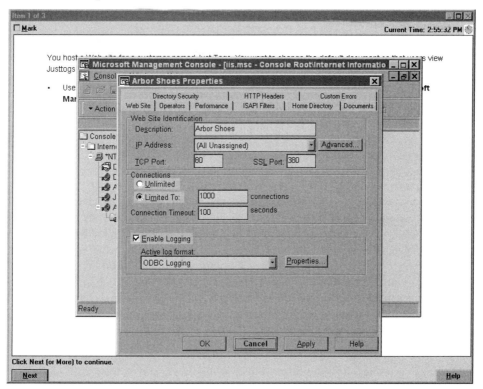

Because of the number of possible errors that can be made on simulations, be sure to consider the following recommendations from Microsoft:

- Do not change any simulation settings that don't pertain to the solution directly.

- When related information has not been provided, assume that the default settings are used.

- Make sure that your entries are spelled correctly.

- Close all the simulation application windows after completing the set of tasks in the simulation.

The best way to prepare for simulation questions is to spend time working with the graphical interface of the product on which you will be tested.

Exam Question Development

Microsoft follows an exam-development process consisting of eight mandatory phases. The process takes an average of seven months and involves more than 150 specific steps. The MCP exam development consists of the following phases:

Phase 1: Job Analysis Phase 1 is an analysis of all the tasks that make up a specific job function, based on tasks performed by people who are currently performing that job function. This phase also identifies the knowledge, skills, and abilities that relate specifically to the performance area being certified.

Phase 2: Objective Domain Definition The results of the job analysis phase provide the framework used to develop objectives. Development of objectives involves translating the job-function tasks into a comprehensive package of specific and measurable knowledge, skills, and abilities. The resulting list of objectives—the *objective domain*—is the basis for the development of both the certification exams and the training materials.

Phase 3: Blueprint Survey The final objective domain is transformed into a blueprint survey in which contributors are asked to rate each objective. These contributors may be MCP candidates, appropriately skilled exam-development volunteers, or Microsoft employees. Based on the contributors' input, the objectives are prioritized and weighted. The actual exam items are written according to the prioritized objectives. Contributors are queried about how they spend their time on the job. If a contributor doesn't spend an adequate amount of time actually performing the specified job function, his or her data is eliminated from the analysis. The blueprint survey phase helps determine which objectives to measure, as well as the appropriate number and types of items to include on the exam.

Phase 4: Item Development A pool of items is developed to measure the blueprinted objective domain. The number and types of items to be written are based on the results of the blueprint survey.

Phase 5: Alpha Review and Item Revision   During this phase, a panel of technical and job-function experts reviews each item for technical accuracy. The panel then answers each item and reaches a consensus on all technical issues. Once the items have been verified as being technically accurate, they are edited to ensure that they are expressed in the clearest language possible.

Phase 6: Beta Exam   The reviewed and edited items are collected into beta exams. Based on the responses of all beta participants, Microsoft performs a statistical analysis to verify the validity of the exam items and to determine which items will be used in the certification exam. Once the analysis has been completed, the items are distributed into multiple parallel forms, or *versions,* of the final certification exam.

Phase 7: Item Selection and Cut-Score Setting   The results of the beta exams are analyzed to determine which items will be included in the certification exam. This determination is based on many factors, including item difficulty and relevance. During this phase, a panel of job-function experts determines the *cut score* (minimum passing score) for the exams. The cut score differs from exam to exam because it is based on an item-by-item determination of the percentage of candidates who answered the item correctly and who would be expected to answer the item correctly.

Phase 8: Live Exam   In the final phase, the exams are given to candidates. MCP exams are administered by Prometric and Virtual University Enterprises (VUE).

Tips For Taking the Designing Security for a Microsoft Windows Server 2003 Network Exam

Here are some general tips for achieving success on your certification exam:

- Arrive early at the exam center so that you can relax and review your study materials. During this final review, you can look over tables and lists of exam-related information.

- Read the questions carefully. Don't be tempted to jump to an early conclusion. Make sure you know *exactly* what the question is asking.

- For questions you're not sure about, use a process of elimination to get rid of the obviously incorrect answers first. This improves your odds of selecting the correct answer when you need to make an educated guess.

Exam Registration

You may take the Microsoft exams at any of more than 1,000 Authorized Prometric Testing Centers (APTCs) and VUE Testing Centers around the world. For the location of a testing center near you, call Prometric at 800-755-EXAM (755-3926), or call VUE at 888-837-8616. Outside the United States and Canada, contact your local Prometric or VUE registration center.

Find out the number of the exam you want to take, and then register with the Prometric or VUE registration center nearest to you. At this point, you will be asked for advance payment for the exam. The exams are $125 each and you must take them within one year of payment. You can schedule exams up to six weeks in advance or as late as one working day prior to the date of the exam. You can cancel or reschedule your exam if you contact the center at least two working days prior to the exam. Same-day registration is available in some locations, subject to space availability. Where same-day registration is available, you must register a minimum of two hours before test time.

You may also register for your exams online at www.prometric.com or www.vue.com.

When you schedule the exam, you will be provided with instructions regarding appointment and cancellation procedures, ID requirements, and information about the testing center location. In addition, you will receive a registration and payment confirmation letter from Prometric or VUE.

Microsoft requires certification candidates to accept the terms of a Non-Disclosure Agreement before taking certification exams.

Is This Book for You?

If you want to acquire a solid foundation in designing security for a Windows Server 2003 network environment and your goal is to prepare for the exam by learning how to design a secure solution for a client using the new operating system, this book is for you. You'll find clear explanations of the fundamental concepts you need to grasp and plenty of help to achieve the high level of professional competency you need to succeed in your chosen field.

If you want to become certified as an MCSE, this book is definitely for you. However, if you just want to attempt to pass the exam without really understanding how Windows Server 2003 security works, this Study Guide is *not* for you. It is written for people who want to acquire hands-on skills and in-depth knowledge of Windows Server 2003 security design.

What's in the Book?

What makes a Sybex Study Guide the book of choice for over 100,000 MCPs? We took into account not only what you need to know to pass the exam, but what you need to know to take what you've learned and apply it in the real world. Each book contains the following:

Objective-by-objective coverage of the topics you need to know Each chapter lists the objectives covered in that chapter.

The topics covered in this Study Guide map directly to Microsoft's official exam objectives. Each exam objective is covered completely.

Assessment Test Directly following this introduction is an Assessment Test that you should take. It is designed to help you determine how much you already know about designing security for Windows Server 2003. Each question is tied to a topic discussed in the book. Using the results of the Assessment Test, you can figure out the areas where you need to focus your study. Of course, we do recommend you read the entire book.

Exam Essentials   To highlight what you learn, you'll find a list of Exam Essentials at the end of each chapter. The Exam Essentials section briefly highlights the topics that need your particular attention as you prepare for the exam.

Key Terms and Glossary   Throughout each chapter, you will be introduced to important terms and concepts that you will need to know for the exam. These terms appear in italic within the chapters, and a list of the Key Terms appears just after the Exam Essentials. At the end of the book, a detailed Glossary gives definitions for these terms, as well as other general terms you should know.

Review Questions, complete with detailed explanations   Each chapter is followed by a set of Review Questions that test what you learned in the chapter. The questions are written with the exam in mind, which means that they will cover the important topics with regard to the exam.

Case Study Questions, complete with detailed explanations   Each chapter also includes a Case Study that is similar in look and feel to the types of questions you will encounter on the design exams. The Case Study in each chapter is designed to test your knowledge of the topics covered in the chapter. Question types are the same as question types in the exam, including multiple choice, exhibits, and select-and-place.

Design Scenarios   Throughout the chapter, you will find scenario-based exercises that are designed to help you think about how you will use the information presented in the chapter in the context of a scenario. They present a Case Study and a few questions that help you think about how you will use the information in the chapter in designing a solution with the Microsoft products.

Real World Scenarios   Because reading a book isn't enough for you to learn how to apply these topics in your everyday duties, we have provided Real World Scenarios in special sidebars. These explain when and why a particular solution would make sense, in a working environment you'd actually encounter.

Interactive CD   Every Sybex Study Guide comes with a CD complete with additional questions, flashcards for use with an interactive device, and the book in electronic format. Details are in the following section.

What's on the CD?

With this new member of our best-selling MCSE Study Guide series, we are including quite an array of training resources. The CD offers bonus exams and flashcards to help you study for the exam. We have also included the complete contents of the Study Guide in electronic form. The CD's resources are described here:

The Sybex E-book for Windows Server 2003 Network Security Design   Many people like the convenience of being able to carry their whole Study Guide on a CD. They also like being able to search the text via computer to find specific information quickly and easily. For these reasons, the entire contents of this Study Guide are supplied on the CD, in PDF. We've also included Adobe Acrobat Reader, which provides the interface for the PDF contents as well as the search capabilities.

The Sybex Test Engine   This is a collection of questions that will help you prepare for your exam. The test engine features:

- Eight Bonus Case Studies designed to simulate the actual live exam. Each Bonus Case Study contains a scenario with 10 questions tied to each Case Study.

- All the Review and Case Study questions from the Study Guide, presented in a test engine for your review.

- The Assessment Test.

Here are two sample screens from the Sybex Test Engine:

Chapter Test: Chapter 2

Chapter 5 Case Study

On the actual Microsoft exam, you will likely be presented with a total of four Case Studies, each with a varying number of questions that correspond to that Case Study. Your grade will be cumulative of all four Case Studies.

Sybex MCSE Flashcards for PCs and Handheld Devices   The "flashcard" style of question offers an effective way to quickly and efficiently test your understanding of the fundamental concepts covered in the exam. The Sybex Flashcards set consists of more than 100 questions presented in a special engine developed specifically for this Study Guide series. Here's what the Sybex Flashcards interface looks like:

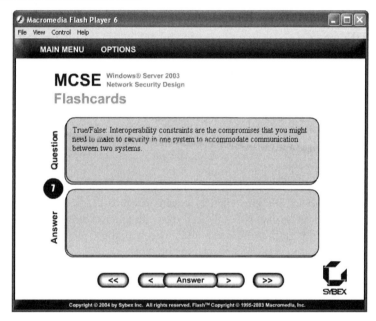

Because of the high demand for a product that will run on handheld devices, we have also developed a version of the flashcard questions that you can take with you on your Palm OS PDA (including the PalmPilot and Handspring's Visor).

How Do You Use This Book?

This book provides a solid foundation for the serious effort of preparing for the exam. To best benefit from this book, you may wish to use the following study method:

1. Take the Assessment Test to identify your weak areas.

2. Study each chapter carefully. Do your best to fully understand the information.

3. Read over the Design Scenarios and Real World Scenarios to improve your understanding of how to use what you learn in the book.

4. Study the Exam Essentials and Key Terms to make sure you are familiar with the areas you need to focus on.

5. Answer the Review and Case Studies at the end of each chapter. If you prefer to answer the questions in a timed and graded format, install the Sybex Test Engine from the book's CD and answer the questions there instead of in the book.

6. Take note of the questions you did not understand, and study the corresponding sections of the book again.

7. Go back over the Exam Essentials and Key Terms.

8. Go through the Study Guide's other training resources, which are included on the book's CD. These include electronic flashcards, the electronic version of the Review and Case Study questions, and the eight Bonus Case Studies.

To learn all the material covered in this book, you will need to study regularly and with discipline. Try to set aside the same time every day to study, and select a comfortable and quiet place in which to do it. If you work hard, you will be surprised at how quickly you learn this material. Good luck!

Hardware and Software Requirements

Most of the exercises in this book are scenario based, which means you will think about the results rather than actually perform steps using the software. Where we felt it would be appropriate to show you how a technology is implemented to clarify its use, we included some hands-on exercises. You will be able to work through the hands-on exercises in this book by using a server with Windows Server 2003 installed as a domain controller. If you desire to gain more experience with the products, then you will need to set up at two computers, one running Windows Server 2003 and one running Windows XP. This will allow you to use various management tools and services to manage security on the network.

You should verify that your computer meets the minimum requirements for installing Windows Server 2003. We suggest that your computer meet or exceed the recommended requirements for a more enjoyable experience.

Contacts and Resources

To find out more about Microsoft Education and Certification materials and programs, to register with Prometric or VUE, or to obtain other useful certification information and additional study resources, check the following resources:

Microsoft Training and Certification Home Page

www.microsoft.com/traincert

This website provides information about the MCP program and exams. You can also order the latest Microsoft Roadmap to Education and Certification.

Microsoft TechNet Technical Information Network

www.microsoft.com/technet

800-344-2121

Use this website or phone number to contact support professionals and system administrators. Outside the United States and Canada, contact your local Microsoft subsidiary for information.

Prometric

www.prometric.com

800-755-3936

Contact Prometric to register to take an MCP exam at any of more than 800 Prometric Testing Centers around the world.

Virtual University Enterprises (VUE)

www.vue.com

888-837-8616

Contact the VUE registration center to register to take an MCP exam at one of the VUE Testing Centers.

MCP Magazine Online

www.mcpmag.com

Microsoft Certified Professional Magazine is a well-respected publication that focuses on Windows certification. This site hosts chats and discussion forums and tracks news related to the MCSE program. Some of the services cost a fee, but they are well worth it.

Windows & .NET Magazine

www.windows2000mag.com

You can subscribe to this magazine or read free articles at the website. The study resource provides general information on Windows Server 2003, Windows XP, and Windows 2000 Server.

Cramsession on Brainbuzz.com

cramsession.brainbuzz.com

Cramsession is an online community focusing on all IT certification programs. In addition to discussion boards and job locators, you can download one of several free cram sessions, which are nice supplements to any study approach you take.

Assessment Test

1. The process of analyzing an organization's assets and determining what needs to be protected versus the cost of protecting the asset and the likelihood that it will be attacked is known as what?

   A. Security threat analysis

   B. Security cost analysis

   C. Security risk analysis

   D. Secure asset analysis

2. Which of the following is a document that explains what assets your organization needs to secure, how to secure them, and what to do if the security is compromised?

   A. Security brief

   B. Security documentation

   C. Security policy

   D. Security manual

3. Threats to the security of a network only come from external attackers.

   A. True

   B. False

4. In order to create a protected network segment, you could include which of the following firewall configurations in your network design? (Choose all that apply.)

   A. Back-to-back configuration

   B. Firewire configuration

   C. Bastion host configuration

   D. Switch configuration

   E. Three-pronged configuration

5. What is the purpose of the IP Security (IPSec) protocol with regard to security? (Choose all that apply.)

   A. It provides encryption of IP packets.

   B. It provides verification that the packets have not been changed in transit.

   C. It provides translation of packets through a firewall.

   D. It provides filtering of packets at the firewall.

6. What are the main vulnerabilities to data transmitted across the network? (Choose all that apply.)

   A. Network monitoring

   B. Identity spoofing

   C. Data modification (man-in-the-middle attack)

   D. Denial of service

7. What two techniques are used to determine if an account is allowed to access a resource? (Choose all that apply.)

   A. Authorization

   B. Replication

   C. Encryption

   D. Authentication

8. A Windows Server 2003 domain cannot trust a Windows NT 4 domain.

   A. True

   B. False

9. Which of the following class of user account pose the greatest threat to security?

   A. Normal user

   B. Power user

   C. Administrative user

   D. Temporary user

10. Trusts between domains within a single tree are transitive.

    A. True

    B. False

11. What feature does Active Directory enable that allows you to give users only the permissions that they require for a specific task?

    A. Encryption

    B. Impersonation

    C. Delegation

    D. Authorization

12. The Encrypting File System makes sure that data is encrypted when it is passed over a network.

    A. True

    B. False

13. What does the acronym PKI stand for?

   A. Public knowledge infrastructure

   B. Private key infrastructure

   C. Public key infrastructure

   D. Public key institution

14. What document is used to verify the identity of a machine or user?

   A. Signature

   B. Digital certificate

   C. Encryption

   D. Password

15. Which of the following is a method of authentication in Internet Information Server 6?

   A. Pluggable Authentication Module (PAM)

   B. Microsoft Passport .NET

   C. Extensible Authentication Protocol (EAP)

   D. MS-CHAPv2

16. What methods can be used update content on an IIS Server? (Choose all that apply.)

   A. WebDAV

   B. FTP

   C. FrontPage Server Extensions

   D. File shares

17. The Security Configuration And Analysis MMC snap-in is used to create and modify security templates.

   A. True

   B. False

18. Which of the following methods is the most appropriate to deploy security settings to a group of computers?

   A. Security Configuration And Analysis MMC snap-in

   B. Group Policy

   C. Local Policy MMC snap-in

   D. `secutil.exe`

19. What server role would be a candidate for the predefined `hisecws.inf` security template? (Choose all that apply.)

    A. Domain controller

    B. Database server

    C. Mail server

    D. Web server

    E. Global Catalog server

20. What technologies supported by Windows Server 2003 can be used to apply patches to a computer? (Choose all that apply.)

    A. Microsoft Windows Update website

    B. Software Update Services (SUS)

    C. Systems Management Server 2003

    D. Group Policy

21. In order to analyze the security patches that have been applied to a computer, you could use the Microsoft Baseline Security Analyzer (MBSA) utility.

    A. True

    B. False

22. What technology could you use so that employees can run only approved applications?

    A. Microsoft Baseline Security Analyzer (MBSA)

    B. Security Configuration And Analysis MMC snap-in

    C. Software restriction policy

    D. Software Update Services (SUS)

23. What technology provides a graphical remote terminal and can be used to securely manage a remote server as if you were sitting at the console?

    A. Secure Shell

    B. Telnet

    C. Remote Desktop for Administration

    D. Remote Assistance

24. What is the main security concern when using remote management tools to manage a server?

    A. Remote management tools allow data and passwords to pass unencrypted over the network.

    B. Remote management tools don't work over slow network connections.

    C. Remote management tools don't work through firewalls or secure routers.

    D. Remote management tools must use remote procedure calls.

Answers to Assessment Test

1. C. Security analysis is the first step in creating an effective security policy. First you determine the cost of the asset in business terms (actual loss, loss of productivity, competitive advantage) and then the risk (the likelihood that a threat would be carried out against the asset). For more information, see Chapter 1.

2. C. This type of document is called a security policy. You would create a security policy after analyzing the risks to the assets on your network. It helps you make decisions about what type of security to implement by defining what an organization's security goals are. For more information, see Chapter 1.

3. B. Vulnerabilities are actually more likely to come from within your organization rather than from outside of it. See Chapter 2 for more information.

4. A, C, E. Back-to-back configuration, three-pronged configuration, and bastion host are all ways to physically secure a network segment using one or more firewalls. Routers and switches do not typically provide this type of functionality. See Chapter 2 for more information.

5. A, B. IPSec provides for the encryption of data and for verification that the packets have not been changed in transit. It does not have anything to do with moving packets through a firewall or filtering packets, although IPSec can be filtered and have translation issues on a firewall. See Chapter 3 for more information.

6. A, B, C, D. All of the options are correct. If packets on a network are captured, their content could be revealed. Identity spoofing involves changing the source IP address, the From address on e-mail, or ICMP packets to fool the receiver. The modification of a packet in transit can make it hard to trust the information or can be used to fool servers into allowing access to privileged data. A denial of service attack involves sending a large volume of packets to a server or sending a special type of packet that will prevent legitimate users from accessing the resource. See Chapter 3 for more information.

7. A, D. Authentication is determining the identity of the account, and authorization is then determining what that account is permitted to access. Replication and encryption do not provide this functionality. See Chapter 4 for more information.

8. B. A trust relationship can be created between a Windows Server 2003 domain and a Windows NT 4 domain. See Chapter 4 for more information.

9. C. An account with administrative permissions will pose the greatest threat because it has the least restrictions on it. See Chapter 4 for more information.

10. A. Trusts between domains within a single tree are transitive. See Chapter 4 for more information.

11. C. Delegation is a feature provided by Active Directory that allows you to give a user explicit control over explicit resources. See Chapter 5 for more information.

12. B. The Encrypting File System keeps data encrypted on disk, not across the network. See Chapter 5 for more information.

13. C. PKI stands for public key infrastructure, which is a means of authenticating users through public and private key combinations and digital certificates. See Chapter 6 for more information.

14. B. You can use a digital certificate to validate a machine's or user's identity. It provides information about the machine or user and contains the signature of the root CA which you can trust or not. See Chapter 6 for more information.

15. B. You can use Microsoft Passport .NET authentication to authenticate with users' Passports, which allows them to have a single logon for the Internet sites that support Microsoft Passport. In addition to using Passport .NET authentication, you can use basic, integrated Windows (which supports NTLM and Kerberos authentication), digest, and forms-based authentication methods or using RADIUS. Extensible Authentication Protocol and MS-CHAPv2 are protocols used to authenticate a VPN or dial-up connection. PAM is a way of providing authentication on the Apache web server, a competitor to IIS. For more information, see Chapter 7.

16. A, B, C, D. All of these methods are available to update an IIS server. The appropriate method that you will use will depend on your security needs and the ease-of-use requirements of your content providers. It can also vary depending on the environment of the server (production, staging, development) and the tools in use. For more information, see Chapter 7.

17. B. The Security Settings MMC snap-in is used to create and modify security templates. The Security Configuration And Analysis MMC snap-in is used to analyze and apply templates. See Chapter 8 for more information.

18. B. The best technique to apply security settings is by setting the security on a Group Policy object and linking it to a container. Once you link the template settings to a GPO, the security settings will be refreshed automatically with Group Policy. See Chapter 8 for more information.

19. B, C, D. Domain controllers would use the `hisecdc.inf` security template instead of the `hisecws.inf` because it has built-in configuration settings for domain controllers. See Chapter 8 for more information.

20. A, B, C, D. All of the listed technologies can be used to apply patches to a computer. See Chapter 9 for more information.

21. A. The Microsoft Baseline Security Analyzer (MBSA) can be scheduled to audit several computers and report their security configuration as well as which critical patches have been applied. See Chapter 9 for more information.

22. C. Software restriction policies allow administrators to explicitly allow or deny software the ability to execute. See Chapter 9 for more information.

23. C. Remote Desktop for Administration is the most common mechanism used to manage Windows Server 2003. It provides secure mechanisms for authentication, and by default, 128-bit encryption is enabled for communications. For more information, see Chapter 10.

24. A. You should be concerned about the secure authentication mechanisms and encryption mechanisms provided by the tools. If a remote management tool does not provide these mechanisms, you should consider another tool or means of providing secure authentication and encryption. For more information, see Chapter 10.

Chapter

1

Analyzing Security Policies, Procedures, and Requirements

MICROSOFT EXAM OBJECTIVES COVERED IN THIS CHAPTER:

✓ **Analyze business requirements for designing security. Considerations include existing policies and procedures, sensitivity of data, cost, legal requirements, end-user impact, interoperability, maintainability, scalability, and risk.**

- Analyze existing security policies and procedures.
- Analyze the organizational requirements for securing data.
- Analyze the security requirements of different types of data.
- Analyze risks to security within the current IT administration structure and security practices.

✓ **Analyze technical constraints when designing security.**

- Identify capabilities of the existing infrastructure.
- Identify technology limitations.
- Analyze interoperability constraints.

Every day, your computer systems and the data they contain are at risk for theft, corruption, or misuse. These risks can come from, for example, malicious crackers outside your organization, internal personnel looking to profit from the data, or careless employees accidentally deleting data. The confidentiality, integrity, and availability of your data need to be protected. Before you can protect your data on a Windows Server 2003 network, you need to know what the policies, procedures, and requirements of the business are for security.

Securing a Windows Server 2003 network means you need to identify the assets that you need to protect, therefore allowing the business to continue to operate without disruptions caused by attackers or viruses. You will also need to evaluate the current security policies and practices to see if they are in line with the security needs of the business. These plans and procedures need to be evaluated and reevaluated as the use of the data and the network changes. This requires that the administrative staff and you understand technical constraints and design security that works within the constraints to meet the needs of the business. Finally, you will need to identify any technical constraints that will be a barrier to providing for the security requirements of the business and how you will overcome them.

In this chapter, you will learn how to evaluate the current IT security policies and procedures and analyze the organization's requirements for securing data. You will also learn how to evaluate risks of current IT practices with regard to security and how the current technologies and requirements of interoperability within the organization impact security.

Analyzing Security Risks

Security risk analysis is the process of reviewing the asset that needs to be protected versus the cost of protecting the asset and the likelihood that the asset will be attacked. The first thing you need to do in determining security risks is to determine what you are trying to protect. The resources you are trying to protect are usually referred to as *assets*. You can identify assets by using the following categories:

Hardware   This can be any type of computer hardware, such as servers, laptops, cables, routers, and switches.

Software   This includes the installed operating systems and applications, source code, and so forth.

Data   Data that needs to be protected includes private employee information, customer information, corporate secrets, and information about pending large transactions, and so on.

Documentation   This includes, for example, security policies and procedures, floor plans, network diagrams, change logs, audit logs, and web logs.

You need to list all assets that can be affected by a security incident in the organization. You should analyze each asset with regard to availability, integrity, and confidentiality to determine where it is at risk. For instance, suppose you run an e-commerce website that uses a SQL Server 2000 database that contains customers' personal information (like credit card numbers), their orders, and the catalog of products. In addition, the website is hosted on a Windows Server 2003 machine using Internet Information Server (IIS). You will need to look at each asset as follows:

Server hardware   If the physical server hardware is compromised then all other security precautions may be worthless. The physical security of the server or servers is important because without it most security can be compromised quickly.

Internet connection   If the Internet connection is compromised, the web application will be offline to customers. The integrity of the data passed over this connection needs to be maintained to prevent someone from changing the information in stream to or from the server. You need to ensure confidentiality of data (presumably credit card numbers and customers' personal information) that passes over the connection.

Internet Information Server (web server)   The web server needs to be protected because it is a great backdoor for attacks, especially if it is not patched. Also, the pages on the site and the code it runs could be defaced or changed. This could affect customer perception or personal information. Information moving through the web server will be confidential, so you'll need to take precautions with the connections to the database and the Internet.

SQL Server 2000   If the database is not working properly, the website will not be available. A database is prone to corruption or misuse, which can affect the integrity of the data. The data is important to the website, so the integrity of the database must be maintained. It would not be good for customer relations if someone manipulated the prices or customers' personal information. The database in this web application stores customers' personal information, so the confidentiality of the data is important.

Windows Server 2003   The server operating system provides applications running on it (IIS and SQL Server in this case), so it needs to be available for the applications to be available. Access to data must be controlled to maintain confidentiality and integrity if it is stored in the file system or Registry. This data usually includes the configuration information of the applications, without which they would not be available.

After you have determined the assets that are at risk, you will need to determine the threats to the assets and the likelihood of the threats being carried out. A *security threat* is anything that will prevent the availability, undermine the integrity, or breach the confidentiality of the asset. The following are some examples of threats to resources:

- A denial of service (DoS) attack on your web server is an example of a threat to the availability of the asset.

- A virus that corrupts data on the file system is a threat to the integrity of the asset.

- Improper application of network permissions that allows a user to access data on the file server is a threat to confidentiality.

We will address threats to specific technologies in the chapters in which the specific technologies are covered.

For example, viruses are really common on the Internet and through e-mail. This is a threat to almost all aspects of your organization's assets and is highly likely to occur. When you take into consideration that a virus has the potential to corrupt, steal, or prevent the availability of data, it's clear that virus protection would be a high priority in your security planning.

You can assess risks using varying approaches, but two of the most common are through quantitative analysis and qualitative analysis.

Quantitative analysis involves estimating the actual value of the asset or what it would cost if the asset was unavailable for a period of time or if it was lost. This kind of analysis is easier for the availability or integrity aspects of risk analysis. For example, you can set a price on the server hardware that might get stolen if the server room is not locked or how much business would be lost if the website were down. Confidentiality of data is more difficult to quantify because the data may be intellectual property, proprietary trade secrets, or private patient information. These assets don't have a definite monitory value but can cost you in terms of lawsuits or lost customers.

Qualitative analysis involves ranking the risks on a scale that reflects the resource's importance to your organization. You usually use two separate numbers for this process to give an accurate assessment of the importance of the resource and the likelihood of a threat being carried out against the resource. We use a scale of from 1 to 10 to put a number on the importance to the business and the chances that the threat will be carried out. We then multiply these numbers together to determine the ranking of the risk in relation to other risks. For example, an online business might assign a rank of 10 to both the importance of its website to the business and the likelihood of a denial of service attack launched against the site, resulting in a score of 100 for the risk. This would be one of the first security risks the organization would address with its available resources.

On the other hand, a small printing company might determine that its website contains only information about the products, services, and location and give it a ranking of 3 while the prospect of a denial of service attack would be given a ranking of 10, resulting in a score of 30 for the risk. This means the company might address other security risks first with its available resources.

You will need to determine the security risks and the likelihood that they will occur from information you have and information you obtain in interviews with key personnel in the organization. You should look at whether the risk has occurred before, because that makes it more likely to occur in the organization. Important risks can then be mitigated by subsequent security planning, as outlined in the next section.

Understanding Types of Attacks

You will need to understand the types of attacks on a network to determine if your systems and infrastructure are vulnerable:

Defenses against these types of attacks will be addressed when we discuss individual technologies in future chapters.

Spoofing   Changing the source information in a packet so that those at the destination cannot determine where it came from or to redirect the response to a request to a different device or to make traffic appear to be from a trusted party.

Man-in-the-middle   Capturing a packet in order to eavesdrop or change some of the information in it and sending it on to the server. Can be used to gain network authentication on some weaker authentication schemes.

Denial of service (DoS)   Sending such a large volume of traffic to a network device that it cannot keep up, changing routing tables or DNS entries, or otherwise affecting the network so legitimate clients cannot get to their network resources.

Replay   Capturing packets and then sending them to a server at a later time. Some protocols are susceptible to this attack if the packets aren't numbered somehow.

Packet sniffing   Using a program that captures packets crossing a device on the network. This type of attack can reveal any information that is weakly or not encrypted.

Social engineering   Using non-computer techniques to obtain passwords or other information about a company. This can involve sifting through trash or conning users into revealing their passwords.

Buffer overflow   Taking advantage of a common bug found in C/C++ programs (which include most services and operating systems). The programmer forgets to check the upper bounds of the data being stored in an array. This means that the attacker can enter data in such a way that it runs past the end of the array and into the same or another program's stack so that the overflow will be executed. In essence, this allows the attacker to insert their own information into your computer's memory, which means they can launch other applications or corrupt data. This is the mechanism that many of the worms use to infiltrate Windows systems. The only way you can guard against it as an administrator is by keeping your systems up-to-date with all critical hotfixes and patches, running only the minimal amount of services needed on the server, and not giving more permissions to the application than is absolutely necessary.

Mail relaying/Spamming   Using an e-mail server to send unsolicited e-mail.

Website vandalism   Altering a website with unauthorized material.

Physical attack   Compromising, vandalizing, or stealing hardware through unauthorized access.

Trojan horse   A program that allows an attacker to take over the host computer or watch what the user is doing.

Worm   A program that uses the Internet to propagate itself.

Virus   A benign or malicious program that self-propagates through other executable files.

Password cracking   Using a brute force dictionary attack (which is trying all possible combinations of passwords, using a dictionary of words and common names) or some weakness in the password encryption algorithm to figure out passwords.

In the "Analyzing Security Risks" Design Scenario, you will analyze the security risks that a company may face.

 **Design Scenario**

Analyzing Security Risks

Infinite Horizons relies on its website for 30 percent of its total orders. This accounts for $200,000 in sales a year, and it is important that the site is up 24/7 so customers don't go to competitors for similar products. Infinite Horizons collects customer information with each sale in a SQL Server 2000 database. Some employees need to use this information to process credit cards offline because Infinite Horizons does not have an online merchants account. Marketing generates reports on the customers and sales information to determine how to position Infinite Horizons's products. Personnel in marketing must not have access to customers' credit card information. In the past, this has occurred. Employees need access to files on an internal file server for their appropriate departments. Employees are also required to log onto the network and has a strong password policy in place.

1. **Question:** Identify the security risks for Infinite Horizons. **Answer:**

    - Denial of service attack on the web server

    - Unauthorized access to credit card information

    - Weak passwords

    - Unavailability of SQL Server

    - Unauthorized access to the file shares

2. **Question:** What are the two primary risks for Infinite Horizons? **Answer:**

    - Denial of service attack on the web server

    - Unauthorized access to credit card information

3. **Question:** Identify the kinds of attacks that can occur on Infinite Horizons. **Answer:**

    - Denial of service attack on the web server

    - Accidental deletion of data on the web server

    - Malicious defacing of the website

    - Physical destruction or theft of the web server or database server

    - Corruption of the SQL Server database

    - Improper access permissions on internal file servers

    - A worm or virus causing data loss or denial of service

- An attacker sniffing packets on the network

- An attacker using social engineering to gain passwords and user IDs from your employees

- Theft of credit card information or changing of prices of products

4. **Question:** How can you mitigate the risks listed in step 3? **Answer:**

Denial of service attack on the web server   Filter unwanted network traffic and employ intrusion detection of the firewall in front of the server. Notify appropriate staff if an attack is noticed because you will usually need to work with the ISP staff to solve this attack.

Accidental deletion of data on the web server   Apply the appropriate permissions to users of the web server to prevent users from deleting data. Make sure you limit access to accounts that can modify permissions to users without proper training from writing or modifying permissions. Make sure you have a current and good backup of the server to recover files if there is a problem. Also, make sure that auditing is enabled.

Malicious defacing of the website   Filter packets heading for your web server on the firewall to reduce the vulnerability footprint. You will need to verify permissions on the files on the web server. You should also filter the types of commands (verbs) that can be issued against your server.

Physical destruction or theft of the web server or database server   Secure the room and building the server is in. Planning for destruction via non-malicious means like a natural disaster can help mitigate this particular risk.

Corruption of the SQL Server database   You need to make sure your SQL Server database has the proper permissions, limit access of the account used to connect from the web server, and preventing SQL injection attacks in the web applications code to prevent corruption. You need to make sure you regularly and successfully back up the database server so you can restore a clean version if you need to.

Improper access permissions on internal file servers   Verify the permissions on the file servers and whether they meet requirements for securing these resources. You could run a baseline security analysis to verify the setup of the file servers.

A worm or virus causing data lose or denial of service   Virus scanning software and education of users will aid in preventing these attacks. If some were to get through, you should have a backup strategy to deal with the data loss.

An attacker sniffing packets on the network   You can thwart a sniffer by using encryption. Infinite Horizons would benefit from using SSL on its website.

An attacker using social engineering to gain passwords and user IDs from your employees   Educate your users about what is expected of them with regard to security.

After you have determined what resources and services are at risk in your organization, you will need to determine if the current security processes are adequate to protect them. This will also give you a clearer picture of what amount of security will give you an adequate return on your investment and whether you are overspending on protecting less-important resources.

Analyzing Existing Security Policies and Procedures

Securing resources in your organization is expensive because it involves additional infrastructure and personnel. In addition, it does not directly affect the bottom line (unless your business is security). In other words, security infrastructure is overhead. You will need to determine what resources need to be secured and whether it would be more cost efficient to protect some resources with an insurance policy. You can begin to determine if the current security is adequate or wasteful by analyzing the current practices in the organization. This information is usually defined in a document called a security policy.

Security policies explain what assets your organization secures, how they are secured, and what to do if the security is compromised. A security policy helps you make decisions about what type of security to implement by defining what an organization's security goals are. By doing so, you can determine what needs to be secured and at what level. You can also use the security policy to communicate these goals to users, administrative staff, and managers. If the organization does not have a security policy, you will need to create one.

After analyzing the risks to assets on a network, you will be able to evaluate and create security policies and procedures. You should create a security policy to ensure that efforts spent on security don't exceed the cost of recovering the assets should it be compromised. Security policies help you determine that your efforts are focused in a cost-effective and not overly burdensome manner to your organization. You need to make sure that the policies you implement adhere to government and industry regulations, so you may need to obtain legal council to verify compliance (HIPAA in the insurance industry or line monitoring in the financial industry, for example). You also need to make sure the policies adhere to the organization's culture and tolerance of procedures and policies, the exposure of resources to employees or customers, threats to the resources of the organization, and security requirements for these resources.

Security policies can be broken into two categories:

Standard security policies   *Standard security policies* are implemented organization wide and represent a baseline of security in the organization. All users must comply with them, and hardware or software can be used to make sure they are enforced and to ease the burden of the security policies on the user. For example, password policies may create difficult-to-crack passwords, but if users need to write the passwords down your policies may not be effective. These policies are required, and any security solution you propose will have to adhere to them. You may need to recommend a change to standard policies if necessary to implement a new service or application.

Recommended security policies   *Recommended security policies* may be necessary for only part of the organization. A division or department may choose to implement an optional security practice if they find it cost effective or determine it applies to their assets. You should take into account any recommended policies that apply to the part of the company you are trying to secure. Also remember that any new security policies you define might be candidates for recommended policies and should be shared with the organization.

Real World Scenario

Adjusting Security Policies to Comply with Government Regulations

One of our coworkers, Dave, recently received an assignment to evaluate a proposed database application for a pharmacy. They decided to create a database that would track the patients and the pharmaceuticals they purchased to make it easier to create internal reports and to address some regulations they have for tracking controlled substances. This reporting required a lot of paperwork and they had decided that automation was the answer.

The database and application was straightforward, but Dave needed to address the Health Insurance Portability and Accountability Act of 1996 (HIPAA). HIPAA requires that patient information be confidential. The pharmacy did not have a security policy that stated that applications need to be in compliance with government regulations. This entailed further discussions about how to bring the database into compliance with HIPAA.

The cost savings of the project need to be evaluated to account for the additional work to bring it into compliance with HIPAA. The project was put into a state of limbo while they reevaluated it and their security policies.

Security policies do not define the technologies used to implement them. This is intentional because their purpose is to define the goals of providing security to the organization. Security policies usually involve the following, as described in RFC 2196, *Site Security Handbook*:

Computer technology purchasing guidelines   Define the required or preferred security features on purchased technology. For example, if authentication in the organization is implemented through two-factor authentication (a form of authentication requiring a device and a password such as smart cards), then smart card readers are required for workstations and servers purchased.

Privacy policy   Defines a user's expectations for privacy with regard to network and phone communications.

Access policy   Defines the rights and permissions associated with resources to protect them from destruction or disclosure. The access policy could define guidelines for connecting to the network, for adding servers or new software to the network, and for notifying users of the policies.

Accountability policy   Defines the responsibilities of the users, administrators, and managers with regard to security incidents and auditing.

Authentication policy   Defines password policy and guidelines for trusted connections to the network.

Availability statement   Sets expectations for availability of resources by defining scheduled downtime, operating hours, and the time it would take to recover resources. This is useful in determining the amount of protection and effort to apply to preventing downtime due to security incidents.

System and network maintenance policy   Defines how internal and external administrators are allowed to maintain the network. You need to determine if remote maintenance is allowed and how it is implemented. This will be covered in more detail in Chapter 10, "Designing Secure Network Management."

Violations reporting policy   Defines what types of network security breaches or violations of security policies need to be reported and to whom.

Once you have defined the security policies for the organization, you will create security procedures to implement the policies. Security procedures define how to comply with policies and provide detailed steps that describe how to implement them. The procedures are where you will apply specific technologies, software, and hardware to the policies. The procedures for implementing security on the Windows Server 2003 family of products will be covered in the rest of this book.

    You can read the entire RFC 2196 at http://ietf.org/rfc/rfc2196.txt.

Security policies are great, but the process of creating a security policy document can be a waste of time if management doesn't enforce the policies or if users and administrators ignore them. Effective security policies have support from all employees in the organization. This means that all the key stakeholders—including management, technical staff, and legal council—should be involved in the process of developing them.

Management will provide the budget to implement the policies and the authority to enforce or provide incentives for employees to follow the policies. It is most important to get management buy-in or the security policies will be difficult to enforce. After all, security policies are an additional burden to the users of the system. For example, it would certainly be easier to use a network if we did not need to worry about passwords.

The technical staff will provide information about limitations of the current technology that is necessary to implement a policy. This is not to say that the policy will not be implemented due to technical limitations. Appropriate means can be used to determine the cost of the risk associated with the policy versus the cost of implementing the policy.

The legal council is involved to make sure the wording of policies is correct, to explain legal problems that may arise from enforcing policies, and to make sure policies include requirements due to regulation and to make sure laws and regulations are followed.

You also need to make sure that the policies don't include too much legal or technical jargon that would make them difficult to understand for both administrators and users. Security policies and procedures should be straightforward and be written in declarative sentences like "All employees must follow the password policy created by the network security group" or "No employee shall have illegal copies of software on their computer." You can then expound on the policy if necessary. You need to remember that policies that are too vague will result in interpretation by employees or, if they are too strict, that employees generally won't be able to do their jobs effectively. Such policies won't be supported by managers and will generally not be enforced.

The security policies (and later changes to them) should be easy to find. You should come up with a method of disseminating the information to the organization. E-mail, company intranet, bulletin

---

Real World Scenario

Pencils and Server Room Doors

A security policy often states that all servers must be in a physically secure server room. But being overly strict about this can cause employees to circumvent the policy to do their job. We were consulting at a credit card bank. The project was being developed on a test server that, due to various test cases, would hang up and need to be physically rebooted. Access was granted via swiping an employee's identification badge on the access pad by the server room door. The problem was that nobody on the development team was allowed into the server room, nor were we allowed to keep the server (even though it only contained test data) outside the server room. This meant that somebody else would have to reboot the computer, and since the server operators were busy with projects of their own, they would open the door and put a pencil in it so we could go back and forth at will without bugging them. This clearly opened the security room to a physical breech of security, but an inflexible and strict security policy that stated only server operators had access to the server room and all servers must be in the server room opened the door (no pun intended) to this kind of security circumvention in the name of productivity.

---

boards in employee lunch rooms, voicemail broadcast, employee reviews, and training programs are all great and varied ways to get the word out. Don't rely on one method because, for example, some employees never visit the intranet site or delete lots of e-mails without reading them.

Also make sure that the policies reflect current administrative practices, which will keep the policies from becoming outdated. Administrators will recognize when security policies are outdated and will deem them worthless. You need to make sure that they do not contain references to old technology or that they are for servers or networks that do not exist. You should make changing the policies part of the policies. You don't create security policies once; it is a constant work in progress as threats, data, or your organization change.

In the "Analyzing Security Policies and Procedures" Design Scenario, you will create the basis for a security policy for a company.

Enforcing Security Policies on Windows Server 2003

The process of creating security policies and procedures will allow you to produce documentation that contains the following:

- The procedures and policies for security in your organization.

- Configuration information and procedures for each server, component, device, and application you have on your network. This should be detailed information that would allow you to create an exact copy of the configurations of the system.

- Change management procedures that define the policies and procedures to follow when changes to the network are made. You would define who needs to know and what needs to be done when changing configuration settings, applying software updates, or applying hotfixes and services packs.

Design Scenario

Analyzing Security Policies and Procedures

The folks at Infinite Horizons pride themselves for maintaining the confidentiality of all customers' data; therefore, security is very important to them. They have implemented password policies and their internal network is protected by a firewall. They have had laptops stolen that contained customer data in the past. They have also had some internal security lapses where shares were assigned incorrect permissions and employees had access to confidential customer data. Infinite Horizons needs to protect data between its customers and its corporate headquarters.

1. **Question:** What are some items that should be included in the security policy for Infinite Horizons? **Answer:**

   - The customers' data must be confidential.

   - Employees must follow the password policy issued by the network administrative staff that includes maintaining complex passwords.

   - Employees must store customer data in a set of folders like a Customer Data folder or a subfolder with EFS enabled on their laptop computers to ensure that it is encrypted.

   - Employees should not be able to access the network data or documents that have not been approved for use for their job function.

   - Employees' actions should be recorded and audited to determine if access controls are adequate and if employees are complying with company policy.

All this will need to be applied to servers as they are built. They will also need to be reviewed regularly to determine if procedures are being followed by administrative staff. You will use the review process to address new threats not originally conceived of when the procedures were put in place. It is best if you schedule reviews to happen at regular intervals through the year.

A *security baseline* details the configuration procedures for each server, device, or application on your network. It contains the configuration of the operating system, settings for applications, permissions assignments, user accounts needed, and any additional settings needed to implement the security procedures. The security baseline is a tool that aids you in re-creating a server with the proper settings or in auditing a server at a later date to see if it is in compliance with the security procedures. It can be as simple as a checklist, or it can be a document that states the steps needed to configure a computer, or it can be something enforced in software (as you will see shortly). Implementing a security baseline can be tedious, so Windows Server 2003 contains the ability to automate the process of applying and auditing your security baseline.

You can apply baseline security at the domain level and the computer level. At the domain level, it involves the settings to all computers that are a member of the domain. This is a good place to implement account policies like password length and authentication types allowed. These settings will override the local computer settings throughout the domain and gives you control over policies in one place.

You can implement a security baseline at the computer level in Windows Server 2003 by using the Security Templates and Security Configuration And Analysis snap-ins, the Local Security Policy administrative tool, or Active Directory Group Policy. These tools allow you to create a new template file or modify one of the existing templates, apply it to the configuration of the server, and test to see if the computer is in compliance with a previously applied template.

The templates are rich in settings that you can apply to the computer. You can define what services are allowed, rights user have to the box, account policies, IPSec policies, and lots of other security settings.

To apply templates and verify the security base of a computer, follow these steps:

1. Log on to Windows Server 2003 if you have not done so already.

2. Click Start ≻ Run.

3. Type **mmc** in the Run dialog box to launch the Microsoft Management Console.

4. Click the File menu and choose Add/Remove Snap-in.

5. Click the Add button on the Add/Remove Snap-in dialog box, which opens the Add Standalone Snap-in dialog box.

6. Add the Security Configuration And Analysis and Security Template snap-ins to the console by clicking on the snap-in name and clicking the Add button.

7. Close the Add Standalone Snap-in dialog box.

8. Close the Add/Remove Snap-in dialog box. You will then see the security policy templates are now displayed in the MMC console.

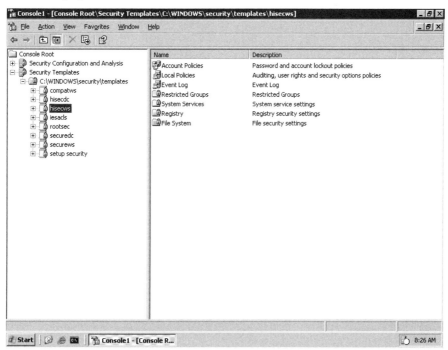

9. Expand the Security Templates console tree. This lists the templates currently installed in the security templates folder (usually located in `WINDOWS\security\templates`).

10. Expand the securedc template. You should see the nodes that you can use to set the security policies for this computer. These policies can be used as part of the security baseline.

11. Expand the Account Policies node and click Password Policy. Notice that there is a default setting for each password policy.

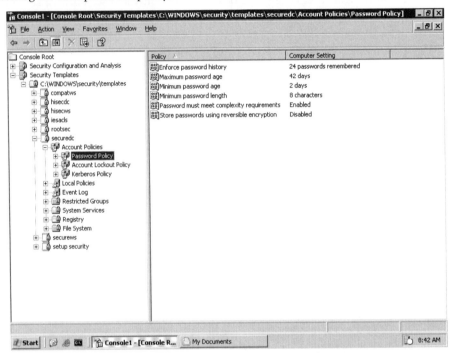

12. You can adjust these properties by double-clicking on the node and changing the value, but before you do, you should make a copy of the default template before you change it. To do this, right-click the securedc template and choose Save As. Type **DC Baseline** for the name of the template and click OK.

13. Open the DC Baseline template by double-clicking the DC Baseline node to expand the node.

Feel free to explore the options you have for setting up the security template. In this case, set a message for users attempting to log in. To do that, follow these steps:

1. Navigate to the Security Options node by expanding the securedc, then the Local Policies node, then the Security Options node.

2. Locate Interactive Logon: Message Text For Users Attempting To Log On in the details pane (the pane on the right listing all the options).

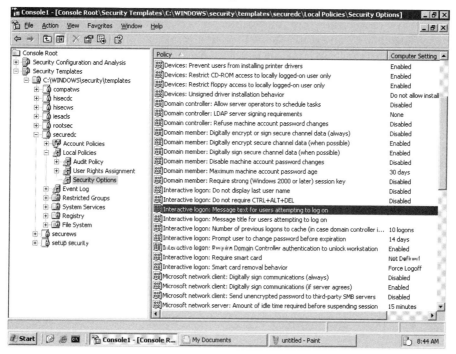

3. Double-click the option to open the Template Security Policy Setting dialog box.

4. Make sure the text box is checked and type the following message:

Unauthorized access to this server is prohibited.

Disconnect now if you have not been authorized to use this server.

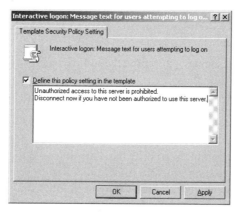

5. Save the template by right-clicking DC Baseline in the tree pane and choosing Save.

You can use security templates to define much more of the security baseline for this classification of servers by using security templates, such as which services are available on the box, Registry and file permissions, account and authentication settings, user rights, and so on.

The Security Configuration And Analysis snap-in is used to apply the template we just created and to later analyze an existing server to see if it is still in compliance with the settings in the template (this makes it easier for you to verify your security baseline for the server through automation). The following steps show you how to use it:

1. Right-click the Security Configuration And Analysis node in the tree pane and choose Open Database.

2. In the Open Database dialog box, name the new template database by typing **DC Baseline** in the File Name field and click OK.

3. The Import Template dialog box appears. Choose the DC Baseline template from the list and click OK. You have loaded the DC Baseline template into the DC Baseline database. You could bring other templates into this database also and apply them all if desired.

4. To configure the server with the template settings, you need to apply it. Right-click the Security Configuration And Analysis node and choose Configure Computer Now.

5. Click OK to accept the default log path in the Choose Log Path dialog box. It may take a while for the template to apply.

6. Close the MMC by selecting Yes when asked to save the console. Save the console as Security Baseline Config.

7. Log off.

8. Press Ctrl+Alt+Del to log on and notice the message that is displayed.

9. Log in to your server using your user ID and password.

Now we will simulate how to verify whether a computer is meeting the security baseline described in the security policy template. To do this, follow these steps:

1. Open the Security Baseline Config console. It should be located in Start ➤ All Programs ➤ Administrative Tools.

2. Right-click the Security Configuration And Analysis node and choose Import Template from the context menu.

3. In the Import Template dialog box, choose the securedc template and click the Open button.

4. Configure the computer with the securedc template settings by right-clicking the Security Configuration And Analysis node and choosing Configure Computer Now.

5. Click the OK button to accept the default log path and wait for it to process the new template.

6. Assume that it is time to audit the security baselines of your domain controllers to see if they comply with the DC Baseline template you created. Right-click on Security Configuration And Analysis node and choose Analyze Computer Now from the context menu.

7. Click the OK button to accept the default log location.

8. After the analysis is completed, navigate to the Message Text For Users Attempting To Log On node (located in `Local Settings\Security Options`). You should see an *X* next to the node, indicating that the security policy has changed. The green check mark by other settings mean they match. A blue icon represents settings that are not defined in the security templates in the database.

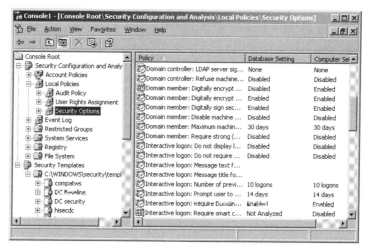

Analyzing Requirements for Securing Data

Organizations depend on the availability of their data. An organization needs to secure its data so that it can do business as usual. *Securing data* means controlling access to the data. Organizations will have different needs when it comes to securing data, so you will need to analyze the organizational requirements for securing data and build a plan. This involves more than just analyzing what access permissions are needed for the data. You need to consider the issues discussed in the following sections.

For more information on securing data, see Chapter 5, "Designing an Access Control Strategy for Network Resources."

Network versus Local Storage of Data

You need to decide whether the data will be stored on the network, locally, or a mixture of both. If you store the data on the network, it will be easier to secure and protect against loss than if it is saved locally. For example, it is easier to back up and physically secure data on a server than on individual desktops. You could then implement file synchronization to keep the server and laptop versions in sync with each other and make the data available to the laptop user when they are not connected to the network. Laptop computers do not stay in one place by their very nature. That means any data on the laptop is vulnerable to being lost or stolen if the laptop is physically taken. This will need to be taken into account and can be somewhat mitigated by the Encrypting File System (EFS). If the data is really important, you should not allow it to be placed on the laptop computers. This would introduce another problem because the data on the server would not be available when laptop users are not connected to the network. You will need to weigh the security concerns with the productivity concerns.

Back Up to Safeguard Against Corruption

You should have a backup strategy in place to guard against lost or corrupted data. If a computer has been compromised, you cannot be certain that it is clean unless you rebuild the system and restore the data from a clean backup. You could have also fallen victim to a virus that corrupts data. A backup policy is an essential requirement to recovering data from corruption, which is one of the three risks to network security. First, you need to decide what data to back up. Important assets such as contracts, reviews, and other documents on the file server should be backed up when changed, whereas other files might need to be backed up once a week. You need to remember that data is stored in other places on the network, such as SQL Server 2000 or Exchange Server 2003 public folders, and not just on a Windows Server 2003 file server. The backup policy should include this data.

You also need to determine the frequency with which the backups should occur. You should use the service level agreement (SLA) to determine this requirement. The SLA should define the amount of data that the organization can tolerate losing. You will need to adjust the backup policies accordingly. For example, a financial organization we consult for requires that no more than an hour of transactions can be lost in a SQL Server–based application they run. We set up a transaction log backup every hour to meet this requirement. This will vary among the different types of data in the organization, so you need to figure out what the policy will be on a case-by-case basis.

You may also consider redundant hardware to guard against data loss. Using a Windows Server 2003 Enterprise Edition cluster or even just using RAID 1, 5, or 1+0 technology can protect against data loss due to hardware failure. You still need to back up your data because hardware technologies do not guard against corruption, whether malicious or accidental.

Auditing Data Access

You need to make sure you determine what type of auditing is necessary for your data. Important resources should be audited, and audit logs should be read on a regular basis to verify that only authorized users are gaining access to the data. In addition, you need to consider the audit log as valuable data and protect it. After gaining access to your data, a clever attacker will try to cover their tracks by cleaning up the audit log. You will also want to set policies that specify the length of time the audit logs need to be kept. This may be influenced by industry regulations, which you must take into account.

     Auditing data will be covered in more detail in Chapter 5.

Access to Data

You need to determine which users need access to data and apply the appropriate permissions to the type of data in question. This could include tasks that range from managing share and NTFS security permissions on a file server to applying physical security that controls access to the server room where the servers that house the data reside. You will also need to document and apply the appropriate permissions for software applications and other application servers on the network.

In a large organization, you will create a standard security policy and then have the database administrators, the e-mail administrators, or the administrator group of the application server craft domain-specific security policies. Once you have defined the permissions, you should create a script or template to reapply permissions at regular intervals. This will correct any unintentional mistakes that an administrator makes in applying permissions or undo any malicious changes. This is also useful in that the security administrators can use a tool to manage permissions that may make their jobs easier.

 You will learn about securing the Windows Server 2003 filesystem, Registry, and Active Directory in Chapter 5.

Data Retention

As part of the security policy, you need to determine how long you will keep data that is generated by your organization. For example, with backup policies in place, backup files will be generated. You need to determine the number of backups you need to keep to successfully recover corrupt data. You can use industry regulations and norms, gut feeling, or tradition for this, but we propose that you keep the backups that you have generated since the last time you verified that a backup was successful. (A backup is successful if you were physically able to recover from the backup to a recovery test server.)

You will need to apply data retention times to audit logs, windows logs, e-mails, backups, and versions of files, to name a few. Whenever possible, consider industry regulations and then consider the nature of the data. For example, how many audit logs do you need to keep to track down malicious user activities for use in a court case? We recommend at least 90 days but this may vary depending on the requirements for your industry and company.

After you have analyzed the organization's requirements for securing data, you will need to look at the security requirements of different types of data, such as data that is stored online, data that is stored locally, backups, audit and system logs, databases, application servers, and data being transferred across a network.

Data that is a common resource (such as for all employees or for clients and employees) is stored online, and requires that the access permissions must be maintained to prevent unauthorized access. You will also need to consider backup strategy and virus scanning to recover and prevent a common source of corruption. Viruses can cause corruption of data and so you will need to use virus scanning to prevent a virus from corrupting the data.

Data stored on a local workstation is not as secure as data stored solely on a central server like a file or web server because it is usually not physically secured. This is especially evident on laptops. This data would need to be encrypted to prevent someone from stealing a laptop and viewing the data. The Encrypting File System included in Windows XP can be used to secure files in this manner. Local application data might need to be addressed separately. You also will need to consider the backup strategy and virus scanning with updated pattern files on the client to prevent corruption.

Backups will need to be secured themselves. If you lose the backup, you have lost everything. You should develop a plan for offsite storage of backup files or a plan that backs up the data to another location. You should also develop a plan to protect backup files that are stored on the network from attack.

The audit and system logs will need to be protected for the information they contain. You also need to determine how long you will keep them and who will have access to them.

Databases contain data used by many of the line-of-business applications of the organization. You need to work with the database administrators to create a policy to protect the database. This will involve access control, backup policies, and audit policies similar to those for file data.

Application servers like COM+, IIS, and even line-of-business applications store data about their configuration that would need to be available to bring the server back up. They also can generate temporary files that could contain sensitive information, and these files should be treated with the same care that you treat the regular data.

Data being transferred over communication wires needs to be secured. This could be files, important e-mails, and credit card information on a website. You need to configure the appropriate type of encryption if this information is confidential and is passing over a public or insecure network. You can use technologies like SSL/TLS to secure HTTP or SMTP data, S/MIME to encrypt e-mail messages, and IPSec to establish a security tunnel to move any type of data.

You need to make sure that you consider all forms that the data will take when analyzing it for security purposes.

In the following Design Scenario, you will analyze the requirements for securing data of a fictitious company called Infinite Horizons.

 Design Scenario

Analyzing the Requirements for Securing Data

An administrator at Infinite Horizons has been reviewing the audit logs and noticed that some data on the file server has been read by employees who are not supposed to have permissions to access it. This data is very important to the business and changes often during the hour. The business has deemed that it would not be cost effective to have to recover more than three hours' worth of data.

1. **Question:** How can Infinite Horizons prevent unauthorized access to data? **Answer:** Make sure the appropriate access permissions are applied to the file server's data. This can be enforced by creating a security template and enforcing it with security policies.

2. **Question:** What should the company do to decrease the likelihood of corruption of data? **Answer:** Centrally store data on a Windows Server 2003 file server and install antivirus software on each client and appropriate servers.

3. **Question:** What else could you do to guard against data corruption? **Answer:** Create a backup policy that backs up the central server every three hours.

Identifying Technical Constraints when Designing Security

Unfortunately, organizations are not homogenous when it comes to the technology that they implement. You will discover a variety of equipment and operating systems in your organization. The capabilities of the equipment, operating systems, and applications might limit your security options. You will need to evaluate the current network technologies used in your organization because they will affect what you can and cannot do with your security policies. If a risk is great and it is likely to occur, you might even need to change the existing infrastructure to accommodate a policy. Suppose, for example, that you would like to enforce software policies through Group Policy. This is most effectively accomplished through combining Group Policy and Active Directory. If you don't have Active Directory, it would be difficult. A short list of the technologies on your network that you need to evaluate follows:

- Authentication infrastructure
- E-mail
- World Wide Web service
- File sharing infrastructure
- Naming services
- Firewall/proxy services
- Custom software and services
- Remote access services
- PKI infrastructure
- Bandwidth
- CPU power of the servers (particularly with regard to encryption because it puts a heavy burden on processor power)

The means for securing each of the technologies in the preceding list will be discussed in greater detail in the appropriate chapter in this book.

You do not want technological limitations to guide your security policies. You should design security policies that would be theoretically best for the organization. You will need to identify areas where the security policies may not be consistent with the network's current technology. The organization can then decide whether it is cost effective to change or update the technology or whether to change the policy. Implementing a security policy that is not consistent with the network's technology puts an additional burden on the user by introducing interoperability constraints.

Interoperability constraints are restrictions brought on when two applications cannot communicate with each other and therefore cannot support the security protocols used to authenticate users on a network. Applications that have interoperability constraints could not support the necessary security

Real World Scenario

Exchange 2000 and Active Directory Distribution List

One situation in which you'll encounter technical constraints (and more specifically, interoperability constraints) is when you're trying to secure distribution group membership on an Exchange 2000 Server machine. If you need to support earlier versions of Windows than 2000 in Active Directory, then you'll need to enable the access group that's compatible with pre–Windows 2000 access groups to simulate the Everyone group in previous versions of Windows. This will allow down-level clients to enumerate the list of users in a distribution list. Unfortunately, it also means that everyone has permissions to view group membership, which leads to a problem with Exchange Server 2000. Because it relies on Windows 2000 Server security and distribution groups for its distribution lists, you will not be able to hide a distribution group's membership as long as you have earlier versions of Windows. You can either upgrade all the clients to Windows 2000 or greater and disable the group that's compatible with earlier versions or live without the ability to hide distribution group membership. You will need to decide, based on the security policy and cost, what you are prepared to do.

protocols used to authenticate users on the network. For example, if your organization's mainframe computer does not support Windows authentication, users would have to use a separate user ID and password to log on to the mainframe. Interoperability constraints can also be an issue when two different versions of an application are used. For example, you might need to use the less-secure protocol NTLM instead of Kerberos to authenticate users in a Windows domain because you need to support users on Windows 98 or Windows NT 4 computers in the domain. You will need to discover and investigate how interoperability constraints will affect your security policies and procedures.

In the following Design Scenario, you will analyze the technical constraints that will impact the security of Infinite Horizons.

Design Scenario

Technical Constraints when Designing Security

Infinite Horizons has an outsourcing program for HR departments of client companies and needs to securely share information contained in its databases with customers. It also has some applications that the customers need to use to enroll employees in their benefits programs. They can also check on the status and current benefits of each employee. Infinite Horizons customers don't always use Windows-based computers, and those that do could be using any version from Windows 3.1 to Windows XP.

1. **Question:** What are the technical limitations to Infinite Horizons's security policy? **Answer:** The client operating systems vary widely in capabilities. The client operating systems vary widely in capabilities, so use will not use the same ways of protecting them. For example, you might want to enforce a password policy that includes strong passwords, passwords longer than 8 characters, and a minimum of 4 days for the password. However, you may find that one of the operating systems that you are using does not support one of these features or you have to purchase a separate package.

2. **Question:** What kind of interoperability issues might arise when clients connect to Infinite Horizons' network? **Answer:** Clients might not support the more secure version of authentication protocols or encryption technology that would be preferred for the sensitive data.

Summary

Analyzing the existing security policy of an organization involves understanding what types of assets the company needs to secure and the cost effectiveness of securing them. Security policies are used to set goals that you will use to secure your assets. They need to be followed by users, IT staff, and managers to be effective. The risk that security policies are not followed can be mitigated through technology and personnel policies of incentives and punishments.

There are risks to hardware, software, people, and the data itself. All these risks can cause problems with availability of data and could ultimately affect a company's profits. It's important to know how to evaluate these risks and how to determine what technologies are needed to mitigate the risks. Some technologies may already be implemented on the existing network. Others may impose interoperability constraints, which will have an impact on what types of security and the level of security you can implement. Being able to recognize these situations and propose cost-effective solutions based on the requirements of the organization is the first step to providing effective security.

Exam Essentials

Know how to evaluate the most important security priorities for an organization. Be able to choose the most important aspects of a company's security needs from the information you are given. You will be given more information than you need.

Understand the requirements for securing data. Know what data needs to be secured and the appropriate techniques for securing it.

Recognize technical constraints or integration issues that are in conflict with security goals. Know what the technical and interoperability constraints a company faces are and be able to take them into account when deciding on the appropriate technologies for policies.

Consider government or industry regulations when designing security policies for a company. You need to make sure that the policies you implement adhere to government and industry regulations. For example, the medical industry has guidelines for privacy of patient records.

Know how to analyze what is successful or unsuccessful about the current security policy. Once you have determined where there are problems with the current security policies, you will need to decide whether to change the policy or update the technology; for example, you may have a password policy that requires 8-character passwords that are rotated every 45 days, but it is difficult to enforce on all of the devices on your network so there are some passwords that don't rotate every 45 days.

Understand how risk is used to determine what needs to be secured.   You will be given many different choices about what to secure in an organization, but you will have limited resources and will need to determine which assets are the most important.

Key Terms

Before you take the exam, be certain you are familiar with the following terms:

assets	security baseline
interoperability constraints	security policies
qualitative analysis	security risk analysis
quantitative analysis	security threat
recommended security policies	standard security policies
securing data	

Review Questions

1. Which of the following describes a security risk analysis?

   A. Using the maximum amount of security possible on each asset in your organization

   B. Reviewing the assets that need to be protected versus the cost of protecting the asset and the likelihood of the asset being attacked

   C. Waiting for an attack to occur and then figuring out what you must do to repair the damage.

   D. Determining what assets are at risk and providing the maximum amount of security to these assets

2. When analyzing the security risks of a network, which of the following categories of assets should you be looking at? (Choose all that apply.)

   A. Data

   B. Hardware

   C. Disks

   D. Software

   E. Backup plans

   F. Documentation

3. Jennifer's company is worried about sensitive company data being used on laptops that are stolen from time to time from the company's sales staff. The company sales force uses the data to sell products, issue quotes, and address customer concerns. There is not always a network connection and it is important that the sales force have the data. Jennifer wants to update the company's security policy to reflect this concern. Which of the following should she include in the security policy?

   A. Laptop users need strong passwords.

   B. Data should not be saved to laptop computers.

   C. Laptop users must use smart cards for authentication.

   D. A suitable form of encryption must be used on sensitive files located on laptop computers.

4. Elliott is concerned about the servers in his company. Many are stored in spare offices or closets and a few have been stolen lately. What type of security should Elliott address in his company's security policy?

   A. Logical

   B. Physical

   C. Data encryption

   D. Password policy

5. Helena needs to connect a Unix server that does not support Active Directory to the network. Which of the following would be a technical constraint of enforcing security on the network by this addition?

    A. Users on the Unix OS will not be able to use resources on the rest of the network.

    B. Users on the Unix OS will not have secure access to files because Unix does not support access control lists (ACLs).

    C. Administrators will be unable to enforce password policies through Group Policy for users on the Unix server.

    D. Users on the Windows Server 2003 network will not be able to connect to the Unix server.

6. Faith works for a small firm that rents medical monitoring instruments to patients. Which of the following would need to be considered the most important part of its security policy?

    A. Backup plan

    B. Lockout period in the user password policy

    C. Protection of data on laptop computers

    D. Government industry regulations

7. Ann is the CTO of a large bank. The bank wants to provide a Web presence where its customers can view their financial records. What is the biggest risk to the customer that Ann should consider?

    A. Controlling access to the internal file servers

    B. Maintaining the privacy of financial records over the Internet

    C. Making sure the users cannot manipulate cookies on their own computers

    D. Avoiding ActiveX controls like Macromedia Flash in the building of its website

8. Dave manages a web application that his company's sales force uses to check on product information, place orders, and manage their customers' information. He only has a web server and FTP server installed. It is vital that this application is up for 24 hours, 7 days a week because it will translate into lost sales and potentially lost customers if it is down. Which of the following attacks should Dave be *most* concerned about?

    A. Man in the middle

    B. Spoofing

    C. Spamming

    D. Denial of service

9. Lenin wants to automate the enforcement of many aspects of his company's security policy. What tools in Windows Server 2003 could he use to accomplish this purpose? (Choose all that apply.)

    A. Active Directory Users And Computers

    B. Security Configuration And Analysis

    C. Security Settings

    D. Security Templates

10. Which of the following should be considered when analyzing the requirements for securing data? (Choose the best answer.)

    A. The type of data

    B. Data synchronization with mobile users

    C. Backup plan for the data

    D. Data access patterns

Answers to Review Questions

1. B. Security risk analysis involves looking at the value of the assets you have. In other words, how much would it cost to replace or live without the asset? This will initiate a discussion of how much security you will need for each asset.

2. A, B, D, F. Data, hardware, software, and documentation are categories of items that should be looked at on a network when determining the network's security risks. The disks and backup plans are specific assets in these categories.

3. D. The policy would reflect that the sales staff will store files on their laptops and that the only real means of protecting sensitive information on laptops is through the use of encryption. A strong password policy and smart cards can be overcome simply by installing another version of Windows on the drive and using it to access the files. Strong passwords really provide security to network resources that are physically secure. The company could choose not to save data to laptops to be secure, but the sales force needs offline access to the data.

4. B. Elliott will need to establish the physical security of his servers. Data encryption and password policies will not protect against theft or vandalism at the physical level. Logical security would represent the software security mechanisms like passwords and access rights.

5. C. This is an example of technical constraints that may affect security on a network. Because the Unix server does not support Active Directory, it would have no information on the network's password policy. The policy would have to be configured separately on the Unix Server and it might not support the same options as Windows Server 2003.

6. D. The biggest cost to the small firm would be from penalties set in government regulations if it is not compliant. Therefore, although a backup plan, password policy, and protection of data on the laptops would also be prudent, government regulation will most likely cost the most in the short term.

7. B. The bank's strongest concern is the privacy of the customer's data sent over the Internet. If this information is not secure, it can cost them in fraud, lost customers, and image.

8. D. Dave should be concerned about a denial of service attack that will prevent legitimate users from accessing the web application. Man in the middle and spoofing involve changing information en route to the server, which may be a concern to Dave but are not his primary focus. Dave is probably not concerned with somebody using him as a spamming server because he is not running an SMTP server.

9. B, D. Using the Security Configuration And Analysis snap-in in combination with the Security Templates snap-in allows Lenin to enforce many aspects of the security policy and to verify that the configured server is still in compliance at a later time. You could push the policy out with Group Policy through Active Directory.

10. C. The data needs to be recoverable if it is to be secure, which means having a backup strategy that will successfully capture the data at regular intervals based on what the service level agreement defines as how much data can be lost. This will minimize the risk of deletion and corruption of the data. The type of data, access patterns, and data synchronization with mobile users are usually indirectly related to access control and encryption.

Case Study

You should give yourself 20 minutes to review this testlet and complete the questions.

Background

Infinite Horizons is a human resources consulting firm. It is located in Rochester, NY. It has been growing at the rate of 20 percent a year and currently has 200 employees at its headquarters in Rochester. Approximately 175 of the 200 employees are consultants. The consultants often work at many of the customers' sites.

Computers

The network headquarters consist of 13 Windows Server 2003 machines and 200 Windows XP Professional workstations. Of the 200 workstations, 175 are laptop users. One of the servers is running SQL Server 2000 to support a Customer Relationship Manager (CRM) for the sales department. The company maintains a firewall. All the users have been granted dial-in permissions. The company maintains a VPN server and dial-up access because most of the employees connect from remote locations to the network. Employees can also use Outlook Web Access (OWA) to check their e-mail via a web browser.

WAN Connectivity

The company has a DSL connection to the Internet at 1.5Mbps.

LAN Connectivity

The LAN runs on a 100Mbps network.

Security

The folks at Infinite Horizons pride themselves in maintaining confidentiality of all customers' data; therefore, security is very important to them. They have implemented password policies and their internal network is protected by a firewall. They have had laptops stolen that contained customer data in the past. They have also had some internal security lapses where shares had the incorrect permissions and employees had access to confidential customer data.

Infinite Horizons needs to protect data between its customers and its corporate headquarters.

CASE STUDY

Network Usage and Roles

Human Resources Department   The HR department uses a database application to maintain resumes and employee information. It also has a file server that stores additional employee confidential information like annual reviews.

IT Department   The IT department maintains and supports the network. Members of this department implement physical and network security.

The help desk resolves first-level support issues and issues with employees' computers.

The server administrators group builds the network and resolves the company's server and network issues.

Sales Department   The sales staff stores shared documents in a share called SALES and personnel sales documents on their local computers. They also need access to a SQL Server 2000 server that hosts their customer relations application and a lead-tracking system. They need to store some of the data on their laptops so it is available whenever they are not connected to the network.

Consultants   Consultants use the network to communicate with each other. They are required to fill out forms in the intranet-based time tracking application. They also need to get access to proposals that certain managers are working on to help author them, and they need secure access to their e-mail through the Web.

Security Policy

All users must securely authenticate on the network.
  Data that is stored on laptop computers must be secure.

Case Study Questions

1. What are the two primary risks to security for Infinite Horizons?
    A. Customer data on stolen laptop computers
    B. Denial of service attack on the Outlook Web Access server
    C. Unauthorized access of the network via the dial-in server
    D. Unauthorized access by employees to network data
    E. Unauthorized access by employees to the customer relationship database
    F. Unauthorized capturing and reading data being transmitted over the VPN connection to the company

2. What are the four security priorities of Infinite Horizons?
    A. Preventing denial of service attacks on the Outlook Web Access server
    B. Preventing unauthorized network access
    C. Securing communications to client sites
    D. Protecting employee data on laptop computers
    E. Isolating the HR network from the rest of the network via an internal firewall
    F. Providing SSL access to intranet resources
    G. Secure authentication of all users
    H. Enabling Windows Only authentication on SQL Server

3. What kind of technology would you use to secure data on the laptop computers?
    A. NTFS permissions
    B. Encrypting file system
    C. Biometric scanner for reading employee fingerprints
    D. A strong password policy

4. What technologies would you implement to guard against data corruption? (Choose all that apply.)
    A. Virus scanner
    B. Backups
    C. Access control
    D. Smart card reads
    E. Data Encryption

5. What security policy statement would apply to Infinite Horizons?

    A. Employees must use strong passwords to access the network as defined by the network administration group.

    B. Employees must not lend their smart card to anyone.

    C. Employees will not store company data on their laptops.

    D. Hardware that requires user interaction must support a smart card reader.

6. What technology should Infinite Horizons employ to make sure data moving between it and its clients is secure?

    A. TCP/IP

    B. Firewall

    C. Encryption

    D. Dial-up

7. What technological limitation will Infinite Horizons face with regard to implementing security?

    A. Password policy cannot be enforced.

    B. Consultants may not be able to connect securely from client sites.

    C. Laptop data will not be secure.

    D. Data exchanged with clients will not be secure.

8. What compromises will Infinite Horizons have to make to integrate security with a customer's network? (Choose all that apply.)

    A. Different password policies

    B. Data not confidentially exchanged

    C. Separate passwords, no single login capability

    D. No access control of the data

9. What is the most important goal when securing assets that Infinite Horizons needs to address in its security policy?

    A. Integrity of the SQL Server 2000 database

    B. Confidentiality of customer data

    C. Physical security of the laptop computers

    D. Availability of the Outlook Web Access server

10. What would be included in the security baseline for a laptop computer at Infinite Horizons?

    A. Employees must use a smart card to log on to the laptop.

    B. Back up the SQL Server database's transaction logs every three hours and perform a full backup every night.

    C. Passwords must have at least eight characters and be complex.

    D. Confidential customer data must be encrypted on a laptop.

Answers to Case Study Questions

1. A, D. All of the answers describe possible risks to the Infinite Horizons network, but you need to consider probability when determining primary risks to the network. Because the company has had laptops with customer data on them stolen in the past and has had issues with employees having unauthorized access to network data, these two options have a higher probability of occurring and need to be mitigated.

2. B, C, D, G. You need to pay attention to any primary security risks that you have identified and the new security features that the customer would like implemented when deciding the security priorities of a company. Infinite Horizons wants to secure communications to client sites and, through strong password policies, secure authentication of users. It also recognized that data is compromised when laptops are stolen or employees have unauthorized access to resources.

3. B. Encryption would afford the best protection to the company's data if it was stolen or lost, which Infinite Horizons considers a risk because it has experienced it in the past. Another option would be to just not allow certain data to be stored on a laptop. NTFS permissions can protect data through access control and are important, but if someone has physical access to the hardware, NTFS permissions can be easily overcome. Likewise, a biometric scanner and strong passwords can be defeated if an attacker has physical access. In the case of Windows, an attacker can just install another copy and use the built-in administrator to access the data, and it is not too difficult to write a program that will read raw data off a hard drive.

4. A, B, C. Virus scanning helps prevent data corruption due to viruses, Trojan horses, and worms. Controlling access to data will prevent unauthorized users from corrupting or deleting the data. However, because neither virus scanning nor access control is one hundred percent successful, you will need to make sure that you have good backups and can successfully restore them when needed. Smart card readers and data encryption don't protect the data from corruption. Smart card readers are used to authenticate the user. This information is certainly useful when creating access control lists, but it is not directly related to preventing data corruption. Data encryption guards against a compromise in confidentiality of the data. Encrypted data can still be corrupted.

5. A. Option A is the only statement that applies to Infinite Horizons according to the scenario. Infinite Horizons does not use smart card technology, so its policy would not mention smart cards. Infinite Horizons allows company data to be stored on laptops and, according to the scenario, wants to address the issue of protecting it because laptops have been stolen.

6. C. Encryption is the way to secure data that is moving through a public network like the Internet. TCP/IP is the protocol of the Internet, but it does nothing to secure data. A firewall can prevent certain data from entering or leaving the company, but once the data is out on the Internet, a firewall is of little use. Dial-up access is usually over a public network and data would still need to be protected with encryption.

7. B. The consultants work at client sites much of the time and may not be able to use a VPN or other secure method to access their company resources. Password policy can be enforced with the Windows Server 2003 Security Configuration And Analysis snap-in. Laptop data can be secured with the Encrypting File System (EFS). Data can be exchanged with clients over an agreed-upon technology like HTTP-S or IPSec.

8. **A, C.** Infinite Horizons will not use the same technology for authentication as its customers use so, due to technical constraints, will need separate passwords for the customer's network. This may lead to employees at Infinite Horizons having to deal with different password policies. Confidential exchange and control of data is a requirement for integration, so no compromises will be made in these areas.

9. **B.** While all these goals are important to Infinite Horizons, the company has stated that the confidentiality of customer data is the most important directive. If there are trade-offs to security due to technical limitations or resources, confidentiality of data will be the priority.

10. **D.** The security baseline would include all of the procedures necessary to implement the security policy for the technology in question. The security policy for Infinite Horizons does not mention smart cards, so smart cards would not be necessary to access laptops. Performing backups of the SQL Server database would be part of the SQL Server baseline but not the baseline for the laptops. The security baseline for accounts would mention the password policy, but again this does not apply to laptop users.

Chapter 2

Identifying and Designing for Potential Security Threats

MICROSOFT EXAM OBJECTIVES COVERED IN THIS CHAPTER:

✓ Design a framework for designing and implementing security. The framework should include prevention, detection, isolation, and recovery.

- Predict threats to your network from internal and external sources.
- Design a process for responding to incidents.
- Design segmented networks.
- Design a process for recovering services.

New threats appear on the Internet all too often. Rarely does a week pass without reading about a new worm, virus, or some other type of security threat that will attack a network. It may seem as if Microsoft products are the ones with the most holes. Actually, most attacks target Microsoft products because Microsoft products are the most popular. A virus that exploits a Eudora mail client will affect not nearly as many people as an attack that exploits Outlook will affect. And because of Microsoft's popularity, the press pays more attention when a vulnerability in a Microsoft product has been exposed. If you manage a network, especially a targeted one like a Windows network, security is one of the most important issues that you will face.

As a security administrator, it is your job to predict and respond to attacks. If you make the assumption that all users accessing your network are trying to breach your security infrastructure, you will have a significant leg up against a true attacker. You must learn how to visualize the attacks that are most likely going to come your way. You will accomplish this by having strategies in place to detect, respond, and remove threats and attacks against your organization.

In this chapter, you will learn how to predict the threats to your network. You will be introduced to the different types of attacks. You will also learn how to design a process that will be used to respond to these attacks should they occur. You will learn how to design segmented networks to keep your assets more secure by making them inaccessible from an insecure network. Finally, you will learn how to design a process for recovering your services.

Predicting Threats to the Network

In order to successfully predict the threats to your network, you will need to understand what motivates the attacker. There are many categories of motives:

Vengeance The attacker may feel harmed by a specific organization and wish to harm it. Commonly, the attacker has an affiliation with the organization, such as former employment. In this case, the risk is elevated because the attacker has inside information about the network, the security practices, and access to the people within the organization.

Corporate or government espionage The attacker may be attempting to compromise a network to try to obtain government or corporate secrets. In this case, the attacker may be motivated by money or their belief system.

Publicity   Many hacking groups attack a network or an application to gain recognition in the industry. Many of these groups publicly take credit for their attacks.

Terrorism   An attacker's goal may be to inflict harm on the target. The attacker may be a part of a group or state-sponsored terror cell. These are the most serious types of attackers because of their willingness to sacrifice the innocent.

To better predict the threats against your organization, you should be aware of the types of vulnerabilities that are used against most networks. In the following sections, you will be introduced to the common security vulnerabilities that plague networks today.

Common Vulnerabilities

Most successful attacks against networks are accomplished by exploiting a well-known weakness. The people who are charged with maintaining the security of a network should be properly trained to recognize vulnerabilities and make it part of their daily routine to learn of new vulnerabilities when they are discovered. Table 2.1 lists some of the most common network vulnerabilities with examples.

TABLE 2.1   Common Network Vulnerabilities

Exposure	Example
Unpatched software	Service packs or hotfixes have not been applied.
Poorly configured hardware or software	Unused services are installed. Defaults are incorporated when software or hardware is installed which eliminates some of the work for an attacker.
Social engineering	Administrator resets password of user without confirming the identity of the user.
Unencrypted data transfer	Critical data being transmitted across a public network in clear text.
Weak password	Blank or default password

Most of the common vulnerabilities are easy to recognize and protect against. One of the main goals of your design is to minimize the attack surface of your organization. Simply translated, you need to remove any services that could be vulnerable to attack unless the services are required. If you have a workstation that will only be used to browse the Internet, it should have no services running other than those that are required. In addition to removing services, you should remove any hardware that isn't required for the workstation to execute its primary function. Removing floppy disk drives or CD-ROM drives can improve security because if someone gets physical access to the workstation, they would have no easy way to install their own software on it.

In the following sections, you will learn how to recognize the types of attacks that are most likely to be used against your organization by internal and external attackers.

Internal Threats

The most severe risks to a system are those that are initiated from within your organization, referred to as *internal threats*. In most organizations, the most common network configurations are those in which the workstations and the servers are on the same segment. Thus, the workstations have unfettered access to the server; there is no firewall or router used to separate the workstations from the servers, and therefore the workstations can attack the server at will. Only in the most secure environments are workstations and servers separated by a firewall. Internal threats occur when a *trusted* user uses their limited access to launch an attack.

 Not all internal incidents are the result of an attack; they could also be the result of user error mixed with administrative carelessness.

The most common motive for an internal security breach is user curiosity. For example, suppose an employee wanted to know how much money a coworker made in a year. They may attempt to access the secure payroll data, which would be a security breach. Other motives exist, ranging from anger at the company to a desire to steal data.

There is nothing more dangerous to your organization than an internal attack by an individual with knowledge of the network configuration and the skill to access it. Internal attacks don't need to be complicated; if the attacker has physical access to parts of the network, they could steal or damage hardware.

Other types of attacks that can be spawned internally are corporate or government espionage. Espionage, as an attack, occurs when the information on your network is either stolen, tampered with, or destroyed. You may think that this type of thing only appears in spy novels and movies, but this type of attack does occasionally occur. It can be quite difficult to track a spy in your organization, especially if you're not affiliated with the government (a government agency would expect these types of attacks). The best technique to detect espionage is to enable auditing and to evaluate the logs frequently. You should especially notice when a specific employee begins to traverse the secure areas of the network.

You'll need to make sure that, in addition to auditing the resources on the network, you are auditing access to the server room. The first line of defense is to physically secure your environment. Failure to accomplish this single task would make any other security technique moot. If your organization has the infrastructure in place to track access to specific rooms, you should request access to these records to see if anyone is attempting access to the room.

Another major problem for security is password security. Many users either share their passwords with other employees or actually have it taped to their monitor so that they won't forget it. In order to prevent this type of breach you need to train your users so that they understand the importance of keeping their passwords secure.

In the "Predicting Internal Threats to Your Network" Design Scenario, you will evaluate a small scenario in order to predict the different types of internal threats.

Design Scenario

Predicting Internal Threats to Your Network

A small company uses Windows Server 2003 on a machine named Server1 to run its line-of-business application. Server1 is located in a locked room with a backup device attached directly to it. In addition to providing the users with the application services, Server1 is also used to store the payroll data. The server is not connected to the Internet and the company uses a consulting firm for major administration tasks; for the day-to-day administration, the office manager has been trained to handle the resetting of passwords of all employees, including the owner. The office manager is also responsible for changing backup tapes.

1. **Question:** What are the threats that can be exploited internally? **Answer:** The office manager could change the password of another user and use that account to spoof the identity of the other user. Once the account is compromised, the office manager can access all information that is privy to that authenticated user. The office manager has physical access to the server and can therefore turn off, or otherwise install or destroy, devices that are attached to the server. The backup tapes contain full copies of all of the data on the server, assuming no encryption; the tapes could be sold to a competitor or destroyed to prevent the data from being restored.

External Threats

Threats that come from outside of your organization's firewall are referred to as *external threats*. The configuration of your network is fundamental in determining whether or not individual servers are vulnerable to attack from the outside. External threats are the ones that are most publicized and those that most organizations spend a majority of their resources on trying to defend against. The motivation of the external attacker is usually quite different than that of an internal attacker.

Assuming the attacker is skillful, they can break into the system, steal or manipulate the data, and to a certain degree, remove all traces of the attack. As you may have guessed, it's impossible to respond to an incident if you are not aware that it occurred.

Most effective attacks against your organization from an attacker who isn't familiar with your network will begin with a systematic probing of your network. This discovery is commonly referred to as *footprinting*. The concept of footprinting, or scouting, is not new. In almost every military conflict, there is a significant amount of discovery that takes place prior to an attack. The attacker, in our context, will evaluate the defenses of the target network or server by determining what systems and services are running. Even a novice attacker can use this information to break into your system.

Figure 2.1 shows what a simple Telnet session to a mail server can reveal about the server that it is running on.

FIGURE 2.1   Telnet session to Exchange Server 2003

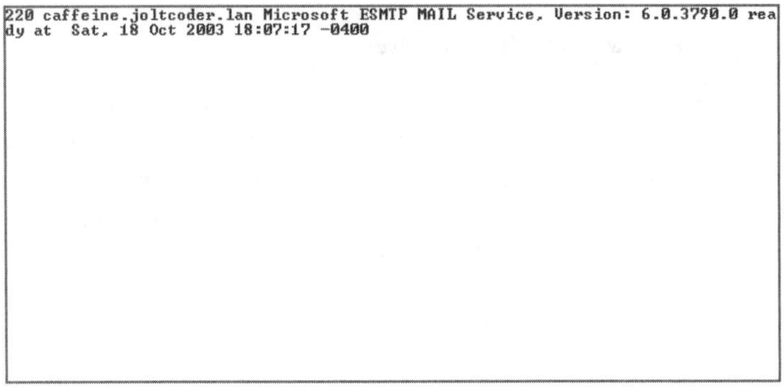

```
220 caffeine.joltcoder.lan Microsoft ESMTP MAIL Service, Version: 6.0.3790.0 rea
dy at  Sat, 18 Oct 2003 18:07:17 -0400
```

As you can see, it tells us the internal name of the server and the full version of the mail service. This information tells the attacker that the server is running Exchange Server 2003 and even includes the minor version information, 6.0.3790.0, which lets the attacker know whether or not service packs have been installed as well as certain hotfixes. A simple Telnet session to a Windows NT 4 web server displays the IIS version, which lets the attacker know the operating system. Figure 2.2 shows a Telnet session to an NT 4 web server (port 80).

FIGURE 2.2   Telnet Session to IIS 4.0

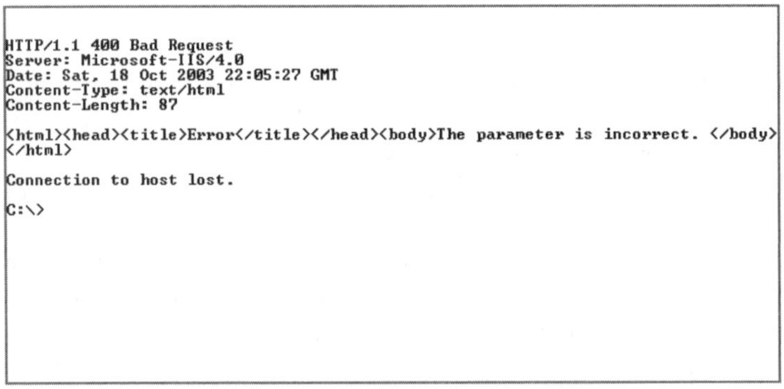

```
HTTP/1.1 400 Bad Request
Server: Microsoft-IIS/4.0
Date: Sat, 18 Oct 2003 22:05:27 GMT
Content-Type: text/html
Content-Length: 87

<html><head><title>Error</title></head><body>The parameter is incorrect. </body>
</html>

Connection to host lost.

C:\>
```

Windows Server 2003 does a better job of shielding the version information, as seen in Figure 2.3.

You'll need to do your best to prevent as much information as possible from getting into an attacker's hands. There are several methods that you can use to change or disable the banners that the services display. The options that are available to you will be determined by the specific service and operating system on the machine you are trying to protect. In addition to using the Telnet utility, there are other more elegant programs such as nmap, a free footprinting utility, and many more. Visit www.insecure.org to get more information about the nmap utility.

FIGURE 2.3   Telnet Session to IIS 6.0

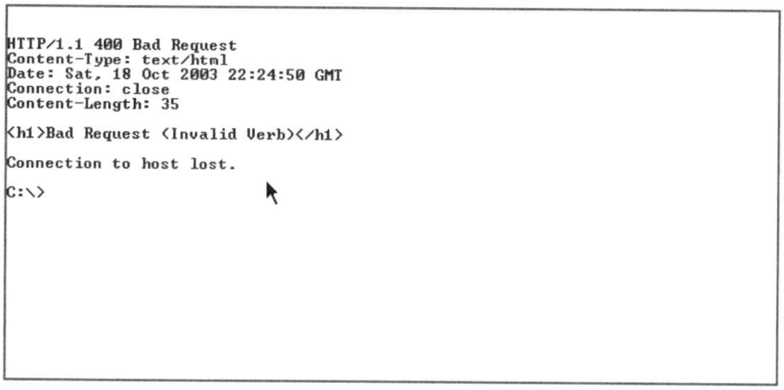

```
HTTP/1.1 400 Bad Request
Content-Type: text/html
Date: Sat, 18 Oct 2003 22:24:50 GMT
Connection: close
Content-Length: 35

<h1>Bad Request (Invalid Verb)</h1>

Connection to host lost.

C:\>
```

In the "Predicting External Threats to Your Network" Design Scenario, you will evaluate a scenario and predict the different types of external threats to the network.

 Design Scenario

Predicting External Threats to Your Network

A large chain of toy stores operates a Web storefront that accepts credit card orders over the Internet for toys to be shipped to the customer. The web server is running IIS 6 on Windows Server 2003, Enterprise Edition. The application uses a SQL Server database, located on another Windows Server 2003 machine, to store the customer, order, and inventory data. The only connections to the web server from the Internet are on port 80 (WWW) and port 443 (SSL).

1. **Question:** What are some of the external threats to this company? **Answer:** One of the external threats that could be brought against this web server is a denial of service attack. The DoS attack could be launched to prevent real customers from accessing the site. Another potential target is the customer's data, including credit card numbers, which could be compromised and disclosed. Once an attacker determines the operating system and the services that are running he or she will try all known vulnerabilities against them, in this case, against IIS and Windows Server 2003, in order to gain access to the server.

Predicting Threats with Threat Modeling

In order to properly allocate your security resources, you should understand which threats are more likely to affect your organization. *Threat modeling* is the process of predicting threats and vulnerabilities to assets in your organization. Determining these threats will make for a more efficient use of your information security resources. Threat modeling can be further eased by categorizing the threats. You can use the STRIDE threat model to categorize the threats against your network. STRIDE is an acronym whose letters stand for the following threat categories:

(S)poofing identity   Identity spoofing can be as simple as an attacker obtaining a username and password of a valid user and then illegally using those authentication credentials to access the resources of the target organization. Another form of spoofing is server spoofing. With server spoofing, an attacker uses a server to simulate another server with the hope of gathering data that would normally only be available to the real server. A common example of server spoofing is web spoofing, which is usually accomplished by taking advantage of mistyped URLs in a browser. The attacker will register the domain amszon.com, which is only one character away from the real Amazon.com, the attacker then creates a website on amszon.com that looks like Amazon.com. When the user's browser loads the erroneous site, it prompts the user for credit card information, or other personal data which the user believes they are sending to Amazon.com, it could even be secure being transmitted over SSL. The point is that the attacker is spoofing the identity of the trusted web server and the user is unaware that they mistyped the URL. This could happen to any e-commerce site where customer data, such as credit card information, would be sent.

(T)ampering with data   This threat category describes situations in which data is maliciously altered on the target machine. For example, data is tampered with when a website gets hacked and the attackers modify the original content and incorporate their own.

(R)epudiation   This occurs when a user denies performing an action and the target has no way of proving otherwise. For example, a file is deleted by a user, the user denies deleting the file, and the administrative team has no logging mechanism to prove that the user did, in fact, delete the file.

(I)nformation disclosure   Information disclosure occurs when someone gains access to data that they should not have access to. An example of information disclosure is when a file containing the salaries of employees is left improperly secured and is viewed by someone who should not have access to it.

(D)enial of service   In a denial of service (DoS) attack, a service is denied to valid users, usually because the service is overwhelmed with requests. An everyday example would be when someone creates a program that auto-dials your work phone number, preventing valid callers from getting through. In network terms, a denial of service occurs when a server or service is overloaded by malicious requests and is prevented from receiving valid requests. If there are multiple attackers, usually because an attacker has taken control over several computers that will be used to launch the attack, it is referred to as a distributed denial of service (DDoS) attack.

(E)scalation of privilege   Escalation of privilege occurs when an unprivileged user gains privileged access illegitimately. When this happens, an attacker can assume the privileges of the trusted system itself. This typically occurs when a service is hijacked to run code of an attacker's choice. If the attacker can force the service to run code on their behalf, the code will run in the security context of the service, which in the case of some services, may be the LocalSystem account or, worse, a domain-level administrative account.

Now that you've learned the categories of the threats that you will face, you'll need to determine where the attack will come from. Although most companies spend most of their security budget securing their network from outside attacks, many studies have shown that attacks are more likely to come from within your organization.

In order to better predict the threats that your organization is likely to encounter, you should use a threat model like the STRIDE threat model. To use a model, you'll need to complete the following steps:

Define the scope   You'll need to first decide what it is that you will be evaluating, specifically which hardware and which software packages will be included in your model. This allows you to focus only on the target of the model as opposed to an entire organization. The scope could be a specific web server, or even a specific application running on the specified server.

Create a team   Next, you will need to build a team that consists of a wide variety of technical skill and experience. By creating a diverse team, you will allow for each object of the model to be evaluated from different perspectives. It is considered best practice to include only those with a limited stake in the outcome of the project to prevent selective disclosure as to the exposed risk. Try to avoid choosing an individual who was responsible for configuring a server that will be evaluated as he or she may not disclose the vulnerabilities that they have caused.

Predict threats   The final step in your model will be to have your team meet and brainstorm to identify all of the potential threats to the subject of the model (such as the web server, the e-mail server, etc.). You should use whiteboards and all pertinent documentation (for example, product documentation, white papers, etc.).

When predicting threats, you will first identify the type of threat, define the threat itself, determine the probability that the threat will be carried out, and determine the degree of the affect an attack will have on your organization. Table 2.2 is a sample STRIDE threat model of an e-commerce web server.

TABLE 2.2   Table 2.2:Predicted Threats Based on STRIDE Model

Type	Threat	Probability	Impact
Spoofing identity	Hacker obtains valid user credentials to access the site.	Medium	Critical
Tampering with data	An attacker changes the prices of products and services listed on the site.	Medium	Moderate
Repudiation	Attacker purchases items from the Web commerce system and later denies the purchase. (No IP logging enabled.)	Low	Low
Information disclosure	Customer credit card data is accessed from the company's website.	Medium	Critical
Denial of service	Attack prevents legitimate customers from accessing the site.	High	Critical
Escalation of privilege	An attacker injects code that runs in the context of a trusted account, such as LocalSystem; the attacker can now operate as the system.	Medium	Critical

Responding to Incidents

To prevent mistakes from happening when responding to security incidents, you should have a well-designed procedure for responding to incidents. Having a procedure in place allows the security response team in your organization to react appropriately when a situation arises. Failure to respond appropriately can cause the incident to worsen. There is the potential to damage or taint the evidence that could lead to the capture and prosecution of the attacker. In the section that follows, you will learn how to design an incident response procedure that will provide your response team with the appropriate steps in the event of a security breach.

Designing an Incident Response Procedure

A recurring concept in information systems management is to have well-designed processes. This is true in all facets of business: the better defined the process, the less ambiguity in the minds of the facilitators.

A plan must be in place that provides you with the information you'll need at the moment that the attack is discovered or suspected. It should contain a list of the names and numbers of those to be notified, especially in an enterprise environment; all site administrators must be aware of the incident so that they can plug or patch the vulnerability that they are probably susceptible to as well.

There are typically two techniques when responding to an attack. One is to shut down or disconnect the system(s) that have been compromised (not the router that they came in through, unless it has been compromised). Shutting down or disconnecting the system(s) allows you to preserve the evidence before the attacker has the opportunity to hide their tracks. The other option is to isolate the system(s) so that you can monitor the activity of the attacker to gather more evidence and at the same time prevent other systems from being attacked. The benefit to this method is that you can monitor the activity of the attacker and can gather even more evidence. This option does, however, come with significant risk. The attacker may notice the changes, eliminate the evidence, and stop the attack. Allowing the attacker to continue, even in an isolated environment, should be an option only for a highly skilled security expert.

There are several situations where the importance of procedures is demonstrated, specifically how not having a procedure can lead to damage in a number of different scenarios. In your procedure you should create a determinate chain of notification, where the information can flow to everyone who may be affected by the incident. One of the best ways to avoid mistakes when reacting to an incident is to have a procedure that spells out how the information should be disseminated to the various members of the team as well as notifying those individuals in need-to-know roles. The Communication procedure is key to the success of your security response team in properly defending and reacting effectively. For example, in a scenario in which you suspect an employee is selling information to competitors typically spurs an internal investigation by the security team to audit the critical resources that are being leaked. Without a procedure specifying whom to notify, the workstation of the employee could be re-imaged by a desktop administrator, which would obviously erase most of the evidence on the machine. Many companies use an imaging solution, such as Symantec's

Real World Scenario

A Incident Response Procedure Will Prevent Mistakes

The first time that I fell victim to an external attack, I panicked and immediately shut down the router that the attacker entered through—I literally unplugged it. That was my knee-jerk reaction under the stress that obviously comes with being attacked. Turning off the router not only disconnected the attacker, it also stopped Internet e-mail from entering our organization and prevented us from sending external e-mail and accessing the Internet entirely. Fortunately, the attackers (I found out later that it was significantly more than one) were only able to gain access to our public FTP servers and simply used them to store and share files across the Internet.

Had there been a well documented procedure dictating my response, I wouldn't have made such monumental mistakes. You will want to make sure that you have a procedure in place to prevent your response staff from making those mistakes.

Ghost, for the hard drives of the workstations in the enterprise, so without proper communication, the workstation of the employee could be re-imaged by a desktop administrator, which would overwrite most of the evidence on the machine. The desktop administrator should be made aware of the breach in security and trained well enough to know that re-imaging the workstation hard drive is not the appropriate response in this situation.

The first step in putting together a Computer Security Incident Response Procedure (CSIRP) is to build a team referred to as a computer security incident response team (CSIRT). It is extremely important that each member of the team be given a finite scope of responsibility. It is always a good idea to include a broad range of skills in the team. A good team would include a network administrator who knows the topology of the network, a server administrator who knows the configuration of the servers, a desktop administrator who knows the configuration of the desktop workstations in the organization, an application specialist who is familiar with the application set that is running on the workstations and the servers, a security specialist whose main focus is on securing the organization, a team leader to facilitate the chain of communication, and a manager who has the authority to make a clutch decision.

Once the entire team has been formed, the next step is to determine the severity level you'll assign to certain types of incidents. As you may imagine, some security incidents may not require the entire team being brought in. For example, an incident such as a small virus infecting a single computer would certainly not warrant the whole CSIRT to resolve the problem. There must be clear definitions of what severity an incident is and therefore who needs to work to resolve the issue. Table 2.3 shows an example of severity classification for ABC Corporation with some examples.

Based on Table 2.3, incidents with a severity of 3 or greater would result in the activation of the CSIRT, while incidents with lower severity levels would be handled without the intervention of the incident response team.

TABLE 2.3   Severity Classification Example

Severity	Example(s)
1	Small number of users receive an e-mail with a virus attachment, which is caught by antivirus software on the computer.
2	Small number of scans detected on perimeter systems along with information concerning which computers will be targeted.
3	Large number of scans detected on perimeter systems; zero affect on production systems. Large number of computers infected with a known computer virus that is handled by antivirus software. Small number of isolated computers infected with unknown computer virus.
4	Breach of perimeter systems or successful denial of service attack with minimal impact on production.
5	Breach of perimeter systems or successful denial of service attack with major impact on production systems; poses a significant chance of financial or public relations damage.

The incident response procedure should include details for the following steps, with as much specific information as possible:

Declare the incident   The response procedure should include the conditions that must be met for an incident to be declared as well as who is responsible for making the declaration. When an incident occurs that requires the team to respond, it should be declared. Typically, the team manager would be the individual making the declaration and would notify upper management that a security incident has occurred. The team manager would also be the person responsible for communicating the incident to the rest of the team.

Analyze the incident   The incident will need to be analyzed to determine the scope of the breach. It is at this stage that the details of the incident will be recorded.

Contain or resolve the incident   Depending on the type of incident that occurs, you may need to quarantine the systems that have been compromised. Should a solution exist that can be applied and alleviate the situation, it should be carried out. Fixing the problem is better than containing it.

Resolve the problem   If the previous step led only to containment, the next step is to resolve the problem. This may begin with cleaning a system and then applying a patch or a service pack.

Prevent reoccurrence of problem   Take the appropriate steps to prevent the system(s) from being compromised again.

Document events   Log all of the events that have taken place, from the discovery of the breach to resolution. This documentation will be used in the post-incident evaluation.

Preserve evidence   Be sure to retain as much evidence as possible. As previously stated, this data can be used by the authorities to capture the attacker. The evidence can also be used to prevent future attacks that exploit similar vulnerabilities.

Conduct a post-incident evaluation   Gather the team after the incident has been resolved to review all of the information that was collected. Identify areas in which the team could improve its response and paths of communication.

 Design Scenario

Designing a Response to an Incident

A virus that propagates from the Internet penetrates the internal LAN of your network. The virus is not immediately identified by all of the administrators. Some of the administrators recognize the virus and manually remove it from the servers that they are responsible for. After the administrators remove the virus, they notice that the servers are immediately infected again.

1. **Question:** What actions should be included in your response procedure for this type of incident? **Answer:** The administrators who recognize the virus should notify the team leader, and the rest of the team, regarding the fix for the virus. The team leader would be responsible for communicating the solution to the rest of the team and to the other departments who need to be aware of the situation. In order to prevent the reoccurrence of the virus, the administrators should take steps to prevent the reinfection of the servers; the steps may include isolation from the LAN, WAN, or Internet.

Planning for Recovering of Services

Now that you've designed a plan for responding to a security incident, you will see how to plan for the recovery of services and/or data. There are many organizations that cannot afford, financially or publicly, to have services unavailable. Imagine if the services provided by Visa or MasterCard were simply unavailable. Purchases across the world would stop. Obviously, these companies have plans in place to recover services regardless of the situation. You'll need to have these plans in place before the security incident occurs.

Once an incident is detected, you will need to take the necessary steps to bring your services back online. Prior to taking any steps, make sure you notify your organization's security response manager. The team should take great care to document each and every step that is taken for recovery. This is one of the most important parts of the recovery process because the documentation will be used for review and will also prevent hasty decisions from hampering the recovery effort. This documentation may also be useful in the event that a legal investigation takes place.

As mentioned previously, the compromised system(s) should be disconnected from the network. All methods of access from the outside world should be included, such as Remote Access Service (RAS), dial-up (unplug the phone line), and the wireless network (it should be disabled). If possible, try to avoid rebooting the system or terminating sessions; this will result in active processes being terminated and can make it more difficult to locate evidence that may be in use at the time of discovery.

It is extremely helpful to make an image or snapshot backup of the compromised system. This snapshot can be used for review in a lab environment to investigate the compromise. There are several third-party utilities that can be used for this type of image; Symantec's Ghost is probably one of the more popular choices. This snapshot can also be used by the legal forensics team to mount an effective case against the attacker(s).

Now that you've protected the data by taking a snapshot of the system at the time that the incident is discovered, you should analyze the intrusion. Check the event logs using Event Viewer and evaluate the configuration information. Figure 2.4 shows the Event Viewer application with security auditing enabled.

FIGURE 2.4   The Event Viewer

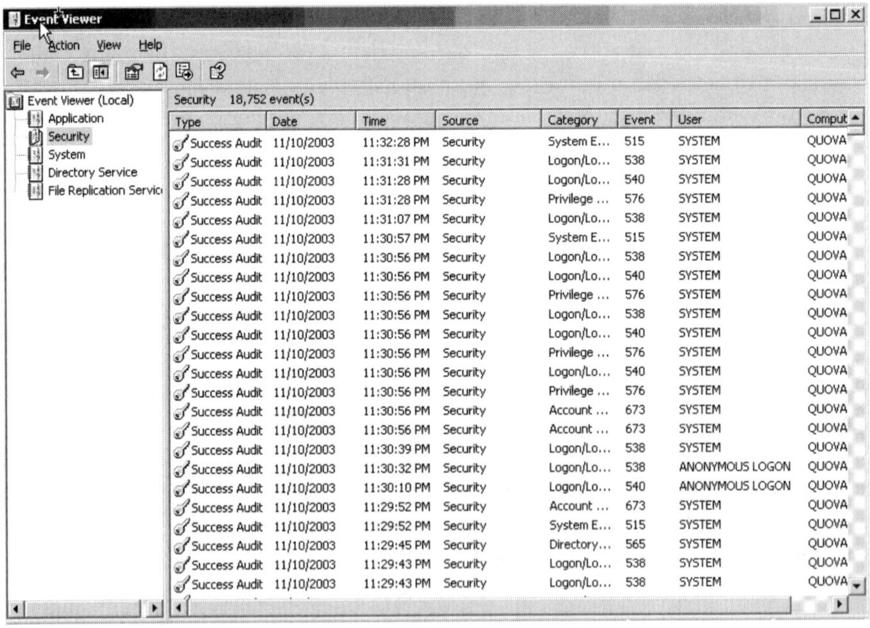

Look especially for modifications made to the operating system or its services. Check for out-of-place users and group memberships; many attacks involve creating a user on the compromised system and granting that user administrative privileges. Check for changes to the system Registry and look for any hidden shares (shares that don't appear in Explorer). You can use the `net share` command at the command prompt to show all of the active shares on the server, as seen in Figure 2.5.

FIGURE 2.5   An example of the net share output

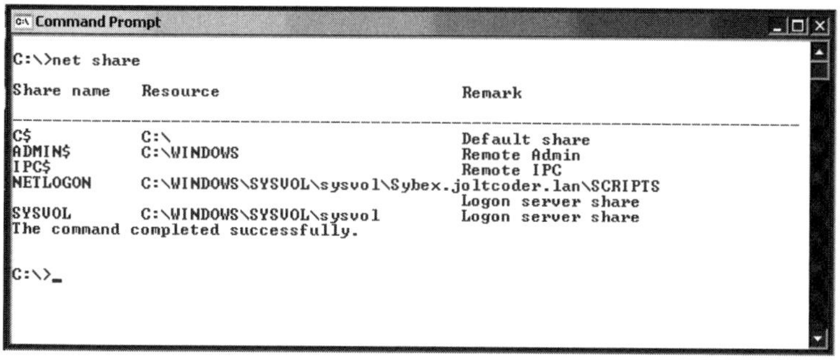

```
Command Prompt                                                    _|□|x|

C:\>net share

Share name    Resource                              Remark
--------------------------------------------------------------------
C$                                                  Default share
ADMIN$        C:\WINDOWS                             Remote Admin
IPC$                                                Remote IPC
NETLOGON      C:\WINDOWS\SYSVOL\sysvol\Sybex.joltcoder.lan\SCRIPTS
                                                    Logon server share
SYSVOL        C:\WINDOWS\SYSVOL\sysvol              Logon server share
The command completed successfully.

C:\>_
```

You should also check for services and processes to see if any are running that shouldn't be. Double-check the name of the executing process; many attackers name the executable of their services to resemble operating system processes or other standard services that are usually running on a server. You should have a list of the services and processes that should be on the system and should be running, including the startup behavior of the services. This can be used to compare the list after an incident to see if there are any changes. Many applications are also run from within other services; svchost.exe is a common executable that is listed in the Windows Task Manager utility and running other applications that may or may not be applications that should be running. In Figure 2.6, you can see that there is more than one instance of SVCHOST.EXE running on the system. You should check to see what applications are running from within svchost.

FIGURE 2.6   Task Manager

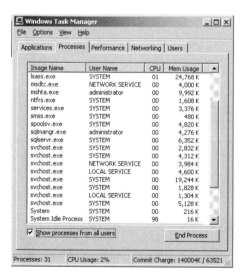

As you can see, it is very difficult to know what is actually running; even certain security software will alert you that `svchost.exe` is accessing the network or the Internet. If you don't know what is running through `svchost.exe`, it is impossible to know for sure whether or not you are allowing a Trojan horse program or some other kind of backdoor attack to get through by allowing it to run. You can use `tasklist /svc` from the command prompt to display the applications that are running within a specific thread and look for unknown processes in the resulting list, as seen in Figure 2.7.

Verify that the data on the server is intact and has not been tampered with. Depending on the role of the compromised server, the data will vary. If the system is a web server, verify that the web pages and other data have not been changed or removed. You'll also want to search for files that may have been left behind by the intruder. Intruders commonly plant network sniffers to record network activity, some of the programs that the intruder plants may be hiding their true functionality in a service or program that appears to be valid. These types of programs are referred to as Trojan horse programs, because they hide their real purpose. You'll also want to check for files that may appear to be system files: `Explore.exe` instead of `explorer.exe`, for example.

Comb through the log files on the system to get an idea of how the system was compromised so that you can take the proper steps to prevent it in the future. In addition to checking the systems that you are sure were compromised, you will want to check the other systems on your network. Think of the compromised server as an infected computer that could be used to infect other machines that it comes in contact with.

FIGURE 2.7 Tasklist output

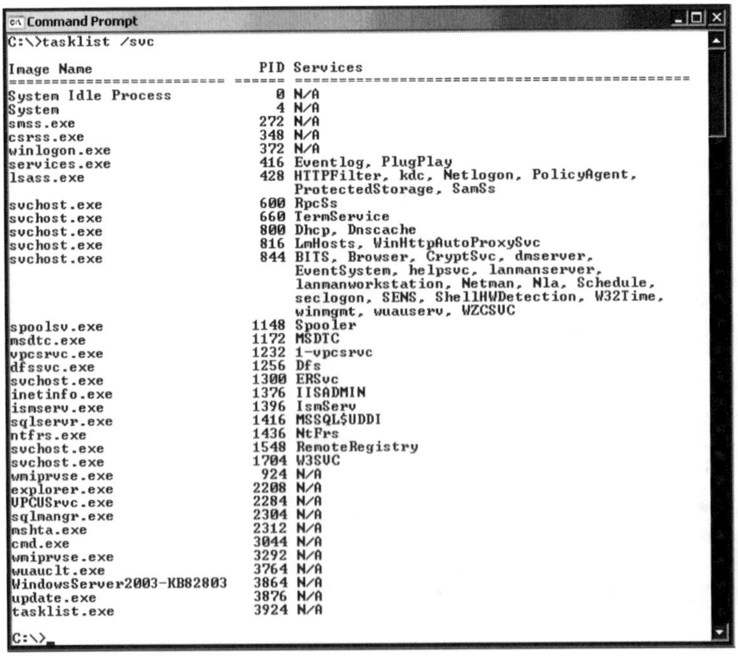

```
Command Prompt
C:\>tasklist /svc

Image Name                     PID Services
========================= ====== =============================================
System Idle Process              0 N/A
System                           4 N/A
smss.exe                       272 N/A
csrss.exe                      348 N/A
winlogon.exe                   372 N/A
services.exe                   416 Eventlog, PlugPlay
lsass.exe                      428 HTTPFilter, kdc, Netlogon, PolicyAgent,
                                   ProtectedStorage, SamSs
svchost.exe                    600 RpcSs
svchost.exe                    660 TermService
svchost.exe                    800 Dhcp, Dnscache
svchost.exe                    816 LmHosts, WinHttpAutoProxySvc
svchost.exe                    844 BITS, Browser, CryptSvc, dmserver,
                                   EventSystem, helpsvc, lanmanserver,
                                   lanmanworkstation, Netman, Nla, Schedule,
                                   seclogon, SENS, ShellHWDetection, W32Time,
                                   winmgmt, wuauserv, WZCSVC
spoolsv.exe                   1148 Spooler
msdtc.exe                     1172 MSDTC
vpcsrvc.exe                   1232 1-vpcsrvc
dfssvc.exe                    1256 Dfs
svchost.exe                   1300 ERSvc
inetinfo.exe                  1376 IISADMIN
ismserv.exe                   1396 IsmServ
sqlservr.exe                  1416 MSSQL$UDDI
ntfrs.exe                     1436 NtFrs
svchost.exe                   1548 RemoteRegistry
svchost.exe                   1704 W3SVC
wmiprvse.exe                   924 N/A
explorer.exe                  2208 N/A
VPCUSrvc.exe                  2284 N/A
sqlmangr.exe                  2304 N/A
mshta.exe                     2312 N/A
cmd.exe                       3044 N/A
wmiprvse.exe                  3292 N/A
wuauclt.exe                   3764 N/A
WindowsServer2003-KB82803     3864 N/A
update.exe                    3876 N/A
tasklist.exe                  3924 N/A

C:\>_
```

Real World Scenario

Recovering Services by Making Hard Decisions

Figment Enterprises is a large-scale organization specializing in providing financial data in real time to its customers through a Web service. The company has sites in Los Angeles, Minneapolis, and Philadelphia and headquarters in Wilmington, Delaware. The computer security incident response team is located at corporate headquarters. Each site maintains service level agreements (SLAs) with its customers guaranteeing that any incident will be properly disclosed and the service will be made available within 15 minutes of the time it became unavailable.

There are LAN administrators that deal with the day-to-day management of network operations at each site. In the event of an emergency security situation, the response team can use remote tools such as Terminal Services or can be flown to the location where the incident has occurred.

During a routine security audit at the Philadelphia office, the security response team discovers that there has been a breach and that one or more attackers have compromised the Philadelphia web server. The team takes the necessary steps, notifying the response manager and removing the network cable from the back of the server. The response team switches the uncompromised backup service into production.

The response team has a meeting to determine how to proceed to get the server back into production. Because this server is critical to the company and needs to be returned to production quickly the decision is made to format the server and reinstall all necessary applications and services from scratch. This solution is the only way to be sure that all of the services that are running on the system are uncompromised. The server will be imaged prior to being formatted so it can be investigated in a lab environment.

Once you have verified that the systems are no longer compromised, you should return them to production, with an emphasis on auditing and logging so that they can be constantly monitored to be sure that there was nothing missed or that they don't get compromised again.

The only way to be 100% sure that there are no more remnants of the intruder is a complete format and restore from a time that was known to be valid and secure.

In the next section, you will learn about segmenting your network to separate the portions that are insecure. This practice is common when the security of the network is critical to ongoing activities in an organization.

Isolating Insecure Networks

Most organizations have a network perimeter, which is any point that connects the internal network to external networks. Network perimeters include the network connection point to the Internet, links to a satellite office, or a remote access server. A screened subnet is also on the perimeter of a network. A *screened subnet* is a protected area on the network that is used to run services that are shared outside of the organization. Business-to-business (B2B) services are typically run from this type of subnet. A DMZ is a type of screened subnet, DMZ stands for demilitarized zone, which is an isolated network segment at the point where a corporate network meets the Internet. Other examples of network perimeters are wireless access point or virtual private network (VPN) connections.

The network perimeter is the part of any network that is most vulnerable to attack. The attack can be random or targeted. Because of the prevalence of threats that affect public network access points, you should take great care to minimize your internal network's exposure to the public network, also referred to as the "wild."

Some companies choose to use firewall services or a screened subnet. As previously mentioned, a demilitarized zone is a specialized type of screened subnet in which the external network is the Internet. Routers and firewalls can be used to screen the traffic that passes into and out of the screened subnet. There are typically three types of configurations that an organization will take when securing its network perimeters:

Bastion host A *bastion host* acts as the only connection for computers on the internal network to use to access the Internet (or other external networks). This configuration is illustrated in Figure 2.8. When configured as a firewall, the bastion host is specially designed to prevent attacks against the internal network. The bastion host uses at least two network adapters; one is connected to the internal network while the other is connected to the external network. This configuration physically separates the internal network from the outside. Its weakness is that it is a single point of failure; should it be compromised, the attacker can gain access to the internal network.

FIGURE 2.8   A bastion host

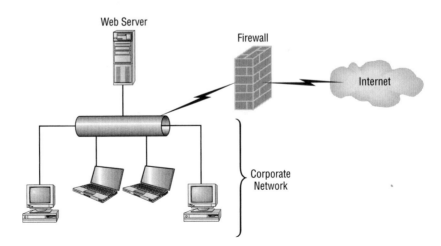

Three-pronged configuration   In a *three-pronged configuration*, the firewall system will have a minimum of three network adapters. One adapter will be connected to the internal network, one to the external or public network, and the third to a screened subnet. This configuration allows for hosts from the public and internal networks to access the available resources in the screened subnet while continuing to isolate the internal network from the wild. Figure 2.9 depicts this configuration.

FIGURE 2.9   A three-pronged configuration

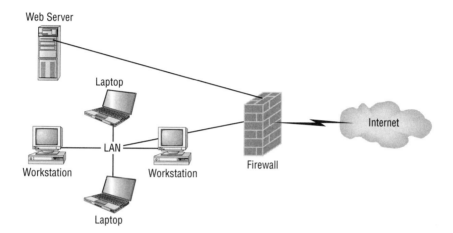

Back-to-back configuration   The *back-to-back configuration* places the screened subnet between two firewalls. The screened subnet is connected through a firewall to the Internet on one end and connected through another firewall to the internal network on the opposite end. This is probably the most secure configuration while still allowing for public resources to be accessed. This would require an attacker to breach both firewalls in order to compromise the internal network. Figure 2.10 shows an illustration of this configuration.

FIGURE 2.10   A back-to-back configuration

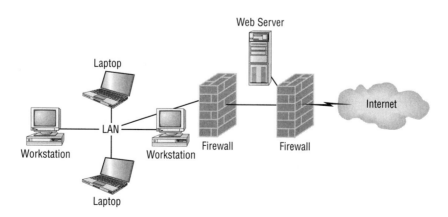

Real World Scenario

The Importance of Perimeter Security

Quovadimus Incorporated is a technology firm specializing in biotechnology. The organization works with educational and government institutions frequently. The CIO tells the network administrator to provide the partnering organizations with access to the company's data. Quovadimus also hosts its own web and mail servers that are accessible from the Internet. The CIO has promised the partnering organizations that the data will be available to them within an hour of their conversation. As a result of not properly preparing for this type of data access, there is no time to develop a secure perimeter.

Using basic techniques like port scanning, an attacker is able to footprint the Quovadimus perimeter network. The attacker learns what operating systems and services are running on the perimeter network. The attacker now has enough information to create an entire diagram of the organization's perimeter. The attacker researches the known vulnerabilities of the services that are running in the perimeter network and can now systematically attack the network. The attacker can now gain access to some or all of the services that are accessible, including those of the organization's partners.

You will need to make sure that the network perimeter is properly secured, especially if there is a possibility of its resources being consumed outside of your organization.

 Design Scenario

Segmenting Networks for Security

ABC Incorporated manufactures explosive space modulators to be sold by its partners. ABC has an Internet website that it hosts on Server1. In addition, ABC's partners need to be able to access the inventory data that is exposed from a web service that is running on Server2. All access to the web service needs to be screened, and the web service and website need to be on separate networks. All of the employees of ABC Incorporated use the corporate network to access their data and to access the other resources. ABC has room in the budget to purchase only one more server to maintain security.

1. **Question:** Which technique should you use in this scenario to meet the requirements and prevent external networks from accessing the internal network? **Answer:** The three-pronged configuration is the only option that meets all of the requirements in the given scenario. There are three separate networks that need to be in place: the network with the website, the network with the web service, and the corporate network. Therefore, the bastion host configuration with only one more computer cannot secure all three networks. Back-to-back configuration requires at least two more computers, configured as firewalls, to be purchased to segregate the DMZ, the LAN, and the Internet. A single server, with three network adapters, will meet the requirements without compromising security.

One of the best techniques in securing the computers that physically leave your network perimeter, such as laptop computers that travel with the user or users who access an organization's resources from their homes (for example, using a dial-up or VPN connection) is to simply educate the users. Make sure the users are using updated antivirus software as well as personal firewall software.

In the "Segmenting Networks for Security" Design Scenario, you will be evaluating a scenario and choosing the best technique to isolate, or segment, the internal network from external networks.

Summary

In this chapter, you learned the different steps involved in predicting threats to your network. The motivation for an attack can range from curiosity to espionage. We showed you how to predict attacks that may be initiated from within your organization or from outside of it. You learned that threat modeling can greatly increase your ability to make appropriate decisions when doling out resources. Categorizing the threats that your organization faces as well as estimating the impact can better prepare you and your team to respond to an incident.

We later showed you that the creation of an incident response procedure can minimize mistakes and allow you to properly respond. Creating organizationally specific severity levels to qualify the attack and its impact further prepares the team with predefined processes to follow when an attack occurs.

After an incident occurs, you will need to take great care to make sure that the appropriate steps are taken. Failure to follow the predetermined plan can lead to mistakes and lost evidence.

Finally, you saw the different techniques that can be employed in order to secure your internal network. You can use a bastion host, a three-pronged configuration, or a back-to-back configuration to better secure your network and still allow some degree of access to services from the public network.

Exam Essentials

Know how to predict the threats to a given network.   Given the makeup of a network, you must be able to predict the threats that could affect its security.

Make sure that you recognize when a network should be segmented.   Take into account the different techniques for segmenting a network to prevent your perimeter network from being exploited, causing your internal network to be compromised.

Know how to design an incident response procedure to minimize downtime and maximize evidence preservation.   Make sure you know what techniques you will use to review an attack, including the system event log, security audit log, and so on. Also know how you will be able to recover from the incident.

Know how to recover the services of your network after an incident has been rectified.   You should also know how to design your organization's services, so that they can proceed uninterrupted even when an incident occurs.

Key Terms

Before you take the exam, be certain you are familiar with the following terms:

back-to-back configuration	internal threats
bastion host	screened subnet
external threats	threat modeling
foot printing	three-pronged configuration

Review Questions

1. Matrix Systems wants to open a new office in St. Paul, Minnesota, to serve as the service center for all offices and resellers. There are two other sites, one in Los Angeles and another in Boston. The St. Paul site will be accessible to the other sites using direct link; in addition, the resellers must be able to access the partner extranet to retrieve inventory data. What type of perimeter security configuration should you use to design the new site?

   A. Back-to-back configuration

   B. Three-pronged configuration

   C. Proxy server configuration

   D. Bastion host

2. When an incident occurs, you must initiate a response procedure. The incident response procedure should include the following steps. Place the steps in the order that they will be carried out by the incident response team.

	Resolve the problem
	Preserve the evidence
	Evaluate the incident response
	Contain the incident
	Analyze the incident
	Document events
	Declare the incident
	Prevent reoccurrence

3. In order to better prepare for a security incident, what actions should you take to predict the threats that your organization could face?

   A. Use a threat model to gauge the type of threats and their impact on your organization.

   B. Create a security response team.

   C. Create a risk and response diagram.

   D. Create a threat diagram.

4. A web server has not properly been patched with a hotfix that alleviates a buffer overrun. In addition, when the server is unable to connect to its database, it displays an error message with the connection information (username and password) that it was using to connect to the database. What parts of the STRIDE threat model describe the threats a situation such as this presents? (Choose all that apply.)

    A. Spoofing identity

    B. Tampering of data

    C. Repudiation

    D. Information disclosure

    E. Denial of service

    F. Elevation of privilege

5. Sojourn Incorporated has several traveling employees who use laptop computers to access the network. In the past, laptops have been infected with a virus while outside of the LAN and later infected the Sojourn corporate environment. What recommendations would you make to prevent this from occurring in the future? (Choose the best answer.)

    A. Require laptop computers to be scanned for viruses by the IT staff prior to accessing the LAN.

    B. Install antivirus software with Live Update enabled on all laptops before they are allowed to leave the premises.

    C. Don't allow laptop computers to access the LAN.

    D. Install Internet Connection Firewall on all Windows XP laptops.

6. Your company has workstations in the lobby that allows guests to access the Internet while awaiting meetings and other appointments. You are worried that someone may be able to access sensitive corporate information by installing a program to record the network packets traveling on the network. What can you do to alleviate this potential threat?

    A. Remove the computer from the lobby and place it in the conference room.

    B. Require users to log in on the workstation.

    C. Remove the floppy and CD/DVD drive from the workstations.

    D. Place this computer outside the corporate firewall so that it is on a different segment than that of the corporate workstations and servers.

7. You are the administrator of a large retail chain with offices in more than 40 states. You need to make sure that all computers are kept up-to-date. Which of the following should you do to eliminate network vulnerabilities? (Choose all that apply.)

   A. Apply service packs

   B. Apply feature packs.

   C. Apply hotfixes.

   D. Uninstall services that are not being used.

   E. All of the above.

8. Your organization is concerned that users may be running Trojan horse applications that may be exposing your infrastructure to security exploits. You must develop a procedure that will be used to determine what services should be running on a computer. Which of the following steps should you complete? (Choose all that apply.)

   A. Create a list of the services that should be running on workstations.

   B. Use the Windows Service Challenge and Response (WSCR) utility to design a security authentication scheme that will validate services prior to accessing resources.

   C. Compare the services running on the machine with those on the list and remove the services that are not on the accepted list.

   D. Remove the user's permissions to run services on the workstations.

9. You are designing a new segment to your network that will include an extranet. The extranet will be accessible to partners and must be secured so that its resources cannot be consumed from the Internet. The corporate LAN's resources should also be inaccessible from both the Internet and the extranet. You want to make sure that all precautions are taken to prevent a breach into your LAN, even if the extranet is breached. Which network segmentation technique should you use?

   A. Bastion host

   B. Three-pronged configuration

   C. Back-to-back configuration

   D. DMZ-Aware Tunnel

10. After an incident occurs and is resolved, which of the following steps should your security response team complete?

    A. Evidence preservation

    B. Incident Declaration

    C. Communication channel exploration

    D. Evaluation

Answers to Review Questions

1. B. As a result of having three separate segments that need to be accessed by a variety of different parties, you should use the three-pronged configuration model because it will allow for each network to be protected centrally while still allowing the appropriate level of access to each of the networks.

2.

Declare the incident
Analyze the incident
Contain the incident
Resolve the problem
Prevent reoccurrence
Document events
Preserve the evidence
Evaluate the incident response

The first step is to declare the incident. Next you analyze the incident so that you can make well thought out decisions in order to move to the next step. Once analyzed you will next contain the incident to prevent other computers from being compromised, next you will resolve the problem. Once the problem has been resolved you will take the appropriate steps to prevent the problem from reoccurring. Finally you will document the events that took place, make the necessary arrangements to preserve any evidence that was collected and lastly you will review the overall incident response so that any problems detected can be avoided in the future.

3. A. A threat model, such as the STRIDE model, can be used to gain insight on the type of attacks that you are susceptible to and what the impact to your organization would be. A security response team is useful when responding to an attack but is not necessary when predicting the threats that could be carried out against your organization. Risk and response and threat diagrams don't exist in this context.

4. A, B, D, F. In a system such as the one described in the question, an attacker would be able to tamper with the data on the web server and, potentially, the database as well. When errors occur on the server, too much information is displayed, including the username and password used to connect to the database; this constitutes information disclosure. The user may be able to gain access to the account used by the web application to access the database, which constitutes an elevation of privilege. Finally, an attacker who accessed the account the web application uses to access the database can authenticate with those credentials, which constitutes spoofing the identity of the service account.

5. B. You should install antivirus software on the laptop computers and train the users on how to keep the virus software updated. If you were to require laptops to be scanned by the IT staff, it could interfere with the IT department's efficiency as well as the efficiency of the user who cannot use their computer while it is being scanned. It is simply unrealistic to forbid the corporate laptops from accessing the network. ICF, or Internet Connection Firewall, doesn't prevent viruses from infecting a computer.

6. D. Physically relocating the computer from the lobby would not alleviate the threat unless it is moved to a separate network segment and this is not specified in answer A, so it is therefore incorrect. Requiring users to log in to the workstation doesn't prevent them from installing software, nor does it provide guests with the ability to access the Internet while waiting for an appointment. Removing the floppy or CD drive will not prevent a user from installing software, that can be downloaded from the internet and installed. The computer must be moved to a segment other than the one that corporate workstations are on. Putting it on the opposite end of a firewall further protects your network from attacks originating from this workstation and therefore answer D is correct.

7. A, C, D. Feature packs introduce new functionality, which could also introduce new bugs; feature packs should be properly tested and installed only if the feature is a service that is required by the server. Applying service packs and hotfixes will patch or fix a bug in an application or service that would otherwise be exploitable. Uninstalling services that aren't necessary makes the attack surface of the network much smaller by only needing to track and protect a smaller number of services.

8. A, C. Your organization is concerned that users may be running Trojan horse applications that may be exposing your infrastructure to security exploits. You must develop a procedure that will be used to determine what services should be running on a computer. Which of the following steps should you complete? (Choose all that apply.)

9. C. Both a bastion host and a three-pronged configuration would permit a breach to the corporate LAN if the firewall is compromised.. The back-to-back configuration would add another firewall between the extranet and the LAN and is therefore the best choice. There is no such product or configuration as a DMZ-Aware Tunnel.

10. D. Once the incident has been resolved, a meeting should take place so the security response team can review and evaluate the steps and methods that were used to resolve the problem. It is this stage of incident response that provides the highest degree of learning. There is no step for the security response team that explores the communication channels.

Case Study

You should give yourself 20 minutes to review this testlet, review the diagram, and complete the questions.

Background

Overview TenGard Security Systems (TSS) is a company who designs, builds, and sells safes.

Physical Locations TSS has an office in Los Angeles, an office in Seattle, and an office in Philadelphia. The office in Los Angeles is connected to the office in Seattle with a dedicated 256K link. A VPN connection connects the Seattle office with the Philadelphia office. The following shows the layout:

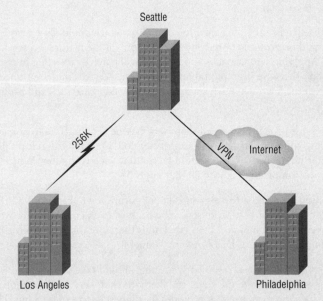

Existing Environment

Directory Services TSS has a domain controller in each office. Active Directory replication takes place between sites at a specified schedule.

Network Infrastructure All servers in the network are running Windows Server 2003, Enterprise Edition. All workstations are running Windows XP. The network also has a perimeter network located in Los Angeles. The perimeter network contains a server named WSB2BSRV1 that is not a member of any Active Directory domain. WSB2BSRV1 hosts a web service that all resellers must have access to for inventory, pricing, and ordering information.

Problem Statements   The server in the perimeter network must be accessible at all times. Currently, if a security incident takes place and requires that WSB2BSRV1 be taken offline, no resellers will be able to sell any of TSS's safes. Users constantly forget to use the Windows Update website to update their computers, which leaves most laptops and workstations vulnerable to emerging exploits.

Interviews

Chief Information Officer   We plan on implementing a wireless network in Seattle so that our users can access the network and its resources with laptop computers without having to locate an Ethernet jack. We need to make sure that users who have laptops don't infect the corporate network should their laptops obtain a virus.

Network Administrator   We need to devise a plan to prevent security incidents from taking place. Should an incident occur, we need to make sure that the appropriate evidence is preserved so that the authorities can follow up legally.

Chief Financial Officer   Regardless of the situation that takes place, our resellers must be able to access our inventory information at all times. We have an agreement that guarantees to our resellers that our data will not be unavailable for more than one hour within a week.

Business Requirements

The following rules must be in place to comply with the guidelines set forth by the government:

- All workstations must have virus protection installed, and it must be updated on a regular basis.
- Internet Information Services should not be installed on any domain controllers.
- The internal network and the demilitarized zone (DMZ) must be segregated so that if an attacker can breach the DMZ, they will still not gain access to the internal network.
- In the event of a security incident, evidence must be maintained so that the authorities can be notified.
- All workstations must have new operating system patches and service packs applied in a timely fashion.
- There must be more than one layer that an attacker has to compromise in order to penetrate the internal network.
- Only essential services should be running on domain controllers.
- Each office should continue to function in the event of an incident with a minimal impact on production.

Case Study Questions

1. How should you configure the connectivity from the internal network to the Internet?

   A. Bastion host

   B. Three-pronged configuration

   C. Back-to-back configuration

   D. None of the above

2. Which of the following actions should you take immediately after an intrusion has been detected?

   A. Create an image copy of the server.

   B. Apply the latest service pack and hotfixes

   C. Check the event logs on the server.

   D. Disconnect the network cable of the affected system(s).

3. You need to make sure that the appropriate patches are applied to all workstations in a timely fashion, even if they are not in the office. Which of the following methods would guarantee this requirement is met? (Choose all that apply.)

   A. Automate Windows Update.

   B. Use Group Policy to push the updates to all users, including those logged in remotely.

   C. Train the users to update their computers regularly, including when they are out of the office.

   D. All of the above.

4. You are going to upgrade a Windows 2000 Server to Windows Server 2003, Enterprise Edition and promote it to a domain controller. You need to make sure that it meets the business requirements. Which of the following would you do? (Choose all that apply.)

   A. Uninstall Internet Information Services from the Windows 2000 Server machine before upgrading it to Windows Server 2003.

   B. Install an antivirus package on it and schedule it to update daily.

   C. Automate Windows Update services.

   D. Remove the SVCHOST service.

   E. Disable all nonessential services.

5. A security breach occurs and you need to make sure that the appropriate authorities get notified and are provided with all the necessary evidence. Which of the following steps should you take while still maintaining the business requirements? (Choose two.)

   A. Image the compromised system.

   B. Close the office.

   C. Shut down the public network connection.

   D. Disconnect the compromised server from the network.

6. You are creating a response procedure to react to the inventory web service server becoming compromised. Which one of the following tasks should you complete in order to maintain your organization's service level agreement with the company's resellers?

   A. Move the inventory service to an uncompromised site or server and notify the resellers of the incident.

   B. Create a team to notify the press regarding the incident.

   C. Activate the response team to begin patching services.

   D. Isolate the inventory service and notify the resellers of the problem.

CASE STUDY

Answers to Case Study Questions

1. C. One of the business requirements states that there must be more than one layer that an attacker must breach in order to penetrate the internal network. Only the back-to-back configuration provides two firewalls, with the DMZ sitting between the public network and the private or internal network.

2. D. The first thing that should be done once an attacker is detected is to disconnect the network cable from the system that has been compromised. Once the network cable is unplugged, you should next create an image copy of the server to be evaluated later or used as evidence. In a lab environment, you could load the image onto a computer and check the logs to trace the exploit. Once the server is deemed unaffected by the breach, you should make sure that the latest patches and service packs are applied.

3. A, B. All of the options *could* be used to meet this requirement. However, training users to do it manually is a good idea, although it won't guarantee that the updates are applied in a timely fashion. Automating Windows Update will allow for the automatic download and installation of patches and hotfixes on a fairly regular basis. Group Policy can also be used to push the updates to the workstations; this is useful when the patches need to be tested before they are rolled out to the users.

4. B, C, E. You should make sure that an antivirus package is installed on the server and that it is updated regularly. Automating Windows Update services allows for the latest security-related patches to be automatically deployed when available. Disabling the nonessential services will make the attack surface smaller and more difficult to penetrate. By default, when you upgrade from Windows 2000 to Windows Server 2003, Enterprise Edition, Internet Information Services is disabled; therefore it is not necessary to manually uninstall it prior to the upgrade. The SVCHOST service runs many essential services and should not be shut down; you can monitor what services are running through it using the `tasklist /svc` command.

5. A, D. The first thing that you should do in this situation is to isolate the compromised system; this is easily achieved by unplugging the Ethernet cable from the switch. Once the system has been isolated, you should create an image backup of it to preserve the evidence. Shutting down the public network connection would affect more than the minimal number of services and violates the business requirements. Closing the office is even worse than shutting off the public network connection.

6. A. Because the business requirements state that you must have the inventory service back up within an hour, you must move it to another server or site while the team responds to the incident.

Chapter 3

Designing Network Infrastructure Security

MICROSOFT EXAM OBJECTIVES COVERED IN THIS CHAPTER:

✓ **Design network infrastructure security.**

- Design IP filtering.
- Design an IPSec policy.
- Design security for data transmission.

✓ **Design security for wireless networks.**

- Design public and private wireless LANs.
- Design 802.1x authentication for wireless networks.

✓ **Design security for communication between networks.**

- Select protocols for VPN access.
- Design VPN connectivity.
- Design demand-dial routing between internal networks.

✓ **Design security for communication with external organizations.**

- Design an extranet infrastructure.

✓ **Design a security strategy for client remote access.**

- Design remote access policies.
- Design access to internal resources.
- Design an authentication provider and accounting strategy for remote network access by using Internet Authentication Service (IAS).

Your network infrastructure is vulnerable to attack at many levels, including the firmware or the physical device itself. You must consider and design for securing the data that resides on a physical device—for example, configuration settings and the data on Ethernet and IP packets that pass through switches and routers on the network. You also need to consider and design for physically securing the network devices, because no matter how strong your security, it can probably be broken by someone who has physical access to it.

Physically securing your own devices is one thing, but on a public network like the Internet, you are not always in control of the devices that your data may pass over. Even internally, you might want to prevent sensitive types of data from being "accidentally" seen as it travels on the network. You need to come up with a security strategy that successfully mitigates the risks to your data moving across networks.

In this chapter, we will explore the vulnerabilities to data transmitted over a network and what protocols are available for mitigating these vulnerabilities. We will then look at designing secure remote access to your network using a virtual private network (VPN) and securely extending your network to external organizations. Finally, we will look at security problems with wireless networks and how you can overcome them.

Designing for a Secure IP Infrastructure

Your network infrastructure is vulnerable to many different kinds of attacks. Attackers can eavesdrop on the data by using a network monitoring tool commonly referred to as a packet sniffer, which is used for legitimate troubleshooting but can also be used maliciously by being placed on a compromised router or network between you and the data's destination. Attackers can take over the administration functionality of a router, switch, or hub and misdirect packets, causing denial of service (DoS) attacks. Attackers can exploit flaws in the firmware or take advantage of known default settings in these devices. They can also launch a DoS attack against a device by trying to overwhelm it with large numbers of packets. These threats to your network will need to be assessed for risk and then mitigated if necessary.

Table 3.1 lists the attacks to which your data is vulnerable.

TABLE 3.1 Common Attacks to Data Transferred across a Network

Attacks	Description of Attacks
Network monitoring	Administrators or an attacker views confidential data contained in packets from a database application or an e-mail application. Passwords that travel on the network unencrypted are viewed and used to infiltrate servers.
Denial of service	An attacker sends an unusual number of packets to the server or exploits a vulnerability that prevents legitimate users from accessing the resource.
Spoofing	An attacker modifies a packet or data to impersonate another resource or person. For example, the attacker forges return addresses on e-mails or source IP addresses on IP packets.
Data alteration	An attacker modifies data between the source and the destination. This could mean changing the data in the packets, redirecting the packets, or forging information to attack network servers. This is used for man-in-the-middle, replay, session hijacking, and packet tampering.

You will need to determine what vulnerabilities will affect a company's network and then consider the importance of the data along with the costs and the technical requirements to secure it. The following is a list of considerations that will help you in deciding what and how to secure data:

Decide what network traffic needs securing.   Securing network traffic requires the use of CPU and network bandwidth, so you will need to figure out what traffic requires security and the level of security that it requires. This can range from setting up a point-to-point connection from the PC that is sending confidential data to the server to establishing a secure connection or tunnel between routers so all traffic that passes through the routers over the segment is encrypted.

Identify the compatibility issues of the operating systems you have installed and the applications running on them.   The version of the OS or application you are running will affect what security options are available for transmitting data. You will need to weigh the cost of upgrading the OS or application with the cost of being less secure.

Make sure that the hardware is secure.   If the hardware is not secure, it doesn't really matter what security measures you are taking on the packets moving across your network. Securing the hardware means making sure you lock the wiring closets and control access to the server room. You can also add more security by using switches rather than hubs on the network. This will make it harder for attackers to "sniff" packets on your network.

Figure out what methods to use to secure data that will be transmitted across a network.
Data is vulnerable as it moves across the physical devices and mediums on the network. You can
not trust devices that you do not exercise full control over, so you will need to take appropriate
precautions with your confidential data. Mainly, you will need to figure out the identity of the
person and/or computer that is transmitting the data and encrypt the data so it cannot be read
on an insecure network. You will also need to take into account laws that restrict encryption
strength and exportation for countries where you will do business. This may mean precluding
data from being transmitted into these countries or using a separate physical network instead
of the less-expensive public network.

Once you have decided what types of attacks your data is vulnerable to, you will need to
come up with a plan to securely transmit data across the network. This may involve coming up
with a method to encrypt the data you are transmitting, verifying that the data has not been
manipulated in transit, and choosing which method you will use to authenticate remote clients
on the network.

Securely Transmitting Data

If you decide that you need to securely transmit data over a network, you have some problems
that need to be mitigated:

- You need to make sure that the data will not be read by any unauthorized individual
  between you and the source.

- You need to verify or authenticate the identity of people who will send packets.

- You need to verify that the data will not be tampered with, meaning the data in a packet
  won't be changed by someone in between you and the packet's source, which is known as
  a man-in-the-middle attack.

You can overcome these problems with transmitting the data securely by encrypting the data,
authenticating the user, and signing the data.

Encrypting Data

You can mitigate the risk of eavesdropping by encrypting the packets that you send over a network. Encrypted packets cannot be read by attackers unless they know the key to decrypt the
data in the packets. Therefore, you will need to take extra precautions to secure the keys that
are necessary to decrypt the information.

There are many types of technology used to secure data transmissions:

- Secure Sockets Layer (SSL), which is used to secure traffic to and from a web server (also
  known as HTTPS).

- Transport Layer Security (TLS), which is based on SSL and can be used to secure all types
  of traffic, from SMTP to database communication.

- IP Security (IPSec), which can be used to establish a secure connection between two devices,
  but does not provide for strong or flexible authentication mechanisms.

- Virtual Private Network (VPN) technology, which uses either PPP or L2TP to authenticate the user and then Point-to-Point Protocol (PPP) encryption or IP Security (IPSec) to encrypt all the content that traverses the network connection between the two end points. We will discuss more about VPNs in the remote access section of this chapter.

In the following sections, we will take a look at the various methods of encrypting packets.

Secure Sockets Layer and Transport Layer Security

Secure Sockets Layer (SSL) and *Transport Layer Security (TLS)* are technologies used to provide session encryption and integrity for packets sent from one computer to another. This could be client-to-server or server-to-server network traffic. It also provides a means for the verification of the server to the client and client to the server through X.509 certificates (digital certificates).

 You will learn more about X.509 certificates in Chapter 6, "Designing a PKI with Certificate Services," when we discuss public key infrastructure.

These protocols use the digital certificates in combination with public/private key and symmetric key encryption to securely exchange keys and encrypt network communications. The benefit of these protocols is that they can guard against malicious or accidental viewing of the contents of packets on a local network or over the Internet. They will also prevent the manipulation of packets sent over a network, so you can be assured that the packet that you receive is the same packet that was sent. They support passing through firewalls, Network Address Translation (NAT) servers, and other network devices without any special considerations other than making sure the proper ports are open on the device. Figure 3.1 shows where SSL would typically be used on a network.

The drawback of SSL and TLS is, like all encryption, they consume CPU resources. Therefore, enabling them will degrade server and client performance. You can get around this limitation by adding special network cards or devices that perform some of the algorithm's work that make up SSL and TLS in hardware, thereby saving your hardware's CPU for other tasks. You could also add CPU to your server to compensate for the increased demands on CPU. You can use Performance Monitor to determine the extent of the performance impact on your hardware.

FIGURE 3.1   The usual place for SSL in a network infrastructure.

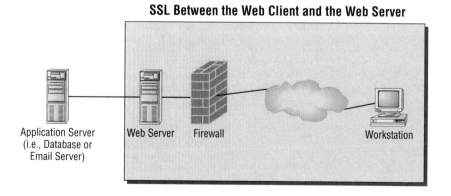

SSL Between the Web Client and the Web Server

SSL is popular for web applications that are extended to public networks like the Internet. This is because it is supported by web browsers and web servers on all platforms and has become the standard for encrypting HTTP traffic. It is also easy to set up and is used on an internal network where web data must be secured. SSL and TLS will have the widest range of compatibility among operating systems and applications because of their use on the Web and are therefore good choices when diverse systems must communicate with each other securely.

 For more information on SSL see http://wp.netscape.com/eng/ssl3/ draft302.txt. For more information on TLS, see RFC 2246 at http://www.ietf.org/rfc/rfc2246.txt.

 You will learn more about designing for SSL and TLS in Chapter 6 and Chapter 7, when we discuss designing a network for public key infrastructure and Internet Information Services (IIS) respectively.

In the following Design Scenario, you will look at design criteria for an SSL solution.

 Design Scenario

Designing for SSL on a Windows Server 2003 Network

Frankfurters, Inc. is a medium-sized company with about 700 employees located in 5 states in the United States. It produces various meat products and is looking to allow access to e-mail for its sales and executive staff throughout the United States. The company is running Windows Server 2003 on its servers and is using Exchange Server 2003 and Active Directory.

During the design process, you interviewed the following members of the company:

CIO   We want to provide e-mail access wherever our sales staff or executives may travel and on whatever computer they may be using. We need to keep the cost low, so we are looking at using the Internet and a national ISP to provide Internet access.

Network Administrator   Users may access their e-mail from their home PCs, from laptops issued by Frankfurters's IT staff, or through computers at other locations.
The e-mail contains important sales projections, client information, and other confidential information, and you need to protect this information in transit, so we need to make sure the solution can deliver the information securely over various network topologies.
We are looking at using the HTTP access in Exchange 2003 called Outlook Web Access (OWA) because it looks easy to use and comes with Exchange 2003.

Sales and Executives   We want a solution that is easy to use. We do not want to deal with set-ting up software or configuration settings for security on the device we may use.

1.   **Question:** What kind of a solution would you propose for Frankfurters, Inc.? **Answer:** Use OWA to provide access to e-mail through HTTP. Enable SSL on the server by generating a public and private key and obtaining a certificate from a company like VeriSign. Provide the users with a URL for accessing the OWA server.

2.   **Question:** Which technology would you use to secure network traffic for the solution? **Answer:** SSL is supported across most operating systems and devices, so it is the best solution for encrypting access to e-mail in this situation. SSL also does not require special intervention by the sales or executive staff. It will also be able to traverse most firewall topologies that support HTTP and SSL.

Point-to-Point Tunneling Protocol with PPP Encryption

Point-to-point Tunneling Protocol (PPTP) can be used to enable an encrypted session between two computers. PPTP tunnels the Point-to-Point Protocol (PPP) over a network like the Internet. This means that you can use the PPP infrastructure and authentication mechanisms to provide secure access to your internal network for partners or employees over the Internet or private connections in much the same way as you can use dial-up access over a modem.

PPTP was developed and standardized by Microsoft to provide a simple mechanism to create a virtual private network (VPN) with Windows NT 4 and Windows 9x clients. Microsoft decided to take advantage of the PPP support in the Windows NT 4 RAS server to authenticate the PPTP session. The resulting session key from the authentication process is used to encrypt the packets that are sent across the tunnel. Encryption is not enabled by default for PPTP, so you will need to enable it through the Security tab of the user's Property dialog box, as shown in Figure 3.2.

FIGURE 3.2   Enabling PPP encryption on Windows Server 2003

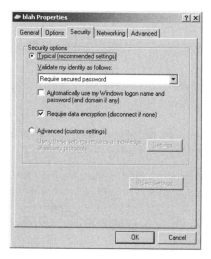

The advantages of this protocol are that it has widespread adoption in Microsoft operating systems, and it is easy to set up on any Windows platform without special downloads. It is also the only way you can set up a VPN connection to a Windows NT 4 RAS server without third-party software. PPTP will traverse all NAT devices because it encapsulates PPP packets inside an IP packet, does not provide IP packet integrity, and does not care if the IP address is changed on the packet. This means that you can use PPTP to establish a tunnel through a NAT server that does not support NAT-Traversal.

There are downfalls associated with using PPTP. Although support on the Windows platform is strong, it has not been as widely or well supported in other operating systems and devices. You would need to verify that the device with which you need to set up a PPTP session supports the protocol. PPTP supports authenticating users but not machines, so you should use it only when you need user authentication and not machine authentication. Another weakness is in the way PPTP does encryption. Its encryption strength is essentially tied to the strength of the password, so you will want to make sure you have strong password policies if you need to use PPTP. This also means if an attacker were to obtain a user's password, they may be able to use this information to decrypt the session. Currently, Microsoft does not recommend using PPTP for VPNs in Windows 2000 or later. Microsoft recommends using Layer 2 Tunneling Protocol (L2TP), for authentication, and IPSec, for encryption, as stronger protocols for secure point-to-point communication, as you will see in the next section.

In the following Design Scenario, you will look at using PPTP to establish a VPN connection to a Windows Server 2003 Routing and Remote Access Services (RRAS) server.

 Design Scenario

Designing for PPTP on a Windows Server 2003 Network

Frankfurters, Inc. is a medium-sized company with about 700 employees located in 5 states in the United States. It produces various meat products and is looking to provide secure access to various applications used by sales and executive staff. It is running Windows Server 2003 with RRAS installed on it. This server sits behind the firewall that provides NAT services. This firewall is not installed on a Windows Server 2003 machine but is a dedicated device.

During the design process, you interviewed the following members of the company:

CIO   We need a solution that will provide secure access to our internal resources. We do not require high security and do not have the budget to install a complicated solution.

Network Administrator   Our firewall does not support NAT-Traversal. We do not have the budget to upgrade the firewall to a product that supports NAT-Traversal. For security reasons, the RRAS server must sit behind the firewall.
The users need to get to the applications from their laptops, client computers, and home computers. These run operating systems varying from Windows 98 to Windows XP.

1.   **Question:** What kind of a solution would you propose for Frankfurters, Inc.? **Answer:** Because its firewall does not support NAT-Traversal and the VPN connection needs to be set up through the firewall, you will need to use PPTP. The company doesn't require high security, so the fact that PPTP relies on passwords for generating encryption keys is not as much of a concern and it keeps the infrastructure simple.

L2TP and IP Security (IPSec)

One of the ways to secure data that is sent across any type of network is with *IP Security (IPSec)*. IPSec is a set of standards that will verify, authenticate, and encrypt data at the IP packet level. IPSec accomplishes this by authenticating the client and the server and exchanging keys that are used to encrypt and sign data. This guards against man-in-the-middle attacks. It also implements the Encapsulating Security Payload (ESP) and Authenticated Header (AH) headers, which use sequence numbers and digital signatures to reduce vulnerability to replay attacks and spoofing attacks, respectively.

The ESP header encrypts and signs each packet. This prevents somebody from reading anything in and above Layer 3 in the OSI model. It will also prevent packet tampering by hashing each packet and encrypting the hash (signing the packet). The receiving computer then verifies the hash by re-computing it and comparing it with the encrypted version contained in the packet. If they don't match, the packet is discarded because it is assumed that it has been tampered with somehow. The AH header will sign traffic but not encrypt it. This means that, for data that does not require encryption, you can guard against packet tampering and man-in-the-middle attacks on a network.

IPSec does this all transparently to the user. It is contained inside of a standard IP packet and routes the same as other IP packets except when it comes into contact with a Network Address Translation (NAT) device. Because NAT needs to alter the IP address in the packet, it will cause the packet to be rejected by the client on the other end (remember the hash). Windows Server 2003 supports NAT-Traversal of IPSec packets. NAT-Traversal is an Internet Engineering Task Force (IETF) draft standard that comes up with a solution for applications like IPSec that are sensitive to the IP packet being altered. NAT-Traversal uses User Datagram Protocol (UDP) encapsulation. This means that the IPSec packet is wrapped inside a UDP/IP header. The NAT device can then change the UDP/IP header's IP address or port number without changing the contents of the IPSec packet; therefore, it will not be rejected on the other end of the connection. You can set up a point-to-point connection with IPSec through a Windows Server 2003 used as a NAT server if the client supports NAT-Traversal also.

The L2TP/IPSec client available for Windows 98, ME, 2000, and XP supports NAT-Traversal. See www.microsoft.com/windows2000/server/evaluation/news/bulletins/l2tpclient.asp for more information.

The advantages of IPSec is that it provides stronger encryption options than PPTP does. Instead of being based on the password, it can be set up to use a preshared key or a certificate-based mechanism, which would provide the strongest encryption. You can also use IPSec to verify the identity of the user (with L2TP) and the machine.

The main disadvantage of IPSec is that it does not support NAT unless NAT-Traversal is available as explained earlier. It can also be more difficult to deploy the solution if you involve preshared keys or certificate-based encryption. You will also need to use L2TP to support user authentication.

When setting up a VPN or providing security for IP traffic in Windows 2000 or later, IPSec is the preferred protocol. IPSec is built into Windows 2000 or later clients and is available for download for Windows 98 and Windows NT 4 from Microsoft's website.

CONFIGURING IPSEC THROUGH SECURITY POLICY

You can enable and configure the IPSec protocol with Group Policy for Windows 2000 or later computers or through the Network Connection Wizard. For a Windows 98, ME, or NT 4 client, you would simply create a new dial-up networking connection and choose Microsoft L2TP/IPSec VPN Adapter (or RASL2TPM on a Windows NT 4 Workstation computer). You can configure rules that a computer will follow in applying IPSec to outgoing and incoming packets. Windows Server 2003 has three built-in IPSec policies:

Client (Respond Only)   The client will use IPSec if the server requests or requires it.

Server (Request Security)   The server will request that an IPSec session be created with the client but will still establish a connection if the client does not support it.

Server (Require Security)   The server will only allow communication with clients that support IPSec. This means that one of the previous two rules needs to be configured.

These settings are located by navigating to the Security Settings section of the Group Policy console or launching the Domain, Domain Controller, or Local Security Policy MMC from the Administrative Tools section of the Start menu. You can click on the IP Security Policies section to reveal the information shown in Figure 3.3.

FIGURE 3.3   The policy settings for IPSec on Windows Server 2003

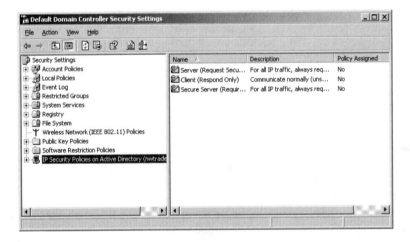

These policies are made up of a default set of rules and are useful for many but not all situations. Therefore, it is also possible to create a custom policy, which is just a collection of rules that form the IPSec policy. You can create rules that define the following:

- A filter that decides what type of traffic (like HTTP or SMTP) to apply the IPSec policy to.
- A filter action that defines what the policy should do when it matches the traffic type defined in the filter. This could be requiring encryption for a protocol or blocking all traffic from a protocol.

- An authentication method that uses one of three mechanisms: Kerberos v5 protocol, PKI certificate, or a preshared key. Kerberos or PKI certificates are the more secure choices but require additional infrastructure. The preshared key does not require Kerberos or PKI infrastructure, but the same key must be entered on each computer. The preshared key option is less secure because it is stored in the policy, which could be compromised, causing difficulty in distributing the key.

- The type of IPSec connection, which is either tunnel or transport mode. Tunnel mode secures traffic between two points (like router to router), and the clients that communicate across the link do not need to support IPSec. Transport mode secures all communication between two hosts but requires the clients to support IPSec.

- The network interface that the IPSec policy applies to, such as a VPN connection or specific network interface.

- The means for exchanging keys over the Internet via Internet Key Exchange (IKE).

It is important to recognize that the default rules do not encrypt all traffic. The following types of traffic are not protected by the filters in the default policies:

- Broadcast traffic

- Multicast traffic

- Internet Key Exchange (IKE)

- Kerberos protocol

- Resource Reservation Protocol (RSVP)

You would need to create your own custom policy rules to accommodate these protocols. You can also create rules that apply IPSec only to certain protocols or only to communication sessions with specific servers. This can allow you to reduce the performance issues associated with IPSec.

There are some limitations and concerns when applying IPSec policies to computers on your network. Windows allows only one IPSec policy to be applied to a computer at a time. This can be a limitation to some security designs that need to be mitigated through third-party support. IPSec is not free in terms of resource usage. You need to consider that IPSec will cause a degradation of performance depending on whether you use encryption, the encrypting protocol you choose, and how many filters you are applying. This will be in terms of CPU usage (although this will not be noticeable unless you are moving a large volume of data on modern systems) and bandwidth (which will only be noticed on low-bandwidth networks). You should enable IPSec only when necessary and then enable encryption only if necessary on top of the AH header. You can also buy network adapters and devices that take the load off the CPU.

You can configure IPSec through IPSec policies by following these steps:

1. From the Start menu, choose All Programs ➤ Administrative Tools and then choose Local Security Settings or Default Domain Controller Security Settings, depending on whether you are using Windows Server 2003 or Windows Server 2003 configured as a domain controller.

2. Click the IP Security Policies On Local Machine to show the rules available in the details pane.

3. Right-click the Secure Server (Require Security) rule and choose Properties, which will bring up the Secure Server (Require Security) Properties dialog box.

FIGURE 3.4   Creating IPSec rules on Windows Server 2003

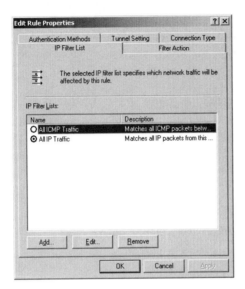

4. In the Secure Server (Require Security) Properties dialog box, click the IP Filter List tab. The IP security rules that are enabled for this policy are listed.

5. Select All IP Traffic by clicking the radio button next to it and click the Edit button, which will display the Edit Rule Properties dialog box.

6. In the Edit Rule Properties dialog box, look at the various authentication and filter settings by clicking the tabs. You define the type of network traffic that will be affected by the rule on the IP Filter List tab (as shown in Figure 3.4), and you can specify how the rule will negotiate and secure communications on the Filter Action tab. You use the Authentication Methods tab to define whether you want to use Kerberos (strong), certificates (strongest), or a preshared key (weakest) for authentication. The Tunnel Setting tab is where you can set up point-to-point communication or a tunnel, and on the Connection Type tab you can define whether the rule applies to all network traffic to and from the server or client, or you can specify that the rule only applies to LAN or remote access traffic.

7. Click the Cancel button so that the IPSec policy will not be changed.

Server Message Block Signing

Server Message Block (SMB) signing adds a keyed hash to each SMB packet. This allows you to guard your network against man-in-the-middle, replay, and session hijacking attacks. But SMB signing does nothing to protect the confidentiality of the data that is passing over the network connection. Signing requires that every packet be signed and verified, which means that you can expect a slowdown when accessing an SMB resource like a file share.

This option is enabled by default on a Windows 2000 Server, Windows XP, and Windows Server 2003. All Windows clients support it except for Windows 95 without the Active Directory client and Windows NT pre–Service Pack 3. If SMB signing is not enabled on the client, it will not be able to connect to a server on which SMB signing is enabled. This will prevent access to Group Policy, printing, and file shares on a domain controller or server with SMB signing enabled. If you have computers that must run these operating systems, then segment all computers that they need to communicate with in their own OU and apply the following Group Policy setting to the OU:

```
Computer Configuration\Windows Settings\Security Settings\Local Policies\
  Security Options\Microsoft Network Server: Digitally sign communications
  (always) = Disabled
```

This can also be applied to a domain, but it will increase the risk of the attacks mentioned earlier. IPSec provides a mechanism to sign all IP traffic and would be a better choice for heterogeneous networks.

See Knowledge Base articles Q230545 and Q161372 for information about enabling SMB signing on Windows NT 4 and Windows 98.

Using Packet and IP Filtering to Secure Your Network

When a computer is connected to a network, anything running on the server is vulnerable to one of the attacks listed in Table 3.1. It would therefore be a prudent step to lock down each server so that it will respond only to network requests for the services that its clients need.

The first rule when locking down your server is that you should install only software that you are using. We have lost count of the number of times we have heard administrators say, "I am not sure what this does, so I will install it anyway because the server might not operate correctly without it." Determining what software is necessary and what is not may take extra time, but it will make your server more secure. You must investigate each and every software package you install on a server and figure out if you really need it in your environment. This can mean even uninstalling software that is installed by default by Windows. Microsoft does not know your environment only you do, so you need to decide what should be on the server. This way, you will maintain the software properly by keeping up with security patches and service packs.

That said, it can be difficult to keep up with all the software that gets installed. For instance, the marketing departments of software companies have their goals (to move product) and the security of your network usually is not one of them. So, as an added layer of protection, you should enable filtering on your servers. There are two types of filters that you can apply to your server: IP address filtering and IP packet filtering.

IP Address Filtering

IP address filtering involves filtering traffic based on the IP address of the client computer. You have two options to enable IP filtering: You can enable all traffic except traffic from the IP addresses listed, or you can exclude all IP addresses and allow only the IP addresses listed.

If you enable IP address filtering, it is recommended that you filter all traffic except the traffic explicitly specified. You also need to realize that an IP address can be "spoofed" (forged), so you should still rely on additional forms of authentication for the users.

You can enable IP address filtering on Windows Server 2003 to specify the traffic you want to filter. To do so, follow these steps:

1. Choose Start ➢ All Programs ➢ Administrative Tools ➢ Internet Information Services (IIS) Manager.

2. Navigate to the Default Web Site node in the tree view.

3. Right-click the Default Web Site node and choose Properties from the context menu.

4. In the Default Web Site Properties dialog box, choose the Directory Security tab.

5. Click the Edit button in the IP Address And Domain Name Restrictions dialog box, shown in Figure 3.5.

6. Click the Add button to add an IP address, domain name, or range of IP addresses to filter.

FIGURE 3.5 Filtering IP addresses using the IP Address And Domain Name Restrictions dialog box

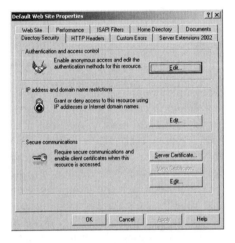

IP Packet Filtering

If you need more granular control than just preventing an IP address from communicating with your server, you can use IP packet filtering. *IP packet filtering* prevents specific packets from reaching their destined ports on the server. This can be effective in guarding against packets for specific services that would not represent legitimate traffic to the server.

You define a filter based on the ports of the protocols of UDP, TCP, or the IP number. Filtering based on UDP or TCP allows you to filter all packets except the packets destined for the ports that you specify. Filtering based on the IP protocol allows you to filter all packets except for those from the IP protocol number that you specify. This would allow you to filter the ARP protocol, for example. It will not allow you to filter ICMP traffic, though.

You can enable IP packet filtering on Windows Server 2003 by following these steps:

1. Right-click the network connection that you would like to enable packet filtering on and select Properties from the context menu to open the Network Connection dialog box.

2. Click Internet Protocol (TCP/IP) in the list box and then click the Properties button.

3. In the Internet Protocol (TCP/IP) Properties dialog box, click the Advanced button and then click the Options tab in the Advanced TCP/IP Settings dialog box.

4. Click on TCP/IP Filtering and then click on the Properties button to open up the TCP/IP Filtering dialog box, shown in Figure 3.6.

5. In the TCP/IP Filtering dialog box, configure the packet filter. Select the Enable TCP/IP Filtering (All Adapters) check box to enable TCP/IP filtering for all the adapters on the box.

6. To configure a filter on the adapter, select the Permit Only option and then click the Add button. Type in the port that you want to filter. For instance, to permit only connections to a web server on the server, click the Permit Only option over the TCP Ports selection, click the Add button, and then type 80 in the TCP Ports list box.

FIGURE 3.6   Filtering IP packets using the TCP/IP Filtering dialog box

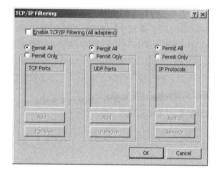

Real World Scenario

A W32.Slammer Worm Attack Prevented Because of Filters

We had a web server that had some of the sample applications installed for some development purposes. This meant that it had Microsoft Data Engine (MSDE) 2000 installed on it and the web server was not being maintained (we were not installing the latest SQL Server 2000 patches on the server). Therefore, the server was vulnerable to attacks due to security holes that are inevitable in any product. This is usually not as much of a problem on a server that is actively maintained. The patches would be installed and the vulnerability would be patched. But this was not the case on this server. We had installed packet filtering on the box as part of the standard setup of the server. We knew that the box would be used for web applications, FTP, and SMTP-based applications. We enabled the filters to allow this traffic along with the capability to authenticate with Active Directory. When the Slammer worm hit, the server was protected because it was not allowing packets to communicate with port UDP 1434, so the Slammer worm was not able to infect the computer. These filters, by being totally exclusive of all traffic except the traffic we allowed, prevented attacks even though the applications were not properly maintained.

In the following Design Scenario, you will create a security design that will include filtering.

 **Design Scenario**

Designing for Filtering

Frankfurters, Inc. has just set up a server that will serve as its web server. The folks in the IT department are concerned about the viruses and worms that are on the Internet. They have been careful to only install the services that they need on their web server. They are still concerned that they may have missed a service.

1.   **Question:** When designing their IP Infrastructure, what would you do to help alleviate their concerns? **Answer:** You could propose enabling IP packet filtering on the server to prevent access to other protocols. You would enable access to port 80 and 443 to support HTTP and SSL. You would also need to consider the ports used to manage the server and to upload new content to the server. A secure design would probably enable these only when needed.

Designing for a Secure Remote Access Infrastructure

Maintaining data security is becoming more important each year as more organizations establish network links between them to share information and increase productivity and as more employees are allowed to work from home. These connections create the need for a mechanism to manage remote access to a network. Because of these security concerns, many security designs include *virtual private networks (VPNs).*

You can set up the Routing and Remote Access Services (RRAS) on Windows Server 2003 to support a VPN. After deciding whether you will allow remote access to your network, you will need to weigh security risks and benefits of the various protocols that are available to you for remote access. This includes the authentication protocols and the data transmission protocols.

A Windows Server 2003 RRAS server uses PPP to establish a wide area network (WAN) connection between two devices. These two devices need to agree upon specific information before they can communicate. The PPP specification sets no particular authentication protocol as a standard. The authentication protocol is negotiated with the Link Control Protocol (LCP) during the Link Establishment phase. During this phase, the two devices establish specific network parameters like the size of a frame, whether to use compression, and the authentication protocol to use for validating the user.

In the following sections we will discuss the various protocols that can be used by Windows Server 2003 to authenticate clients or servers on your network.

Authentication Protocols

Windows Server 2003 has many built-in protocols. In the following sections, we'll describe the protocols that can be used for authentication.

Password Authentication Protocol (PAP)

With *Password Authentication Protocol (PAP)*, the user ID and password are transmitted in clear text to the server, where it is compared to the server's version of the same information. This is not a secure means of authenticating a user and should be avoided in most environments.

Shiva Password Authentication Protocol (SPAP)

Shiva Password Authentication Protocol (SPAP) was developed for the ShivaLAN Rover product. It transmits the password in a reversible encryption format. This means that this protocol is subject to replay and server impersonation attacks. The password encryption format is also easy to break. This protocol should not be enabled because there are better protocols supported by Windows Server 2003 and this is only here for backward compatibility with devices that support only SPAP.

Challenge Handshake Authentication Protocol (CHAP)

Challenge Handshake Authentication Protocol (CHAP) is the industry standard protocol for performing PPP authentication and is popular among Internet Service Providers (ISPs). This protocol uses the challenge-and-response mechanism for validating the user. When the client and server try to initialize a PPP session, the server sends a challenge to the client in the form of a random number and a session number. The client concatenates the user's password to the challenge and hashes it using an MD5 algorithm with a shared secret to generate a 128-bit response.

 A hash is a fixed-length value that is a nonreversible form of encryption. The value is sent through a function referred to as a hash function and a unique value is returned. It is sometimes referred to as a one-way hash. This means that there is no way to determine the information in the hash from the hash itself.

The server compares the hash that it receives with the one it generates. In the case of a Windows Server 2003 RRAS server, it would make a request to the domain controller for the user's password and concatenate it to the challenge it sent to the client. It would then hash the challenge and compare it with the response it received from the client. If they match, the user is authenticated and a PPP data connection is established to the RRAS server. The user is not authenticated on the network until they log in to the domain. In other words, when you connect to the RRAS server, you authenticate your remote access connection, using a form of CHAP or smart card authentication through EAP; once you are connected, you will have to authenticate to access network resources. If you are using a Windows 2000 or later client, you will access network resources using Kerberos authentication; otherwise, you will use a form of NT LAN Manager (NTLM) authentication.

The shared secret for the hash algorithm should not be sent over the network connection, or it should be encrypted by setting up a trust between the client and the server, which would establish a key on both sides through some mechanism not defined in the CHAP protocol. The secret can be variable (just as long as the server and client stay in sync) to discourage replay attacks. The secret also can allow for setting a time limit of use between challenges so that it will expire and you can limit the time of exposure to any single attack because the attacker would need to figure out the new secret.

The advantages to using the CHAP protocol for authentication is that it is a standard that is supported on many platforms. PAP is supported on many platforms also, but it has the disadvantage of passing the password over the network. CHAP does not send the password to the server; it hashes it, which provides for the encryption of the password.

A disadvantage to CHAP is that it requires that you store the passwords in a reversible encryption format so that the domain controller can return the password to the RRAS server. This makes the server susceptible to attackers using tools like l0phtcrack that crack passwords based on hashing values and compare them to the hash. If you must use this form of encryption, make sure you secure all copies of your accounts database, including backups, and that you limit physical access to the server. In addition, the passwords are passed over the network to the RRAS server, making them susceptible to attack, so you will need to consider encrypting the connection between the domain controller and the RRAS server.

 CHAP is defined in RFC 1994, entitled *PPP Challenge Handshake Authentication Protocol (CHAP)*.

Microsoft Challenge Handshake Authentication Protocol (MS-CHAP)

Microsoft Challenge Handshake Authentication Protocol (MS-CHAP) is Microsoft's version of CHAP. It uses the MD4 algorithm for the hash and the Data Encryption Standard (DES) encryption algorithm to generated the hash. It also provides a mechanism for changing passwords and reporting errors with the authentication process. MS-CHAP was developed for Windows 3.1 and the original version of Windows 95. It has been replaced with MS-CHAPv2 (discussed next) due to some security issues, such as sending two parallel hashes: LAN Manager and NT LAN Manager. The LAN Manager hash was much weaker and easily broken by network tools. This then aided in an attack on the NT LAN Manager hash. It also did not authenticate the server, so it was subject to man-in-the-middle attacks and replay attacks. These were addressed in MS-CHAPv2.

 MS-CHAP is defined in RFC 2488, entitled *Microsoft PPP CHAP Extensions*.

Microsoft Challenge Handshake Authentication Protocol Version 2 (MS-CHAPv2)

In response to security issues discovered in the MS-CHAP protocol, Microsoft released *Microsoft Challenge Handshake Authentication Protocol Version 2 (MS-CHAPv2)*. This is the strongest password protocol supported by Windows Server 2003 for remote access and should be used when smart cards or certificates are not an option. MS-CHAPv2 disables LAN Manager Security, which means that the original Windows 95 and older clients will not be able to authenticate. It uses a 16-byte authenticator response to verify that the Windows Server 2003 RRAS server is responding with a SUCCESS message. These and other improvements make this fairly strong, but it still suffers from being based on user password complexity like other forms of password authentication. It would be a good practice to use a strong password policy when using MS-CHAPv2.

Bruce Schneier of Counterpane Systems and Mudge from L0pht Heavy Industries have two articles on Bruce Schneier's website detailing the security vulnerabilities of MS-CHAP and MS-CHAPv2. You can find the articles at www.schneier.com/paper-pptp.html and www.schneier.com/paper-pptpv2.html.

Extensible Authentication Protocol (EAP)

Extensible Authentication Protocol (EAP) is a standard way of adding additional authentication protocols to PPP. EAP provides support for certificate-based authentication, smart cards, and other protocols like RSA's SecurID. It allows third-party companies to provide even stronger authentication protocols to meet your company's security needs. Windows Server 2003 comes with an EAP package for using smart cards or MS-CHAPv2.

Windows Server 2003 comes with two EAP packages: MD5-CHAP and Certificate or Smart Card. The MD5-CHAP is just a test package used to troubleshoot EAP connections and should not be used in production.

Smart Cards

A smart card is a card that has a chip in it that securely stores data. This data usually consists of digital certificates and the user's private keys. Smart cards use a two-tiered authentication mechanism, so the certificates and keys are not accessible to someone if they were to steal the smart card without the user's PIN. You can use a smart card to establish a PPP data connection with the RRAS server, but the user will still need to log into the network with both a user ID and password or through the smart card. Using smart cards requires a Public Key Infrastructure (PKI) to manage the certificates used to authenticate users. PKI, certificates, and smart cards are discussed in detail in Chapter 6.

Deciding on Which Authentication Strategy to Choose

There are some things that you need to consider when designing for authentication security for a remote access infrastructure. You should avoid the use of PAP or SPAP on your RRAS server. Both of these protocols send the password over the wire, which means it can be captured and cracked. You are better off using one of the versions of CHAP or EAP. Due to security problems with MS-CHAP, Microsoft recommends that you use EAP or MS-CHAPv2 for authentication, preferably EAP if you have a public key infrastructure. In fact, by default, Windows Server 2003 installs RRAS with CHAP and MS-CHAP disabled.

If you must use PAP, SPAP, or CHAP to integrate with third-party products or non-Windows clients that do not support MS-CHAPv2 or a common EAP mechanism, you will need to enable reversible encryption in Windows Server 2003 Active Directory. This is done one of two ways: using the Account tab on the user's Properties dialog box or using the Domain Security Policy snap-in.

To enable reversible encryption from the user's Properties dialog box, follow these steps:

1. Open the Active Directory Users And Computers snap-in.

2. Open the property page for the user account that requires reversible encryption by right-clicking the user account and choosing Properties from the context menu.

3. In the user Properties dialog box, select the Account tab.

4. Select the Store Password Using Reversible Encryption option in the Account Options list box, as seen in Figure 3.7.

5. Click the OK button to enable reversible encryption.

FIGURE 3.7 Selecting the Store Password Using Reversible Encryption option

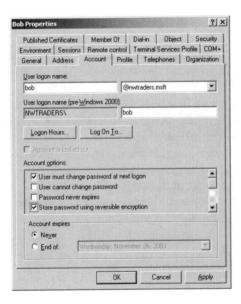

To enable reversible encryption from the Domain Policy snap-in, follow these steps:

1. Open the Domain Security Policy snap-in (you could also do this in the default domain group policy).

2. Select Security Settings ➤ Account Policies ➤ Password Policy.

3. Enable the Store Passwords Using Reversible Encryption For All Users in the domain policy.

If you need to enable reversible encryption, you should try to minimize the number of accounts affected by enabling it for specific users only. You would then want to make sure that these users have difficult passwords to guard against brute force attacks or dictionary attacks on the passwords. You would do this for the domain only if most of your users were Macintosh or Linux users because you would need to support the CHAP protocol or if you are an ISP and not sure what OS your users will be using. You should investigate using EAP if you need a more secure solution for integrating various operating systems.

You should determine how important security is for your remote access infrastructure. You will need to factor in what types of clients you are using and the costs associated with the security technology. If security is the most important thing, then you should use the EAP option. This means that you could use smart cards or SecurID to provide authentication. You will also need a PKI to support smart cards, as well as make sure the smart card solution covers all of your client operating systems and devices.

If you don't deem security important enough to warrant smart cards and a PKI because the associated costs for physical hardware and administration are too much for your organization, you should choose MS-CHAPv2 if you have Windows clients and make sure all the other protocols are disabled. You should strive to use only the most secure authentication method for your clients. If you have non-Windows OSes, then you may need to enable CHAP if you do not choose to use a smart card solution or can't find a version of the PPP protocol that supports MS-CHAPv2 for the client.

In summary, you should consider the following when choosing an authentication strategy:

- You should choose EAP using smart cards to provide for two-factor authentication. Smart cards will have a certificate that in combination with the user's password or PIN will validate the user. If the person trying to authenticate does not have both, then they will not be validated. The drawback of EAP is that it requires a PKI, which means higher management costs and more complexity in the network infrastructure.

- You should choose MS-CHAPv2 in an environment in which you have Windows 98 or greater clients and do not want to maintain a complex PKI infrastructure.

- You should choose CHAP or PAP when you need to support a diverse set of OSes and devices and do not require strong security.

In the "Choosing an Authentication Strategy" Design Scenario, you will design an authentication strategy for a Windows Server 2003 network.

Design Scenario

Choosing an Authentication Strategy

Frankfurters, Inc. needs to set up a VPN to allow employees to access a terminal server that runs various applications they can use to do work on the road and at home.

During the design process, you interviewed the following members of the company:

CFO   There is no budget to purchase servers or hire additional staff in this cycle. We will need a solution that allows us to use our current hardware and staff.

CIO   Frankfurters has a small IT staff that is already overextended keeping up with the applications and servers that are currently installed on the network.

Network Administrator   We have a strong password policy that is enforced by a password policy in Active Directory. We have standardized all our clients on Windows 2000 or greater.

1. **Question:** You need to come up with an authentication strategy for Frankfurters. What would you recommend? **Answer:** You should recommend the use of MS-CHAPv2 because Frankfurters does not have the budget to implement PKI, which would be necessary with EAP. The main weakness of MS-CHAPv2 is that it relies on passwords to generate session keys, so you will want to stress the importance to Frankfurters staff of maintaining its strong password policy.

Determining What Encryption Method to Use

After you have determined the authentication strategy for your remote access clients, your VPN will still be vulnerable to data alteration and network monitoring. You will need to decide how you will encrypt the data traveling over the connection to prevent these attacks. This is especially important in the case of a VPN that is using the Internet as a means of connection. The encrypting of data over the public network is what makes the connection private. You can choose between three different ways to set up encryption for your VPN connection, and each has its strengths and weaknesses:

Point-to-Point Tunneling Protocol (PPTP)   PPTP is a Layer 2 tunneling protocol that encapsulates PPP packets into IP datagrams. The resulting datagram can be routed over IP-based networks and take advantage of the authentication, compression, and encryption services provided by PPP to authenticate a user with the RRAS server supporting PPTP. PPTP provides for encrypting traffic through the Microsoft Point-to-Point Encryption (MPPE) protocol. The session keys for encrypting the traffic are generated from the MS-CHAP or EAP passwords; therefore, you must be using MS-CHAP, MS-CHAPv2, or EAP to support encryption with PPTP.

Layer 2 Tunneling Protocol/IP Security protocol (L2TP/IPSec)   L2TP also encapsulates PPP packets in an IP datagram as PPTP does. This means that it can take advantage of the services provided by PPP, like authentication or compression. However, it does not use the MPPE protocol to provide for encryption of the PPP packet. MPPE is considered a proprietary section of PPP, so it leads to compatibility problems between OSes and devices. Instead, L2TP takes advantage of IPSec to provide encryption. IPSec supports many types of encrypting technology and is not limited by one technology as PPTP is. L2TP provides for user authentication, as PPTP does, but also provides for computer authentication through Kerberos, certificates, or pre-shared keys because it relies on IPSec. The combination of L2TP and IPSec is sometimes referred to as IPSec transport mode. It is also more widely supported on non-Windows-based operating systems and devices. L2TP\IPSec is now supported on Windows 98 or later operating systems and is available for download from Microsoft.

You can download the latest L2TP\IPSec client for Windows 98 or later at www.microsoft.com/windows2000/server/evaluation/news/bulletins/l2tpclient.asp.

IP Security (IPSec) protocol   IPSec can be used alone to establish an encrypted VPN connection between two devices, which is referred to as IPSec tunnel mode. IPSec tunnel mode provides for machine authentication through Kerberos, PKI certificates, or a pre-shared key. It does not provide for user authentication, so it is not as useful for client-to-server VPN connections. It is typically used in a gateway-to-gateway connection in which one of the end points does not support L2TP.

You need to consider different aspects of your network infrastructure and the devices that you use when designing an authentication and encryption strategy for your VPN. You should consider the following items in your VPN design:

Compatibility with NAT   Because PPTP encrypts the data in the PPP packet only, it is immune to NAT and the IP datagrams can be manipulated and without you having to worry about them being discarded at the other end. L2TP is not compatible with NAT because it uses IPSec to secure its IP packets. This means that after the NAT server tries to update the IP address or the port of the packet, it will fail the integrity check and the packet will be discarded. You can get around this limitation with a Windows Server 2003 RRAS server because it supports a technology called NAT-Traversal. NAT-Traversal encapsulates the IPSec packet into a UDP datagram that can then traverse the NAT device, much like PPTP is packaged in a PPP packet. The clients and the server need to support NAT-Traversal for this to work.

User authentication   PPTP and L2TP/IPSec support user authentication on a Windows platform through the authentication protocols discussed earlier. IPSec tunnel mode does not support user authentication.

Computer authentication   PPTP does not support machine authentication. L2TP/IPSec does because it relies on IPSec to provide its encryption. IPSec supports verifying the identity of the machine through one of three mechanisms: Kerberos, PKI certificates, or a pre-shared key. The PKI certificate is considered the strongest of the three, but it requires a PKI infrastructure.

Kerberos is second and just requires an Active Directory domain in a Windows Server 2003 network with a Windows 2000 or greater client. Pre-shared keys are the easiest to configure because they require no additional infrastructure, but there are logistic problems for distributing the keys securely and most should be used in a test lab or on small networks when there are no other options.

Compatibility with most network devices   PPTP is primarily used on Windows-based networks. L2TP/IPSec is widely supported by many devices and OSes. You will choose L2TP and IPSec to connect with non-Windows servers and devices.

In summary, when designing an encryption strategy for your network, the following points may be helpful:

- You should use L2TP/IPSec as a VPN solution whenever possible. It provides the most security options and Microsoft recommends using it for remote access. It also gives you the most compatibility with other network devices and OSes.

- For maximum security, you should choose EAP with smart card support for the user authentication protocol, PKI certificates installed on the machine to provide machine authentication, and IPSec with 128-bit encryption. This solution would require a PKI and the most amount of administrative overhead. PKI will be covered in more depth in Chapter 6.

- You can scale back on the administrative overhead of PKI and still provide a reasonably secure solution by using MS-CHAPv2 for the user authentication protocol, Kerberos for the machine authentication through Active Directory, and IPSec for the encryption protocol with 128-bit encryption. This would not require any extra servers but still provide a reasonably secure environment for most users.

- You should use PPTP if you have an all-Windows-client network and want to support Windows 95 clients or later. You can also use it if you do not want to install the L2TP/IPSec client on Windows 98, ME, and NT 4. In addition, you can use PPTP to provide a VPN tunnel through a NAT device if it does not support NAT-Traversal.

- L2TP/IPSec and IPSec can be tunneled through a NAT device (like a firewall or Windows Server 2003 RRAS server that is providing NAT) only if the NAT device and the client supports NAT-Traversal. If not, you will need to use PPTP or set up a connection from the NAT device to the gateway on the other network through an IPSec tunnel mode or L2TP/IPSec if both sides support it.

- You should use IPSec tunnel mode only if one of the devices does not support L2TP; otherwise, take advantage of the security provided by the additional user authentication.

In the "Designing a VPN Solution" Design Scenario, you will design a VPN encryption solution. VPNs can also be used to establish secure connections to internal networks. You would then use Kerberos or NTLM to authenticate on the internal network for access to network resources. This would be especially true when connecting to internal networks through a demand-dial routing connection.

Design Scenario

Designing a VPN Solution

Frankfurters, Inc. has implemented a new customer relations management application to improve customer service. Most of the sales staff work from home or on the road. The company has issued notebook computers to its sales staff. The notebooks are running Windows XP Professional. The network uses Windows Server 2003 Active Directory to authenticate the users. The data that is in the customer service application is sensitive customer information and needs to be protected. The company wants to use the cheap access to the Internet to provide access to the company's network.

1. **Question:** What encryption technology should you propose for the VPN? **Answer:** Frankfurters should set up a VPN solution to use L2TP/IPSec.

Designing Demand-Dial Routing for Internal Networks

Broadband connections are seemingly pervasive in the United States nowadays. But there are still many locations where they are not available or are too costly. In addition, most will face higher prices for broadband abroad, if it is available at all. In these cases, you can take advantage of the Windows Server 2003 RRAS demand-dial feature. You can have Windows Server 2003 dial an ISP or a phone number connected to a modem at a remote office when packets need to be routed to another location.

Windows Server 2003 can use Plain Old Telephone Service (POTS), Integrated Services Digital Network (ISDN), or Asynchronous Digital Subscriber Lines (ADSL) lines through new support for Point-to-Point Protocol Over Ethernet (PPPoE) with the appropriate modem type (POTS, ISDN, or DSL) for demand-dial. You can configure the type of demand-dial interface by launching the Demand-Dial Interface Wizard through the following steps:

1. Navigate to the Routing And Remote Access MMC by selecting Start ≻ All Programs ≻ Administrative Tools ≻ Routing And Remote Access.

2. Right-click your server name in the left pane and choose Configure And Enable Routing And Remote Access from the context menu.

3. In the Routing And Remote Access Server Setup Wizard, select Next.

4. Choose the Secure Connection Between Two Private Networks option.

5. Choose the Yes option for the question Do You Want To Use Demand-Dial Connections To Access Remote Networks?

6. Choose how you would like to assign IP addresses to remote clients.

7. Click the Finish button to launch the Demand-Dial Interface Wizard.

8. Click the Next button to advance to the Interface Name screen. Give the interface a name.

9. Choose the type of demand-dial connection, as shown in Figure 3.8. Click Next.

FIGURE 3.8 Various demand-dial connection types that can be used for the demand-dial interface

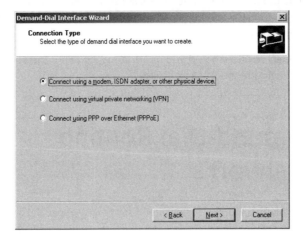

10. Choose the modem or interface over which the connection will be established. Click Next.

11. Enter the phone number that will be used to establish the connection. Click Next.

12. Choose the transport and security options available for the connection. You will have the choice to route IP packets over this connection, to add a user account so that a remote router can dial into the demand-dial RRAS server and authenticate, to send a plain-text password to the computer on the other end if necessary, or to use scripting to complete the connection with the remote router. Click Next.

13. You will need to establish a static route to enable the demand-dial interface. This should encompass the networks on the other side of the connection. Click Next.

14. Specify the connection credentials that will be used to authenticate with the demand-dial server on the other end of the connection. This provides security by specifying who can establish a demand-dial connection with the server on the other end. Click Next.

15. Click Finish to complete the Demand-Dial Interface Wizard.

Once you create a demand-dial connection, it is essentially the same as if you had a routed Internet or network connection. Therefore, you should design security for your dial-up connection as if it were a permanent connection to the Internet.

Determining the Type of Demand-Dial Connection to Use

The first thing that you need to decide is whether you are going to dial an ISP or dial directly to your company or branch office. This will be a decision for which you'll need to consider the level of security desired versus the cost of managing and maintaining your own phone lines and modems. You have more security if you dial into your own lines because you'll avoid sending your data over the Internet where it can be viewed or manipulated and you'll have control over your own lines. However, don't think that you are secure in using your own lines. There are ways to eavesdrop on data traveling over all types of connections, so you will need to take the same precautions in encrypting your data and authenticating the client as you would for any remote access client, earlier in this chapter. Having your own lines will make it more difficult for the attacker to get to the devices and infrastructure.

If you decide to use the Internet to make your connection, you will need to consider how you are going to authenticate and encrypt data that travels over the Internet. You can treat this connection to your branch office just as you would handle a remote client authentication and establish a VPN for the information you need to send over the connection. You can use IPSec to establish a tunnel or use L2TP/IPSec to perform point-to-point communication, as discussed in the section "Designing for a Secure Remote Access Infrastructure." Just make sure you also treat this connection as if it were a broadband connection to the Internet, and remember that it is a two-way connection. Just as you should never have your network exposed to the Internet, you should consider setting your demand-dial router behind a NAT server at a minimum or, even better, use a firewall. You can, at the very least, use a new feature of Windows Sever 2003 called Internet Connection Firewall (ICF) to enable a basic firewall on the demand-dial router.

Setting up a dial-up broadband connection to an internal branch network means that you have predictability because the client on the other side is at a set location. This means that you can use RRAS features like caller ID verification and various callback options for the dial-up adapter properties configuration, as shown in Figure 3.9.

FIGURE 3.9   Setting up caller ID and callback.

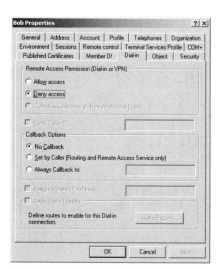

You should take advantage of both of these features on a demand-dial router because they call from a fixed number. Caller ID and callback can be set up using remote access policies on the Windows account used to authorize the connection.

The account used to authenticate a connection can be either a client computer connection or a demand-dial router connection. Typically, you will only want to allow the demand-dial account to connect to a demand-dial router. Windows Server 2003 will differentiate between a demand-dial router and a client connection by looking at the account used by the connecting client to authenticate. If the user ID is the same as the user ID configured for the answering router, it is a demand-dial router connection. You should set the user ID used by the demand-dial router to be the same as the user ID for the demand-dial interface on the answering router.

You also should consider the following when configuring a demand-dial connection: You need to configure the connection on both ends to enable communication in both directions; otherwise, it will be a one-direction communication. You should avoid using dynamic routing protocols like RIP over a demand-dial interface, because they add unnecessary overhead and an added security risk. This means that you would need to configure static routes on the interface. Microsoft has provided an option called auto-static update mode to update routes if you would rather not do it manually.

Designing Security for Demand-Dial Routing

When designing demand-dial routing, you need to consider whether the connection is required on demand or is a persistent connection. An on-demand connection is generally used if the bandwidth is paid based on time connected, and it's common to ISDN and long-distance calls. This will affect some of your security design when setting up the connection. You have a choice to use a modem to connect or a VPN. The on-demand option will not always be up, so it has less of an attack footprint and you could take advantage of caller ID or callback technology in many cases. The persistent connection option will generally use a VPN connection, so you will need to consider the security of the VPN or installing one if it does not exist.

You will also need to decide whether the connection will be one-way or two-way initiated connections. In two-way connections, both routers must be able to accept and initiate connections, so both sides must be configured. In a one-way connection, you would not configure the answering demand-dial interface to dial out because it is used only to answer calls. This helps you go beyond authenticating the demand-dial router.

Demand-dial routers will need to be authenticated just like a client that was connecting to the network. This means that you need to make sure you use a user account to validate the connection between the branch office and the central office. You can indicate to the answering RRAS router that this is a demand-dial router call by naming the demand-dial interface on the answering RRAS demand-dial router with the same name as the user account that is used by the calling router to authenticate.

The user account that you use for your demand-dial connections will need to be given some consideration. By default, it will have its remote access permission set to allow access even if you want to control it with the remote access policy through the Routing And Remote Access MMC or in the user's Properties dialog box under the Dial-In tab. The remote access policy allows you to control who can connect to an RRAS server. You will also need to consider the password strength used for this account. The domain password policy will be enforced on the account, but you might want to consider making it stronger (for example, 14 characters instead of the usual 8 for user accounts) because this connection is vulnerable. You need to do the following on the General tab of the user's Properties dialog box:

- Clear the setting for User Must Change Password At Next Logon because the demand-dial interface is not able to change the password and will not be able to connect because it is not an interactive process. If you use the Demand-Dial Interface Wizard, this will be set automatically.

- Check the Password Never Expires check box to make sure that the password will not have to be changed at an inopportune time. The password expiring will cause the demand-dial connection to fail. You should establish a password rotation policy that you control to make sure the passwords get changed on a regular basis.

Designing for Demand-Dial Authentication

When setting up a demand-dial connection, you should use the strongest authentication possible on Windows Server 2003, which is EAP-TLS with certificates. If you don't have a PKI, you should use MS-CHAPv2 and enforce a strong password policy to guard against attacks.

The EAP-TLS solution will require that you install a user certificate on the calling router and a machine certificate on the answering router to verify the identities of the routers to each other. You will need to consider a method of deploying the certificates in your design. You can distribute the certificates on a floppy disk and then import them on the demand-dial routers after physically delivering the routers. You can also use smart cards as a means of distributing the certificates.

If you use EAP-TLS, you will also need to make sure that the demand-dial routers can see the certificate revocation list (CRL) on a server, which means the certificate authority (CA) must be available. Or, if you published the list into Active Directory, you can use a local domain controller computer. You will need to use the latter if you will not be able to see the certificate authority until after you have established the demand-dial connection.

You can also verify the identity of the calling router by using a Remote Authentication Dial-In User Service (RADIUS) server. This can be used to provide accounting and auditing for your demand-dial activity, and it supports MS-CHAPv2 and EAP with smart cards or machine certificates for authentication. This is particularly useful if you need to dial into a router that is not running Windows Server 2003 RRAS or if you need to establish a VPN connection by first dialing up an ISP, authenticating against the corporate network, and then establishing the VPN. In addition to strong authentication, you can use encryption to enhance security over your demand-dial connection.

You can encrypt data over your demand-dial link with either link encryption or end-to-end encryption. Link encryption is sometimes referred to as tunnel mode and will only encrypt the data between two routers. End-to-end encryption protects data from the source host to its final destination. You will typically use link encryption for a demand-dial router connection unless you are dialing through a VPN to establish the connection. IPSec is the industry standard protocol for setting up link encryption. IPSec should be used in conjunction with L2TP to establish end-to-end encryption and stronger authentication on the connection.

You would use the security protocols previously discussed to provide for the VPN demand-dial tunnel because you have all the same encryption options with demand-dial routers as you have with VPNs. If you use the L2TP/IPSec solution, you will need to distribute the certificates that are used to authenticate the IPSec security association. You also need to make sure that your design provides for a firewall at the branch office and that you allow L2TP/IPSec traffic to pass between the corporate and branch offices. If you are using L2TP, the gateway IP address cannot be set because L2TP is a point-to-point protocol. You will need to set up a static route to the branch and/or corporate office, which will make sure the appropriate traffic will be forwarded to the correct interface.

The default settings for a demand-dial connection is to require data encrypting using MS-CHAP or MS-CHAPv2. The type of encryption will be negotiated by the client and server before the connection is established. You should not clear the Require Data Encryption (Disconnect If None) check box in the Remote Router Properties dialog box, which is accessed from the Routing And Remote Access MMC. You can also configure the use of a particular encryption algorithm by using the Encryption tab of the property page for the remote access policy for the account used on the calling routers.

Controlling Connections to a Demand-Dial Router

You can control when a demand-dial router can use the connection through two properties of the demand-dial interface: demand-dial filtering and dial-out hours. Demand-dial filtering allows you to specify the types of IP traffic that will cause a connection to be made. All other types of IP traffic will not establish a connection. The dial-out hours option allows you to restrict the hours in which the demand-dial router is able to make a demand-dial connection. This will guard against attacks that could occur when, for example, a branch office is closed and the connection is not needed.

You can also apply IP packet filters to the interface, as discussed in the section "IP Packet Filtering" earlier in this chapter. You need to realize that demand-dial filters are applied before the connection is made and IP packet filters are applied after the connection is made. Make sure you don't allow IP filters to pass through the demand-dial filters only to be discarded by IP filtering on the firewall or IP packet filtering on the server. It is recommended that you apply the same filters to each type of filtering.

In summary, you should consider the following points when securing your demand-dial connection:

- If you need more security for your connection, you can rent a leased line that is dedicated to you and not shared as the Internet is. This should not lull you into thinking your data is safe. You should still be concerned with the eavesdropping or manipulation of packets, either by the phone company or more likely internal employees, so you should use encryption.

- Use remote access policies to manage the remote access settings for your network so you can control the authentication protocol used, the types of connections allowed, who can connect with the RRAS server, and the encryption level.

- Use demand-dial filters, IP packet filters, and dial-in hours to gain control over who can access the server and when.

- Use strong passwords on the accounts used for remote access. Consider using EAP to use certificate-based authentication in conjunction with a password to provide two-factor authentication for demand-dial routers.

- For packet encryption and integrity, use L2TP/IPSec to establish a tunnel between two demand-dial routers if the connection is over the Internet.

In the following Design Scenario, you will design a demand-dial solution for a branch office.

 Design Scenario

Designing a Demand-Dial Solution for a Branch Office

Frankfurters has two offices in South America that oversee its main beef production facilities. The main office, located in Rio de Janeiro, has a high-speed connection to the corporate office in the United States. The other office is located on a large ranch in a remote location in Brazil. There are a few employees there and a server with some applications installed on it that are used to support the ranching operation. There is a need for the office in Rio de Janeiro to access the remote office on the ranch. The IT manager states that he does not want to support modems at each desktop that needs to communicate with the remote location. He also mentions that it would be a violation of the security policy. The same security policy also states that all precautions should be taken in securing modem communications. The users are worried about the performance of the applications over the modem. You determine that the applications are web based and geared for low-bandwidth environments, but you don't want to add too much overhead. High-speed bandwidth is not available to the remote site. The company does not have a PKI.

1. **Question:** What solution should you propose to connect the two offices together and what authentication protocols would you use to verify the identity of the server? **Answer:** You should propose the use of a demand-dial router solution because the clients cannot directly connect to the location with a modem. This solution would need to be configured to be a one-way connection to the ranch. The demand-dial gateway at the ranch should be configured to use caller ID to validate the incoming call. You should require that the demand-dial router authenticate with the remote location by using a secure authentication protocol like MS-CHAPv2 because PKI is not available. You should enable demand-dial filters to prevent undesired traffic from traveling to the ranch through the demand-dial interface. This can help guard against worms.

Designing for Secure Communications with External Organizations

Many times you need to extend your network to communicate with external organizations. The data your organization will send over these connections is often confidential and needs to be protected. Guarding against eavesdropping and tampering and authenticating the identity of the source of the packets you exchange between your organization and an external organization is vital.

One of the ways to ensure secure communication between your organization and an external organization is to set up a VPN and use L2TP/IPSec as discussed earlier. In addition, you will need to authenticate the external organization, which can be a problem because duplicating user accounts for another organization would surely be a management headache. However, you can use the existing accounts that are in the other (and presumably trusted) organization by setting up a RADIUS client that points to the other organization. You would not need to establish or manage accounts in your organization; all of this would be handled by the other organization.

In addition to the solutions presented in the preceding paragraph, you could set up a dedicated VPN tunnel. Using this approach, the router end points would authenticate each other with, ideally, a certificate obtained from a PKI or Kerberos for maximum security. If security is not as much of a concern you can use a preshared key to establish the dedicated VPN tunnel. You also need to design a way to securely communicate key changes between organizations. This process can be automated with the installation of a PKI because you can set up a secure connection between the organizations. You would use the same kind of technologies used in the demand-dial solution discussed in the previous section.

The main difference between a business's client computer or branch office connecting with a VPN and connecting with an external organization is the need to authenticate accounts in the external organization. To do this, you can use a RADIUS server, which on Windows Server 2003 is called Internet Authentication Service (IAS), to validate accounts that are located in another organization. This requires that you set up a PKI. You can then use a new feature of Windows Server 2003 known as an IAS proxy to forward the request to a RRAS Server in another forest.

In the following Design Scenario, you will design a security solution for connecting to an external organization.

 Design Scenario

Designing a Connection Strategy with an External Organization

Frankfurters, Inc. has decided to expand its business by purchasing a small sausage maker called the Kielbasa Factory. As part of the purchase, the folks in the IT department are integrating the network at the Kielbasa Factory with Frankfurters, Inc.'s network. Employees at Frankfurters will need to access the inventory, accounting, customer, and shipping systems located at the Kielbasa Factory. Frankfurters does not want to spend money on leased lines to the Kielbasa Factory because Frankfurters already has DSL access to the Internet. The Kielbasa Factory has its own Windows Server 2003 forest and infrastructure in place.

1. **Question:** What should you propose to provide external access to the Kielbasa Factory's network resources from Frankfurters's network? **Answer:** You would establish a VPN tunnel between the Kielbasa Factory and Frankfurters, Inc. to encrypt and protect traffic between the companies. The VPN tunnel would use the Internet as a vehicle for connections to avoid the use of leased lines. You would enable IP packet filtering on the interface to allow only the necessary traffic to pass between the networks to protect assets located at the company. You would need to establish a trust between the forests so that employees in one company could access resources in the other without having to log in again.

Designing for a Secure Wireless Network

Wireless network technology is very beneficial in allowing employees to work from a number of different locations. People use cell phones to check their voicemail from their car or use a device like a Blackberry to check their e-mail on the golf course. Wireless technology allows people to connect notebooks and other portable devices to a network without the need to find a physical network port. In fact, we are taking advantage of the wireless technology as we work on this book at various locations to aid in research. But with all of these benefits, wireless technology poses a greater security risk to the data that is transferred because the information is broadcast to anyone within range of the signal.

Wireless networks are everywhere. The mobile phone networks, pager networks, and infrared devices all use wireless networking. But the common wireless network in business nowadays is known as *wi-fi*, which stands for wireless fidelity. There are three major wireless standards for wireless networking defined as wi-fi by the Institute of Electrical and Electronics Engineers (IEEE):

802.11a   *802.11a* can transmit data at speeds as fast as 54Mbps but at a shorter range than the other more popular standards. It also uses a different part of the electromagnetic spectrum and so is not compatible with either 802.11b or 802.11g. Its short range, and non-overlapping 12 channels means that it is a specification that is more appropriate for densely populated areas.

802.11b   *802.11b* is currently the most popular specification for wireless networking. It supports speeds up to 11Mbps over a longer range than 802.11a. Devices that support 802.11b tend to be less expensive, hence the popularity.

802.11g   *802.11g* supports speeds up to 54Mbps and is compatible with 802.11b because they both use the same part of the radio spectrum. It does have a shorter range than 802.11b to get the full 54Mbps speed.

The 802.11 standards support two methods or modes of communication: ad hoc mode and infrastructure mode. *Ad hoc mode* is a peer-to-peer communication mode in that clients communicate directly with each other. Clients can be configured to allow incoming connections and support ad hoc mode. With *infrastructure mode,* the clients connect to a wireless device that acts as a bridge between a wireless and wired network called an *access point.* Security for a wireless network is simple, but it can be a problem to manage the configuration.

Security Options in the 802.11 Standard

People search for unsecured wireless access points through a process called "war driving," which consists of using a notebook computer or a PDA with a wireless network card and a utility like NetStumbler or MiniStumbler and driving around looking for unsecured access points. Once an access point is found they publish this information on the Internet or leave marks that indicate an insecure wireless point. This means that anybody could be using your wireless access point to access the Internet or your network. They can also capture packets that you may be sending over the wireless network to reveal passwords or confidential information. There are three security mechanisms that you can implement to guard against unauthorized use of your access point and eavesdropping on your wireless traffic.

The first security mechanism that the 802.11 standards use is a *Service Set Identifier (SSID),* which is an identification that uniquely identifies a wireless network. The SSID is used as a means of preventing clients from connecting. Only clients that have been configured with the same SSID as each other or the access point can connect. This is not very secure because most access points will broadcast the SSID to all the clients for ease of configuration. You can turn off this feature so that the access point runs in stealth mode, which means that the client would have to be configured with the correct SSID before it can connect.

You can also use MAC address filtering to control which MAC addresses can communicate with the access point. This would require you to set up MAC filtering to specify which clients you want to allow to connect. This can be a management headache if there are a large number of clients. Wireless packets can also be captured, revealing the MAC addresses that are allowed. An attacker can use MAC address spoofing to overcome this restriction.

The third security mechanism you can use in the wireless standard addresses security issues by using the *Wireless Equivalent Privacy (WEP).* WEP uses the RC4 symmetric key encryption to authenticate clients and provide for the encryption of transmitted data. WEP uses a symmetric key, which means that the client and the access point require the same shared secret key. There is no standard on providing the shared secret key to the client, and it usually must be done manually, as shown in Figure 3.10. The administrator will also have to rotate the keys on a regular basis to guard against unauthorized use, and as you can imagine, this will be a tedious process.

Beyond the SSID, MAC filtering, and WEP keys, there is no additional form of authentication. Therefore, as you can see, the mechanisms provided by the 802.11 standards are insecure because you could figure out the SSID by capturing the broadcast wireless signal or socially engineering them. The packets also travel through the air and are susceptible to being read, spoofed, or altered.

FIGURE 3.10 Configuring WEP keys in Windows Server 2003

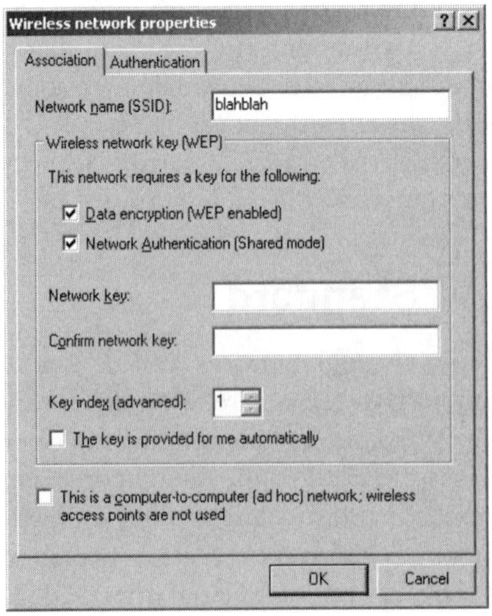

Designing for a Secure Wireless Network Using the 802.1x

The 802.1x standard was developed to help administrators provide greater security to wireless networks (although it will work with wired networks as well). 802.1x uses EAP-TLS to authenticate the user and encrypt the connection between the client and the server. This authentication mechanism uses certificates on the client and server to provide for mutual authentication. This will require PKI to be put in place to manage the creation, distribution, and revocation of certificates (see Chapter 6 for more information). It will also provide for encryption of each connection using TLS. This means that the keys for encryption can be negotiated per session. 802.1x also allows for many means of authenticating the client on the network, such as smart cards, SecurID, or passwords.

You can configure the 802.1x through Group Policy Security Settings. You can use Group Policy Security Settings to manage many clients at once with Active Directory, which will solve some of the management problems with 802.11. You can get to the Group Policy Security Settings for 802.1x by following these steps:

1. Open the Security Settings section of Group Policy by navigating to the Domain Security Policy MMC. To do so, choose Start ➢ All Programs ➢ Administrative Tools ➢ Domain Security Policy, to reveal the screen shown in Figure 3.11.

   You can use the Wireless Network (IEEE 802.11) Policies node to configure 802.11 and 802.1x configuration settings.

2. Right-click on the Wireless Network (IEEE 802.11) Policies node and choose Create Wireless Network Policy from the context menu to configure a wireless policy.

FIGURE 3.11   The wireless network policy settings container

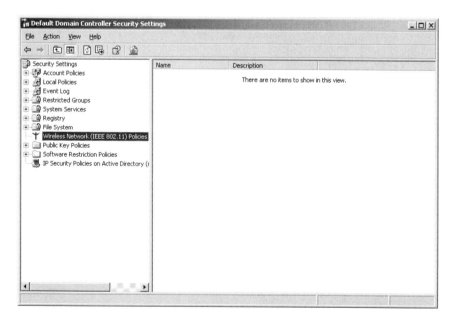

3. This will launch a Wireless Network Policy Wizard that will ask you to enter the name of the wireless policy and then ask if you would like to edit the wireless policy. Give the policy a useful name and then click Next.

4. Click the Finish button to end the Wireless Network Policy Wizard and reveal the Wireless Network Policy Properties dialog box.

You can enable the client computer to use 802.1x without using Group Policy by following these steps:

1. Select Start ➢ Settings ➢ Control Panel ➢ Network Connections.

2. Right-click your wireless network connection and choose Properties from the context menu.

3. In the wireless connection's Properties dialog box, click the Wireless Networks tab to reveal the property page for configuring wireless networks for the client, as shown in Figure 3.12.

4. Choose the wireless network configuration in the Preferred Networks list box and click the Properties button.

5. In the preferred network's Properties dialog box, click the Authentication tab.

6. Click the Enable IEEE 802.1x Authentication For This Network check box, as shown in Figure 3.13, to enable 802.1x for this client.

FIGURE 3.12 The Wireless Networks tab on the wireless network's Properties dialog box

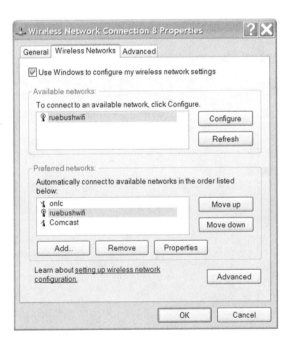

FIGURE 3.13   Enabling 802.1x on a client

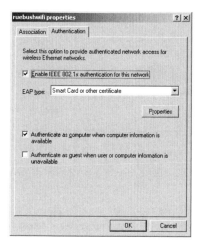

Using Protected Extensible Authentication Protocol to Secure

For those who don't have the extensive public key infrastructure, you can use a protocol called *Protected Extensible Authentication Protocol (PEAP)*. This protocol is not as strong as smart card or some other form of certificates used on the clients, which is required with EAP-TLS. PEAP allows the client to use a password to authenticate the user on the wireless network. This makes it easier to set up 802.1x, but at a cost of degrading security. Remember, however, that you are always weighing the cost of a solution with the loss that would be incurred if security was breached. PEAP would need to be enabled on the client and the server to support this form of authentication for the network. You would use the EAP Type drop-down box on the Authentication tab in the preferred wireless network Properties dialog box to enable PEAP on the client side, as shown in Figure 3.14.

FIGURE 3.14   Enabling PEAP for 802.1x authentication

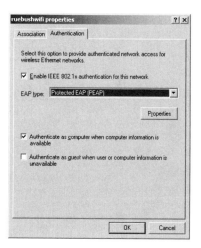

On the server you would need to navigate to the Wireless Network (IEEE 802.1x) Policies node and open up the Properties dialog box for the policy that you would like to enable PEAP and then click the IEEE 802.1x tab to find the EAP Type drop-down box.

The following steps describe how to get to this property page:

1. Open the Security Settings section of Group Policy.

2. Right-click the New Wireless Network Policy node in the right-hand pane and choose Properties from the context menu to configure a wireless policy.

3. In the New Wireless Network Policy Properties dialog box, click the Preferred Networks tab.

4. Click the Add… button to reveal the New Preferred Setting Properties.

5. Click the IEEE 802.1x tab to reveal the EAP type setting.

6. In the IEEE 802.1x Properties dialog box page, select Protected EAP (PEAP) from the EAP type drop-down box, as shown in Figure 3.15.

Regardless of whether you choose to use certificates or PEAP to authenticate with the wireless access point, 802.1x uses RADIUS to authenticate the requests to connect to an access point. The access point acts as a RADIUS client that will forward all requests to connect to the RADIUS server, which in Windows Server 2003's case is called Internet Authentication Service (IAS). The RADIUS server will check to see if the client has been allowed access to the wireless access point, which ensures that the client is authenticated to gain access to the network and can prevent unauthorized access points. RADIUS also provides extensive auditing and accounting that can also be used to maintain security. These logs can be reviewed to verify the usage patterns of accounts and recognize if there has been a security violation.

FIGURE 3.15   Enabling PEAP on Windows Server 2003

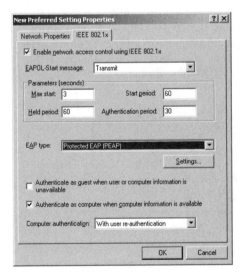

Designing for an Open Access Point

Using the 802.1x, standard, you can create a secure private wireless network that will provide for data encryption and integrity but there are many times that you would want to provide open access to the Internet for clients, consultants, or the general public. This should be on a network that was shielded from your internal network by a firewall. You should also control the types of traffic that could be passed to the Internet on the open wireless access point by using a router, firewall, or an intrusion detection system to prevent abuse of the public system. In addition, you will need to make it clear to those using the open access point that their traffic is not secure and they should use it at their own risk. Figure 3.16 shows how you would lay out a wireless network with an open access point.

Identifying Wireless Network Vulnerabilities

Wireless networks by their very nature are vulnerable, so you should pay close attention to designing a secure network. The following list includes some of the vulnerabilities you need to consider:

- WEP keys must be manually configured in many devices and there is no standard to manage them. You have to usually set them up on the client manually.

- Packet checksums, which are the result of a mathematical calculation on the packet that is added to a packet to verify the integrity of the packet, are not encrypted, so an attacker could manipulate the packets in transit.

- The destination or source of a packet can be changed.

- Shared key authentication is all that is available without 802.1x.

- There is no user or machine authentication option with 802.11 protocols, so you only need to know the SSID to connect (if WEP is not enabled).

- Many access points have a well-known default setting. For example, a LinkSys wireless access point's default SSID is LINKSYS. An attacker will guess the defaults on popular devices first to determine if they can gain access.

FIGURE 3.16   Network layout with an open access point

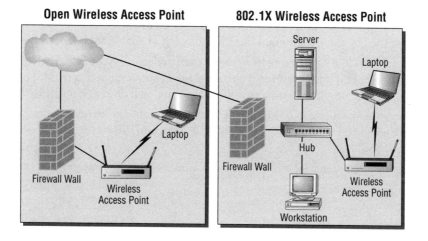

The following list includes the main threats to a wireless infrastructure:

- Attackers can eavesdrop on wireless packets because they are broadcast. You are broadcasting more or less to the world if you don't use encryption.

- Employees or attackers can add unauthorized access points to a network to provide access to it. These access points normally will not be secure, opening up a vulnerability on your network.

- DoS attacks can be launched by broadcasting a stronger signal, jamming the air with noise, redirecting packets, or disconnecting clients.

- Attackers can figure out your SSID or valid MAC addresses by intercepting wireless packets even if you disable SSID broadcasting or enable MAC filtering.

Guarding Against Wireless Vulnerabilities on Windows Server 2003

You can secure wireless communications on a Windows Server 2003 network by implementing the following:

- Use the strongest security you possibly can. Try using 802.1x if your hardware is compatible. If it is not compatible with your company's existing equipment and your company cannot afford to upgrade, use IPSec to maximize your protection against eavesdropping and manipulation of packets. At a minimum, use WEP for some protection.

- Don't use the default SSID of an access point and disable SSID broadcasting on the access point. This will prevent attackers from discovering the SSID by simply coming within range of the access point or guessing the SSID from a known list of default SSIDs for the access point. They can still read it from the packets, but you are increasing the difficulty of accessing the network.

- You should adjust the range of the access point if possible. The access point should cover only the area necessary; otherwise, running at full power, it might cover the street below, additional floors in the building, or even the next building. You usually have to adjust the range through SNMP commands sent to the access point. You will need to use site surveys to verify the coverage of your access points. A site survey is similar to what we described as war driving earlier, only it's obviously done for security purposes. A site survey can be accomplished by using a program like NetStumbler, available at www.netstumbler.org.

- You should also use site surveys from time to time to locate unauthorized access points on your network. Employees or even an attacker might sneak an access point onto the network. This access point will usually not be secure and will pose as a threat to the network.

- Use infrastructure mode to centralize the management of security on the access point. You can take advantage of 802.1x, centralized WEP keys, and SSID settings by disabling broadcasting of SSIDs.

In the next Design Scenario, you will design a wireless security strategy.

Design Scenario

Designing Wireless Security

You need to set up a wireless network for boardrooms in your company. There will be many types of presentations and other data transferred across this network. You have determined that it must be secure because some of the information passing over the network would be sensitive in nature.

1. **Question:** What would you do to secure these access points? **Answer:** First, you need to purchase access points that support 802.1x. You should install Internet Authentication Service (IAS) (Windows RADIUS server) and configure the wireless access point to act as a RADIUS client to the IAS server. Next, set up a public key infrastructure to enable certificates on the client and server, and then enable EAP-TLS for authentication and encryption of packets on the network. You disable SSID broadcasting and change the default SSID on the access points and configure the clients with these SSIDs through Active Directory Group Policy. Finally, enable access to the wireless network through Active Directory Group Policy.

Summary

In this chapter, you learned about the various vulnerabilities that are present when transmitting data on networks and how to protect your Windows Server 2003 network against threats. We showed you what protocols are available for authentication on a Windows Server 2003 network and discussed the strengths and weaknesses of each one. You will need to focus on CHAP, MS-CHAPv2, and EAP as the main protocols used for authentication on Windows Server 2003.

After you authenticate, you will need to worry about the security of the information you are sending across your network. When designing a solution for transmitting data, you need to consider eavesdropping and manipulation of the packets. These types of attacks can be avoided by encrypting and signing the packets with technologies like IPSec or PPTP.

You can combine an encryption technology like IPSec with a protocol to negotiate the authentication protocol like L2TP. A combination like L2TP/IPSec or PPTP with PPP encryption is the basis for creating a Virtual Private Network (VPN). A VPN allows you to create a secure connection over an insecure network like the Internet or a wireless connection.

With regard to the security design principles in connecting to a partner organization, we discussed aspects of the various methods you can use to connect to the organization and the authentication and data security problems you will encounter. This included using demand-dial and VPN technology to connect to another organization.

Wireless networks also present a problem when it comes to securing the transmission of data and controlling authentication to the network. You learned how to use the SSID and WEP to begin to secure access points and then how you could use 802.1x to provide for stronger and more manageable authentication and encryption through RADIUS and certificates obtained through your public key infrastructure.

Exam Essentials

Know that the preferred VPN technology on Microsoft platforms is L2TP/IPSec. L2TP/IPSec provides the strongest mechanisms for authentication, encryption, and packet integrity.

Understand the various authentication protocols used on Windows Server 2003. EAP-TLS is the strongest and most versatile authentication protocol, but not everyone will be able to maintain the PKI infrastructure to support it. MS-CHAPv2 is not as strong, but it is simpler to set up than EAP-TLS. You should choose MS-CHAPv2 when EAP-TLS is not available due to lack of infrastructure. You would use EAP-TLS or CHAP to authenticate non-Windows clients.

Recognize that not all data will need to be encrypted. Be able to determine what data should be encrypted and, to conserve resources, apply encryption to just those situations.

Design security for the vulnerabilities that the company's data may face. Consider eavesdropping, DoS, data alteration, and spoofing in your data security design. Know what technologies can overcome these vulnerabilities in a given situation.

Remember to take advantage of the caller ID and callback functions to increase demand-dial strength. You don't want to rely on just the authentication mechanism to provide authentication if you don't have to.

Understand how to secure a wireless network. Windows Server 2003 provides authentication through the 802.1x standard. This requires an 802.1x-compliant access point, IAS installed on the Windows Server 2003 network, and a public infrastructure to support EAP-TLS. You can avoid having to use smart cards or client certificates by using PEAP. At the very least, you should disable broadcasting of the SSID and enable WEP.

Key Terms

Before you take the exam, be certain you are familiar with the following terms:

802.11a	Microsoft Challenge Handshake Authentication Protocol Version 2 (MS-CHAPv2)
802.11b	Password Authentication Protocol (PAP)
802.11g	Protected Extensible Authentication Protocol (PEAP)
access point	Point-to-point Tunneling Protocol (PPTP)
Ad hoc mode	Secure Sockets Layer (SSL)
Challenge Handshake Authentication Protocol (CHAP)	Server Message Block (SMB) signing
Extensible Authentication Protocol (EAP)	Service Set Identifier (SSID)
infrastructure mode	Shiva Password Authentication Protocol (SPAP)
IP address filtering	Transport Layer Security (TLS)
IP packet filtering	virtual private networks (VPNs)
IP Security (IPSec)	wi-fi
Microsoft Challenge Handshake Authentication Protocol (MS-CHAP)	Wireless Equivalent Privacy (WEP)

Review Questions

1. What are two main vulnerabilities to transmitting data across a network? (Choose the two best answers.)

   A. Eavesdropping on packets

   B. Illegal access to files on the network

   C. Manipulating packets in transit

   D. Denial of service to network devices

2. Which of the following technologies will protect data transmitted across the Internet from eavesdropping or manipulation?

   A. PAP

   B. WEP

   C. CHAP

   D. IPSec

3. You have a need to provide strong encryption and authentication for users of a wireless access point. What standard should you use?

   A. 802.11b

   B. 802.1x

   C. 802.11g

   D. 802.11a

4. You have set up an access point that supports 802.1x. You want to take advantage of the stronger authentication and encryption standard. What services should you install on your Windows Server 2003 network to take advantage of the 802.1x standard? (Choose all that apply.)

   A. Windows time service

   B. Internet Authentication Service (IAS)

   C. Certificate service

   D. Web service

5. You have a network that does not have a public key infrastructure set up. The cost of implementing and maintaining PKI is not worth the security it provides to your company. What protocol should you use to authenticate users on your VPN?

   A. MS-CHAP

   B. PAP

   C. MS-CHAPv2

   D. EAP

6. You are using a Windows XP client to connect to a Windows Server 2003 RRAS server. You want to maximize the security of the data that you are transmitting over the VPN. What protocols would you use? (Choose all that apply.)

    A. L2TP

    B. PPTP

    C. IPSec

    D. PAP

7. You need to establish a VPN connection through a NAT server that is running Windows Server 2003. You want to use the strongest available technology for the VPN. What technology would you choose for the VPN?

    A. PPTP

    B. IPSec

    C. L2TP/IPSec

    D. CHAP

8. You are setting up a Windows Server 2003 machine as a RRAS server that will be used for dial-up connections from a demand-dial router. This demand-dial router is running the Linux operating system. Which protocols should you use to authenticate with Windows Server 2003? (Choose the two best answers.)

    A. PAP

    B. CHAP

    C. MS-CHAPv2

    D. EAP

9. You are designing a VPN solution that uses IPSec. You decide that the default rules of an IPSec policy are appropriate, except you want to make sure that the IPSec session is always negotiated. Which default rule would you select to meet this criteria on the server?

    A. Server (Requires Security)

    B. Server (Request Security)

    C. Client (Respond Only)

    D. A custom rule because the default rules don't support requiring IPSec

10. You need to give VPN access to the sales and executive groups, but no one else. You have a Windows Server 2003 network running Active Directory. How would you easily accomplish this task?

    A. Add users that require remote access to the built-in Remote Access group.

    B. Use Group Policy to apply the Allow Remote Access Account policy to the domain.

    C. Use Group Policy to apply the Allow Remote Access Account policy to the domain. Filter the group policy based on membership to the sales and executive groups.

    D. Go into every account that needs remote access and verify that each member of the sales and executives groups has remote access.

Answers to Review Questions

1. A, C. You need to pay attention to the company's need to prevent eavesdropping and packets being manipulated in transit on the network. Some companies might not need this kind of protection for certain types of data, and it's important to keep this in mind because protecting data is a complex and time-consuming task and therefore costly.

2. D. IPSec prevents the contents of packets from being read and manipulated through the Encapsulating Security Protocol (ESP) because it will both encrypt and sign the packets. PAP and CHAP are used for authenticating users on a VPN or network. WEP can be used to prevent eavesdropping on packets on a wireless network, but it does not encrypt the checksum, so a determined attacker could manipulate the packet.

3. B. The 802.1x standard provides for the authentication of users on the wireless network. It also provides strong encryption for data transferred across the network. The 802.11a, b, and g standards can also be used to provide connection, but without the strong authentication and encryption standards of 802.1x.

4. B, C. You will need to have the RADIUS server—in this case, ISA—installed so that the RADIUS client will be built into the access point. This will provide for authentication that can be mapped against your accounts in Active Directory. You will also need to establish that PKI and certificate services will be part of that infrastructure. The certificates are used for setting up TLS encryption and authenticating the client and the server.

5. C. MS-CHAPv2 is an authentication protocol that does not pass the password across the network, thereby protecting it. This is the strongest authentication protocol for Windows without the use of EAP-TLS, which requires a PKI. MS-CHAP uses LAN Manager security and can be attacked with a man-in-the-middle attack. Also, the password can be cracked without brute force methods, so MS-CHAP was ultimately replaced with MS-CHAPv2. PAP passes the password in clear text over the network and is not secure. EAP is one of the strongest forms of authentication and requires the most investment in resources to set up certificates for each client.

6. A, C. The L2TP combined with the IPSec protocol provides for strong authentication of the user based on a variety of protocols and strong encryption standards. This is the choice Microsoft recommends when you're using an OS that supports L2TP/IPSec. PPTP will work on Windows 95 clients if you need to support them. PAP is an insecure authentication protocol.

7. C. L2TP/IPSec is the ideal choice. In the past, with Windows 2000, you were limited in that IPSec would not pass through a NAT server and you would have then chosen PPTP for the VPN technology. With Windows Server 2003, NAT-Traversal is supported, so IPSec traffic will pass through the NAT box. However, IPSec alone does not provide for the user authentication that is required for a VPN which is provided by L2TP. CHAP is an authentication protocol that is used by many operating systems that hash the password, so the password is not sent clear text and is only used for authenticating with non-Microsoft systems. PPTP is a tunneling technology that could be used, but it is not recommended by Microsoft for use anymore when you have Windows 2000 or greater servers and clients. L2TP/IPSec is a stronger form of VPN technology than PPTP.

8. B, D. You could use one of the standard protocols for setting up a PPP session, which are PAP, CHAP, and EAP. However, PAP is considered insecure because it passes passwords over the wire unprotected. This means that you are left with CHAP and EAP. If you can get it to work, EAP would be the strongest, but CHAP would be easier to set up. MS-CHAPv2 is Microsoft's version of CHAP for authenticating Windows clients.

9. A. You would set the server to Server (Requires Security) and the client to Client (Respond Only) to make sure that connections to the server are created only over IPSec. All the other options will make it so that the connection does not need IPSec in some situations.

10. C. You would apply the group policy that allows remote access to the domain and then filter it so that it applies only to the sales and executive groups. Applying it to everyone in the domain would give remote access to everyone in the domain. There is no built-in Remote Access group to give users remote access. Going into every account would be too tedious, from both a creation and management perspective.

Case Study

You should give yourself 20 minutes to review this testlet, review the table, and complete the questions.

Overview

Odin Sports is a company that designs, manufactures, and distributes sports equipment to most countries in the world.

Locations

The company is headquartered in Albuquerque. In addition to the headquarters, the company has four other locations that operate as branch offices. These are located in New York, Beijing, Paris, and Rio de Janeiro. The company has approximately 4500 employees distributed as follows among the locations:

Location	Employees	Departments
Albuquerque	2500	Accounting, Marketing, HR, R&D, IT
New York	300	Sales
Beijing	500	Manufacturing, Sales
Paris	700	Design, Sales
Rio de Janeiro	500	Manufacturing, Sales

Current Environment

Odin Sports has two Active Directory domains: one for production and a test domain that is used to try new products and concepts. The production domain has two domain controllers in each location. The OU structure reflects the locations of the company and then the departments at that location. All computer, resource, and user accounts are kept in the OU for the department at that location. Active Directory is centrally managed by the IT staff.

The company prides itself in being up-to-date with technology. Windows Server 2003 is running on most of its servers, and the company has just finished deploying Windows XP to all desktops in Albuquerque, New York, and Paris. There is a mixture of Windows 98 and Windows XP in Beijing and Rio de Janeiro to support some legacy manufacturing applications, but the company is looking at technology to remove this dependence on Windows 98 due to maintenance headaches.

The internal network has a variety of applications, including a recently revamped intranet portal running on IIS 6 using ASP.NET.

Confidential research and development data is accessed through applications installed on terminal servers located in Albuquerque. That way, it does not get stored on local user hard drives that are difficult to secure.

Web applications in Albuquerque are used to exchange secure data between Odin Sports and its suppliers.

Interviews

CIO   We have plans to roll out a wireless network in Albuquerque to support the staff from the boardrooms. We also have an upgrade to one of our manufacturing applications that will help us get rid of Windows 98 and make it possible to use Pocket PC devices to access the application from the manufacturing floor. This means we will be installing wireless in Beijing and Rio de Janeiro.

Network Administrator   We are overworked maintaining the systems we have. There are no plans to hire more staff, so any solutions must be simple to maintain.

Chief Security Officer   We are concerned about wireless security and need to implement a public key infrastructure to issue digital certificates for wireless authentication. The root certificate authority needs to be protected because, if it is compromised, our certificates are no good. We need to maintain and deploy certificates through this infrastructure without making more work for the network administrative staff.

We also need to make sure that all wireless communication is encrypted and secure. Trade secrets will be moved across the network. Again, we need to accomplish this without increasing work for the network administrators.

Business Requirements

The company's security policy is written with the following requirements:

- All users must be authenticated by a domain controller before accessing network resources.
- Data used for research and development must have the highest level of protection for the company to stay competitive.
- Wireless networks will not be deployed until the necessary security measures are in place.

Case Study Questions

1. You must design an authentication method for the R&D personnel in Albuquerque and Paris to access the applications and file servers they use. What should you do?

    A. Require all R&D personnel to connect to the network with a L2TP/IPSec connection from their Windows clients.

    B. Require all R&D personnel to connect to the network with a PPTP connection from their Windows clients.

    C. Require all R&D personnel to have computer certificates installed on their workstations and then validate each workstation's certificate before allowing access to services.

    D. Require all R&D personnel to have smart card readers installed on their machines. Require a smart card logon to gain access to a terminal server computer that will be used to access resources on the network.

2. You need to allow users in Albuquerque, Beijing, and Rio de Janeiro to access the wireless network. What should you do?

    A. Configure WEP on the wireless access points and then on the client computers.

    B. Configure the wireless access points to use 802.1x to authenticate users.

    C. Set up IPSec on the client computers. Make sure that servers on the network require security so that the clients connect using IPSec.

    D. Configure EAP-TLS authentication on the RADIUS server (in this case, Internet Authentication Service). Configure the wireless access points and client computers to use 802.1x authentication.

3. You need to make sure that data sent over the wireless connection is encrypted. The wireless solution needs to meet the concerns of the Chief Security Officer. What should you do?

    A. Create a Group Policy object (GPO) that is linked to the appropriate OUs. Create a wireless policy and use it to enable data encryption and dynamic key assignment.

    B. Configure the wireless network settings at the interface on each client computer to require encryption.

    C. Configure the wireless access point to not broadcast its SSID.

    D. Create a logon script. Have the script configure the wireless network settings on the local computers to use encryption and assign keys.

4. You need to design an IPSec policy so employees connecting to terminal servers and web servers in the Albuquerque office can work with confidential data from work or home. You need to decide what policy settings are necessary for IPSec. What should you do?

    Drag the appropriate policy setting from the Policy Setting section to the correct location(s) in the Work Area section.

Type of Traffic	Servers To and From the Internet	Servers To and From Client Computers	Policy Setting
HTTP/HTTPS			No Policy
Remote Desktop Protocol (RDP)			Allow
All other protocols			Deny

5. You need to design a secure connection strategy between the R&D and design departments' resources. Your solution must minimize the impact on client, server, and network performance. What should you do?

    A. Use IPSec to encrypt all communications between Albuquerque and Paris.

    B. Configure the clients to use EAP-TLS and smart cards for authentication and encryption with the other location.

    C. Configure SSL on all web servers at both locations.

    D. Require all clients to establish a VPN connection using L2TP/IPSec to the other location.

Answers to Case Study Questions

1. D. The security policy requires that R&D data and applications are protected by the highest level of protection. Using smart cards with EAP-TLS for authentication and encryption and using Terminal Services to prevent downloading of data is the strongest protection.

2. D. You will need to authenticate the users on the network. Because security is a concern and the effort has been made to install PKI, you can use it in your wireless solution. You would avoid the WEP solution because managing the preshared keys would be too much work for the IT staff. You would need to add a RADIUS server to the network to use 802.1x authentication so B is not as complete as D. IPSec will encrypt the network traffic, but there is no authentication mechanism built into it, so C is not a solution to the company's wireless requirements.

3. A. You would use the Active Directory to push out a GPO that sets up the wireless network settings. This would require the least amount of work for the network administrators but still provide for setting up encryption.

4.

Type of Traffic	Servers To and From the Internet	Servers To and From Client Computers
HTTP/HTTPS	No Policy	No Policy
Remote Desktop Protocol (RDP)	Allow	Allow
All other protocols	Deny	

You would not apply an IPSec policy to the HTTP/HTTPS traffic because you would use HTTPS to provide encryption and authentication for the application and would not need IPSec. You would want to encrypt the RDP traffic with IPSec for the RDP protocol to the terminal services for protection. All other traffic would be denied for IPSec to the servers from the Internet.

5. A. To minimize the performance impact on the networks and the client and server CPUs, you should establish an IPSec tunnel between Albuquerque and Paris. This will encrypt only the network traffic that will travel over the link, limiting the network overhead, and will not use the client or server CPUs for encryption. Options B, C, and D would require each computer to perform encryption, which will degrade performance.

Chapter

4

Designing an Authentication Strategy for Active Directory

MICROSOFT EXAM OBJECTIVES COVERED IN THIS CHAPTER:

✓ **Design a logical authentication strategy.**

- Design forest and domain trust models.
- Design security that meets interoperability requirements.
- Establish account and password requirements for security.

✓ **Design a client authentication strategy.**

- Analyze authentication requirements.
- Establish account and password security requirements.

In this chapter, we will show you how to design an authentication strategy. You will learn about the different trust models and about the interoperability of authentication types between different operating systems. In the latter section of this chapter, we will discuss password requirements and the different techniques that you can use to employ them in a Windows Server 2003 environment.

Designing Authentication for Active Directory

In a server-based networked environment, where resources are centrally stored and managed on servers, there are typically two functions to securing resources:

- *Authentication,* which is the process of determining an identity (for example, a user)
- *Authorization,* which is the process of determining the resources the user can access once authenticated

You must consider the authentication requirements of your entire organization when designing the authentication infrastructure. This includes services that your company exposes, applications that contain their own authentication mechanism, even the level of remote access that you intend to support. Obviously, a heterogeneous environment can add a level of complexity to your design considerations, but even on an all-Microsoft network, there are several authentication methods that are used. Users may authenticate locally, remotely, or over the Internet.

Authentication security is critical in thwarting potential vulnerabilities of your organization. It is common for an attacker to attempt to obtain valid credentials from a machine or service that they have already compromised.

You will need to make sure that your passwords are kept secure no matter how or where they're stored. One of the most egregious violations of this is when the user writes their network password on a piece of notepaper and tapes it to their monitor.

Any user that takes resources off site will need to be properly trained on the storing of passwords and other sensitive material. Specifically, users with laptops will need to learn about the different techniques that they can employ to further secure the data on their computer. The Windows Encrypting File System (EFS) is an excellent way to further secure data on a mobile computer that is not physically secured on site.

EFS is covered in Chapter 5, "Designing an Access Control Strategy for Network Resources."

There are three types of vulnerabilities that pertain to authentication, and all can be used to compromise an entire organization:

Passwords   The importance of keeping passwords secure goes without saying; you need to make sure that you avoid the common vulnerabilities of passwords. One of the main goals in your password security strategy should be to prevent passwords from falling into the hands of unauthorized individuals. There are many utilities available that give a computer on a network the capability to record all of the packets that are being transmitted across the network. There are several resources that accept the username and password in cleartext; this is especially common across the Internet. The cleartext transmission is usually a result of IIS configured to use basic authentication when receiving the credentials from the user. Unfortunately, other types of IIS authentication are not supported by most browsers. You should prevent passwords from being transmitted in cleartext. An attacker could sniff the authentication packets, and a simple analysis of the packets would reveal the logon credentials, password included.

If you allow users to log in to your network from outside of the office, including accessing Outlook Web Access (OWA) or a secure Internet website, you will need to make sure that the credentials being transmitted are encrypted to prevent passwords from being sniffed. You can secure this type of remote access by using Secure Sockets Layer (SSL) to encrypt all of the traffic to your Internet site or by requiring that all access to the network's resources be through a virtual private network (VPN) connection. SSL is used when accessing websites using the HTTPS protocol as opposed to the non-encrypted HTTP protocol.

Consider the Real-World Scenario "Cleartext Passwords Across a Network" when gauging the vulnerability of passwords being transmitted in clear- or plaintext.

There are also several examples of Trojan horse applications or keystroke logging utilities that store and forward passwords to an attacker. You'll need to make sure that you have appropriate policies in place to prevent this software from getting installed. There are also products that need only the hash of the password in order to break the password. One of the best examples of this is L0phtcrack from @stake, or LC4 as it is now called, which can sniff the hash on the network and then attack it using dictionary or brute force attacks. To prevent this from happening in your organization you'll want to make sure that the password hashes are not sent across the network.

You can see LC4 in Figure 4.1 after only a few seconds of processing a typical network password list. Using a utility like LC4, most passwords are broken in the first few minutes. You can minimize its usefulness by not storing passwords on the local machine and preventing its installation on a machine that has access to your network.

There are several available network utilities that will let you detect when a network card is placed in promiscuous mode, which allows it to record all packets—including those not destined for it. Also, certain types of network hardware can prevent most sniffing utilities from working easily. One of the best ways to prevent all types of attacks is to prevent an unknown computer from gaining access to your network. The same notion can be applied to software. Don't let unknown software be installed on any computer that accesses your network.

FIGURE 4.1 LC4 password recovery

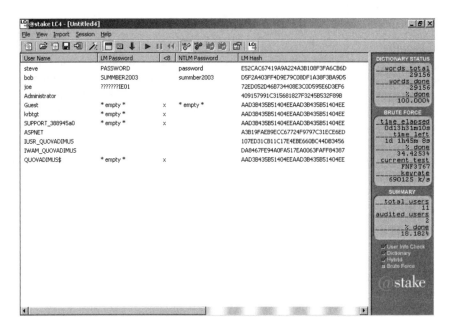

🌐 **Real World Scenario**

Cleartext Passwords Across a Network.

Jim is a traveling salesman for InnaTech banking software and accesses his e-mail remotely, including from his home, where he has cable modem access. InnaTech has enabled Outlook Web Access (OWA) and made it available outside the corporate firewall. The IIS web server is configured to use basic authentication through HTTP (port 80) so that Jim and the other salespeople can access their e-mail, calendar, and contacts from anywhere.

Because InnaTech uses both basic authentication and an insecure communications channel, anyone on the network that Jim uses to check his e-mail would be able to sniff his credentials from the network and the credentials will be in cleartext. If Jim uses his home computer, in many cases his neighbors would be able to sniff his network packets traveling to and from his provider. In addition to the vulnerabilities associated with a cable modem, they could also be sniffed from a wireless network at a coffee shop or in an airport.

If Jim and the other salespeople truly need this access, you should, at a minimum, require SSL and use a higher level of authentication such as Integrated or Digest.

Real World Scenario

Stored Credentials Are Easy to Exploit

Marc is the server administrator at a small consulting company named WTF Consultants. Marc manages all of the Windows 2000 and Windows Server 2003 servers for his company and does most of the management, patch installation, service pack installation, and so on from his laptop computer using a Terminal Services session. Marc is tired of entering the long and complex passwords required for him to log on to these servers remotely and decides that he will store the password in an RDP file on his notebook along with the other settings for the connection to the server. The following screen shot shows the Remote Desktop Connection Editor.

His credentials are cached in the file, which is now stored on his laptop. The file does encrypt the password. Should someone open it using a text editor, they would see something similar to this.

```
demo.RDP - Notepad
File  Edit  Format  View  Help
screen mode id:i:2
desktopwidth:i:800
desktopheight:i:600
session bpp:i:16
winposstr:s:0,3,0,0,800,600
full address:s:Server01
compression:i:1
keyboardhook:i:2
audiomode:i:0
redirectdrives:i:0
redirectprinters:i:1
redirectcomports:i:0
redirectsmartcards:i:1
displayconnectionbar:i:1
autoreconnection enabled:i:1
username:s:administrator
domain:s:myDomain
alternate shell:s:
shell working directory:s:
disable wallpaper:i:1
disable full window drag:i:1
disable menu anims:i:1
disable themes:i:0
disable cursor setting:i:0
bitmapcachepersistenable:i:1
password |
51:b:01000000D008C9DDF0115D1118C7A00C04FC297EB01000000413C106448F34A4783EA2BF391F5048B000000000800
0000700073007700000003660000A800000001000000003EF3833B9DB5E220342599CCCFFA8693000000000480000A0000
00010000000CDD1F113444FB39D56146827A78E35980802000017E62596F45C23CA9CC20AC5C15FB62B857FF903B5050
47B25D247DA2ED67F8E8565BA0C5CEEB7A2CF13625A56C3DB9EEBC8E0080F0167A3F94EA20BE0C5DF68BA7929F6692BC6
D905BBE7580B6B5DA43DC929A33B4034544FE2DB0C08BBFD8B4CE26723DB793039EC660D96159AC24E50F8C5B4546A857
C2E4E7FED39B770CD270C20A0878A2C69BA0CDDE03405D180F7F2157D92D2FF6BEC8E33CDABDCF7D641805FFC3171E94A
1141A221849C5598F537873BB8F872D131244E46CB6D2F7BC8EC80D73CE5433907E5526D0A977AF64C1C0B03DA3E04EFE
39A663980D9772EF5E8AD2CEA17D5265F9F771715F1DA73AFF92A78481525F16B9E61328BDCBFB392C6CA8278E1C2B6B9
89ECBC1B7EC049CF85E496D453C848039A79C5BC925A1FCC50D1244D752147AE2B661D2A5F26437D77FA92FC2111B180F
75C81443B139AEFA5D3943F236BA9C74572C87F88914476F85E5FCF2D0F99C915045E8782C85172FFADA7F79F8B7DC8A5
20E89613B1B5C6CBFFCBDD2E228D8AC55AD76B0B8283808F7710CBD41AE2366851B811BD1DAF415CE1BBB82BE0FA99B054
1A3BD63A035EB3744FADBEB06EE4A6BE67088CCB17A77A16D99F36B85058663F5C97E7A4816CEDE2FF7DC053B3BFD36EA
116F198F1EF1A82C4576580BAC4447D9738EFB81DBDDD96787B76CF9CE04658CE73D2189FD5D54EEF421CAB47AAE1F0C1
A24BEDD787FB832CCA566339140000006622D307BE564F9103D128A7A6F3B348AE5C8544F0
```

Now that this file exists on his laptop, he simply double-clicks the previously saved RDP file and his terminal session opens and logs him on.

Marc has exposed himself and his server to a couple of vulnerabilities. First, should someone gain access to the RDP file, they would be able to use his credentials to log on to WTF's servers without even trying to break the password. In addition, even though the password is encrypted, it is stored in the file and could be broken in time.

One rule of thumb that you should maintain is that, whenever possible, do not store credentials. It may be a nuisance to enter the password, which is thankfully complex, but it would be a bigger nuisance to have to recover from an attack.

Interoperability and Compatibility   If you are using older systems or software, you are only as secure as the weakest system. As you will learn later in this chapter, a trust relationship between a Windows Server 2003 domain and a Windows NT 4 domain is much less secure than between Windows 2003 domains. In addition, if you must have authentication in place that is compatible with a non-Microsoft network operating system, you may be forced to lower the functionality of your authentication in the name of compatibility.

Encryption   Passwords that are stored somewhere need to be using a strong encryption algorithm. Older authentication methods tend to use weak encryption, which is only marginally better than no encryption at all. Many older applications or operating systems use weak encryption that can be easily broken.

In the "Evaluating Windows Authentication Methods" Design Scenario, you will be evaluating a scenario and determining the potential decisions that you will need to make regarding authentication in Active Directory.

Once an account is successfully authenticated, with either the correct username and password combinations or a valid smart card, there is little that can be done to determine the validity of the person using the account. To prevent these incidents from occurring you must design a secure authentication strategy. This is accomplished by designing security for authentication. In the next section, you will learn how to design a secure authentication strategy that is in line with your organization's business requirements.

Determining Authentication Requirements

When determining your organization's authentication requirements, you'll need to analyze its business requirements. There are two fundamental steps in determining the authentication requirements of your network: first you must determine the effect of the business requirements on your network, and then you must determine the interoperability requirements.

Many organizations have strict authentication requirements that must be in accordance with government regulations. You'll want to discover these types of requirements in the early stages of design because your business's viability may be dependent on meeting them. You will need to talk

Design Scenario

Evaluating Windows Authentication Methods

You are the administrator for a small certified public accounting firm, Hunter Cliffs Incorporated, that works primarily with individuals. The company has been in business for over 50 years and is in the process of reengineering the way that its employees interact with its customer base. The company wants to attract new and diverse customers by updating its business model to do business across the Internet. Hunter Cliffs has three Windows Server 2003 servers participating in a native Windows 2003 domain. The application developer on staff has decided to create a web application that will allow customers to fill out their financial information on a web page and submit it over the Internet to the customer database. This will allow for an automated evaluation followed by an employee evaluation before the tax form is finalized. You need to design a solution that will give each customer secure access to the new web system.

The proposed solution is to create a text file that will store the tax data for each customer on the web server. When users access the secure tax information page, they enter their credentials using a web form at the following address: http://www.hctaxescorp.com/taxdata.asp. On the web server, basic authentication has been enabled and you must create user accounts for all customers wishing to access this system.

1. **Question:** Is this proposed solution a secure one? Why or why not? **Answer:** The site that the users enter their credentials on is insecure because HTTP is used instead of HTTPS. In addition, basic authentication is in place, which means that the usernames and passwords will be transmitted from the customer to your web server in plaintext and would be an excellent target for an attack.

to your supervisor to determine if there are external security requirements that your design must adhere to. If there is a department dedicated to standards and practices, the department members may have the information that you require. When you are conducting your interviews, you'll want to pay attention to any statement that guarantees security or privacy. A marketing vice president, for example, may mention a privacy policy that guarantees "…that customer information will be viewed only by valid corporate representatives." This type of statement would require that customer data be specifically addressed in the authentication design.

Once you have established external authentication constraints, you need to determine the interoperability requirements with older operating systems. If you must incorporate Windows 95 or Windows NT 4 workstations into your design, it will play a role in determining the type of authentication that can be used. You must also determine any application compatibility requirements; many applications require a specific authentication mechanism. To determine what operating systems you must support, you'll need to audit your company's computing infrastructure. You will need to learn the applications and services running in your organization so that you can make the appropriate interoperability design considerations.

Once you've discovered all of this information, you will be in a better position to begin the design phase. In the section that follows, you will be introduced to the different protocols that are used for network authentication as well as the issues that each one introduces to your environment.

Selecting the Authentication Protocols to support

There are several techniques that Windows supports for authentication on a local area network (LAN). It's important to determine, given your environment, which authentication protocol to support. Typically, the new types of authentication are stronger but are less likely to be compatible with older applications and environments. In Windows 2000 and higher, the Security Support Provider Interface (SSPI) will determine which authentication protocol should be used for account validation.

The following network authentication protocols are supported in Windows Server 2003 (LAN Manager–based protocols are less secure than Kerberos v5, explained later in this section):

LAN Manager   The *LAN Manager* protocol is used by older Microsoft operating systems such as MS-DOS and Windows 95. This authentication protocol is the least secure method supported in Windows 2000 and Windows Server 2003 and therefore should be used only if the computers must access resources being served by computers running MS-DOS, Windows 95, or Windows 98 operating systems. If your organization does not require LAN Manager, you should remove the LAN Manager password hashes from the account database because an attacker can easily crack a LAN Manager password hash. You should remove the hashes using Group Policy or simply require that passwords be greater than 14 characters long.

NT LAN Manager (NTLM)   The *NT LAN Manager (NTLM)* protocol does a better job of storing passwords than LAN Manager does. NTLM is the default authentication protocol for Windows NT 4 domains and for local SAM accounts in Windows 2000 and Windows XP.

NTLM Version 2 (NTLMv2)   The *NTLM Version 2 (NTLMv2)* protocol is the most secure of the LAN Manager–based protocols in Windows 2000 and Windows XP. This protocol is also available for Windows 95 and newer Microsoft operating systems if the Active Directory client extensions are installed. The NTLMv2 protocol performs mutual authentication and can be more secure when session security is added. Session security will cause the connection to fail if the NTLMv2 protocol is not negotiated.

You can select how the computers in your environment will use the LAN Manager and NTLM authentication by configuring the LAN Manager compatibility level through Group Policy or manually editing the Windows Registry. You should always choose the highest level that your infrastructure and applications support. Table 4.2 explains each level.

You can configure the LAN Manager compatibility level using the Group Policy or local security MMC snap-ins under `Computer Configuration\Windows Settings\Security Settings\Local Policies\Security Options\LAN Manager Authentication Level` in Windows Server 2003 and `Computer Configuration\Windows Settings\Security Settings\Local Policies\Security Options\Network Security: LAN Manager Authentication Level` in Windows XP.

TABLE 4.1   Table 4.2 LAN Manager Compatibility Levels

Level	Description
0	Clients use LAN Manager and NTLM authentication and never NTLMv2 session security.
1	Clients use LAN Manager and NTLM authentication and will use NTLMv2 session security if it is supported by the authenticating server.
2	Clients use only NTLM authentication and will use NTLMv2 session security if it is supported by the authenticating server.
3	Clients use NTLMv2 authentication and will use NTLMv2 session security if it is supported by the authenticating server.
4	Clients use NTLM authentication and use NTLMv2 session security if the authenticating server supports it. Domain controllers will reject NTLM and LAN Manager authentication, only accepting NTLMv2.
5	Clients use NTLMv2 authentication and will use NTLMv2 session security if it is supported by the authenticating server. Domain controllers will reject NTLM and LAN Manager authentication, only accepting NTLMv2.

There is no way to disable NTLM-based authentication completely in Windows 2000 or Windows XP.

The most secure authentication protocol supported by Windows Server 2003 is Kerberos version 5.

The *Kerberos v5* authentication protocol is the default authentication protocol for computers running Windows 2000 or higher that are in Active Directory domains. When coupled with strong passwords, the Kerberos v5 protocol is considered the strongest authentication protocol in the Windows arsenal. The Kerberos protocol supports smart cards for multifactor authentication and adheres to RFC 1510. When you use Kerberos, you can interoperate with Unix-based operating systems by creating a trust relationship with a Kerberos realm. Kerberos authentication, to prevent the replay of the information, requires that all computers involved have their time synchronized within a defined threshold (5 minutes in Active Directory).

In the next Design Scenario, you'll learn how to design client authentication.

In the next section, you will learn about the trust models that apply to both domain and forest design. You'll learn which trusts are created automatically and which you have to create by hand. You will also determine which of the non-default trusts would better suit a specific infrastructure.

Design Scenario

Designing Client Authentication

Luke Worrall & Associates is a national accounting firm with over 12,000 employees nationwide. LW&A has offices in Dover, Philadelphia, Miami, Minneapolis, and San Francisco. Each office has its own IT staff that reports to the corporate IT staff located at the corporate headquarters in Dover. LW&A has upgraded all of its domain controllers to Windows Server 2003 and has implemented Active Directory running in Windows 2003 Native mode. There are several different operating systems that employees use. LW&A is in the process of standardizing on Windows XP Professional. The offices in Dover, Philadelphia, and Minneapolis are all running Windows XP Professional. The office in Miami has mostly Windows XP Professional, but there are still some desktops running Windows 98, Second Edition and Windows NT 4 Workstation. The office in San Francisco was recently acquired from a competing firm and has two Unix servers. The Unix servers run specific software that the employees in the San Francisco office need to access. All other servers in San Francisco are running Windows Server 2003 and all of the workstations are running Windows XP Professional.

Each office has its own domain organized as in the following graphic:

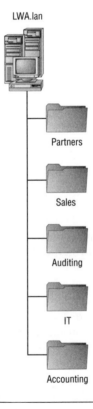

1. **Question:** You decide to implement NTLMv2 as the least-secure protocol that will be accepted by the domain controllers in your Dover, Miami, and Minneapolis offices to ensure a secure computing environment. What are potential problems and incompatibilities that may result from this implementation and how would you rectify them? **Answer:** There are no issues with regard to Dover and Minneapolis. All servers are running Windows Server 2003 and all workstations are running Windows XP Professional, which natively supports NTLMv2. In Miami, however, the Windows 98, Second Edition and Windows NT 4 workstations cannot authenticate using NTLMv2 and requiring NTLMv2 as the least-secure protocol that will be accepted on the servers in Miami will prevent these older operating systems from authenticating to the domain. To resolve the problems stated, you would need to install the Active Directory client extensions on the machines running Windows 98, Second Edition and Windows NT 4 or upgrade their operating systems to Windows 2000 or XP Professional.

2. **Question:** You must incorporate the Unix servers in San Francisco into your network strategy and cannot require the users in that office to have more than a single logon. The users at the San Francisco office must be able to access the data and the services published from the Unix servers. What tasks do you need to complete in order for this problem to be resolved? **Answer:** You could use Kerberos v5 authentication and create a trust relationship between the San Francisco domain and the Kerberos Unix realm.

Designing Forest and Domain Trust Models

One of the most important decisions you will make when designing your Active Directory infrastructure is the extent to which you intend to utilize forests and domains. Will you have a single forest or multiple forests, and within each forest, will you have a single domain or multiple domains? Each decision that you make along the way will impact the level of the security in place in your environment. There are several advantages and disadvantages with respect to security that you must understand before designing your domain or forest model.

A *trust model* will represent the configuration of the trusts between your Active Directory domain or forest and another environment. One of the first things you will need to bear in mind is that the operating system on the external environment will have a significant impact as to the level of security that is used to maintain the trust.

Domain trusts, which are trusts between Windows domains, can be between domains within the same tree, in separate trees, or in separate forests; they can even be between stand-alone domains. All domains within a tree trust each other, directly or indirectly, due to the transitive trust relationship that all domains have with their immediate parent domain. The transitive trust "climbs" the tree from the very bottom domain to the forest root domain. This trust model is displayed in Figure 4.2. Notice that all trusts go in both directions, and remember that, because the trusts are transitive (for example, if Joltcoder.lan trusts Sales.Joltcoder.lan and Joltcoder.lan trusts HR.Joltcoder.lan, then Sales.Joltcoder.lan trusts HR.Joltcoder.lan), all domains trust each other, by default, within the tree.

FIGURE 4.2 Transitive trust model

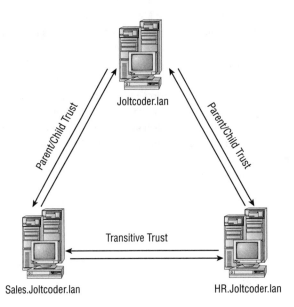

In the following sections, you will learn the implications associated with each of the trust types.

Default Trusts

There are two types of default trusts (both two way and transitive):

Parent/child trusts *Parent/child trusts* are by default created automatically when a new child domain is added to a preexisting domain tree.

Tree-root trusts *Tree-root trusts* are created automatically when a new tree is created in an existing forest. It is a trust between the tree-root domains of each tree.

Non-Default Trusts

There are other types of trusts that can be created manually and are not all two way and transitive. The following list describes the other types of trusts:

External trust An *external trust* is a nontransitive trust between an Active Directory domain and an external Windows domain, such as an NT 4 domain or a domain that is in a separate forest and doesn't have a forest trust with the source domain. An external trust can go in one or both directions.

Realm trust A *realm trust* is a trust between a Windows Server 2003 domain and a non-Windows Kerberos realm. A realm trust can be either transitive or nontransitive and can go in one or both directions.

Forest trust   A *forest trust* is a transitive trust that is between separate forests and can be either one or two way. If the forest trust is a two-way trust, then authentication requests made from either forest can reach the other forest.

Windows 2000 uses the Kerberos protocol to secure trusts within a forest. However, for external trusts, Windows 2000 uses the more primitive NT LAN Manager (NTLM) to secure trusts with Windows NT 4 domains as well as between Windows 2000 domains that are in separate forests. Because Windows 2000 uses NTLM to secure trusts between domains that are in separate forests, a trust relationship between a Windows Server 2003 domain and a Windows 2000 domain in a different forest will use NTLM rather than the Kerberos protocol for authentication, while a trust between two Windows Server 2003 forests will use Kerberos.

In the "Designing Trust Models" Design Scenario, you will be evaluating two scenarios and determining the most appropriate trust model and how the trust should be designed.

In the next section, you will learn how to analyze account and password security requirements.

Design Scenario

Designing Trust Models

Scenario 1

ABC Inc. has a single Windows 2003 forest with a root domain named abc.lan. There are three satellite offices that are each configured as Windows NT 4 domains. You have interviewed the IT manager and she stated that all of the satellite offices will be upgrading their domain controllers to Windows Server 2003 within the next two months. You need to design a trust model for the present configuration that will allow the Windows Server 2003 domain and the Windows NT 4 domain to share resources. You must also make sure that the model you design can continue to expose resources to the existing Windows Server 2003 domain after the upgrade with a minimal amount of administrative effort.

1.   **Question:** How would you configure trusts between the different domains? **Answer:** You should create a two-way external trust between the Windows Server 2003 domain and each of the three satellite offices. The Windows Server 2003 domain will trust the Windows NT 4 domain, and the NT 4 domain will trust the Windows Server 2003 domain.

Scenario 2

RTM Corporation is a publisher of technical manuals with offices in Phoenix, Philadelphia, and Miami. The Phoenix office has a Windows 2000 Active Directory domain running in Native mode. All of the domain controllers in Phoenix are running Windows 2000 Advanced Server and are up-to-date with patches and service packs. The office in Philadelphia is running a Windows Server 2003 Active Directory domain running in 2003 Native mode. All domain controllers in Philadelphia are running Windows Server 2003. In Miami, the network is running a strict Unix network configured as a Kerberos realm.

You have resources in Philadelphia that need to be accessed in all of the remote locations. Currently, there are no trust relationships of any kind between any of the offices. The RTM corporate headquarters is in Phoenix and should be at the top of the domain namespace. You need to create trusts that provide the maximum level of security for authentication. One of your business partners requires that you use Kerberos as the authentication protocol for all of the trusts.

1.   **Question:** What tasks must you complete in order to facilitate the authentication requirement of your business partner? **Answer:** Your first task will be to upgrade all of the domain controllers in Phoenix to Windows Server 2003 and switch the domain to Windows 2003 Native mode. Windows 2000 doesn't use Kerberos authentication between forests; therefore, you must upgrade Active Directory to 2003 Native mode. You can then create a trust between the Windows Server 2003 domain and the Unix Kerberos realm.

Analyzing Account and Password Security Requirements

Network accounts are used to give users access to the data that is stored on the various network resources. Should an attacker be able to take over an account, they would be able to perform any tasks that the user could perform. In addition, an attacker could simply break the password that is associated with an account, and would be able to perform the operations that are assigned to it.

In the following section, you will learn how to analyze accounts and passwords and recognize the potential risks to them. You will be able to list the common vulnerabilities of varying types of accounts and understand the requirements of each type of account based on its role and the type of access that it will require.

There are three basic types of accounts:

External users   Users that are outside of your organization, such as anonymous Internet users, users from a business partner, or even authenticated Internet users.

Internal users   Users that are employees, consultants, temporary workers, and so on who work directly for your company. These users typically have physical access to the network.

Administrative   Employees, consultants, and services with administrative permissions assigned to the accounts that they use.

Obviously, different types of accounts are going to have different security requirements. In the following section, you will learn how to identify the requirements of the different types of accounts.

Identifying Account Requirements

User accounts are used to determine what actions a particular user can perform. That being said, different types of accounts will require different levels of security. Each account type has an escalating level of trust and access to the system:

- External users have very limited access; it is good practice to consider that external users are potential attackers and lock them down accordingly. These accounts should have only the permissions that they require and no more because they are the accounts that are most likely to be exploited.

- Internal users have a higher level of access to the organization's resources because they typically represent employees with access to the organizational assets. Although it may be tempting to treat internal users as if they were attackers and prevent them from having access to everything, that usually has a significant impact on the productivity of the organization.

- Administrative accounts represent an ideal target to the would-be attacker because they have advanced rights on the system. An administrative account can be used to create other accounts or to run an application service and therefore must be as secure as possible.

Accounts receive their access rights from several different sources:

User rights User rights are the rights that are assigned to users. They allow the user to perform specific actions, such as logging on locally or as a service. Figure 4.3 shows the user rights assignments portion of the domain policy snap-in.

FIGURE 4.3 User Rights Assignment

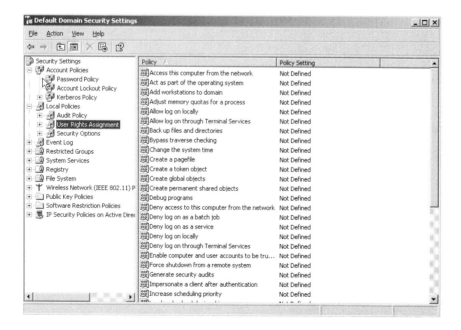

Permissions   Permissions are assigned using discretionary access control lists (DACLs) and are assigned for resources in Active Directory and NTFS. DACLS are made up of access control entries (ACEs) that specify the permissions on the identified object.

   ACEs are covered in more detail in Chapter 5.

Account scope   The account scope determines where the account has authority. In a Windows network, there are two types of accounts: local accounts and domain accounts. Local accounts can be assigned permissions only on the computer that contains them, while domain accounts can be assigned permissions to any resource within the domain or a domain with a trust relationship with the containing domain.

Group membership   Windows security groups allow you to assign permissions to a large number of users at a single time. This facilitates a consistent assignment of permissions to several similar users. Using groups to assign permissions makes the management and auditing of users more efficient. There are several types of groups within an Active Directory forest. Table 4.3 shows the different groups and what can be a member of each of the group types.

TABLE 4.2   Windows Group Types

Group Type	Membership	Scope
Universal	Native mode: Accounts, Global groups, other Universal groups.	Forest
	Mixed mode: Not Available.	
Global	Native mode: Accounts or Global groups from same domain.	Domain
	Mixed mode: Accounts from same domain.	
Domain Local	Native mode: Accounts, Global groups, and Universal groups from any domain, as well as other Domain Local groups from the same domain.	Domain
	Mixed mode: Accounts and Global groups from any domain.	

The recommended practice for assigning permissions using groups in Windows networks is to follow the practice of AG(G)DLP. The following explains this process:

1. Place (A)ccounts in (G)lobal groups.
2. Optionally, nest (G)lobal groups.
3. Place the Global groups in (D)omain (L)ocal groups.
4. Assign (P)ermissions for the resource to the Domain Local group.

The acronym AG(G)DLP is a great way to remember this process. However, the last task you should perform is placing the Global groups in the Domain Local groups. You do this task last so that an account can't use a permission until all of the permissions have been assigned.

Universal groups are covered in detail in Chapter 5.

There are several techniques that you can employ to minimize your exposure to an attack on an account. The best thing that you can do is to not give an account any more authority than it requires. This concept is called the *Principle of Least Privilege (PoLP)*. It states that an account should have the minimum permissions required to accomplish a task. User accounts should be granted only the privileges required to perform their job, service accounts should be granted only the privileges required to run the service, and only one service account should be granted per network service. You should have one service account that is used to run all SQL Server services across the domain and another service account for your Exchange Server services, and so on. Administrative accounts should be used only when administrative permissions are required to perform a task.

People who are in the role of a network administrator should have more than one account; one of them should be a typical user account with only the permissions of a normal user. The normal account should be the account that the administrator uses to log on to the system, check their e-mail, browse the Internet, and so on. In addition to the normal user account, the administrator should have an account with administrative permissions that is only used in conjunction with the runas command to run only those programs that require administrative level permissions.

The runas command does not work with smart cards. The administrator would be required to log off as the normal user and log on using the smart card with an administrative account. Once the administrator performs the administrative tasks, they would log off the administrative account and log back on as the normal user.

In the "Analyzing Accounts" Design Scenario, you will be analyzing the security requirements of accounts in the given scenarios.

There are several vulnerable aspects of accounts that, when exploited, provide an attacker the access they are looking for. Passwords, as you might have guessed, represent a common target for an attacker. There are several password-specific issues that can be exploited to allow an attacker to hijack an account. As previously mentioned, a weak password is susceptible to brute force or dictionary attacks and can be easily broken. Many users use the same password for multiple resources, which usually have different levels of authentication security requirements. If one of the systems is compromised, the account can be hacked on multiple systems.

Take, for instance, a PIN for an ATM card, which operates like a password. Many users use the same PIN on several credit cards accounts, bank accounts, voicemail accounts, and so on. In this scenario, if an attacker can compromise one of the systems and learn the PIN, all of the systems are compromised.

 **Design Scenario**

Analyzing Accounts

Scenario 1

Your network is running a SQL Server 2000 database that requires access to remote file shares stored on other computers in the domain. The service account that runs this service is currently configured as LocalSystem.

1. **Question:** What should you do to configure the SQL Server Service account to be able to access the remote file share while maintaining a highly secure environment? **Answer:** You should create a domain user account that has only the permissions required to execute the required tasks of SQL Server. It must be added to the ACL of the directory that contains the SQL Server data files and all other file system resources that the service will need to access. The SQL Service account would need to be given explicit user rights, such as the Login As A Service right on the server(s) running SQL Server. The account would also need the necessary ACEs to the Windows Registry ACLs for the keys that SQL Server needs to access. The reason for the domain account is because the service will need to access shares on remote servers and thus must authenticate over the network. If the SQL Server machine does not need to connect over the network to other servers, you should use a local user account, not an administrator or the LocalSystem account.

Scenario 2

You are the network administrator for an organization that has a main office in Pompano Beach, Florida. There are satellite offices in West Palm Beach and Miami that you must manage. You need to be able to manage all of the servers in your network no matter which location you are physically connected to. You've installed the Windows administration tools on your workstation (AdminPak.msi) to enable remote administration and your account is a member of the Domain Administrators group.

1. **Question:** What should you do to further secure your remote administration by protecting both the servers and the network as a whole? **Answer:** You should create a second account that you use to log on and access the non-administrative software (for example, Outlook, Internet Explorer, and any other applications that doesn't require administrative permissions in order to function). You can then use that account to log on to the various sites and use the runas command when you need to launch any of the Active Directory administrative tools.

Another target for an attacker is an account that is assigned excessive privileges. This is obviously why the PoLP is so important. Users who have local administrator privileges or services that run as an administrator on a machine are examples of this vulnerability. SQL Server's service account, in many cases, does not need to be a member of the local Administrators group. If the account is given elevated privileges, it can be exploited from within SQL Server as well as from within the application that uses SQL Server.

When it comes to determining the risks to accounts, you will need to evaluate the cost of the vulnerability to your organization and the cost to alleviate it. You may find that there is more than one solution to any given problem. Determining the most effective solution will be your goal. In a business environment, the effectiveness of the solution will probably be determined by how much money you can save. One of the most important things for management to keep in mind is return on investment (ROI).

With these vulnerabilities in mind, you need to know how to analyze a situation and determine the best way to deal with it. In the "Analyzing Account Risks by Cost Analysis" Design Scenario, you will evaluate a situation and determine the best solution.

In the next section, you will see some of the different techniques that you can employ to increase the security of these account vulnerabilities.

Designing Password Policies

In order to better secure passwords, you'll need to know how the passwords are stored for each account. Kerberos passwords are stored in Active Directory as part of the user's long-term key. NTLM passwords are stored as an MD4 hash value. LAN Manager passwords are case insensitive, and long passwords (up to 14 characters) are split into 7-character chunks and are then used to encrypt a constant value using the Data Encryption Standard (DES). The constant value is then stored. Service account passwords are stored persistently in cleartext as a Local Security Authority (LSA) account, while cached logon credentials are not stored persistently at all.

If attackers can gain physical access to a computer, they would be able to extract the NTLM and LAN Manager passwords from the Security Accounts Manager (SAM) database and then attack the hashes with well-known brute force and dictionary password tools. To prevent this type of breach, remove the LAN Manager password hashes from the computer and use strong passwords. You can use Group Policy to implement these policies, including the NoLMHash policy. The NoLMHash policy will disable the storage of LM hashes of a user's password in the local computer's SAM database or in a Windows Server 2003 Active Directory environment. To configure the Group Policy method, complete the following steps:

1. In Group Policy, expand Computer Configuration ➢ Windows Settings ➢ Security Settings ➢ Local Policies and click Security Options.

2. Double-click Network Security: Do Not Store LAN Manager Hash Value On Next Password Change.

3. Click Enabled, and then click OK.

On a single machine you can enforce this policy by following the preceding instructions but using the Local Security Policy MMC snap-in under Administrative Tools. You can also prevent the LM hash by requiring passwords that are longer than 14 characters or using certain Alt characters in your password.

 For more information on LM hash storage and techniques for removing LM hash storage, see Microsoft Knowledge Base article 299656 on the Microsoft support website.

 **Design Scenario**

Analyzing Account Risks by Cost Analysis

It has been determined that weak passwords are affecting the overall security of your organization. The organization has estimated that, for each incident in which an attacker is able to guess the password that a particular account uses, it costs approximately $12,000. This cost includes all of the resources that are used in determining an incident has occurred and reacting to it. Your organization has also estimated that this type of attack occurs about eight times per year.

Your computer security incident response team has proposed three separate solutions, and you must determine which solution is the most appropriate given all of the information involved:

Solution 1   A security policy will be created and applied to all accounts in the organization. The policy will require complex passwords as defined by a custom filter that guarantees that strong passwords are the only type that are accepted. The help desk determines that it will cost the organization about $2,000 to implement this solution and that it will reduce the number of compromised passwords by 25 percent.

Solution 2   Solution 1 will be used, and in addition, all users and administrators will attend mandatory password training to assure that there are fewer calls to the help desk and that all users affected by an attack will understand what types of passwords are expected when they must select a new one. Password auditing will also take place on random samples of users to make sure that passwords are not easily located. The IT staff estimates that the total cost of this solution is $10,000 and that it would reduce the number of password-related security incidents by 50 percent.

Solution 3   Solution 1 will be used, and in addition, you will require that all users reset their passwords every 25 days. The help desk estimates that this will increase the support calls for password issues by 50 percent, cost $50,000 more per year for increased staff, and reduce the number of password-related incidents by 75 percent.

1.   **Question:** Which is the best solution? **Answer:** With no solution in place, the organization spends approximately $96,000 correcting the problem. Solution 1 will add $2,000 to the cost of the correcting the problem but will decrease the quantity of incidents to approximately six per year, which would cost $72,000. Solution 1 makes the cost of the incidents $74,000 per year. Solution 2 will add $10,000 to the cost of implementation and will decrease the quantity of password-related security incidents to approximately four per year. Solution 2 reduces the cost of the password security incidents to $58,000 per year. Solution 3 adds $50,000 to the cost of the solution and reduces the incidents to two per year, which makes the total cost of related incidents $64,000 per year. Based on cost, Solution 2 is the best answer in this situation.

Windows 2000 and above allow for policies to be set to require strong passwords. The options that are exposed using these policies are as follow:

Maximum Password Age   The value you set for the Maximum Password Age policy represents the number of days that a password is valid until the user is required to change it. All passwords can be broken given enough time and the correct tool. With that in mind, one of your goals should be to require passwords that are complex and complicated enough so that they will take more time to break than the maximum password age. For example, if you suspect that a user's password can be broken in 40 to 60 days, then the maximum password age should be less than the minimum amount of time that the password could be broken. For example, you could set the Maximum Password Age policy to 30 or 35 and feel confident that it won't be broken before it must be changed.

Enforce Password History   The value you set for the Enforce Password History policy is the number of unique passwords remembered by the system for the specified account. These passwords cannot be reused, so users will not be able to reuse a password that they have used previously.

Minimum Password Age   The Minimum Password Age policy determines the number of days that a password must be used prior to it being changed. The default value for this option is zero. If Maximum Password Age is set to 30 and Enforce Password History is set to 12, the policy's goal is to prevent a password from being used again for a year. Many users simply change their password 13 times as soon as it expires, allowing them to keep the original password. The Minimum Password policy prevents a user from circumventing the purpose of the Maximum Password Age and Enforce Password History policies by requiring that a new password must be in place for specified period of time before it can be changed.

Minimum Password Length   The Minimum Password Length policy determines the minimum number of characters that must be used for a password. The default value is zero. Remember that if this value is greater than 14, the LM hashes will not be stored locally.

Passwords Must Meet Complexity Requirements   The Passwords Must Meet Complexity Requirements policy requires passwords that do not contain the user's name or login name, are at least six characters long, and contains characters from three of the following four groups:

- Uppercase letters
- Lowercase letters
- Numbers
- Special, non alphanumeric characters such as " < * & > ? / ; - _ = | \ . , ` ~ ^ % $ # @ !

Store Passwords Using Reversible Encryption   Enabling the Store Passwords Using Reversible Encryption policy provides support for applications that use protocols that require knowledge of the user's password for authentication purposes. Enabling this policy is essentially the same as storing cleartext versions of the passwords. Because of this weakness, this policy should not be enabled unless the specific application's requirements are of greater importance than the need to protect the integrity of the passwords.

This policy must be enabled if you are using Digest Authentication in Internet Information Services (IIS) or Challenge-Handshake Authentication Protocol (CHAP) authentication through remote access or Internet Authentication Service (IAS).

Remote access is covered in Chapter 3 and IIS is covered in Chapter 7.

Account Lockout   The Account Lockout policy disables an account when the number of failed authentication attempts exceeds a threshold. This policy can increase the number of help desk calls and wind up costing your organization money. For this reason, complex passwords and good auditing should be used to recognize a brute force attack on an account. The account lockout policy consists of three elements:

> **Account Lockout Duration**   The Account Lockout Duration policy sets the number of minutes that an account will be locked before it is automatically unlocked. Many environments set this for a short amount of time. The time period is usually in place to minimize calls to the help desk by allowing the user to simply wait and try again after the lockout time period has passed. Obviously this would slow down a brute force attack because the attacker would be able to attempt only a set number of passwords before the account would be locked.

> **Account Lockout Threshold**   The Account Lockout Threshold policy sets the number of invalid attempts that can occur before the account is locked. Many environments prefer to set this at 3, which is typically enough to allow a user to realize that they left their Caps Lock key on and still prevent a brute force program from testing a large number of passwords.

> **Reset Account Lockout After**   The Reset Account Lockout After option sets the duration, in minutes, from an invalid logon attempt until the count resets itself back to zero.

The combination of these three account policy options, if used in concert, will minimize the attack surface of many brute force programs. Assuming Account Lockout Duration is set to 30 minutes, Account Lockout Threshold is set to 5, and Reset Account Lockout After is set to 15 minutes, an attacker would be able to attempt only 10 passwords per hour as opposed to many thousand per minute if no lockout policy is configured.

   To better respond to potential attacks, you should make sure auditing is configured and evaluated on a regular basis.

In the "Analyzing and Securing Accounts with Account Policies" Design Scenario, you will analyze a scenario and use account policies to configure the accounts for the network in the scenario.

Account Logon Hours

A useful account setting that you can and should implement is setting valid logon hours. This feature exists in most network operating systems, including Windows Server 2003. The setting is configured using the account's properties dialog box from the Active Directory Users And Computers MMC. It allows an administrator to specify when a user is allowed to access the network.

Suppose, for example, that a company has an employee whose job it is to take customer orders over the phone and enter them into an order application during business hours. There should be no reason for this user to be able to log on to the network outside of business hours (since he shouldn't be on the phone).

 **Design Scenario**

Analyzing and Securing Accounts with Account Policies

You are the administrator of a small network that does business with the government. Because of the partnership with the government, the security that must be in place must meet certain regulations. The regulations require that all accounts with access to sensitive data have complex passwords.

You have agreed to enforce a strong password policy on the users who have access to the government-related resources. You need to take the necessary precautions to prevent a brute force password cracking utility from attempting several password combinations to authenticate as a valid user.

1. **Question:** As the administrator of this network, you must configure account policies for the user accounts. Which of the following policies should you enable or define a value for?

    ▪ Passwords Must Meet Complexity Requirements

    ▪ Maximum Password Age

    ▪ Enforce Password History

    ▪ Account Lockout Duration

    ▪ Account Lockout Threshold

    ▪ Reset Account Lockout Counter After

    ▪ Store Passwords Using Reversible Encryption

    Answer: To enforce a strong password policy, you should enable the Passwords Must Meet Complexity Requirements option. To prevent an attacker from hijacking accounts, you should configure the accounts to be locked out after a set number of invalid logon attempts by enabling and setting a value for the Account Lockout Threshold policy. To facilitate this requirement, you'll need to specify the time span that the account will be locked out, using the Account Lockout Duration policy.

Summary

In this chapter, you learned about the importance of authentication in Active Directory. The most common ways to increase the security of authentication are by securing passwords, properly configuring interoperability, and using encryption. We looked at the different authentication protocols and their respective strengths and weaknesses as well as which ones are compatible with each other.

There are different types of trusts that can be configured and some are more secure than others. You learned the nuances of using authentication protocols with different trusts. Specifically, you learned which trusts are default trusts and which ones must be manually configured.

We showed you how to analyze the requirements of accounts and their passwords. You should be able to distinguish among internal, external, and administrator accounts and know the difference in the approach to the requirements of each. We later explained how to design a secure password policy for your organization's accounts.

Exam Essentials

Know the different types of authentication protocols. Make sure you know the circumstances under which LAN Manager, NTLM, NTLMv2, and Kerberos should be used as well as the strengths and weaknesses of each.

Make sure you are comfortable with the different trust types. You should understand which trusts are more secure than others as well as when to use each one. You'll need to know which trusts are one and which are two way as well as which are transitive. Finally, know when it is appropriate to create an external trust.

Know the common vulnerabilities of accounts and how to defend against them. You should be able to recognize the common account vulnerabilities, such as weak passwords and excessive permissions.

Know how to design secure password policies. Password policies should include requiring strong passwords. Setting the various password policies can increase the security of the account.

Key Terms

Before you take the exam, be certain you are familiar with the following terms:

authentication	NT LAN Manager (NTLM)
authorization	NTLM Version 2 (NTLMv2)
domain trusts	parent/child trusts
external trust	Principle of Least Privilege (PoLP)
forest trust	realm trust
Kerberos v5	tree-root trusts
LAN Manager	trust model

Review Questions

1. Which of the following authentication protocols is used in a forest trust between a Windows 2003 forest and a Windows 2000 forest?

    A. LAN Manager

    B. NTLM

    C. NTLMv2

    D. Kerberos v5

2. To secure passwords stored in the SAM database of a Windows Server 2003 that is not a member of the domain which of the following policies should you configure in Local Security Policy?

    A. Set the minimum password length to 15.

    B. Set the minimum password length to 10.

    C. Set the maximum password length to 10.

    D. Set the maximum password length to 15.

3. You need to create a policy that minimizes the chance that a password can be cracked using a brute force password cracking utility and then used to log on to the network. Which of the following policies should you configure or enable? (Choose all that apply.)

    A. Maximum Password Age

    B. Enforce Password History

    C. Minimum Password Age

    D. Account Lockout Duration

    E. Account Lockout Threshold

    F. Reset Account Lockout After n

    G. Passwords Must Meet Complexity Requirements

4. Which authentication protocol is the most secure option to Windows Server 2003?

    A. LM Hash

    B. NTLMv2

    C. IPSec

    D. EFS

    E. Kerberos v5

5. You design a secure password policy by enabling the Passwords Must Meet Complexity Requirements policy. Which of the following passwords are valid for a user whose name is John Rico and username is JRico? (Choose two.)

   A. RiCo*3_1

   B. F%2_=87ba^

   C. t4(8^rt\

   D. p@s$word

6. According to best practices, which group scope should have permissions assigned to it?

   A. Universal

   B. Global

   C. Domain Local

   D. Enterprise

   E. Domain

7. When analyzing the authentication requirements of the network, which topics will play the most significant role? (Choose two.)

   A. Business requirements

   B. Service pack level

   C. Interoperability requirements

   D. Industry standards

8. You need to access a printer that is shared from an NT 4 server that is a domain controller in an NT 4 domain. Which authentication protocol will be used?

   A. LAN Manager

   B. NTLM

   C. NTLMv2

   D. Kerberos v5

9. You need to devise a grouping strategy for your Windows Active Directory organization. The Active Directory is made up of four domains. Some of the domain controllers are running Windows NT 4 and Windows 2000 in addition to Windows Server 2003. You need to create a group that can be used in any of the domains. Which of the following group types should you create?

   A. Universal

   B. Global

   C. Domain Local

   D. Enterprise

10. Which of the following Windows Active Directory trusts are transitive by default? (Choose all that apply.)

   A. Forest trust

   B. Tree-root trust

   C. External Trust

   D. Realm trust

   E. Parent/child trust

Answers to Review Questions

1. C. Windows 2000 supports only the Kerberos v5 protocol for trusts within a forest, not between them. The strongest authentication protocol that Windows 2000 forests can use with a trust relationship is NTLMv2. LAN Manager and NTLM are used by earlier versions of Windows and are not used in this type of trust.

2. A. The LM hash will split a password that is up to 14 characters and store it locally. Creating a password that is greater than 14 characters will prevent the hash from being stored locally. There is no Maximum Password Length policy that can be configured.

3. A, B, C, G. The account-related policies will prevent an attacker from using a utility to attempt to log on to an authentication server. The policies will not thwart a password cracking utility from guessing the password hash once the hash is stored; rather they will make the guessed password obsolete by the time it has been decrypted. Setting the Maximum Password Age will require that a user change their password, ideally before the utility can obtain the password. The Enforce Password History and Minimum Password Age policies are used to prevent the user from changing their password back to one of their recently used passwords. These settings will make the password that the utility obtains obsolete. Setting the Passwords Must Meet Complexity Requirements policy will make the utility work harder and take longer to get the password.

4. E. LM Hashes are used by LAN Manager related authentication protocols, they are not themselves a protocol. NTLMv2 is supported for authentication under Windows Server 2003, but it is less secure than the Kerberos v5 authentication protocol. IPSec is used to encrypt data on the wire and EFS is used to encrypt data on the file system.

5. B, C. For a password to meet the security policy stated, it must contain three of the four types of characters: uppercase letters, lowercase letters, numbers, and special characters. In addition, the password cannot contain the user's name or username. Option A contains the user's last name and option D meets only two of the character requirements, so they are not valid. Answers B and C are valid complex passwords.

6. C. According to best practices, you should follow the AG(G)DLP method, where accounts are placed in Global groups, Global groups are optionally nested, Global groups are placed in Universal groups (If you are using Enterprise level grouping), Universal groups, if used, are added to Domain Local groups or the Global groups will be added to the Domain Local groups, and Domain Local groups are assigned permissions. There is no group scope named Enterprise or Domain.

7. A, C. Options A and C are correct because they will have the largest impact on the decisions that you will make as you design the security infrastructure in your network. Service pack levels and industry standards are not as important to the overall security design as the business or interoperability requirements are.

8. B. Windows NT 4 supports only NTLM. NTLMv2 is supported on Windows 2000 Server and Windows XP, and Kerberos v5 is the default authentication protocol for Windows 2000 Server and Windows Server 2003 native domains.

9. B. Universal groups are only supported when all domain controllers are running Windows 2000 Server and Windows Server 2003 and Active Directory is in Native mode. Windows NT 4 domain controllers only support Global groups.

10. A, B, E. Forest trusts, tree-root trusts, and parent/child trusts are the only trusts that are transitive by default. A realm trust could be transitive, but not by default.

Case Study

You should give yourself 20 minutes to review this testlet, review the table, and complete the questions.

Overview

Towely Incorporated designs, manufactures, and markets industrial strength towels. Towely Inc. is currently the largest supplier of towels to hotels in the world.

Physical Locations

The organization has three offices, as shown in the following table. The main office is in Philadelphia, and there are branch offices in Los Angeles and Miami. Employees and the business units are distributed as referenced in the table.

Office Locations	Employee Quantity	Business Units	Onsite IT support
Philadelphia	5,000	Executive, Marketing, HR, and IT	IT staff
Los Angeles	750	Accounting and Research and Development	5 IT administrators
Miami	100	Manufacturing	1 IT administrator and 1 help desk operator

Existing Environment

Directory Services   Towely Incorporated consists of a single Active Directory domain named TowelyInc.com. The company's organizational unit (OU) structure is shown in the OU structure exhibit (in the section "Case Study Exhibits").

There are domain controllers in each of the offices: Philadelphia, Miami, and Los Angeles.

A global security group named PHLExecs contains all of the executive employees in the Philadelphia office. A global security group named MIAManufacture contains all of the manufacturing employees in the Miami office.

Network Infrastructure   All of the servers are running Windows Server 2003, Enterprise Edition. All of the client workstations in all of the sites are running Windows XP Professional. All computers have the most recent service packs applied. Client workstations access websites through a proxy server.

Towely Incorporated uses an internal website to handle most of the human resources as well as other organizational business. Only employees should be allowed to access the intranet and the organization's information.

There is also a perimeter network. The perimeter network houses a server named ExServer4. ExServer4 is not a member of the Active Directory domain. ExServer4 hosts a website that is used by the various hotel chains to order more towels for their respective hotels. The website is maintained in Internet Information Services 6.0 running an ASP .NET application.

All of the Research and Development data is located on a single server named RD_Data, located in Los Angeles.

Problem Statements

The following organizational problems must be considered:

- Whenever a significant outage occurs, the help desk operator in Miami gets inundated with calls.

- The employees in the Los Angeles office have a history of installing unsupported drivers on their workstations. In addition, you have discovered that unauthorized software has been installed on some of the workstations by employees. Some of applications that have been installed have caused incompatibilities with some of the line-of-business applications.

- Users frequently forget to lock or log out of their client computers. This is a security risk and should be prevented from happening.

Interviews

Chief Information Officer   We plan on implementing a secure infrastructure to prevent our competitors from gaining access to our research information.

On occasion, we monitor logon traffic to our domain controllers and inspect the logs randomly. This inspection needs to occur on a more regular basis.

Chief Operating Officer   The last time the IT department implemented a widespread policy shift, it took the users several weeks to adjust and production decreased significantly. Any changes that are made that affect production need to have a minimum impact on the bottom line.

Network Administrator   We need to test software and make sure that it is compatible with our current desktop image. Users should not be able to install software on their own client computers without administrative oversight.

Last year more than 10 users had their passwords compromised because they were easily guessed. Our team spent weeks recovering from each of the incidents and we want to, at least, minimize the occurrence of passwords being compromised.

Currently there are no logon policies in place.

Business Requirements

Organizational Goals   Currently the IT Staff manages user, group, and computer accounts centrally in Philadelphia. The help desk operator in Miami needs to have the authority to manage the users in Miami only.

Security   The company's security policy contains the following requirements:

- Manufacturing data must not be accessible over the network through shared folders. The highest level of authentication must be used for all access to the data.

- Access to the RD_Data folder must be restricted to only members of the research team. The research team should be able to make all types of changes to the contents of the files.

- Before business partners are allowed to access the partner site, the source IP address needs to be recorded and be in a specific list of allowed source addresses.

The following security requirements apply specifically to the websites and servers for the organization.

- IIS cannot be installed on domain controllers.

- All access to the internal website should be restricted to only allow authenticated users in the domain.

Case Study Exhibits

The following shows the physical locations and connectivity diagram:

Los Angeles   Philadelphia   Miami

The following shows the Active Directory organizational unit structure:

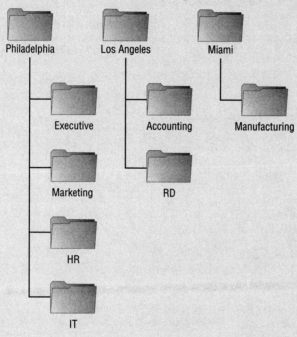

Case Study Questions

1. You need to give permissions to the employees in the research team so that they can access the research data. Which of the following tasks should you complete? (Choose all that apply.)

    A. Create a Domain Local group named dl_ResearchData.

    B. Add the research accounts to the Domain Local group dl_ResearchData.

    C. Assign permissions to the Global group g_ResearchData.

    D. Create a Universal group and add the research accounts to the Universal group u_AllResearch.

    E. Create a Global group named g_ResearchData.

2. You decide to implement strong password requirements for all of the users in the Miami office. You need to make sure that no password cracking utility can access LM hashes on the local machines. What additional steps should you take? (Choose all that apply.)

    A. Add a lockout policy for 3 invalid logons within a 30-minute timeframe.

    B. Create a Group Policy Object that removes the LM Hashes from the local machines and link the policy to the Miami container.

    C. Install a third-party monitoring system to evaluate the strength of the passwords and determine how long the passwords should be in order to thwart any brute force attacks.

    D. Automate an alert notification to be sent when an incorrect username or password combination is supplied.

    E. Set the Minimum Password Length policy to 15 for all users in Miami.

3. Towely Incorporated has hired some new research and development employees that need to have access to the research data. What must you do to assure that the new employees can access the data to perform their job?

    A. Add the new employee accounts to the Domain Local group for the research data.

    B. Add the new employee accounts to the Universal group for the research data.

    C. Add the new employee accounts to the research Global group that has access to the research data.

    D. Add the new employee accounts to the Domain Users Global Domain group.

4. Towely Incorporated has just acquired Leaf Soap LLP. Leaf Soap runs a Windows 2000 Active Directory domain that is running in Native mode. You need to configure the two domains to talk to each other so that resources are available to users in both domains. You need to configure the trust relationship to use Kerberos v5. What additional tasks must you perform? (Choose all that apply.)

    A. Convert the Windows 2000 Active Directory domain to a Kerberos realm.

    B. Create a two-way trust relationship from the Towely domain to the Leaf Soap domain.

    C. Make the trust use Kerberos v5 by configuring the Registry on both bridgehead servers.

    D. Upgrade the domain controllers at Leaf Soap to Windows Server 2003 and change Active Directory to run in Windows 2003 Native mode.

5. With the acquisition of Leaf Soap, your IT staff now must secure additional servers. After auditing the new network, it is determined that Exchange Server is running in the Leaf Soap domain. The service accounts for Exchange are running in the context of the LocalSystem account. You would like the service to run custom scripts that record log information to a remote share. You need to make sure that accounts have only the absolute minimum permissions that they require in order to function. Which one of the following should you do?

A. Remove the permissions to resources that are not needed for Exchange from the Local-System account.

B. Create an account on the server that is running Exchange and assign it only the permissions that are required to run the Exchange Server services.

C. Create an account in the Leaf Soap domain and assign it only the permissions that are required to run the Exchange Server services.

D. Create an account in the Leaf Soap domain and assign it to the local Administrators group on the Exchange Server machine.

6. You fear that the accounts in the Leaf Soap domain are less secure due to weak password requirements. Which of the following policies should you enable in order to require stronger passwords? (Choose all that apply.)

A. Maximum Password Age

B. Minimum Password Length

C. Minimum Password Age

D. Enforce Password History

E. Passwords Must Meet Complexity Requirements

7. You want to make sure that users in the Philadelphia office can only log on during normal business hours. What can you do in order to enforce this rule?

A. Enable and configure logon hours in the account's properties dialog box.

B. Enable the Logon Hours policy for the domain.

C. Enable the Store Logon Hours With Credentials option on the domain controller.

D. Enable the Account Lockout Threshold and the Account Lockout Duration options.

8. Your security team has alerted you that in the early morning hours, several attempts are made to authenticate as various accounts and these attempts are obviously not being made by employees. What additional security policies must you enable to prevent this from being exploited into a brute force password attack? (Choose two.)

A. Account Lockout Duration

B. Reset Account Lockout After

C. Enforce Password History

D. Account Lockout Threshold

9. In your organization, a user, Winston Smith, whose logon is wsmith, attempts to set his password to WiNsTOn98. You have configured the default password filter by enabling the Passwords Must Meet Complexity Requirements policy. The password is rejected citing password requirements. Why?

   A. The password doesn't contain each of the four required character types (uppercase, lowercase, numeric, and special characters).

   B. The password contains the user's logon name.

   C. The password contains the user's name.

   D. The password contains less than the minimum number of characters defined in the filter.

10. One of your partners needs to provide resources to some of your users. The partner runs Unix and has a Kerberos realm configured. You need to make sure that your organizational resources cannot be accessed by your partner's accounts. What should you do?

    A. Create an external one-way trust with the partner's domain trusting your domain.

    B. Create an external two-way trust between your domain and the partner's domain.

    C. Create an external one-way trust with your domain trusting your partner's domain.

    D. Create in your domain accounts for the users in the partner's domain and assign them the appropriate permissions on the required resources.

11. To prevent users from being able to install software on their workstations, which one of the following tasks should you complete?

    A. Remove the users from the Domain Users Global group.

    B. Remove the users from the Local Users group on their client workstations.

    C. Remove the users from the Administrators Local group on their client workstations.

    D. Add the users to the Restricted group on the local workstations.

Answers to Case Study Questions

1. A, E. The proper way to assign permissions to resources is to use the AG(G)DLP technique. Put accounts in Global groups, optionally nest Global groups, place Global groups into Domain Local groups, and assign permissions to the Domain Local group. Option B is incorrect because accounts shouldn't be added to a Domain Local group. Option C is incorrect because permissions shouldn't be assigned to Global groups. Option D is incorrect because accounts shouldn't be added directly to Universal groups. Options A and E fall into the AG(G)DLP rule.

2. B, E. To prevent LM hashes of passwords from being stored, you will need to modify the local security policy of all the workstations in Miami. To do this in the most effective manner, you should create a Group Policy Object (GPO) that prevents the storing of LM hashes locally and link it to the Miami OU. Or, you can require that passwords be more than 14 characters long, which also prevents the LM hash from being stored. Therefore options B and E are correct. Options A, C, and D are incorrect because none of them have any effect on the storing of LM hashes.

3. C. To give the new employees access to the appropriate resources, you should add them to the Global group for the research users. Accounts should be added to Global groups, not Domain Local or Universal groups. All users are automatically added to the Domain Users group, which doesn't have access to the specific resources for the Research and Development department.

4. B, D. For the trust relationship to use Kerberos v5, both domains must be running Windows 2003 Active Directory in Native mode. The Leaf Soap domain controllers must be upgraded to Windows Server 2003 in order to facilitate the Kerberos trust relationship. Once you've upgraded Active Directory in the Leaf Soap domain, you should create a two-way trust relationship between the two domains. Option A is incorrect because a Windows 2000 Active Directory domain cannot be converted to a Kerberos realm. Option C is incorrect because there is no Registry setting that provides this functionality and bridgehead servers are the primary path connecting sites for replication; they do not play a direct role in trust relationships or Kerberos authentication.

5. C. To make sure that the account has only the permissions that are required, it should be a domain user account that is assigned the minimum permissions to run the service. Option A is incorrect because the LocalSystem account should not be used for services that could be targets for attack. Option B is incorrect because a local account is not sufficient to access the remote share. Option D is incorrect because giving the account administrator privileges is giving excessive permissions and causes the attack surface to widen instead of become smaller.

6. B, E. Only options B and E will force the passwords to be stronger. Setting a maximum or minimum password age or setting the Enforce Password History policy will make the accounts more secure but not make the passwords stronger, which is the requirement in the question.

7. A. To restrict when users are allowed to log on, you will need to configure the logon hours using the Active Directory Users And Computers tool and configure the policy in the account's properties dialog box. Option B is incorrect because there is no Logon Hours domain policy. Nor is there a Store Logon Hours With Credentials option, and therefore option C is incorrect. Option D is incorrect because account lockout settings don't enforce logon hour rules.

8. A, D. You must configure the Account Lockout Duration option and the Account Lockout Threshold option in order to prevent a brute force attack against your accounts. Option B could be configured, but it isn't required. In the current configuration, an administrator will need to unlock the account manually rather than let it automatically unlock itself after a prescribed time period. Option C is incorrect because enforcing password history won't prevent a brute force attack.

9. C. The default filter requires that a password meet three of the four required character types, which the supplied password does. Therefore option A is incorrect. The password does not contain the user's logon name, which is wsmith. The minimum number of characters for a password as defined in the default filter is 6, and the supplied password exceeds 6 characters. The only possibility is that the user's name is Winston (either first or last).

10. A. Option B is incorrect because you should configure a one-way trust only where the Unix realm trusts your Active Directory domain. Option C is wrong because the trust is going in the wrong direction. Option D is wrong because the resources are located at the partner site, not yours, and therefore the partner needs to assign the permissions to the resources, not your organization. Option A is correct because you need to create a trust relationship between your Windows domain and a non–Windows domain, in this case UNIX, using a Kerberos realm trust. The question states that you need to make sure that the resources in your domain are not to be accessible to the users of the UNIX realm therefore the trust should only go one way: from the UNIX realm to your Active Directory domain.

11. C. The users are able to install software because they have excessive permissions on their workstations. Option A is incorrect because all users should be members of the global Domain Users group. Answer B is incorrect because, if the users aren't members of the local Users group, they won't have the required permissions to use their client computer. Option D is incorrect because there is no Restricted group on local workstations.

Chapter

5

Designing an Access Control Strategy for Network Resources

MICROSOFT EXAM OBJECTIVE COVERED IN THIS CHAPTER:

✓ **Design an access control strategy for directory services.**

- Create a delegation strategy.
- Analyze auditing requirements.
- Design the appropriate group strategy for accessing resources.
- Design a permission structure for directory service objects.

✓ **Design an access control strategy for files and folders.**

- Design a strategy for the encryption and decryption of files and folders.
- Design a permission structure for files and folders.
- Design security for a backup and recovery strategy.
- Analyze auditing requirements.

✓ **Design an access control strategy for the registry.**

- Design a permission structure for registry objects.
- Analyze auditing requirements.

In this chapter, you will learn how to design an access control strategy. You will learn the details of discretionary, role-based, and mandatory access control and be able to explain the process that occurs when a user logs on and receives an access token, which is used when the user attempts to access a resource. You will see how the operating system enforces access control and some of the best practices when it pertains to administrative accounts. We will explain the basic guidelines for auditing the use of permissions as well as user rights.

We will show you what access control entails and why it is such an important topic. You will be able to recognize the differences between user-based and password-based access control as well as the difference between user rights and a user's permissions.

Designing Access Control Strategies

Access control is defined as the process of authorizing users or groups to access resources, such as files or printers on the network. As stated in Chapter 4, "Designing an Authentication Strategy for Active Directory," network security is based on two fundamental concepts:

Authentication   Authentication is the process of determining the identity of something or someone.

Authorization   Authorization is determining what the authenticated identity is allowed to do.

The key concepts that define access control are explained in the following topics:

Ownership of objects   When an object is created, Windows assigns it an owner. The owner, by default, is the creator of the object (e.g., the user who creates the printer object in the directory).

Permissions assigned to objects   The principal technique for implementing access control is permissions. *Permissions* are used to grant or deny users and groups a specified action. The permissions are implemented, typically, through the use of security descriptors. *Security descriptors* are attributes attached to an object that specify the permissions granted to users and groups, the security events to be audited, and the owner of the object. An example of a permission assigned to an object is the Read permission on a specific file assigned to a security group.

A security descriptor contains two *access control lists (ACLs)*. An access control list is a list of security protections that apply to an entire object, to a set of the object's properties, or to an individual property of an object. Simply put, the ACL contains all of the permission attributes regarding an object, including who is explicitly granted access as well as those explicitly denied access to the object. There are two types of ACLs:

Discretionary access control lists (DACLs)   The *discretionary access control list (DACL)* is the part of the security descriptor that grants or denies specific users and groups access to the object. Only the owner of the object can change permissions granted or denied in the DACL.

System access control lists (SACLs)   The *system access control list (SACL)* is the part of the security descriptor that dictates which events are to be audited for specific users or groups.

Both the DACL and the SACL consist of *access control entries (ACEs),* which contain each user's or group's attributes on the object. In order to view the DACLs and SACLs, you must enable Advanced Features from the Active Directory Users And Computers tool's View menu.

Inheritance of permissions   Inheritance, implemented by Windows, causes an object created in a container to inherit the permissions of its parent container. For example, when files are created within a folder, they will inherit the permissions that are assigned to the folder.

Object managers   When individual permissions need to be adjusted, you will use the appropriate tool to manage the object type. For example, to modify the permissions of a folder, you would use Windows Explorer and right-click the folder and then choose the Properties menu option. The Permissions tab would then be used to change the permissions for the folder.

Object auditing   Windows provides the ability to audit users' access to objects. You can use the security log to view these events.

Designing Access Control for Active Directory

Access control, as mentioned previously, is used to manage access to resources for security purposes. In Active Directory, specifically, access control is administered at the object level. This is accomplished by configuring different levels of permissions or access to objects. The permissions could be Full Control, Write, Read, and so on.

Access control for Active Directory objects relies on the Windows access control model, which is made up of the two basic components:

Access tokens   *Access tokens* contain the information regarding a logged-on user.

Security descriptors   *Security descriptors* contain the security information that protects an object.

When a user logs on successfully, the system will produce an access token that includes the identity and privileges of the user account. The system then uses the token to identify the user when their thread interacts with a securable object or attempts to perform some action that requires privileges. The following is a partial list of the elements that are contained in an access token:

- The Security ID (SID)

- SIDs for the groups of which the user is a member

- Logon SID, which is a SID that persists only for the duration of the active logon session

- List of the privileges possessed by the user or the groups to which the user belongs
- An owner SID
- The SID for the user's primary group
- The default DACL, which includes the creator/owner permissions, that is used when the user creates a securable object
- The source of the access token
- A value that indicates whether the token is a primary or an impersonation token

As a result of this information being assigned when a user logs on, certain conditions may require a user to log off and then back on in order to gain access to a recently modified permission. For example, a user is added to a security group while they are currently logged on. The access token that they have already received does not contain the SID for the newly assigned group and the user's current thread will not be a member of the group. To rectify this situation, the user must acquire a new access token, which can easily be accomplished by logging off and back on again.

Table 5.1 shows the basic outline of the Windows (NT-based) access control model.

TABLE 5.1   Windows Access Control Model

Element	Description
Security descriptor	Every object in Active Directory has its own security descriptor that contains the security information that determines the access to the object. The descriptor can contain ACEs in DACLs.
Security context	When an attempt to access an object is made, the application will supply the credentials of the security principal that is making the access request. Once authenticated, the credentials that were supplied will determine the security context of the running application. The security context includes the group membership and the privileges that are associated with the originally supplied security principal.
Access check	The system will permit access to an object only if the security descriptor for the object grants the necessary access rights to the requesting security principal or to a group in which the principal has membership.

Simply stated, the Windows access control model will not allow a principal to access an object that they have not been granted access to.

In the next sections, we will introduce to you the different types of permissions that are available for Active Directory objects. You will learn the best practices for assigning them and how to make dealing with assigned and inherited permissions more manageable.

Understanding Active Directory Object Permissions

In Active Directory, every object has its own security descriptor that specifies which accounts have permission to access the object as well as what type of access is permitted. The object permissions are what provide you with the capability to control who can access individual objects or an object's attributes within the directory. Typically, you will use permissions to assign privileges to an organizational unit; however, you can assign permissions to any single object.

Active Directory has several types of permissions; the standard permissions are composed of those that are the most commonly assigned. Table 5.2 lists the standard permissions.

TABLE 5.2   Active Directory Standard Permissions

Permission	Description
Full Control	Includes Change Permissions and Take Ownership, as well as all other standard permissions
Write	Provides the ability to change an object's attributes
Read	Provides the ability to view objects, object attributes, the owner, and the Active Directory permissions
Create All Child Objects	Provides the ability to create any type of object in a container, typically an organizational unit (OU)
Delete All Child Objects	Provides the ability to remove any type of child object from a container

The standard permissions are a logical combination of special permissions. The special permissions that are available are different depending on the resource that you are attempting to secure. They include Read Attributes, Read Extended Attributes, Write Attributes, Read Permissions, Change Permissions, etc. For example, if the resource that you are trying to secure is a file on an NTFS volume, you may grant a security group the special permission of Execute File.

NOTE   You can access the special permissions by clicking the Advanced button from the security tab of the object's properties window.

Prior to a user gaining access to an object, an administrator or the object owner must grant permissions to the user. These permissions are stored in the DACL.

Active Directory object permissions can be granted or denied (either implicitly or explicitly), set as standard or special permissions, and set at the object level or inherited from a parent object.

Real World Scenario

Avoiding Deny Permissions

Steve is the network administrator for a large management consulting firm. There are two types of partners that run the firm: equity and nonequity partners. Nonequity partners should have access to everything that equity partners can access with the exception of the firm's financial information. To facilitate this access, Steve decides to create a Global group named All-Partners that has all of the partners' accounts as members. In order to assure that the nonequity partners cannot view the financial information, he creates ACEs on the FinancialData folder for each of the nonequity partner's accounts and denies each one the Read permission.

Over time, the nonequity partners may buy in to the firm and become full equity partners. When this occurs, Steve must remove the ACE denying the individual accounts. In addition to the administrative burden of managing these permissions on individual accounts, the more ACEs on an ACL, the worse the performance will be when accessing the folder.

In order to resolve these problems, Steve creates two additional Global groups: EquityPartners and NonEquityPartners. The EquityPartners group is granted the Read permission to the FinancialData folder and the NonEquityPartners group is not. This makes maintaining these groups in the future easy and it keeps the ACL on the FinancialData folder small.

Deny permissions always take precedence over any other permission. The only time you would need to use a Deny permission is when a user is granted a permission elsewhere and needs to be trumped. Users are not allowed to access an object unless they have been granted access either directly or indirectly. Therefore, with proper planning, there should be little reason to deny a permission if it was never granted in the first place. Some organizations may require the explicit denial of a permission in order to guarantee that a user or group will never have access to a resource, even if the permission is granted in the future. This situation commonly arises when specific business rules must be maintained.

If a permission is not explicitly granted, it is implicitly denied. For example, if the Sales group is granted Read permission to a user object and no other principal is stored in the DACL for the printer object, users who are not members of the Sales group are implicitly denied access. An explicit Deny is when an ACE that states a denied permission is added to the DACL that states a denied permission. For example, you may have a user named Collin who is a member of the Human Resources group. The HR group is granted the ability to create and remove child objects for a specified OU; however, Collin should not be granted this right. You can prevent Collin from performing these actions by explicitly denying the Create All Child Objects and Delete All Child Objects permissions. While all other permissions are cumulative, combining anything with a Deny permission results in the permission being denied.

There are some other types of permissions that are available for Active Directory objects. In the following list, extended rights, validated writes, and property sets are all explained:

Extended rights   *Extended rights* are used for special operations that apply to specific types of Active Directory objects. For example, the Active Directory right Send As applied to an Exchange Server right allows for a user or group to send mail as the specified mailbox.

Validated writes   A *validated write* is different from a Write permission in that it evaluates the content of the write and determines if the value supplied conforms with the specified semantics. An example here is the Add/Remove Self As Member permission that applies to groups. This permission allows users to add or remove themselves as members of the group, providing a more granular level of control than just the ability to add and remove anyone from the group.

Property sets   A *property set* is a group of interrelated attributes. The added value of property sets is that access rights can be granted to a property set as a whole rather than to individual attributes, which in turn improves the responsiveness and overall performance of the access control infrastructure. In addition to performance benefits, they also simplify security management. For example, there is a property set named Domain Password, which encompasses the following Domain attributes:

- `lockOutObservationWindow`
- `lockoutDuration`
- `lockoutThreshold`
- `maxPwdAge`
- `minPwdAge`
- `minPwdLength`
- `Pwd-Properties`

As you can see, it is easier to grant a user the ability to manage the property set than to manage each individual attribute.

In the following Design Scenario, you will design an access control strategy for Active Directory objects.

 Design Scenario

Designing an Access Control Strategy for Active Directory Objects

You are the network administrator for a medium-sized business management company whose main office is located in Phoenix. The company also has offices in Philadelphia and Miami. There are no network administrators or any other IT staff members located in the satellite offices. The help desk is located in Phoenix, and you have noticed that there is a large volume of incoming calls from the remote users who need to have their passwords reset. You want to reduce the burden on the help desk and allow each of the satellite offices to have more autonomy as it relates to password lockout problems. Each office is configured as its own domain. The office manager at each location is reasonably computer savvy and the decision has been made to grant the office manager the ability to unlock accounts and configure the domain passwords to the requirements of the office.

1.   **Question:** Which of the following actions should you complete? (Choose the best answer.)

- Assign each office manager the Domain Password permission set.

- Add each office manager to the Domain Admins group for their domain.

- Create a group named OfficeMgrs in each domain and grant the group the Domain Password permission set.

- Create a Universal group in the domain named OfficeMgrs and grant it administrative permissions at the root domain container.

Answer: Based on the available options, the best solution is to use a permission set and assign it to a group. The first option would work, but it is always recommended that you assign permissions to groups, not to users directly. The second option would not work because it is never a valid solution to grant a user administrative privileges unless they require all of them. The last option also would not work because a Universal group is not required based on the specified scenario.

Along the theme of ease of management, in the next section you will learn the best ways to design your security group infrastructure.

Designing a Security Group Strategy for Active Directory

As you learned in Chapter 4, there are different group types with different levels of visibility or scope across the domain or forest. In Active Directory, when in Windows 2000 Native mode or higher, you will have access to a new group scope: Universal.

 If the Active Directory mode is Windows 2000 Mixed, Universal groups are not available.

A *Universal group* can have members that include accounts, Global groups, and Universal groups from any domain and can be assigned permissions in any domain in the domain tree or forest.

Universal groups can be used to consolidate groups whose logical membership should span domains. In order to accomplish this, you add the accounts to Global groups in their respective domain and then nest the Global groups within Universal groups. This is the recommended strategy because changes in the membership of the Global group will not cause changes in the Universal group, which typically would require replication of the global catalog to each global catalog server in the forest.

With the addition of Universal groups to the AG(G)DLP guideline discussed in Chapter 4, the recommendation becomes AG(G)UDLP, as seen in the following list:

1. Place (A)ccounts in (G)lobal groups.

2. Optionally nest (G)lobal groups.

3. Place (G)lobal groups into (U)niversal Groups.

4. Place (U)niversal groups into (D)omain (L)ocal groups.

5. Assign (P)ermissions to the (D)omain (L)ocal group

Real World Scenario

Taking Advantage of Universal Groups

Thatcher is the network administrator for a large consulting company. The company's Active Directory is made up of three domains: TJR.lan, east.TJR.lan, and west.TJR.lan. In each domain, there are human resource records that all HR personnel need to be able to modify. There are HR accounts in each of the domains and Thatcher wants to keep the ACLs short and easy to maintain. In addition, he needs to minimize replication traffic between domains.

Thatcher creates a global group in each domain—glCorpHR, glEastHR, and glWestHR—and then adds them to the dlHR domain local group in each domain. Each time membership changes in any of the Global groups, forestwide replication would be required. Also, the ACL would have three access control entries (ACEs).

To reduce replication, Thatcher creates a Universal group named uHR. He then adds the glCorpHR, glEastHR, and glWestHR Global groups to uHR. Next, Thatcher grants each of the dlHR Domain Local groups (one for each domain) the appropriate permissions on the HR data. Once that step is completed, he adds the uHR Universal group as a member the dlHR groups in each domain. Now as membership changes in the Global groups, replication will only need to occur within each domain and not between them.

In the following Design Scenario, you will evaluate the scenario provided and create the appropriate groups to provide the required access.

Design Scenario

Planning an Appropriate Group Strategy

You are the Windows Active Directory architect for a large toy manufacturer. Ralph needs to design a grouping strategy for the accountants in the toyshop.com domain. There are two domains: the headquarters, which is toyshop.com, and the U.S. business, which is US.toyshop.com. The company has been very successful and intends to expand into other countries in the future. You need to devise a strategy for your groups that provides the least administrative overhead with the maximum security. There are accountants in both domains and they are members of the AccountsReceivable and/or AccountsPayable Global groups in their respective domains. All accountants need access to the AccountsData share in each domain.

Question: From the following, choose the additional tasks you should complete in order to design the appropriate grouping strategy.

- Create a Global group named glAccountants in each domain; add AccountsReceivable and AccountsPayable as members.

- Create a Domain Local group named dlAccountsData in each domain; add the glAccountants groups as members.

- Create a Universal group named AllAccountants; add glAccountants from each domain as members.

- Create a Domain Local group named dlAccounts in each domain; add the Universal group AllAccountants as a member of the group.

- Grant the Domain Local group dlAccounts in each domain the permissions to access the AccountsData folder.

- Grant the Global group glAccountants permissions to both domains' AccountsData share.

Answer: In order to adhere to the AG(G)UDLP guideline, you should create a domainwide Accounting group in each domain with the AR and AP groups as members. Each domain's Global Accounting group should then be added to a Universal group, in this case named AllAccountants. In each domain, a Domain Local group should be created and granted permissions to the AccountsData share and the Universal group AllAccountants should be added to the Domain Local groups.

Best Practices for Assigning Permissions to Objects

The following list includes some of the best practices that you should keep in mind when assigning permissions to Active Directory objects.

Avoid changing the default permissions on Active Directory objects.   In some circumstances, unforeseen problems can occur or could lead to reduced security on the object(s).

Avoid assigning a security principal, user, or group Full Control of an object, especially an organizational unit.   The Full Control permission includes the Take Ownership and the Change Permissions permission, which, if used improperly, can be exploited so that a user granted Full Control can assign another principal the permissions on the child objects in the hierarchy. As stated in Chapter 4, assign only the minimum required permissions (Principle of Least Privilege).

Limit the quantity of access control entries that apply to child objects.   If you use the Apply Onto option when controlling inheritance, all of the child objects of those that you have specified will receive their own copy of the ACE. As the number of objects that receive copies increases, there can be significant performance issues across the network.

Assign the same set of permissions to multiple objects.   Windows Server 2003 includes a feature called single-instancing with regard to access control lists. If several objects have identical ACLs, Active Directory will store only one instance of the ACL, thus preserving resources.

Assign access rights broadly instead of granularly.   With a smaller number of access control entries, the overall system performance will increase. For example, you should use property sets rather than individual properties; doing so provides for a smaller number of ACEs. There are times when it is necessary to assign permissions to an individual property; however, you should try to minimize that granular a permission assignment.

Assign permissions to groups instead of user accounts. You can utilize groups to minimize administrative overhead and design flaws that can lead to a lowered overall security. You should use the AG(G)UDLP technique for the maximum blend of maintenance and security. Using groups also limits the overall quantity of ACEs on a given object. For example, you could use a single ACE to represent all managers rather than a single ACE for each user account that is a manager.

In the next section, you will learn about delegation and how you can use it in your Active Directory design to increase security.

Designing a Delegation Strategy

In a Windows NT 4 domain, in order to have the right to change a user's password, you had to be a member of the Domain Administrators group (excluding third-party offerings). This solution posed a significant quandary: Do you give Domain Administrator permissions to users who should not normally have them, or do you require your upper-level domain administrator to take action each time a user needs to have their password reset. In most situations, neither result was acceptable. *Delegation* provides the ability to assign specific tasks to the appropriate users or groups without giving them any more rights than they require to perform the task you have delegated to them.

Active Directory facilitates the efficient management of its objects by allowing for the delegation of administrative control. *Delegation of control* is the ability to assign the responsibility of managing Active Directory objects to another user, group, or organization. By delegating control, you negate the need to have several high-level administrative accounts, because any user or group can be delegated control of an object without it being added to an administrator group.

You can delegate the permissions to create or modify objects in a specified organizational unit. For example, you can give the human resources department the ability to create and modify user accounts in Active Directory. You can also delegate the ability to modify specific attributes of an object, such as granting a group the ability to reset the passwords of users within a specific OU.

Delegating administrative control will lessen the administrative burden of managing the enterprise by distributing the administrative load across the entire organization. Taking advantage of delegation, you can increase the security of your organization by reducing the number of members in the administrative groups.

To delegate control for common administrative tasks, follow these steps:

1. Open the Active Directory Users And Computers MMC and click the organizational unit for which you intend to delegate control.

2. From the Action menu, select Delegate Control.

3. The Delegation Of Control Wizard begins. On the Welcome page, click Next.

4. From the Users Or Groups page, select the user or the group to which you want to grant permissions and then click Next.

5. On the Tasks To Delegate page, select one or more of the following tasks to delegate:

   - Create, delete, and manage user accounts

   - Reset user passwords and force password change at next logon

   - Read all user information

   - Create, delete, and manage groups

- Modify the membership of a group
- Manage Group Policy links

6. Click Next.

7. From the Completing The Delegation Of Control Wizard page, click Finish.

In the "Delegating Permissions" Design Scenario, you will evaluate a scenario and determine the best use of delegation.

 Design Scenario

Delegating Permissions

You are the IT administrator of a large television marketing company that has over 15,000 employees nationwide. In addition to the offices in the U.S., there is a satellite office in Mexico City with 100 employees. The Mexican office is where all of the management training occurs, so the number of employees tends to fluctuate. There is only a single help desk support technician in the Mexico City office to support the employees who work from the office as trainers and support staff. All of the servers in all of the offices run Windows Server 2003, Enterprise Edition, and all workstations are running Windows XP Professional.

The users in the Mexico City office have been installing unauthorized software that has caused compatibility problems with one of the important line-of-business applications. You need to make sure that the users in Mexico City cannot install software themselves. Instead, only the Mexico City help desk technician should be able to install software on the workstations there. The help desk technician should also be able to create and manage all user, group, and computer accounts that are located in Mexico City.

The OU structure for the Mexico City site is displayed in the following graphic:

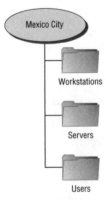

1.   **Question:** You need to design a method to grant the Mexico City help desk technician the necessary permissions to perform his job. What should you do? **Answer:** You should delegate the required permissions to the Puerto Rico help desk technician account on the Puerto Rico OU.

Designing Access Control for Files and Folders

Just as with Active Directory objects, there are different types of permissions that apply to files and folders. In this section, you will learn how to control access to files and folders locally or by using NTFS permissions, and then you will learn how to work shared folders into your overall design.

There are standard and special permissions for all securable objects that exist in the Windows network system. The standard permissions are those that are most frequently assigned, while special permissions provide for more granular control over resources. For example the NTFS Read permission includes the following special permissions: List Folder/Read Data, Read Attributes, Read Extended Attributes, and Read Permissions.

The standard permissions that are provided for NTFS are as follows:

- Full Control
- Modify
- Read & Execute
- List Folder Contents
- Read
- Write

In earlier versions of Windows, the default file permissions were inadequate because they gave all users Full Control. As a result of the new focus at Microsoft on security, specifically Microsoft is now implementing secure defaults whenever possible; for example, the Users group, by default, receives only the Read permissions. If you've worked with the earlier versions of Windows, you will need to remember that in Windows Server 2003, when creating a file structure, you do not need to remove the Everyone group from the ACL. However, by default the Administrators group and the special SYSTEM group will inherit Full Control from the volume root. The Users group will inherit Read & Execute, List Folder Contents, and Read permissions from the volume root. If these permissions are not the ones that you require, you'll need to remove the default ACEs from the DACL.

Windows Server 2003 organizes the files into directories that are represented in Windows Explorer as folders. NTFS file permissions, or NTFS permissions for short, are always checked when an attempt is made to access a resource on the file system. NTFS permissions will be cumulated whether the principal is requesting the file locally (logged in directly at the server) or remotely from their workstation. There is another level of access control that only applies when the resource is being accessed remotely: Share permissions. When designing the access control for files and folders, you will need to remember that Share permissions determine the maximum access that is allowed into the file system remotely. The NTFS permissions that are assigned to the requesting principal are combined with the Share permissions and the most restrictive permission passes through. For example, Server5 is sharing a folder named myShare and has explicitly granted the Domain Users group Read permission to the share. The Domain Users group is also explicitly granted the Full Control NTFS permission. If the user is accessing a file using the share

(Server5\myShare), members of the Domain Users group will only have Read permission because it is the most restrictive permission when comparing the NTFS to the Share permissions.

When a folder is shared, the Read permission is granted to the Everyone special group as the default permission. You will want to remove this and only grant permissions to the required principals. As you grant specific users or groups rights to the share, their default permission is Read.

You can create hidden shares, which will not be displayed in Windows Explorer if a client navigates to the server using its UNC path. Hidden shares do not add any layer of security, nor should you assume that they are not visible to a potential attacker. You can create a hidden share simply by appending a dollar sign ($) to the name of the share when you create it as you would any other share such as Accounting$. Windows Server 2003 will automatically share folders that are required for certain administrative tasks. By default, these administrative shares assign Full Control permission to the Administrators group and you cannot modify the permissions of administrative shares.

Table 5.3 shows the administrative shares and describes what they are typically used for.

TABLE 5.3 Administrative Shares

Share Name	Local Folder	Description
C$, D$, E$, ...	C, D, E, ...	The root of each partition with a drive letter assigned to it is automatically shared. Through this root share, an administrator will have remote access to the entire partition tree.
Admin$	Systemroot (e.g., C:\Windows)	This is the operating system root. Administrators can use this hidden share to access the Windows installation without knowing the drive or path that Windows was installed to.
Print$	Systemroot\System32\Spool\Drivers	When a printer is shared on the server, this share is created to store the operating system drivers required to print to the printer. The Everyone group has Read permission and the Administrators, Server Operators, and Print Operators all have the Full Control permission. If no printer is shared on a server, this share will not exist.
IPC$		This folder is used when administering the server remotely.

You can view all of the folders that are shared, including the administrative hidden shares, by typing **net share** at the command prompt, as seen in Figure 5.1.

FIGURE 5.1   The net share command

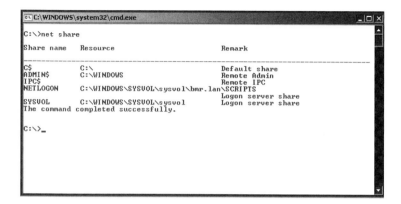

You can also use the Computer Management MMC, shown in Figure 5.2, to view the shares.

FIGURE 5.2   Viewing shared folders in Computer Management

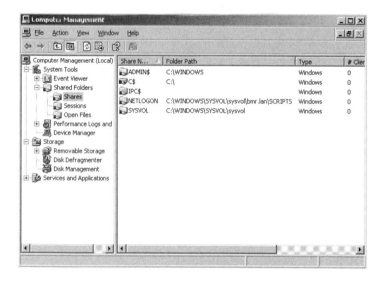

You can remove certain administrative shares; however, the next time the Server service is started, they will be re-created.

You should combine Share and NTFS permissions to control the access to your organization's data. Make sure that you remember that all objects on an NTFS volume have an owner and that owner always has the permission to change the permissions on the object. This can be exploited to undermine the security policies configured by the IT staff. For example, a user in the Human Resources group creates a spreadsheet on the HR server that allows only Human Resources employees to access the data. The user who created the spreadsheet has the Full Control permission to it as its owner, and that user can grant another user the Full Control permission, even if the other user is not a member of the Human Resources group. To counter this, you should grant Change Permissions to the Human Resources group on the shared folder on the HR server. The user can still create new files on the server but cannot grant Full Control permissions to any other user unless they are logged on locally to the HR server.

In the following Design Scenario, you will evaluate a scenario and make the appropriate decisions to control access to the files and folders within the specified organization.

 Design Scenario

Designing an Access Control Strategy for Files and Folders

You are the network administrator for a small architecture firm named Brady Corp. Brady Corp. has an office in Miami and another in Boston. The Brady Corp. network is made up of a single Active Directory domain named Bradycorp.com. There are two domain controllers in each office.

A Global security group named MiaResidentialArchitects contains the members of the architecture department in the Miami office and a Global security group named BosResidentialArchitects contains the members of the architecture department in the Boston office. All of the servers are running Windows Server 2003, Enterprise Edition. All of the workstations are running Windows XP Professional and have the most recent service packs applied. All of the architectural data is located on a server named ArchBrady in a folder named ArchData, which is located in Miami.

The company's security policy specifies the following requirements:

- Access to the ArchData folder must be restricted to only members of the MiaResidentialArchitects and the BosResidentialArchitects.

- The members of these groups need to be able to add and modify the files in the folder, but they should not be able to take ownership or change the permissions of other members' files in the ArchData folder.

1. **Question:** You need to design an access control strategy for the ArchData folder and the files and folders that are contained within it. What should you do to secure the folder according to the business requirements? **Answer:** You should assign the MiaResidentialArchitects and the BosResidentialArchitects groups the Allow-Modify permission. In addition, you will need to remove the Administrators, SYSTEM, and Users group from the DACL.

Designing a File Encryption Strategy

Now that you've learned to restrict access to file and folder resources, you will take a look at securing resources that are out of the realm of your control. Laptops that must leave the environment must have their data secured from theft and other risks and you must work with the Encrypting File System (EFS) features of Windows.

EFS enables you to encrypt files on an NTFS volume automatically, and by default, no additional administration is required. EFS is based on the Cryptography Application Programming Interface (CryptoAPI), which is built into the Windows Server 2003 operating system.

The EFS encrypts only the files that are on disk; files that are transmitted over the network are decrypted before they are sent. In order to encrypt data in transit, you should use IPSec or SSL.

EFS-protected files are encrypted at the file-system level, and the files are only accessible with the appropriate private key and certificate. Even if an attacker reinstalls the operating system, the file will be unreadable without the decryption key.

 Encryption and compression are mutually exclusive.

In order to encrypt a file or folder, you simply right-click the object and select Properties from the context menu and select the Encrypt contents to secure data option. When the Properties window is displayed, click Advanced to display the Advanced Attributes dialog box, shown in Figure 5.3.

Implementing the Encrypting File System

The EFS is a very powerful technique in securing your data, but if misused, it can lead to legitimate users being prevented from accessing their data. You should have a policy in place for encrypting files to prevent encryption from inadvertently causing a loss of data. For example, an administrator encrypts all of the files in a folder and later deletes the administrative account.

FIGURE 5.3   The Advanced Attributes dialog box

For maximum security, you should encrypt folders before creating sensitive files in them. This assures that the files are never written to the disk as plaintext. When folders, rather than individual files, are encrypted, files that are created within them are also encrypted, even those created by an application or service.

You should also create a policy for the recovery of encrypted files. The policy should include the guidelines and steps for file recovery as well the standard operating procedure for the storage and use of the private recovery key. An administrator may leave the floppy disk that contains the data recovery agent's private key, which could then be used to decrypt any encrypted file. The policy should outline the appropriate methods for working with the recovery key.

In addition to creating procedures for the encryption and decryption of the files requiring this level of security, it is always recommended that users be trained on EFS and understand what it can and can't do. Proper education will minimize the use of the recovery agent as well as the likelihood that a user will encrypt a file with no means of recovering it or believe that when the file is copied to another location, such as a floppy disk, it will remain encrypted and secure.

To recover an encrypted file, any recovery agent on the domain can simply remove the encryption attribute or open the file. You should take great care in securing the private key of the recovery agent.

Designing Access Control for the Windows Registry

The Windows Registry contains sensitive information about the entire system, its applications, and its users. If an attacker can gain access to the Registry, they would be able to cause severe damage to the computer. It is for this reason that you should maintain a high level of security on the Windows Registry.

The Windows Registry is highly secure by default, with the Administrators group having Full Control permission to just about all keys in the Registry. Users have full access to the keys that pertain to their accounts (HKEY_CURRENT_USER) and read-only rights to the keys related to the system and its software; they have no access to information stored for other users. Users who are assigned the appropriate permissions for a key can make changes to the permissions that are similar to the permissions within the file system.

The Windows Registry, like the resources you've seen up to this point, has its access permissions stored in DACLs and SACLs. To modify the permissions on Registry keys, you can use the Registry Editor, shown in Figure 5.4.

You should make sure that, whether the data is an Active Directory object, part of the file system, or in the Windows Registry, accounts are given only the minimum permissions required to complete their tasks. Never give more permissions than those that are explicitly required.

Analyzing the Auditing Requirements for Data

When you implement network security in your organization, you do so typically by attempting to prevent attacks. A proper security design will mitigate many of the common attacks. However, with persistence, an attacker will eventually be able to penetrate your security infrastructure. The quicker that you can detect the penetration, the quicker you can respond to it. To minimize the damage inflicted at the hands of an intruder, you must detect it early.

One of the most important techniques for early detection is auditing your network and systems so that you can react promptly when an anomaly is noticed. In this section, you will learn the value of auditing and of having an auditing policy in place. You will then learn how to design an auditing policy for your organization.

Network auditing is the process of recording specific events on a network. Auditing the events that occur on systems and the applications that they run will provide you with the information that you would need in order to compare the behavior of a user to that of an attacker.

In order for the audit information to be useful, you will need to have a baseline of what a user, computer, or application is supposed to be doing. Having the baseline allows you to better discover an intruder. For example, we have running on a server an ASP.NET web application that should only be accessing a Microsoft SQL Server database and its own application directory. With auditing enabled, we can detect when the application attempts to access another directory or server on our network. The attempt to access the other directory may be due to an attacker compromising the application. In short, knowing what your systems should be doing is important to detecting an intruder.

Now that you have learned just how important auditing is, in the following sections, you'll learn how to create an audit policy as well as a process for an audit review.

FIGURE 5.4 The Registry Editor

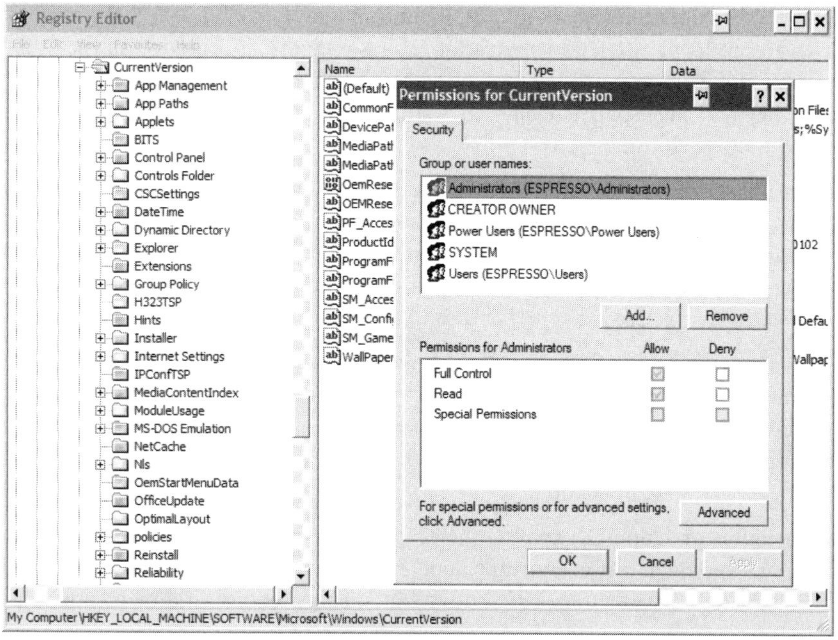

> 🌐 **Real World Scenario**
>
> ### Preventing Internal Attacks through Auditing
>
> A medium-sized investment firm uses Microsoft Exchange Server. All of the network administrators are members of the Domain Admins group for the domain. One of the administrators is able to open and read all of the other users' mail, which causes users to occasionally report that mail that they have not read is shown as having been already read in Outlook. The administrators may brush this off when the users complain because it may appear as a minor inconvenience. However, if auditing is enabled (the auditing of Microsoft Exchange opening another user's mailbox is enabled by default) and monitored, this issue could have been stopped before sensitive information was leaked, because someone would have seen the entries showing an administrator opening other users' mail.

Designing an Audit Policy

As you may have guessed, there is more to an audit policy than flipping a switch and turning it on. You'll need to properly plan your strategy for the best results. You'll need to complete the following steps in order to plan your audit policy:

Determine which events to audit.   Having an audit log that contains thousands of events per hour will make it difficult at best, and impossible at worst, to sift through the unimportant audit event entries to locate something substantive. To keep the information in the audit log meaningful, you will want to work with both the business and technical teams in your organization because they will have specific insight as to the normal operations that their respective applications and users perform.

Select the appropriate auditing tools.   Select the most appropriate tool for the job. This can be applied to many different situations and is extremely important when it comes to auditing the events that occur in your organization. Depending on what needs to be audited, you will need to use different tools to gather the data, and you may even require a separate tool to view the audit log. The various tools are listed in Table 5.5 later in this section.

Design a method for reviewing event logs. You'll need to work with the different teams to assign the responsibility of monitoring the logs. Obviously, the reviewer of the business application logs should have an understanding of the business application and how it works. For example, a typical IT staffer won't understand whether or not the general ledger should be accessed by a specific user of an accounting application.

Design a course of action to examine the suspicious events.   You should also define a process by which to investigate the events that appear to be out of the norm. The process should be in the form of a written policy that includes items such as who should be notified.

Create a retention policy for audit logs.   In many cases, there is a history or pattern that led to the attacker being discovered. This history can be evaluated for future prevention or as evidence to provide to authorities. To access the historical data, you'll want to have a policy defined for the archival of the security logs. This policy could be consulted when you need to view an audit log from last year, for example.

There are some best practices when it comes to auditing that you will want to adhere to, both for performance and to keep the size of the audit log to a minimum. To facilitate this, it is recommended that you create audit statements that will define the general type of event that needs to be tracked, the details that need to be recorded, and what system or resource that will be audited. Table 5.4 is an example of an audit statement.

TABLE 5.4 Audit Statement Example

Audit Statement Component	Example
Event Type	Track logon attempts to authenticate to the network.
Event Details	Record failed logon attempts, time of occurrence, remote system attempting to log on.
Audit Resource	Only record for members of the IT_Administrators group on domain controllers

There are a number of tools that you can use for auditing; their usefulness will depend on the resource that is being audited. Table 5.5 contains a partial list of the common resources that require auditing and some of the tools that can be used to produce an audit log.

TABLE 5.5 Common Auditing Resources and Utilities

Resource to Audit	Application or Resource Containing Audit Data
Operating system	Event Viewer, Microsoft Operations Manager, custom scripts
Web applications	IIS logs, URLScan
Network perimeters	Router log, firewall log, packet filtering log, intrusion detection system log, network monitor
Application specific	Application-specific logs, intrusion detection log, antivirus log, Microsoft Operations Manager

Once the audit log has been generated there should be a procedure designed for its review. In the next section, you will learn the steps that you should complete in order to design the audit review procedure for your organization.

Designing a Process for Audit Review

When evaluating the audit data, you should define the following:

The principal who is responsible for analyzing the events   You need to make sure that those charged with managing and analyzing the audit logs are accountable and do their job. They should be able to recognize the difference between normal operating events and suspicious activity as recorded in the log. You should also look into custom applications or scripts to better search through the logs looking for events that have already been defined by your organization as suspicious.

Audit review schedule   You'll need to create a schedule for audit log analysis. There must be more than one person assigned to this task, and it is a good idea to verify this by planting suspicious data in the log in order to verify that your process for discovering suspicious events is functional and is being followed. There should be a maximum interval of time that is permitted to pass between log reviews, and you'll want to make sure that this interval is short enough to prevent significant damage to your infrastructure should an attacker have access to your system for this duration.

Suspicious event notification procedures   You should explicitly define how those who analyze the logs are to report the information to the security response team or manager for further investigation. There should be a defined escalation policy if the notification is not accepted within a specified time period.

Evidence preservation procedure   As explained in earlier chapters, you will want to be able to provide as much data to law enforcement as possible to aid in the conviction of the offense. You will need to make sure that the audit logs are gathered and used appropriately to aid the investigation and possibly the ensuing trial.

In the "Designing an Audit Policy" Design Scenario, you will evaluate a scenario and design the appropriate audit policy to facilitate early detection.

 Design Scenario

Designing an Audit Policy

You are the network administrator for a contractor that does business with the government. It is specified in the government contract that you must not only secure access to the data located in the GovData folder, but you must also maintain a record each time an attempt is made to read or write to/from the contents of an existing file, even if the attempt is unsuccessful. You need to design a monitoring strategy for the GovData folder. You also need to track when someone attempts to change the permissions on a file or folder in the GovData directory.

1.   **Question:** What should you do? **Answer:** You should audit success and failures for reading, writing, and appending data on the GovData folder. You will also track the success and failures for Change Permissions and Take Ownership. The auditing policies will be for all users.

Creating a Secure Backup and Recovery Strategy

Securing the data in your organization is critical, for obvious reasons, but many overlook the fact that almost of your organization's data is stored on backup media. Usually, access to the data on a backup device is not audited in the same manner that access to the file system of Windows is monitored by event auditing. It is for this reason that you will need to have a secure backup and restore strategy. In this section, you will learn the essentials of designing a secure backup strategy and you will be able to create a plan for secure backups and restores.

To build a secure strategy for backups, you must implement the following:

Secure offsite storage   To ensure that your system can be recovered, there must be a recent copy of your data at a location other than where it originated. The offsite location should be secure and not susceptible to its own disasters or theft.

Secure onsite storage   In addition to having backup media off site, you will also want to keep a copy of your data that is easier for you to access. It should not, however, be stored with the original data. For example, you should store your backup media in a different room or floor so that, should a disaster occur to only the original data, the onsite backup will not be compromised. If the backup contains sensitive data, which it usually does, keep it in a locked area such as a safe. For enhanced protection, store it in a fireproof, heat-resistant safe. A fireproof safe is not enough; most media will melt when it reaches a certain temperature.

Write protection   To make sure that backup media is not accidentally overwritten, you should write-protect the media. Many backup utilities provide functionality that writes an expiration date to the media header that, by default, will prevent the backup media from being used again until after the expiration date.

Data classification   When a disaster occurs, you will want to bring the most critical services and data up first. This task can be eased by classifying the backups based on the recovery priority. Your organization's mission-critical data will have a shorter recovery time priority than other data, for example.

Appropriate backup centralization   Security is usually easier to maintain on backups if they are all handled centrally, but for business reasons, this may not be possible. You will need to take both business and recoverability into account when determining where backups should occur.

Secure backup schedule   You will need to create a schedule that includes incremental, differential, and complete backups to provide for recovery in an appropriate amount of time. Most media can be used reliably 20 times before it begins to degrade, so you should devise a schedule that deals with this sufficiently. For example, in a round-robin scheme, a separate tape is used for each day of the week. After 20 weeks, a new tape is used and the original is archived. Other types of backup schedules include grandfathering and equal rotation.

In the following sections we will show you the guidelines when backing up or restoring your data.

Secure Backup Guidelines

There are certain best practices that will increase your level of security as it pertains to the media you are backing up to. The following list includes some of the most common techniques that should be used to secure your backup media:

Use the best backup media that you can afford, taking into account a proper rotation. Backup media is not the place to save on your IT budget.

Physically secure the backup media so that only the appropriate persons can gain access to it. Every day the media used to back up data gets smaller and smaller, making it almost impossible to detect in someone's bag or pocket. You can, in some cases, encrypt the data on the media to prevent unauthorized access to it. If it's encrypted, make sure that you have the necessary means to decrypt it should it be required.

Keep the media labeled appropriately.   Label the media based on the classification that represents the data on the media. For example, "Mission Critical 3/29/2004 3:17AM" would be an appropriate label.

Do not change the classification of backup media once it has been used to store a backup. Even data that has been erased or overwritten may still be retrievable.

Remove media from rotation prior to failure and destroy it completely to prevent unauthorized theft from your company's waste.   Destroy media completely by crushing, incinerating, shredding, or even melting it. If you intend on reusing media, erase it first using a secure data erasure utility.

Keep track of all backup media.   Make sure that all media is signed in and out so that at any given moment, you can find out the location of each and every piece of media.

Periodically verify the integrity of the media.   Make sure the media is devoid of viruses, worms, and other security compromises. If you detect a virus on your system, you should verify that the data is not also infected.

In the event that the data cannot be restored, consider sending it to data recovery organizations that can usually recover data for a fee.

Centralize the backup strategy as much as possible.   Know that some of the users may back up their own data on an insecure medium. Any sensitive data should be kept off of the workstations in your environment. Emergency repair disks contain the Security Account Manager (SAM) database for the local machine and can be used to crack the passwords in it using a utility like LC4.

Secure Restore Guidelines

There are some important steps that you should take to securely restore data. The following list includes some of the most common techniques:

Test the restore process.   The only way that you can be certain that the backup is effective and working is to restore from it. You should do periodic recovery drills, similar to a building's fire drill, to evaluate the effectiveness of the restore process and the validity of the data. Regardless of what a backup log states, you don't have a verifiably successful backup until it has been tested and proven to work.

Perform recovery drills in a secure location to prevent unauthorized access to the data that has been restored.   Make sure that the machines that you are restoring your data to are properly secured. The restore servers will have the sensitive data on them at the conclusion of the restore and should be secured just as much as the production server.

Evaluate backup logs regularly.   Many backup applications will report a "success" even when several files are skipped.

Once sensitive data has been restored to the secure test server, use a secure erasure utility to remove all traces of the data from its disks.   In some cases, you may want to follow the Department of Defense standard (DoD 5200.28-STD) for how to completely remove traces of data.

Summary

In this chapter, you learned some of the methods that you can utilize in order to design an access control strategy for a multitude of resources that are made available via a Windows network. You were reintroduced to some old concepts such as ACLs and ACEs. You learned about the different types of Active Directory object permissions and the best techniques to use when assigning them. The best practices for group design, at the forest and domain levels, is another topic that was included in this chapter.

Later in the chapter, you learned about the importance of delegation and how it can be used to better design a secure management environment. We also showed the best practices as they pertain to the file, folder, and share permissions as well as how permissions can work together in order to provide for a more secure remote and local data repository. To protect the data that may be stored on a laptop or some other computer that cannot be physically secured, you can encrypt the files on the disk using the Encrypting File System (EFS). When EFS is properly configured, it can prevent an unauthorized individual from being able to read the files, even with physical access to the hard drive, by requiring the appropriate information to decrypt the files.

To better secure your organization, it is important to see how the different resources are being accessed. Should you enable auditing, on by default on Windows Server 2003 domain controllers, you can better protect your resources because you will be able to see the difference between regular traffic and special, abnormal traffic.

Finally, we explained the importance of a secure backup and recovery strategy to assure the security of the data that is on disk as well as the data that is on the removable media (for example, a tape device).

Exam Essentials

Know the best techniques for implementing and organizing security groups. You should be able to read a scenario and design the security grouping, which includes determining which groups will have permissions assigned to them. The best practice follows the AG(G)UDLP model.

Know when to use delegation instead of membership in administrative groups. You need to be able to recognize when it is more appropriate to delegate to a user or a group the ability to manage a container (for example, an organizational unit) rather than adding the respective user or group to an administrative group (for example, Domain Administrators).

Know the different permissions and how they apply to the securable objects. Know how to secure an NTFS volume locally and remotely, as well as the best ways to secure Active Directory objects.

Be comfortable designing a secure backup and recovery design. Remember that the data on the tape must be secured when it is active as well as when it is no longer useful.

Understand when the Encrypting File System (EFS) is useful. You will need to know what situations would be most advantageous for use with the Encrypting File System (EFS) and when it may not be suitable. Specifically machines that fall outside of the organization's physical control, such as laptop computers, would typically be good candidates for the EFS.

Make sure that you know how to configure an audit policy based on requirements dictated in a scenario. You will need to be able to make the appropriate decisions as far as what resources to audit, whether you should audit success or failure, and what principals you will be auditing. Remember that on Windows Server 2003 domain controllers, auditing is turned on by default.

Key Terms

Before you take the exam, be certain you are familiar with the following terms:

access control entries (ACEs)	permissions
access control lists (ACLs)	property set
access tokens	security descriptors
delegation	system access control list (SACL)
delegation of control	Universal group
discretionary access control list (DACL)	validated write
extended rights	

Review Questions

1. Which part of the security descriptor is used to grant or deny users and groups access to an object?
    A. Discretionary access control list (DACL)
    B. System access control list (SACL)
    C. Access token
    D. Security ID (SID)

2. Following best practices, put the following tasks in the order that they should be completed when designing a security group strategy.

	Place Accounts in Global groups.
	Assign Permissions to Domain Local groups.
	Nest your Global groups.
	Put the Universal group in the Domain Local group.
	Place Global groups in a Universal group.

3. Which of the following permissions are a part of the standard NTFS permissions? (Choose all that apply.)
    A. Full Control
    B. Modify
    C. Read & Execute
    D. Open
    E. Change

4. What are the default permissions on a share when it is created?
    A. Users Allow-Read
    B. Everyone Deny-Full Control
    C. Everyone Allow-Full Control
    D. Users Allow-Full Control
    E. Everyone Allow-Read

5. Which of the following Active Directory features can you use to minimize the number of individuals who are granted administrative permissions?
    A. Impersonation
    B. Delegation
    C. Microsoft Baseline Security Analyzer (MBSA)
    D. Group Policy

6. Many of the users in your organization use laptops that are running Windows XP Professional and take them out of the office. There is some confidential information that is stored on the laptops, and you need to make sure that if the laptops get lost or stolen, the data is not compromised. What should you do?

   A. Enable the Encrypting File System (EFS) on the folder that the files are stored in.

   B. Use NTFS to secure the folder that the files are stored in.

   C. Configure IPSec to encrypt the data on the disk.

   D. Configure SSL to encrypt the data on the disk.

7. You are administering a folder that all of the users in the Accountants groups use. The users need to be able to create, modify, and delete files in the AcctData folder. What permissions should you add to the ACL for the Accountants group when you grant them access to the AcctData folder? (Choose all that apply.)

   A. Full Control

   B. Modify

   C. Read & Execute

   D. List Folder Contents

   E. Read

   F. Write

8. Which of the following users can assign permissions on a file by default? (Choose all that apply.)

   A. An administrator

   B. The last user to modify the file

   C. The Users group

   D. The creator/owner of the file

9. You are a member of the security group name AcctGroup. The AcctGroup has been granted Full Control to the AcctData share. The AcctData share contains a folder, named MonthlyData, to which the AcctGroup has been assigned the Modify NTFS permission. When accessing files over the network, what permissions do you have? (Choose all that apply.)

   A. Full Control

   B. Modify

   C. Read & Execute

   D. List Folder Contents

   E. Read

   F. Write

10. You are a member of the Administrators group and the Employees group. The Employees group has been granted the Change permission to the EmpData share. The EmpData share contains a folder, named VacationData, to which the Employee group has been assigned the Read and List Folder Contents NTFS permission. The Administrators group was removed from the ACL on the share. When accessing files over the network using the EmpData share, what permissions do you have? (Choose all that apply.)

    A. Full Control

    B. Modify

    C. Read & Execute

    D. List Folder Contents

    E. Read

    F. Write

Answers to Review Questions

1. **A.** The DACL is the part of the security descriptor that is used to grant or deny specific users and groups access to the object. The SACL is used to determine which events are to be audited for specific users or groups. An access token contains the information regarding a logged-on user. The Security ID (SID) is used to uniquely identify objects in Active Directory.

2.

Place Accounts in Global groups.
Nest your Global groups.
Place Global groups in a Universal group.
Assign Permissions to Domain Local groups.
Put the Universal group in the Domain Local group.

   Follow the AG(G)UDLP method, but the placement of the Universal group in the Domain Local group should be last. By doing this task last, you prevent anyone from accessing the resources until they have been completely secured.

3. **A, B, C.** The standard NTFS permissions are Full Control, Modify, Read & Execute, List Folder Contents, Read, and Write.

4. **C.** When a share is created by default, the Everyone group is granted Full Control through the share.

5. **B.** Rather than making a user such as a help desk technician a member of the Administrators or Domain Administrators group, you can use delegation to grant the user or group control over an object or an entire Active Directory container, thus minimizing the number of users or groups who require membership in the administrative groups.

6. **A.** EFS is the technology that should be used to secure the data on disk. NTFS will not prevent access to the files and folders if the disk is physically obtained by someone else. IPSec and SSL are used to encrypt data over the network, not on disk.

7. **B, C, D, E, F.** The only permission that you should not assign to the Accountants group is Full Control because it includes the ability to change permissions and take ownership, which is not required in the scenario presented in the question.

8. **A, D.** By default, an administrator and the creator/owner of the file would have the Full Control permission, which includes the Change Permissions special permission.

9. **B, C, D, E, F.** You will have the Modify permission across the network. Full Control is not granted at the folder level; therefore, it will never propagate through the share.

10. **B, C, D, E, F.** By default, the Everyone group is granted the Read permission on a share. The scenario states that the Employees group is granted the Change permission on the share. When combining Share and NTFS permissions, the most restrictive is what is effective. Administrators have, by default, the Full Control NTFS permission on all folders. When combined with the Change permission on the share, Change is the only permission granted to the Administrators group when accessing files and folders through the share.

Case Study

You should give yourself 20 minutes to review this testlet, review the exhibits, and complete the questions.

Overview

IntelliAgent Management provides management and consulting services to customers in North and South America.

Physical Locations

The company's corporate headquarters is located in Miami. The company has four satellite offices in the following cities:

- Los Angeles
- New York
- Rio de Janeiro, Brazil
- Santiago, Chile

Planned Changes

IntelliAgent Management is entering into a partnership with JC Enterprises, a worldwide management conglomerate. The JC Enterprises network is made up of a Windows 2000 Active Directory domain, and JC Enterprises has no plans to upgrade its servers to Windows Server 2003.

The partnership between the two companies will exist exclusively over the Internet. Marketing users from both companies will require access to a shared folder named `CustomerData`, which is housed on a Windows Server 2003 server within the IntelliAgent corporate network.

Existing Environment

Directory Services   The existing Active Directory forest for IntelliAgent Management is shown in the Active Directory Infrastructure exhibit in the case study exhibits section.

The IntelliAgent network consists of a single Windows Server 2003 Active Directory forest. The forest contains three domains named IntelliAgent.com, na.IntelliAgent.com, and sa.IntelliAgent.com.

Network Infrastructure   The company's existing network infrastructure is shown in the Network Infrastructure exhibit in the case study exhibits section.

A Windows Server 2003 database server is located in the Los Angeles office perimeter network. All of the workstations in North America run Windows XP Professional with Service Pack 1. Each office has a domain controller, which also serves as a file server.

CASE STUDY

Problem Statements

The following business problems must be considered:

- The IT staff is having difficulties maintaining all client computers with the latest security patches and service packs.

- Unauthorized users have been able to modify data on some of the IntelliAgent servers. Unauthorized users must not be able to modify the data on the company's servers.

- Access to the resources is currently assigned on a per-user basis, which causes an immense amount of administrative overhead.

Interviews

Chief Information Officer   Over the course of the last six months, we have been focusing our security on internal threats. Now we realize that, because we are relying on the Internet to maintain the partnership with JC Enterprises, we must focus on external threats to keep the connection points secure.

One of our competitors has recently been hacked and their confidential customer information was posted to the public. Occurrences such as these need to be prevented. We also suspect that some users are attempting to access the server and delete files that they are not authorized to delete.

Network Administrator   There is no IT staff in the South American offices, and when the users there lose their password, they need to contact the Help Desk in the Los Angeles office.

Business Requirements

The following business requirements must be considered:

- Any solutions implemented must minimize administrative overhead.

- You must be able to track users' access to the file servers.

- The marketing department for each company must be able to access the customer information.

Written Security Policy

The company's written security policy includes the following requirements:

- All customer information must be kept confidential. Access to customer data must be tracked.

- Certain marketing information is available to the general public. Modifications to this public information must be tracked.

Case Study Exhibits

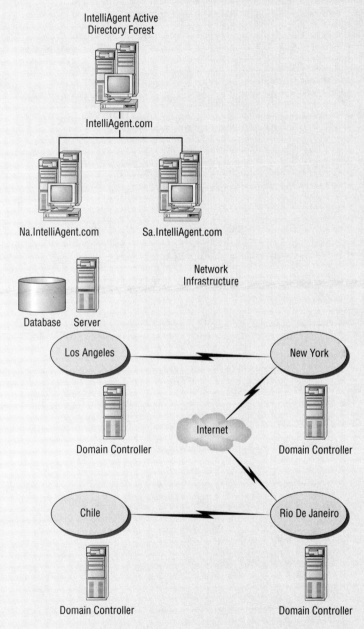

IntelliAgent Active
Directory Forest

IntelliAgent.com

Na.IntelliAgent.com   Sa.IntelliAgent.com

Network
Infrastructure

Database   Server

Los Angeles   New York

Domain Controller   Domain Controller

Internet

Chile   Rio De Janeiro

Domain Controller   Domain Controller

Case Study Questions

1. You need to design a resource access solution for the marketing department that meets business and technical requirements. A one-way trust has been created where the IntelliAgent forest trusts the JC Enterprises forest. Which actions should you perform? (Each answer presents part of the solution. Choose two options.)

   A. Add the marketing department users to a new Global group named GlobalMktg in each domain. Add the GlobalMktg group from each domain to a new Universal group named AllMktg in the JC Enterprises forest.

   B. Add the marketing department users to a new Global group named mktgGroup. Add the mktgGroup Global group to the Domain Local group for the customer data.

   C. Add the marketing department users to a new Universal group named AllMktg. Add the AllMktg Universal group to the local groups on the Miami servers.

   D. Add the marketing department users to a new Global group named GlobalMktg in each domain. Add the GlobalMktg group from each domain to a new Universal group named AllMktg in the IntelliAgent forest.

   E. Add the AllMktg Universal group to the Domain Local group for the customer data and grant the permissions to the Domain Local group.

2. You need to design a method to grant permissions to the office manager in each of the South American satellite offices so that they can reset passwords for other employees at each site. What should you do?

   A. Add the office managers' accounts to the Domain Administrator's group for their respective domain.

   B. Add the office managers' accounts to the DACL for their respective site. Then assign the necessary permissions to this account.

   C. Delegate the necessary permissions to the office managers' accounts on their respective offices' OU.

   D. Grant the office managers' accounts the ability to create new objects in their respective offices' OU.

3. You need to design a method to track changes that users make to the North America servers' data. What should you do?

   A. On the file servers in North America, enable Audit Privilege Use Success And Failure Auditing.

   B. On the file servers in North America, use the Security Configuration And Analysis tool to enable Audit Directory Service Access Failure Auditing.

   C. On each server, configure the `NTConfig.pol` file to restrict access to the Registry.

   D. Create a Group Policy object (GPO) that will apply a custom security template that restricts access to the Registry. Apply the GPO to all of the servers in North America.

   E. On the file servers in North America, enable success and failure auditing on each server's shared folder.

4. You need to design a method to track access to customer data. Your solution must comply with the written security policy. What should you do?

A. Write a script to evaluate effective permissions on the marketing files.

B. Schedule Microsoft Baseline Security Analyzer (MBSA) to run periodically.

C. Audit marketing files for successful and failed attempts to access the data by all users.

D. Audit marketing files for failed attempts to modify the data by all users.

5. You need to design an access control strategy that meets business and security requirements. Your solution must minimize forestwide replication. What should you do?

A. Create a Global group for each location. Add users to their respective location groups as members. Assign the location Global groups to file and printer resources in their respective domains, and then assign permissions for the file resources using the location Global groups.

B. Create a Global group for each location and add the respective users as members. Create Domain Local groups for the file resources in each domain. Add the Global groups to the respective Domain Local groups. Then assign permissions to the file resources by using the Domain Local groups.

C. Create a local group on each server and add the authorized users as members. Assign appropriate permissions for the file and printer resources to the local groups.

D. Create a Universal group for each location and add the respective users as members. Assign the Universal groups to file and printer resources. Then assign permissions by using the Universal groups.

E. Create a Global group for each location and add the respective users as members. Create a Universal group and add the location Global groups as members. Create a Domain Local group on the Miami server and assign it the appropriate permissions to access the customer data. Add the Universal group to the Domain Local group as a member.

Answers to Case Study Questions

1. D, E. Following best practices, options D and E are correct. Option A is incorrect because the Universal group is created in the JC Enterprises forest and not the forest that holds the resource to be shared. Option B is incorrect because it doesn't minimize administration overhead. Option C is incorrect because accounts should not be members of a Universal group when the AG(G)UDLP best practice is followed.

2. C. To minimize administrative overhead, you should use delegation to allow the office managers in the remote locations to reset the passwords for the employees in their respective offices. Granting the office managers administrator privileges gives them more than the required permissions, so it is not a secure solution. Granting the office managers' accounts the permissions to create new objects in an OU does not allow them to reset the password for other employees at the site, so option D is incorrect.

3. E. To track the changes made remotely to the data on the servers in North America, you should enable auditing on the shares on the server in Miami. Privilege use is too broad, therefore option A is incorrect. You need to track access to the file system, not access to the directory, therefore option B is incorrect. NTConfig.pol was used in Windows NT 4 for policies, which won't play a role in Windows Server 2003. Creating a GPO restricting access to the Registry has no effect on the tracking of remote access to files, so option D is incorrect.

4. C. You will need to audit successful and failed attempts to access the data rather than just the failed attempts as stated in option D. Option A has no impact on the tracking requirements in the written security policy. The MBSA will not do anything automatically as a result of it being run periodically.

5. E. Using a Universal group with Global groups as its members means that, changes in membership in the Global groups will not cause forestwide replication to be required, only domainwide replication.

Chapter

6

Designing a Public Key Infrastructure with Certificate Services

---

MICROSOFT EXAM OBJECTIVES COVERED IN THIS CHAPTER:

✓ **Design a public key infrastructure (PKI) that uses Certificate Services.**

- Design a certification authority (CA) hierarchy implementation. Types include geographical, organizational, and trusted.

- Design enrollment and distribution processes.

- Establish renewal, revocation and auditing processes.

- Design security for CA servers.

✓ **Design a logical authentication strategy.**

- Design certificate distribution.

✓ **Design security for communication with external organizations.**

- Design a strategy for cross-certification of Certificate Services.

The Internet is full of all kinds of people and companies that you have never personally met. Some may claim to be somebody they are not to fool you into revealing information about yourself, into allowing them to access your network, or into running their code. You need a mechanism for validating the identity of someone you will work with over a network whether you have met them or not. After all, how can you tell that the company you just received an important security patch from is really Microsoft and not somebody who just wants to trick you into installing a Trojan horse? This mechanism would ideally allow you to encrypt and sign content also. A public key infrastructure (PKI) is the mechanism that provides the services and components to validate the identity of a user and store the keys needed to encrypt and sign data.

In this chapter, you will learn about the elements that make up a PKI. You will learn about the server types required for a PKI and the management requirements for PKI. You will also look at extending the PKI to trust other organizations.

Introduction to Certificates and Public Key Infrastructure

There are three problems with exchanging information over a network:

- How do I know you really are who you say you are?
- How can I keep the information that we exchange secret?
- How do I confirm that the information you sent hasn't been modified in transit?

These questions can be addressed with technology known as *public key encryption* and *X.509 certificates (digital certificates)*. In the following sections we will be discussing public key encryption and the digital certificate technology that makes it possible. We will also look at what a public key infrastructure is and how it is used to manage digital certificates.

Public Key Encryption and Digital Certificates

Public key encryption is an encryption scheme based on the Diffie-Hellman algorithm, which was first released in 1976. It allows users to share encryption keys without the need for a secure channel. You generally use a tool to generate a public and private key combination. The public key is used to encrypt a message and can safely be shared with others over a non-secure connection because it contains no information about how to decrypt the message. The private key is used to decrypt the message and should be kept secret by the owner. Any message you encrypt with the public key of the combination can only be decrypted with the corresponding private key. If you wanted two-way encryption, you would need to exchange public keys or, as in the case of Secure Sockets Layer (SSL) and Transport Layer Security (TLS), use a symmetric key that is generated by the client and sent to the server encrypted with the server's public key (see Figure 6.1 to see how PKI works when applied to SSL). Digital signatures are also handled with a public and private key combination; in this case, the private key signs the data and the public key is used to verify the signature. A digital signature is a hash of the data (the most popular algorithms for hashing are MD5 and SHA-1) that is encrypted using the private key. The public key is used to decrypt the hash and verify that the document has not changed and that the signature really came from the corresponding key of the pair.

FIGURE 6.1   How PKI works when applied to SSL

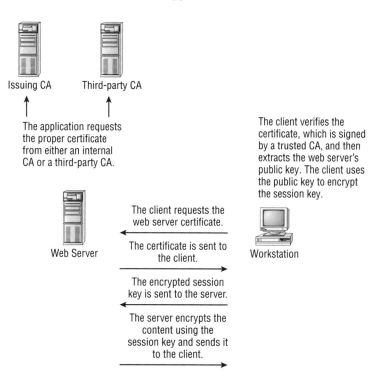

X.509 certificates, also known as digital certificates or just certificates, are electronic documents that contain information about the owner of the certificate, the public key of the owner, and the signature of the validator of the information in the certificate (the validator is called a certificate authority). The X.509 certificate contains a number of fields, including these most common ones (see Figure 6.5):

- Version number
- Serial number
- Algorithm identifier

- Issuer name
- Validity
- Subject name
- Subject public key information
- Issuer unique identifier
- Subject unique identifier
- Key identifier

There are different types of certificates for different applications. These applications will use certificates for everything from encrypting e-mail and securing web communications to encrypting files. Windows Server 2003 provides templates for generating certificates for various applications; these are called *certificate templates*. They provide the fields necessary for the application that uses the certificate. Table 6.1 shows the various certificate templates available for issuing certificates from Windows Server 2003 and the applications that use the certificates.

TABLE 6.1   Available Certificate Templates

Certificate Template	Applications That Use This Type of Certificate
Directory Email Replication	directory service e-mail replication
Domain Controller Authentication	client authentication, server authentication, smart card logon
EFS Recovery Agent	file recovery
Basic EFS	encrypting file system
Domain Controller	client authentication, server authentication
Web Server	server authentication
Computer	client authentication, server authentication
User	encrypting file system, secure e-mail, client authentication
Subordinate Certificate Authority	certificate authority
Administrator	Microsoft trust system, encrypting file system, secure e-mail, client authentication
Authenticated Session	client authentication
CA Exchange	private key archival
CEP Encryption	certificate request agent

TABLE 6.1 Available Certificate Templates *(continued)*

Certificate Template	Applications That Use This Type of Certificate
Code Signing	code signing
Cross Certification Authority	certificate authority
Enrollment Agent	certificate request agent
Enrollment Agent (Computer)	certificate request agent
Exchange Enrollment Agent (Offline Request)	certificate request agent
Exchange Signature Only	secure e-mail
Exchange User	secure e-mail
IPSec	IP security IKE intermediate
Key Recovery Agent	key recovery agent
RAS and IAS Server	client authentication, server authentication
Router (offline request)	client authentication
Smartcard Logon	client authentication, smart card authentication
Smartcard User	secure e-mail, client authentication, smart card logon
Trust List Signing Microsoft Trust List	Microsoft trust list signing
User Signature Only Secure Email, Client Authentication	only signing e-mail (no encryption), client authentication
Workstation Authentication Client Authentication	client authentication

The main function of a certificate is to link a public key to the information about a user or computer contained in the certificate. Of course, you cannot trust the information in the certificate because it could have been forged or manipulated in transit. For instance, anybody can create a certificate and say that they are from Microsoft or from any other company. The strength of certificates comes from a trusted third-party certifying that the certificate information is valid and the document has not been altered in transit. The creation, verification, and revocation of certificates requires an infrastructure to help manage it.

Public Key Infrastructure

A public key infrastructure (PKI) is the technology, software, and services that allow an organization or organizations to securely exchange information and validate the identity of users, computers, and services. This infrastructure is made up of a variety of services and components, as the following list illustrates:

- Digital certificates

- Certification authority (CA)

- Certificate revocation list (CRL)

- Technology to distribute certificates and certificate revocation list

- Tools to manage the PKI

- Software that uses PKI (web browsers, web servers, encrypting file system (EFS), Routing and Remote Access Server (RRAS), Virtual Private Network (VPN), Internet Authentication Server (IAS) for authentication, Active Directory, etc.)

- Certificate templates

These services are responsible for issuing, managing, revoking, and verifying digital certificates that are used on your network.

At the heart of the PKI is the certificate authority (CA), which verifies the information in the certificate and then digitally signs the certificate with its public key. A CA can be public (third-party like Verisign, Thawte, or RSA), or you can set up a private CA in your own organization by installing a root CA on Windows Server 2003 in your organization. By signing the certificate, the CA is essentially making a statement that the person sending the certificate is who they say they are based on the proof of identity that the CA required. PKI-enabled applications must be set up to trust the CA, which means that you trust the certificate.

A certificate is created through a separate tool or a tool contained in a PKI-enabled application. The certificate contains the public key of the requestor and the proper fields for the type of certificate requested. The certificate is then submitted to the CA (through a website, e-mail, or other means) which verifies the information, signs the certificate if the information checks out, and returns the certificate to you. Verification can come in many forms, from confirming that you own the DNS domain for your web application to requiring you to meet in person with a representative and provide two or three forms of identification like a driver's license, Social Security card, or passport. The amount of verification depends on the type and use of the certificate. You then install the certificate into your application to provide identity validation and encryption.

Of course, a certificate can't vouch for the character of the person or company, but at least you know they are who they say they are. If someone tries to alter the certificate, you will be alerted by the PKI-enabled application (like a web browser) that participates in the PKI process because the hash in the signature will not match the one in the certificate, so you can detect a forged certificate. You can view and configure certificates in PKI-enabled applications. The client-side certificates used by Internet Explorer or Outlook Express can be managed through Internet Explorer by following these steps:

1. Start Internet Explorer.

2. Choose Tools ➢ Internet Options to open the Internet Options dialog box.

3. Click the Content tab, shown in Figure 6.2.

4. Click the Certificates button to open the Certificates dialog box.

5. Click the Trusted Root Certification Authorities tab, shown in Figure 6.3. Here, you will see all the certificates that are trusted.

FIGURE 6.2 The Content tab of the Internet Options dialog box

FIGURE 6.3 The Trusted Root Certification Authorities tab of the Certificates dialog box

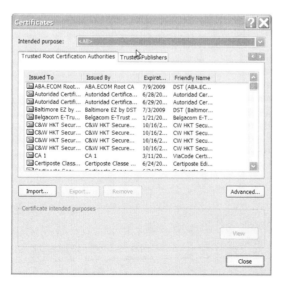

6. Double-click any one of the certificates listed in the list box to open the Certificate dialog box, shown in Figure 6.4.

7. Click the Details tab to view the fields that are contained in the certificate (see Figure 6.5).

FIGURE 6.4   The General tab of the Certificate dialog box

FIGURE 6.5   The Details tab of the Certificate dialog box

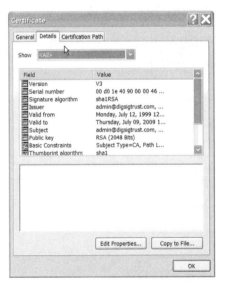

8. Close the Certificate dialog box.

9. Close the Certificates dialog box.

10. Close the Internet Options dialog box.

Certificates can also be configured on the server side through the Internet Information Services MMC. The tool allows you to generate a web server certificate, submit the certificate to a CA, and install the certificate on the web server. You can then use the tool to identify the virtual directories on which you want to enable encryption through the virtual directory Properties dialog box.

When identifying systems that need the added protection of PKI, you need to analyze the cost of implementing PKI versus the value of the data that needs to be protected. PKI can be used to secure e-mail and communications with customers, employees, and other organizations over the Internet or to implement digital signatures for software components. You should implement some kind of PKI if you need to rely on the following technologies in your applications:

- Smart cards
- Extensible Authentication Protocol–Transport Layer Security (EAP-TLS)
- IP Security (IPSec)
- Secure Sockets Layer (SSL)
- Digital signatures
- 802.1x
- Encrypting File System (EFS)
- Software code signing
- Authentication
- Secure e-mail

To better illustrate the use of certificates, let's look at a familiar technology that is based on PKI, *Secure Sockets Layer (SSL)*. This technology solves two problems that occur when trying to secure a transaction over the Internet: verifying the vendor's identity and securely transmitting data:

SSL begins with the merchant creating a certificate.   The process of creating the certificate may vary from vendor to vendor, but they all need to provide a tool to produce a public and private key pair and collect some information about the creator.

Suppose you buy something online for your significant other's birthday. You navigate to the website and select your product and then select checkout, which starts a secure session. You can now enter your personal information and credit card information without the risk of someone eavesdropping on the network connection and stealing the information (although you may still be vulnerable to being conned, or the vendor's database could be infiltrated through lax security measures, problems that SSL does not fix).

The client requests the secure site by using the HTTPS protocol.   This will establish a connection to the server on port 443 by default. The client will request the certificate from the server (see Figure 6.7). It will look at the CA information and verify that the certificate has not been altered since it was signed by the CA, that it has not been revoked by the CA, and that it is a trusted CA. If something does not check out, you will get a warning similar to the one in Figure 6.6 and you can decide how to proceed.

If you don't get a warning, you can assume the server operator is associated with the DNS domain that contains the website. The server could also at this point request a certificate from the client to verify the client's identity. This is an optional step in SSL and usually only used if you are working with a partner organization or a smart card technology.

The client will then extract the public key and use it to encrypt a session key that the client generates.   This can be seen in Figure 6.8. The session key will be sent to the server encrypted with the public key (see Figure 6.9). This key is a symmetric encryption key that the server will then use to send encrypted information back to the client. The client will use the key to decrypt the information and send any response back to the server by encrypting the information first and then sending it to the server. You have now encrypted the data without revealing your keys, thereby making it safer.

FIGURE 6.6   Warning in Internet Explorer

FIGURE 6.7   Client requesting certificate from the server

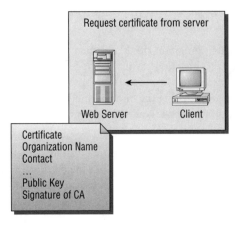

Generally, if you were setting up a secure public website, you would pay for a certificate from a trusted root CA like Verisign. Browsers ship with the CA's certificate installed in them, so the user will not receive a warning when they try to connect to the site, which is why you should use a third-party CA on your public servers. But there are cases in which you want to use certificates with partners or even internally in your company. You can use a third-party CA, but because you may require a lot of certificates, that could cost your company a lot of money for internal use. You trust yourself, so you could become the CA by installing certificate services on Windows Server 2003. You would need to know how to design and secure a PKI infrastructure if you need to become your own CA.

FIGURE 6.8 Client verifies certificate signature and uses public key to encrypt response.

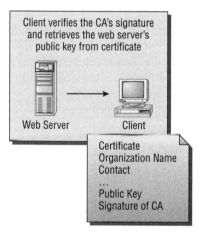

FIGURE 6.9 An encrypted response with the session key is sent to the server.

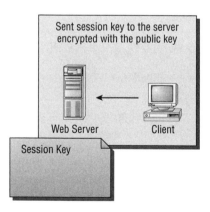

Designing a Certificate Authority Implementation

A certificate authority (CA) needs to perform the following roles:

- Maintain a root certificate to distribute its public key.

- Identify the certificate requestor and validate their identity. This can vary from simply verifying that the domain is correct to doing a background check and having someone physically verify the identity of the requestor.

- Issue certificates to requestors.

- Maintain a database of registered users (certificates issued).

- Generate and maintain a certificate revocation list (CRL).

When designing a CA implementation, you need to consider what types of applications you will use to require certificates. You will then need to determine what clients will need certificates. You will also need to define the certificate security requirements. Finally, you will need to decide on the appropriate certificate server roles and hierarchy.

Determining Certificate Requirements

Applications that use PKI will require a number of types of certificates to be installed. You will need to decide which applications will require certificates and what types of certificates those applications will require. Table 6.2 list technologies that rely on certificates and the ways applications might use certificates.

TABLE 6.2   Common Technologies That Rely on Certificates

Technology	Applications
Client authentication	Validating computers or clients on the network
Digital signatures	Signing a document to verify that it came from the appropriate user
Encrypting File System (EFS)	Securing files on the file system of a computer
IP Security (IPSec)	Securing remote access to network over a public network through encryption and authentication of machines
Secure email (S/MIME)	Encrypting and signing e-mail messages

TABLE 6.2   Common Technologies That Rely on Certificates *(continued)*

Technology	Applications
Secure Sockets Layer (SSL)	Encrypting traffic to and from a website; verifying the identity of the web site
Server authentication	Verifying the identity of the server
Smart card logon	Providing for two-factor authentication with smart card technology
Software code signing	Verifying that the source of the code and the code has not been altered since it was released
802.1x	Authenticating clients and encrypting traffic
Extensible Authentication Protocol–Transport Layer Security (EAP-TLS)	Providing encryption and identity verification

After you have determined what applications you need to secure, you will need to decide to implement a private CA or utilize a commercial CA. There are different reasons you might choose one or the other. You would set up a private CA if you have the need to control and administer your own certificates. You would also do so if you needed to deploy many certificates because doing so with a commercial CA would be costly. Implementing your own root CA and additional hierarchy means you can cross-certify with a partner organization, which allows you to create a limited trust of certificates from a partner organization that they manage separately.

 Cross-certification will be discussed later in this chapter, in the section "Trusting Certificates from Other Organizations."

The disadvantage to implementing a private CA is that it will likely require additional staff and servers to install and manage. You would have to also consider the methods for deploying the certificates. You could then use Group Policy and Active Directory to deploy the certificates to clients on your network, but deploying them outside of your network is more difficult.

A commercial authority is widely trusted, so clients will not have to complicate things by having to install a certificate. You would use a commercial CA if you need to have a certificate trusted outside your organization. For example, suppose your company has built an application that will be used over the Web. Part of the application will require that private or sensitive information be sent over the Internet. You would obtain a certificate from a commercial CA to implement SSL on your website because the commercial CA's certificate will be contained in the client's browser. The drawback is that you cannot administer your own certificates. You also cannot cross-certify with a partner organization because you do not have control over the root server.

In the "Choosing Where to Host Certificates" Design Scenario, you will determine where to host certificates for a company.

Design Scenario

Choosing Where to Host Certificates

Trinity Importers, Ltd. is a retailer that specializes in importing Asian goods into the United States and selling them through retailers throughout the East Coast. The company has decided to expand to the Internet to expand its market. It has hired a web development company to develop and host the e-commerce site.

Network Administrator   We are overworked supporting the servers and the POS systems already in place in the organization. We are not increasing the staff for supporting the e-commerce site because the company has outsourced the hosting of the site. We do not want any additional administrative duties for the application.

CIO   We are testing out the popularity of an Internet presence for our company. We want the customers to have an easy time using the site. We do not want to support any kind of complex installs.

CSO   The clients of the website will be sending private information to the website, like credit card information and additional information that we collect. We want customers to feel confident that their information will not be compromised.

1.   **Question:** Trinity needs to implement SSL to secure data transmitted over the Internet. Of the following, what kind of PKI should you recommend to Trinity Importers? **Answer:** You should choose a commercial CA for issuing the certificate because of the requirement of not wanting a solution that is a burden for the network administrators and because the CIO doesn't want to have to worry about distributing the private root CA certificate.

2.   **Question:** Why would you need a certificate for Trinity Importers? **Answer:** You need a certificate to implement Secure Sockets Layer in the application. The certificate will prove to the client that the server comes from Trinity's domain if the client trusts the issuing root CA. It also contains the public key of the web server so the client can send an encrypted message to the server to initialize the SSL session key.

Designing the Roles of Certificate Authorities

When you establish a PKI in your own organization, you will need to choose the roles of the CA servers that you install. You have a choice of three different server roles:

Root CA role   The first CA you install in your organization is the *root CA*. The root CA server is the ultimate CA in the organization. It is responsible for signing all other subordinate CA certificates. The root CA is the only server role that trusts itself by signing its own certificate and issuing this root certificate to itself. The role of the root CA is to authorize other CAs in the organization. Therefore, if your clients trust the root CA, then they trust the certificates issued by the root's subordinate CAs. When an application receives a certificate, it will verify that the certificate is issued by a trusted root CA; otherwise, it will warn the user that there is a problem with the certificate. You can issue root certificates to the Windows client trusted root certificate store by using Active Directory or Domain Group Policy or through a website or file share where users can download the trusted root certificate. The root CA is very important and it would be detrimental to network security if it was infiltrated, so it is recommended that it be kept offline.

Intermediate CA role Generally, it is recommended that the root CA be kept offline, so it is not available to approve and issue certificates. The root CA can certify the subordinate CAs to accept, approve, and issue certificates on its behalf. The *intermediate CA* can be used to certify requests for certificates. This will reduce the number of times that the root CA's private key is exposed. The intermediate CA (also known as a policy CA) is the CA that approves client requests for certificates known as enrollment requests.

Issuing CA role After the intermediate CA, you would install an *issuing CA* to enroll, deploy, and renew the certificates. The issuing CA is the CA that will communicate with the client applications and computers. The issuing CA is the server that needs to be available all of the time for proper CA functionality.

You will want to design for multiple CAs in your organization to provide availability and secure publishing points in your organization. You should not go more than three levels deep with your CA design and two levels will be adequate for most organizations.

You also have the choice of installing an *enterprise CA* or a *stand-alone CA* on a Windows Server 2003 server. An enterprise CA will take advantage of Active Directory to control the enrollment process. This means that you can use Group Policy to manage and distribute client certificates. You can also use the certificate templates to create a certificate. A stand-alone CA does not take advantage of Active Directory. You will not be able to use Group Policy to manage certificates and will be limited to a web-based or command-line utility enrollment.

You build a chain of trust or a certificate path when issuing certificates. The certificate that a user or a computer receives can be trusted because the issuing CA received its certificate from another CA or directly from the root CA. Because the root CA issues the certificates used by subordinate CAs, and eventually the client's certificates, as long as you trust the root CA and it is kept secure, you can verify the identity of the certificate. If the root CA is compromised, then all certificates issued by the root CA or any subordinate can be considered invalid because they can be forged by someone. You should keep the root CA secure.

You can install the different CA roles into one of three basic hierarchies. A single server would have the root CA approving and issuing certificates. This is the least secure of the three hierarchies because it exposes the root CA to attackers, which can be dangerous if the private key used to sign certificates is compromised. You can help mitigate this risk by installing a two-tier hierarchy.

A two-tier hierarchy allows you to keep the root CA offline except when you install new CAs. The root would have one or more subordinates, but it would have no more than two levels, as shown in Figure 6.10.

The subordinate would be the intermediate and issuing CA, which can be kept online to handle the day-to-day certificate maintenance requirements without exposing the root CA's private key. This is usually the best cost-versus-security combination.

A three-tier hierarchy can further secure your CA by separating the intermediate CA from the issuing CA, as shown in Figure 6.11.

FIGURE 6.10 A two-tier hierarchy

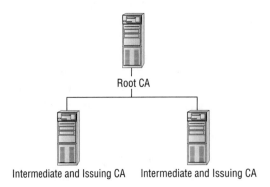

FIGURE 6.11 A three-tier hierarchy

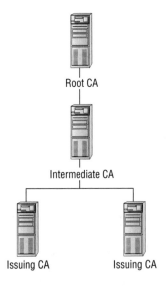

The three-tier hierarchy allows you to add an additional layer of CAs between the client and the root CA. This will allow you to create separate issuing CAs for different groups of clients. For example, internal clients can obtain their certificates from a different CA than the one external clients obtain theirs from.

Most organizations will not require a three-tier hierarchy for security of their applications. You will need to weigh the cost of server licenses and managing the extra servers against the importance of security requirements for your CAs. The root and intermediate CAs are centralized, so when we talk about designing a CA hierarchy, we are generally referring to issuing CAs.

Determining Appropriate CA Hierarchies

You will need to determine where and how you will want to group your issuing CAs. You have four design choices when determining how to lay them out:

Organizational CA hierarchy   You can design a CA hierarchy based on the classifications of employees in your organization. You would use an *organizational CA hierarchy* if you need to use different policies for issuing certificates to employees, contractors, administrators, partners, and various other classifications of users. Users would obtain certificates from the proper issuing CA for their classification. For example, you could decide that a contractor must provide two forms of government ID, while an employee might only need to log on to the network with their user ID and password.

Department CA hierarchy   If your organization's administration is decentralized, then you can let each department control their own issuing CAs. Using the *department CA hierarchy*, you could let the marketing department or the accounting department decide what certificates they want to deploy. They can control the issuing of certificates for their PKI-based applications or they can meet the unique legal requirements of their departments. You could have both a policy CA and an issuing CA in the department if the department requires different policies for issuing certificates.

Function CA hierarchy   You can design a CA hierarchy based on the type of certificates that you wish to issue. With the *function CA hierarchy*, you would have a separate issuing CA for each certificate type or application that requires PKI. You would use this design if you need to separate the management of different certificate types. For example, the group that manages the Exchange servers for e-mail may require control over the certificates that are issues for S/MIME digital signatures and encryption. You would then create an issuing CA for S/MIME certificates and allow the Exchange group to manage the certificates that it issues. You may have legal requirements for different certificate types. This may involve the length of issuance or the issuing policies for particular certificate types or applications.

Geographic CA hierarchy   You can decide that it is necessary to base the distribution, enrollment, and management of certificates on geographic locations of your organization. With the *geographic CA hierarchy*, you would install issuing CAs at each geographic location in your company. Factors that would influence this decision would be legal requirements, such as a requirement that all PKI activity must be maintained within country boundaries, or availability requirements, such as needing a local CA server if the WAN links are potentially down.

When designing for the different CA hierarchies, you will find that legal requirements will determine the type of hierarchy you choose. Certain industries will have requirements about how long documents must be kept, therefore encryption keys cannot be changed or recycled during that period. Countries will have different legal requirements for encryption and you would need to make sure issued certificates do not violate these laws. You would need to create three documents to help determine the appropriate hierarchy for your organization: the security policy, the certificate policy, and the certification practice statement.

The security policy for the organization   The security policy is a document that defines the security practices that are used in the organization, as we discussed in Chapter 1, "Analyzing

Security Policies, Procedures, and Requirements." The security policy would define the security concerns of the organization, what they need to protect, and what resources the organization wants to dedicate to security. The security policy should include information about the PKI in use in the organization. You would use this information to document procedures and practices with regard to CAs, their certificates, the level of trust that each certificate should have, and the legal liabilities if the different certificates are compromised.

The certificate policy   The certificate policy defines how a certificate subject (user or computer) is verified before it is assigned a certificate, where the private keys will be stored (separate hardware device or a computer hard drive), the process for responding to lost keys, the enrollment and renewal process, the maximum monetary or intrinsic value that can be protected by this certificate, the types of actions that can be performed with the certificate, and any additional requirements surrounding a certificate that is issued in your organization.

The certification practice statement (CPS)   The CPS is a document that specifically defines how to implement the certificate policy on the organization's CA hierarchy. You would define the users, computers, and applications that will require certificates. You also can include authentication and identification methods for enrollment and renewal, the obligations and liabilities of the organization with regard to the CA hierarchy, the audit policy for ensuring that the CPS is followed, operational requirements for the CAs in the organization, the types and versions of certificates that will be issued, and the procedures for securing CAs in the organization. The CPS essentially defines the management of the CAs that are in the organization, while the certificate policy defines the procedures for managing certificates. The CPS can then be published to the policy CAs through the use of a `CAPolicy.inf` file. The CPS will then be published to all subordinate CAs.

In the "Choosing a CA Hierarchy" Design Scenario, you will decide what would be the appropriate CA hierarchy for an organization.

 Design Scenario

Choosing a CA Hierarchy

Trinity Imports, Ltd. has offices in Asia, Europe, and New York. The company uses a multiple-domain model with one domain for each of the locations. Each location has its own administrative staff. These locations also have different legal requirements when it comes to strength of encryption that may be used. Trinity needs to implement a CA hierarchy. The folks at Trinity have decided that their design will have the root CA and policy CA for the organization in New York. They now want to design the rest of the hierarchy.

1. **Question:** What hierarchy would you recommend for Trinity and why? **Answer:** Trinity should build a hierarchy based on the geographic location of each of its sites because the organization requires different legal requirements for regions or countries.

Trusting Certificates from Other Organizations

There are situations in which you will need to trust users in other organizations. You could issue certificates from your own CA servers to users in the other organization. If you need maximum control over who gets a certificate or you don't trust the security policies of the other companies, you would issue and revoke certificates from your own CAs. The other organization could be integrated into your CA hierarchy. The drawback to this is that you will need to manage the certificates for the other organization. This would mean that you will need to decide on a method to securely distribute certificates to the other organization. You will also need to revoke certificates for people that leave the other organization or certificates that are lost on a smart card or computer. You will need to have processes in place to manage changes in the organization that will impact the CA hierarchy.

 Real World Scenario

Establishing a Cross-Certificate Trust

Jenny is in charge of security at VanderDoes and Fenton, a large law firm in Philadelphia. The law firm takes security very seriously and has a PKI for two-factor authentication and wireless authentication of clients. The law firm is aggressively growing, which means it is merging with other law firms to increase its size and caseload.

VanderDoes and Fenton recently acquired a medium-sized law firm. This law firm has its own PKI in place to support its applications and two-factor authentication.

In addition to the acquisition, VanderDoes and Fenton has just purchased a new application that allows its clients to view the progress of a case from a website. The lawyers from both firms are pushing for access to each other's systems and the clients want access to the website, but they want assurances that their transactions will be secure.

Because VanderDoes and Fenton has an existing PKI, Jenny decides that, rather than reissue all the lawyers' and personnel certificates from their CAs, it would be faster to set up a cross-certification so that each PKI trusts the root from the other organization. This means that users will be able to gain access to the information in each domain with the minimal amount of work for Jenny and her staff. She also decides to lease a certificate from a commercial CA to provide SSL to the web application. She decides to require 128-bit encryption to maintain security over the Internet to the application. She authenticates the clients through the web server with basic authentication over SSL.

Many organizations will not be ready to take on that much coordination and overhead, which will constitute greater cost. There is an alternative to having to manage the certificates for the other organization: have the other organization manage their own certificates and trust the certificates that they issue. You can establish a *cross-certification* to trust the certificates that are issued in the other organization. A cross-certification will allow two organizations to trust each other and rely on each other's certificates and keys as if they were issued from their own certificate authorities. The two CAs would exchange cross-certificates to enable users in each organization to interact securely with each other.

A certificate will need to be issued and distributed to users, computers, or services on the network. At some point, the certificate will expire depending on the policy under which it was issued, at which time the certificate will need to be renewed. Certificates that have had the corresponding private key compromised or that have expired will need to be revoked.

Creating an Enrollment and Distribution Strategy

You eventually will need to decide how to issue certificates to the users, computers, and services that participate in the PKI. The process of requesting and installing the certificates for the user, computers, or services is called the *enrollment strategy*. There are many types of enrollment methods that you can use, depending on the type of CAs (enterprise or stand-alone), the client computer operating system, the issuing policy requirements, and where the CAs are located in relation to the clients.

The first step in enrollment is issuing the request. You can issue a request to the CA server and obtain a certificate through a web page, the Certificates MMC, a command-line utility, and autoenrollment by the underlying OS. The enrollment strategy you use depends on three factors:

The client's operating system   The underlying operating systems for the clients that will participate will affect the means you can use to enroll and renew a certificate. For example, non-Windows OSes will need to use the web page for enrollment, and autoenrollment is supported by only Windows XP and Windows Server 2003.

The type of CA you will be running   There are two types CAs: a stand-alone CA and an enterprise CA. The enterprise CA supports autoenrollment for certificates and the use of Group Policy and certificate templates to control the request and deployment of certificates. Windows Server 2003 and Windows XP support only autoenrollment. A stand-alone server will only support web-based enrollment or command-line enrollment.

The types of user, service, or computer accounts that will receive the certificates.   You need to determine if the accounts or computers are connected to Active Directory. Also, are the accounts contained in your organization or external to your organization?

You will need to determine how you will distribute certificates, which is called enrollment. In the following sections you will learn how to enroll clients and servers for certificates through the Web, Certificates MMC, command-line, and autoenrollment. We will then look at automatic and manual enrollment and what user interfaces are available to you for enrollment.

Using Web-Based Enrollment

Web-based enrollment allows you to obtain a certificate or the CA's certificate through the use of a web browser (see Figure 6.12). This is the primary interface to a Windows Server 2003 CA server. The web-based version is useful for navigating firewalls or for obtaining certificates for non-Windows clients. You can use web-based enrollment if you are trying to enroll for a certificate with a stand-alone CA or an enterprise CA. Web-based enrollment will be installed on any CA by default, but you can also install it on any other Windows Server 2003 server. The web-based enrollment can generate almost any certificate that you can generate through other means except for the smart card logon and autoenrollment certificates because these certificates are issued only from an enterprise CA directly to the client. Web enrollment does not support certificate templates, so all the information for the user and the type of certificate need to be provided by the user. You can request a user certificate through the standard options of the web interface. You can use the advanced options to export a certificate, renew a certificate, request a certificate for another user, and generate keys on the client for a certificate request.

Web-based enrollment also allows you to enroll and renew certificates for smart cards through a smart card enrollment station. A smart card enrollment station will allow you to enroll for certificates on behalf of a user. You would need an Enrollment Agent certificate to enroll for a certificate on behalf of a user. This will allow you to issue smart cards to your users without requiring them to enroll for the certificates that will be stored on their smart cards on their own.

FIGURE 6.12   Web-based certificate administration

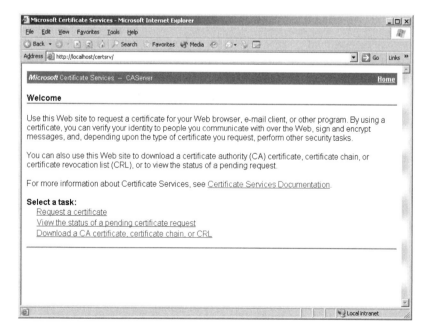

FIGURE 6.13   The Automatic Certificate Request Setup Wizard

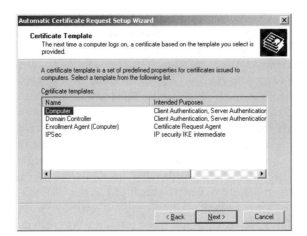

Using the Certificates MMC For Enrollment

The Certificates MMC allows you to enroll for a certificate using the Automatic Certificate Request Setup Wizard (see Figure 6.13). This will only work with enterprise CAs and for Windows 2000, Windows XP, and Windows Server 2003 users, computers, and services. You can use the Certificates MMC to manage the certificate requests on a stand-alone CA but not to make a request through the Automatic Certificate Request Setup Wizard. You can use the MMC only to obtain a certificate for the current user of the application, or if you are an administrator, you can get certificates for yourself, the local computer, or local services on the computer.

Using Command-Line Certificate Enrollment

The `certreq.exe` command-line utility will allow you to create, submit, accept, and retrieve certificates. Because it is a command-line utility, it can be used from batch files or scripts. You can use it to create and sign cross-certification certificate requests to establish a trust with another CA hierarchy. `Certreq.exe` will allow you to map the CA certificate to the policy that you will use to set constraints for the Cross Certificate Authority certificate. You can use `certreq.exe` to request a certificate from a stand-alone CA and enterprise CAs.

Using Autoenrollment

Autoenrollment for certificates is supported on Windows XP clients and Windows Server 2003 against a Windows Enterprise Server 2003 enterprise CA. You can autoenroll for smart card logon, EFS, SSL, and S/MIME certificates for users and computers that log onto an Active Directory environment. Group Policy on the user or computer is used to manage autoenrolled certificates, and the permissions on the certificate template control what certificates a user can request. Autoenrollment will allow you to request user, computer, and smart card certificates. This is a cost-effective way to deploy EFS, smart card, and S/MIME certificates in an Active Directory environment with Windows XP and Windows Server 2003 servers. You choose the certificates that you want the clients to have through Group Policy, as shown in Figure 6.14. You can also control certificates that are issued by controlling the permissions on the certificate template using Global or Universal groups. This will require that you have an enterprise CA and is not supported with a stand-alone CA. If your certificate requires only one authorizing signature, you can use autoenrollment; otherwise autoenrollment will be disabled.

Understanding the Difference between Automatic and Manual Enrollment

Whether you choose automatic or manual enrollment will depend on the number of clients you want to enroll, the types of clients, and the security level of the certificate. For example, you might want to install a computer certificate on every client in your organization to validate each computer. This would be a tedious process to do manually, so this would be a case for autoenrollment. In fact, autoenrollment is most useful when you want to enroll clients for computer and IPSec certificates. On the other hand, you might have administrators who use smart card authentication to authenticate with servers for remote management. Because the user authentication certificates stored on the smart card are considered high security, you could require the administrators to manually apply for the certificates to have more control over the approval process. Figure 6.15 shows how you would enable the autoenroll feature on the CA server.

FIGURE 6.14   The automatic certificate request settings in the Group Policy Editor

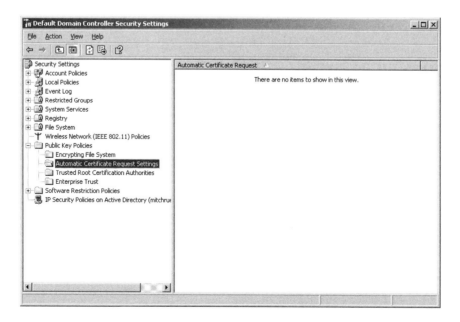

FIGURE 6.15 The Autoenroll setting on the Security tab

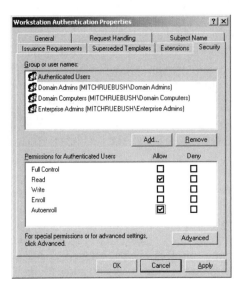

In addition to automatically enrolling a client for certificates, you can choose to manually or automatically approve certificate requests. After the client requests a certificate, you can manually approve the certificate as an administrator using the Certificates MMC or you can develop a complex policy to approve it, which is usually preferred for certificates that require high security. You can also let the certificate request be approved automatically. This works well if you first validate the clients through a domain logon. Automatically approving requests is a good mechanism for providing certificates that are routinely issued or issued in high volume.

Choosing a User Interface

The user interface that you choose for certificate processing will depend on whether you choose automatic or manual certificate enrollment and approval methods. If you choose to use the automatic request, which is through autoenrollment, you will not have a user interface for enrollment. A manual enrollment and approval process will allow you to choose between using a web enrollment page or the Automatic Certificate Request Setup Wizard. A designated administrator or a user can use a web enrollment page to do the following:

- Request a certificate by using a certificate request file.
- Renew certificates by using a certificate renewal request file.
- Request and deploy a basic user certificate.
- Request and deploy other types of certificates.
- Save a certificate request to a file.
- Save the issued certificate to a file.

- Check on pending certificate requests.

- Retrieve a CA certificate.

- Retrieve the latest certificate revocation list.

- Request smart card certificates on behalf of other users if you have been given the proper permissions (have an Enrollment Agent certificate).

You can perform similar tasks using the Certificate Request And Renewal Wizard through the Certificates MMC. However, administrators might prefer to use the Automatic Certificate Request Setup Wizard to create an automatic certificate request for clients. You can start either wizard from the Certificates MMC, which is a tool to request, renew, and manage certificates.

Your decision about what tool to use is simplified if there is a firewall between you and the CA. The Certificates MMC requires DCOM to communicate with the server, and the firewall administrator will most likely not open TCP and UDP ports 135 due to security concerns, so you would need to use a web enrollment page.

Storing Issued Certificates

You will need to store certificates that you create through your CA server in one of the following locations:

Smart card   *Smart cards* are devices that are the size of credit cards and are used to provide security solutions for authentication, e-mail, and data encryption. Smart cards store certificates and the corresponding private key in a secure manner. You can access the private key only through use of a valid PIN. Smart cards use *two-factor authentication*, meaning that you must have the physical smart card and the valid PIN to authenticate on the network or digitally sign an e-mail message, for example. Smarts cards can enhance network security through these means.

File   Certificates can be exported to a file for transfer to another location or to protect a private key by removing it from a computer. Certificates can be exported to file in one of two formats on Windows: Public Key Cryptography Standard (PKCS) #12, which will write the public and private key out to the file, and the PKCS #7 Distinguished Encoding Rules and Base-64, which stores the certificate only.

Computer   Certificates for Windows accounts can be securely stored on a computer by encrypting the certificate. That way, only the Windows account will have access to the certificate.

Active Directory   You can store server certificates, certificate revocation list certificates, and CA certificates in Active Directory. This makes it easier for Windows clients to access the certificate in a secure manner.

Website   You can publish certificates to a website where they can be downloaded to the clients. This is a good idea for certificates that need to be used by partner or customer computers or that need to be checked for revocation from the Internet.

In the "Designing an Enrollment and Distribution Strategy" Design Scenario, you will design an enrollment and distribution strategy for a company.

Design Scenario

Designing an Enrollment and Distribution Strategy

Trinity Imports has a chain of 200 stores throughout the eastern United States and Canada. Each of these stores has a computer that connects to the central office in Philadelphia via a dial-up connection to a local ISP number and then establishes a VPN connection using IPSec to the central office. The central office validates the computer based on its computer certificate. The computer certificates need to be acquired and distributed to the computers. All clients are running Windows XP, and they have an Active Directory domain for each location.

IT Manager   The IT staff is already stretched to the limit with the current infrastructure that they support. They can't take on too much additional responsibility.

CSO   We need to validate the computers that dial in for security purposes. The computers will authenticate over IPSec with Kerberos and use a L2TP\IPSec.

1. **Question:** What would be the best way to deploy certificates that will meet both of their needs? **Answer:** You would install your issuing CA servers as enterprise CAs on a Windows Server 2003 server. You could then take advantage of autoenrollment through the organization for the computer certificates.

Renewing, Revoking, and Auditing Certificates

After you decide how you will distribute certificates, you will need to manage and track the certificates. Certificates are only issued for a period of time; then they will expire, so you will need to come up with a strategy for renewing them. Renewing the certificate and associated key pair can help prevent the key from becoming compromised, but sometimes that key *is* compromised, so you will need to come up with a strategy for revoking certificates. Revoking a certificate will let clients know that the certificate is no longer trustworthy. Finally, you will need to track what users and administrators are doing with the CAs and certificates by using auditing on the servers.

Renewing Certificates

Certificates are issued for a finite lifetime, which means that they will expire. The lifetime of the certificate will depend on the type of certificate and the policy that the CA has set for the certificates. Certificates will need to be renewed when the lifetime ends. When you renew a certificate, you can choose to keep the same public/private key or generate a new key pair. The longer a key is active, the more vulnerable it is to being compromised. You can reduce the risk of key compromise by renewing the public/private key combination each time you renew a certificate instead of at the maximum lifetime of the key pair. At least, you should never renew the certificate past the lifetime of the key pair. You can also increase the length of the key when you renew a certificate. This means you can use the renewal process to strengthen the key if you determine that it no longer meets your security policy. It is recommended that the key length be somewhere between 1024 and 4096 bits.

CAs also have certificates that are issued from their parent CA or, in the case of the root CA, issued to itself. When these certificates expire, the CA can no longer issue certificates and all certificates that the CA issued will expire. You should remember that when a CA's certificate expires, all subordinate CAs' certificates expire. When you renew a CA's certificate, all subordinate CAs' certificates will need to be renewed. You will need to come up with a strategy to renew the CA certificates or any certificate before they expire. When renewing CA certificates, you should always generate a new key pair.

The following questions will need to be answered before you can determine a renewal strategy for your certificates:

- Which certificates are you allowed to renew?

- How often can a certificate be renewed before its key is retired?

You can justify longer lifetimes for certificates if they are infrequently used and have strong keys, because a potential cracker won't have many opportunities to capture them. If the certificate is captured it will be nearly impossible to crack the strong key. You can continue to renew the signature for the certificate up to the issuing CA certificate's lifetime. On the other hand, if the certificate has a weaker key or is used more frequently, you will want a shorter lifetime. You should renew these certificates more frequently but never beyond the lifetime of the CA certificate.

The following steps will allow you to renew a certificate on a CA:

1. Navigate to Start ➤ Program Files ➤ Administrative Tools ➤ Certificate Authority to open the Certificate Authority console.

2. Right-click on the certificate authority on which you would like to renew the certificate to open the context menu.

3. Choose All Tasks ➤ Renew CA Certificate to renew the CA's certificate.

4. You will then be prompted about changing the length of the key pair used in this certificate. Choose Yes to generate a new key pair or No to keep the existing key pair.

You need to plan on the renewal of the CA certificates before they expire to guarantee uninterrupted certificate services. This has to be done manually for certificates that were requested through a web enrollment page or the Certificate Request And Enrollment Wizard. Clients will not be able to renew or acquire certificates if the CA certificate has expired. You can use the same mechanisms that client computers use to obtain certificates to renew a CA certificate. CA certificates are important and you should use a manual process to renew them. You should pay attention to the length of your public/private key pair. If the key length is inadequate, during the renewal of the certificate you can lengthen it. The key pair has a lifetime that should be set based on the length of the key. Longer key pairs can have a longer life because they are less likely to be cracked. You should generate a new key pair when renewing a CA certificate if the key has expired. This will mean that all certificates based on these keys will need to be renewed, so this will require a great deal of planning for the root CA certificate.

Autoenrollment is the only option that supports automatic renewal of the certificates before they become invalid. It will also support the issuance of pending certificates.

Revoking a Certificate

Sometimes you may have a problem with a certificate; for example, the private key might be compromised or an employee might quit and you no longer want the certificate to be valid. You can invalidate a certificate on the CA and then publish the CRL to the root CA and subordinate CAs. This will allow clients to download the revocation list and verify that the certificate is still valid if it is not on the list. There are many situations that can cause you to revoke a certificate, but the following is a list of possible reasons:

- The CA has been compromised.

- The private key has been compromised.

- A new certificate that replaces the previous certificate has been issued. Perhaps you have a need to update information in the certificate.

- You have decommissioned or replaced the CA.

If you find yourself revoking certificates based on a CA or private keys being compromised, you would be wasting energy revoking and renewing certificates. You should strongly protect the CAs and private keys.

You can configure clients to check the CRL before they accept a certificate. The client can then be configured to either reject the connection or just show a warning box that will state that the certificate has been revoked and ask if the user would like to proceed.

You can publish the revocation list to either the Active Directory or a website. You will need to revoke the certificate(s) before publishing the CRL. The location will be stored in the certificate. Applications must be configured to check the CRL at the publishing point chosen, so this means that the application will need to support the chosen publication point.

The following steps will take you through the process of revoking certificates:

1. Open up the Certification Authority console by navigating to Start ➤ Administrative Tools ➤ Certification Authority.

2. Expand the CA that contains the certificate that you want revoked.

3. Click on the Issued Certificates container to show the certificates issued by the server.

4. Right-click on the certificate that you wish to revoke and choose All Tasks➤ Revoke Certificate from the context menu.

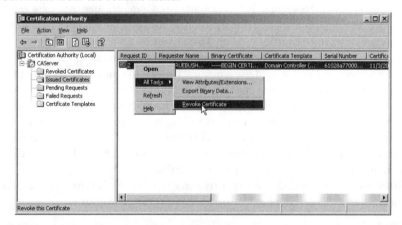

5. Publish the certificate revocation list to the CA hierarchy by right-clicking on the Revoked Certificates container and choosing All Tasks ➢ Publish.

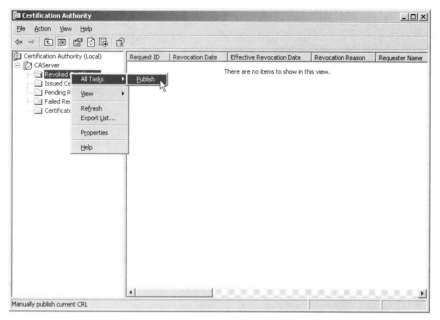

If a CA or the private key store is compromised, it can mean that all your certificates are invalid or the policies used to enroll for certificates have been compromised. This means that you need to protect your CAs. The root CA is the most important, and as we discussed earlier, it should be kept offline and only used when it is necessary to add a CA to the network. You will need to assume that someone can bypass your security measures—after all, even trusted administrators may have reason to compromise security—and track access to the CAs.

Auditing Certificate Authorities

You can track access to the files, Registry settings, and CA settings through auditing, so you can track a compromise or attempted compromise of the CA server. You will need to decide what event categories you will need to audit in your organization. This should be based on the security requirements of the organization. You will need to balance the amount of information that you choose to audit. If you audit too little information, you will have great difficulty in determining what happened during a security incident. If you choose to audit too much information, you will either fill up the audit logs with too much useless information that will be difficult to sift through or fill them up to the point that there is no more room and you won't be to collect data at the time of a security incident. Once you decide how much to audit, you can use a product like Microsoft Operations Manager or performance alerts to set up alerts on the varying event IDs generated by the audit settings to automate the discovery of security incidents.

Your audit policy will contain event categories for the Registry, the file system, and the CA servers. These will be logged to the local security log on the server and can be viewed through the Event Viewer tool.

You can get to the specific auditing settings of a CA by following these steps:

1. Open up the Certification Authority console by navigating to Start ≻ Administrative Tools ≻ Certification Authority.

2. Right-click on the CA server for which you want to configure the auditing settings and choose Properties from the context menu.

3. Click the Auditing tab to reveal the auditing options.

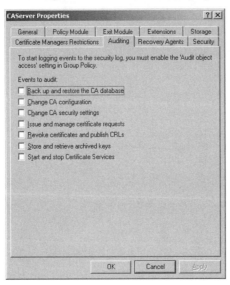

It is recommended that you enable all of the settings for auditing on a CA.

You should also audit Registry access because, if someone gains access to the Registry, they will have access to the configuration and control over the application. The follow settings are recommended for auditing the Registry:

HKEY_LOCAL_MACHINE\SYSTEM\CurrentControlSet\Services\Certsvc\Configuration
You should audit any failed access for the Everyone account for all permissions.

HKEY_LOCAL_MACHINE\SYSTEM\CurrentControlSet\Services\Certsvc\Configuration
You should audit any successful access for the Everyone account for all of the permissions.

The following is a list of the different audit settings you would want to consider when auditing a CA infrastructure:

For more information on securing Windows in general, see "Threats and Countermeasures: Security Settings in Windows Server 2003 and Windows XP," available at www.microsoft.com/technet/security/topics/hardsys/tcg/tcgch00.mspx.

Audit Account Logon Events   You would use the Audit Account Logon Events setting to log each instance of a user logging on to or off of a computer. The event will be logged into the security log of the computer that validates the account. For example, a domain controller would log the appropriate event for domain accounts, whereas logging on to a computer with a local account will log the appropriate event to the local security log. A local login will not log an account logoff event to the security log. You can set it to Success, Fail, or No Audit to log successful authentications and failed authentications or to not track them at all. You should set Audit Account Logon Events to Success for the domain. That way, if someone accesses the network through an existing user's account, you can track when it happened. You can also track failed logon attempts to determine if someone is trying to log on to your network. This is not usually recommended, though, because it can lead to a denial of service (DoS) attack, where the attacker just attempts to fill up your security logs with failed logon attempts. Most attackers will not keep trying to log on to the system but will use another means to get passwords.

Audit Account Management Events   The Audit Account Management Events setting will allow you to track when someone makes a change to an account. You can track when a user account or group is created, changed, or deleted; when a user account is renamed, disabled, or enabled; or when a password is set or changed. You can use this setting to verify that administrators are following company account policies, to detect if an administrator is trying to elevate permissions, or to detect if someone is trying to attack you by injecting a new account. You would want to set this to audit both successes and failures to log the changes made and attempts to make changes to accounts.

Audit Directory Service Access   The Audit Directory Service Access setting will allow you to track changes and access of directory service objects. You would then configure the directory service object's system access control list (SACL) to specify the auditing condition. You would need to change the setting on this to Success and Failure to be able to audit access to directory service objects.

Audit Object Access   The Audit Object Access setting will enable you to specify the audit settings for objects like files, folders, printers, CAs, and Registry settings. The Audit Object Access setting does not enable auditing of objects itself, but it must be set to Success and Failure to audit successful and failed events on each individual object. You need to specify the SACL for each object that you wish to audit to generate events specifically for access to this object. You should choose the specific settings that you want to track on each object. Specifically, for a CA, you will need to audit the following file paths to audit failed attempts to read or modify or successful modifications from any user:

Folder	When to Audit	User	Type of Access
C:\CertSrv	Success	Everyone	Modify
C:\CertLog	Success	Everyone	Modify
C:\Windows\system32\CertSrv	Success	Everyone	Modify
C:\Windows\system32\CertLog	Fail	Everyone	Full Control

You can also turn on auditing for the CA server after you have turned on object auditing.

Audit Policy Change   The Audit Policy Change setting will let you log changes to the user rights assignment policies, audit policies, or trust policies. This means that you will be able to track changes to the audit policy or track whether a user account is given a right like Login Locally. You should set this setting to Success only because the Failure setting does not provide useful information. You would want to specifically look at the user rights assignments around the management and operations of a certificate server. The following user rights could impact the security of the CA: Backup Files And Directories and Restore Files And Directories, which allows back up and restore of certificate stores; and Manage Auditing And Security Log, which allows you to configure and view security-related events.

Audit System Events   The Audit System Events setting controls the auditing of restart, shutdown, system time change, and other events that affect the system security log. You should set this to Success on the system to audit changes to the system. You would not need to enable Audit Process Tracking and Audit Privilege Use unless a business need justified it. The audit policy is only part of the overall security that you should plan for your CAs.

In the "Designing a Renewing and Revocation Strategy" Design Scenario, you will decide on an audit policy for an organization.

Securing for Certificate Authority Servers

Your CA server is vulnerable to attacks. You will need to harden it to prevent the risks to your authentication and encryption infrastructure if you choose to use a PKI solution. Hardening a CA server means looking at the additional services that are required. For example, you will have to install Internet Information Services (IIS) on your issuing CA servers. IIS is used to issue certificates to non-Windows clients, issue certificate revocation lists, and distribute certificate authority certificates. This means that you will need to harden IIS on these computers along with hardening the CA server.

You will learn about hardening IIS in Chapter 7, "Designing Security for Internet Information Services."

 Design Scenario

Designing a Renewing and Revocation Strategy

Trinity Importers, Ltd. needs to decide how long the certificate should last and what the renewal process should be. The CSO states that the information in the POS is important but not sensitive.

1.   **Question:** What should you suggest for a renewal strategy? **Answer:** You should recommend using a stronger key and renewing less frequently because the data is not sensitive. You would probably renew it two or three times before the key expires. The use of the stronger key should be enough to protect it. You should renew the key when the key expires.

Hardening your server will require the use of many of the security features included in Windows Server 2003. You will need to properly configure file system permissions on your CA, and you will need to pay attention to the administrative roles for the CAs. You will also need to secure well-known accounts on the CA servers, run only the services required on the server, and provide physical security for the server, and as we discussed earlier, you will need to audit the server.

You will want to pay attention to securing the root CA in your CA hierarchy. If the root CA is compromised, then all certificates issued by the root CA are compromised and will need to be revoked and renewed. Because the root CA is responsible for all certificates issued in your organization, this would mean a great deal of work. It is recommended that you install the root CA as a stand-alone CA that you keep physically secure and offline. You will need to bring it online only when you need to add a new CA server. This will minimize the chances for the root CA to be attacked.

Administrative access to a Windows Server 2003 CA server can be controlled through four roles:

- CA Administrator
- Certificate Manager
- Backup Operator
- Auditor

One person can assume all of these roles, but to minimize your exposure if one of these accounts is compromised, you should have different accounts associated with each role. The first two roles can be set using the Security tab of the CA server Properties dialog box, as shown in Figure 6.16. The third and fourth roles are granted through user rights that are set with the Group Policy MMC and are used to grant backup capabilities and rights to read and manage the audit logs.

FIGURE 6.16 The Security tab of a CA server Properties dialog box

The *CA Administrator* role is associated with the Manage CA permission on the CA server. This role will allow the account to configure the CA server, manage permissions, and renew CA certificates. The *Certificate Manager* role is associated with the Issue And Manage Certificates permission. This role will allow the account to initiate a key recovery, manage certificate enrollment, and revoke certificates.

You can also secure a CA server by limiting access to it. The Certificate Managers Restrictions tab of the CA Server Properties dialog box allows you to allow or deny groups and accounts that can manage certificates on the server, as shown in Figure 6.17. This is particularly useful to creating a CA hierarchy based on the organization.

Files on the file system are protected by using access control lists (ACLs) to prevent unauthorized access to the important files on your CA server. Encryption is a stronger form of protection for files that need to be used by only a single user. The NTFS file system provides for ACLs and encryption on a Windows Server 2003 server. The following table lists two paths that will need special attention when securing a CA server and the permissions required:

File path	Permissions
Systemroot\system32\CertLog	Administrators (Full Control), SYSTEM (Full Control)
Systemroot\system32\CertSrv	Administrators (Full Control), SYSTEM (Full Control), Users (Read, Execute, List Folder Contents)

FIGURE 6.17   The Certificate Managers Restrictions tab

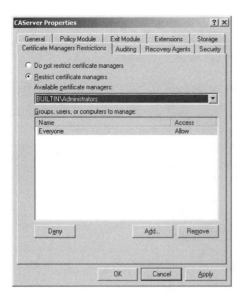

You will need to secure well-known accounts like Administrator and Guest, which cannot be deleted. You should rename these accounts to prevent unauthorized attempts to use them to log on. You would also leave the Guest account disabled. You should not allow anyone to log on as the built-in administrator account. You will then audit the logon access with the unique name given to this account. Many scripts use the Security ID (SID) of the built-in administrator account to attempt attacks on the server. You will also want to use a different password and name for the built-in administrator account on each server to prevent access to more than one server on your network to contain the damage of a broken password.

You should never configure the accounts used by the services to run under a domain security context, unless you must for reasons of authenticating with other services in the domain or if it is required by the service you are using. If an attacker is able to gain physical access to the server, the domain account can be compromised by a SAM password-breaking utility like L0phtcrack.

You should limit the services that are running on the server because it will limit the attack footprint of the server. You should install only the services necessary for the CA server by installing just the certificate services to the server and installing IIS only on the servers that support enrolling and distributing certificates.

You should provide physical security for the CA servers. Preferably, this security would be in a secure location that requires a key card to provide entry. You would also want to restrict access to the CD-RW drive and the floppy drive to those that are logged on locally so nobody can access the drives over the network. This is because sensitive information can be copied to a floppy or CD-RW (such as when backing up a private key used by the server), and if the box was infiltrated, the attacker might be able to read the information on the disk.

You will also want to change the default location for the CA installation. This will mean that the attacker cannot simply enter a well-known default path to the CA database or executables on your system. They would have to determine where the files are located, which would make the attack more difficult.

You should start by applying an appropriate security template through the Microsoft Server Baseline Policy (MSBP). Microsoft provides Legacy Client, Enterprise Client, and High Security Client templates. MSBP uses .inf file security templates to apply baseline security settings to the Windows Server 2003 roles. This is very useful tool to set up the auditing policy, event logging policy, group policies, and installed services.

You will learn more about this tool in Chapter 8, "Designing Security for Servers With Specific Roles."

In the "Designing Security for a CA" Design Scenario, you will design security for a CA server.

Design Scenario

Designing Security for a CA

Trinity Importers is worried about security for its root CA server. The company doesn't want to incur the cost of renewing all the certificates in the organization if the root CA server is compromised.

1. **Question:** What should be done to protect the root CA server? **Answer:** Trinity should install the root CA on a stand-alone CA server and lock it in a physically secure location, disconnected from the network. The server can be brought online whenever there is a need to sign a certificate with the root certificate or when it is time to renew the root CA certificate.

Summary

Certificates are used to identify users, computers, and services on the network. A certificate contains the public key and identifying information of the owner plus a digital signature of the certificate authority. There are three types of CAs: the root CA, policy CAs, and issuing CAs. Each of these CA roles can be installed on the same server or different servers. The root CA is the only CA that can assign and sign its own certificate. It is responsible for signing all other certificates in the PKI of the organization. The client trusts the signature of the root CA, which means that it trusts all the certificates issued by subordinate CAs. The policy CA is a subordinate CA that is responsible for approving or denying certificate requests. This can be automated or can be manually performed by a security administrator. The issuing CA is a subordinate CA that is responsible for issuing certificates to the client when the client enrolls or renews a certificate.

You need to decide who in your organization will have control over certificates that are being issued for users, computers, or applications. There may also be legal or company security policy issues that require certificates to be handled in differing fashions. You can choose from essentially four different designs for a certificate hierarchy: function, organization, department, or geography.

When you install a CA, you can decide to install it as a stand-alone CA or enterprise CA. The stand-alone CA does not integrate with Active Directory and therefore does not support integration with Group Policy to configure clients for certificates. A stand-alone server also does not use a certificate template, which means that the client will need to supply all the information necessary for a certificate. The enterprise CA is integrated with Active Directory and supports using Group Policy and certificate templates to deliver certificates to the clients. Stand-alone and enterprise CAs also differ in the means you can use to enroll and renew certificates.

You can enroll or renew certificates through a web interface, autoenrollment, the Certificate Request Wizard in the Certificates MMC, through the command line, or through script with `certreq.exe`. A stand-alone CA supports web-based enrollment only. The enterprise CA supports web-based enrollment, autoenrollment, and Certificate Request Wizard through `certreq.exe`. There are operating system limitations for using autoenrollment and the Certificate Request Wizard.

Autoenrollment is only supported on the Windows Server 2003 and Windows XP operating systems for user and computer certificates (you can autoenroll computer certificate in Windows 2000). After you issue a certificate, you may need to revoke it at a later date.

You can revoke a certificate that has been issued by your CA hierarchy. When you revoke a certificate, you publish it to the certificate revocation list (CRL). The CRL is a certificate that clients can request to find out if a certificate that they are presented with is valid. The CRL will notify users or applications if a certificate is no longer valid. You will need to make sure the clients can request the CRL, which means that if you have clients that will access certificates over the Internet, they will need to be able to communicate with at least one CA to obtain the CRL.

You will also need to secure your CA infrastructure so that you and your clients can trust certificates in your organization. You must keep your root CA secure because if it is compromised, all other certificates in the PKI of your organization will be compromised. You should install the root CA on a stand-alone CA and keep it offline, off the network, and in a secure location. You would use subordinate CAs to issue certificates to other CAs and clients. You will also need to protect the private keys that are generated for the certificates. You can protect the keys by using a cryptographic service provider (CSP). There are three types of CSPs: software CSPs, hardware CSPs, and smart cards. These will provide a mechanism to securely store private keys for private keys. The mechanism that you choose will affect the lifetime that you choose for the public/private key pair. Hardware CSPs tend to be more difficult to crack than a software CSP, so you can have longer key lifetimes. This is generally because the hardware CSP keeps the keys out of memory so they are not accessible in dump files or on the hard drive.

No matter how much security you provide, you can never assume that your security precautions will not be broken. You will need to set up auditing on the servers to detect changes on the server as well as who did what. Auditing will provide information that can be vital in a legal case against the cracker and in determining what resources have been compromised.

Exam Essentials

Know what types of applications require the use of a public key infrastructure.   You will need to utilize a PKI if you need to perform smart card logons, SSL, IPSec, EFS, S/MIME, or use any applications that require encryption or digital signatures.

Know the forms of enrollment that are available and when they are used.   There are several ways you can enroll for a certificate: web-based enrollment, the Certificate MMC, the command line with `certreq.exe`, and autoenrollment. Web-based enrollment is the most accessible form and can be used for enrollment at all times. The Certificates MMC's Automatic Certificate Request Setup wizard can be used from Windows 2000, Windows XP, and Windows Server 2003. The command line can be used to script certificate requests for automation. Autoenrollment is the easiest way to obtain and renew certificates in an organization that wants to have the least amount of administrative overhead if you are using Windows XP and Windows Server 2003 server.

Understand what the term two-factor authentication means.   A technology like smart cards consists of hardware devices that store private keys and certificates. The user would need to have a password or PIN to use the smart card. This is the first level of authentication. The second part will be the certificate on the smart card that validates the identity of the user.

Know the different types of CAs that you can install and what their role is in PKI.   The root CA is the server that issues the initial certificate in the hierarchy. All other certificates in the organization are signed by the root CA's certificate, so if you trust the root CA, you will trust all certificates in your infrastructure. The intermediate (or policy) CA is responsible for the procedures that are used to approve certificate requests. The issuing CA is the server the clients communicate with to enroll or renew a certificate.

Remember that there are two types of server roles for CAs in a Windows Server 2003 infrastructure: enterprise CA and stand-alone CA.   The enterprise CA is integrated with Active Directory and you can use Group Policy to issue certificates to clients. Windows XP and Windows Server 2003 use a Windows Server 2003 enterprise CA to support autoenrollment. This type of CA needs to be connected to the network. A stand-alone CA supports web-based enrollment only but can be removed from the network without causing problems. Stand-alone CAs do not use certificate templates, so the information must be provided during enrollment.

Know how to secure the server roles in a CA hierarchy.   You would want to install the root CA on a stand-alone CA that can be removed from the network and stored in a physically secure location. If the root CA is compromised, then all certificates in the PKI would be compromised. The intermediate CA is used to approve request for certificates. You would want to secure this server because an attacker could generate certificates if it was infiltrated. The issuing CA server is the only server that should be exposed to the Internet or the clients.

Remember that you can create a CA hierarchy based on function, organization, departments, and geography.   A CA hierarchy based on function will create subordinate CAs for each type of application that the PKI supports, like S/MIME, IPSec, and EFS. A CA hierarchy based on organization will divide certificate servers among the classifications of personnel in the organization, like employee, contractor, and partner. A CA hierarchy based on departments will create CAs for each department, like accounting, marketing, and engineering. This will work well if the administration of the organization is decentralized but still maintains a centralized PKI. It can also be used if departments have differing requirements for issuing certificates. A CA hierarchy based on geography would give personnel in regions or countries control over the appropriate subordinate CAs; this kind of CA hierarchy is generally used to meet the legal requirements of the countries involved on certificates and encryption, but it can also be used to provide availability. While each of these designs usually include issuing CAs, they can also include policy CAs if you need to control granting the certificate request for any of the design strategies.

Key Terms

Before you take the exam, be certain you are familiar with the following terms:

CA Administrator	geographic CA hierarchy
Certificate Manager	organizational CA hierarchy
certificate templates	public key encryption (PKE)
cross-certification	Secure Sockets Layer (SSL)
department CA hierarchy	smart cards
enrollment strategy	stand-alone CA
enterprise CA	X.509 digital certificates
function CA hierarchy	

Review Questions

1. What is a X.509 digital certificate?

   A. An entity that list the policies that are used for security on the network

   B. An electronic document that contains information about the owner of the certificate and the public key of the owner and the signature of the certificate authority

   C. A means of updating Active Directory with user information

   D. A way to provide information to the server about the security mechanism needed to establish the connection

2. Which of the following applications would require that a PKI architecture be in place? (Choose all the apply.)

   A. Smart card logon

   B. Encrypting File System

   C. File sharing

   D. IP security

   E. E-mail

   F. Secure e-mail

3. What are the four possible ways of designing a CA hierarchy?

   A. Organization

   B. Groups

   C. Geography

   D. Function

   E. Department

   F. Users

4. Which of the following ways can you use to enroll for a certificate with a stand-alone CA?

   A. Web enrollment page

   B. Autoenrollment

   C. `certreq.exe`

   D. Certificate Request Wizard

5. Which operating systems can be used to perform autoenrollment with an enterprise CA? (Choose all that apply.)

   A. Windows XP

   B. Windows ME

   C. Windows Server 2003

   D. Windows 2000

6. What are the three possible roles for a CA in the organization?

   A. Root CA

   B. Intermediate CA

   C. Enrollment CA

   D. Issuing CA

   E. Renewal CA

7. What auditing setting must be enabled to allow CA-specific auditing through the Certification Authority console?

   A. Audit Account Login Events

   B. Audit Object Access

   C. Audit System Events

   D. Audit Process Tracking

8. Which of the following reasons would you use in choosing to revoke a certificate? (Choose all that apply.)

   A. The CA has been compromised.

   B. The certificate has been renewed.

   C. The CA certificate has been renewed.

   D. The private key was stolen.

   E. The certificate was used for signing.

   F. The certificate authority has been retired.

9. What are the four roles that perform administrative tasks on a Windows Server 2003 CA server?

   A. PKI Manager

   B. Certificate Manager

   C. PKI Administrator

   D. Auditor

   E. Administrator

   F. Backup Operator

   G. CA Administrator

10. Why should you perform role separation on a CA server?

   A. To separate the types of CA servers so that renewal and enrollment take place on different servers

   B. To minimize damage done to the certificate hierarchy should an attacker infiltrate the administrator account

   C. To split the roles of the server for renewal and enrollment of certificates

   D. To provide a mechanism to increase the availability of the PKI structure

Answers to Review Questions

1. B. A certificate contains fields that identify the subject (owner of the certificate) and the subject's public key. The certificate is then signed by a certificate authority that verified the information so all clients that trust the CA can trust the information in the certificate.

2. A, B, D, F. You would need to use certificates in applications that require authentication of the user, a digital signature, or encryption without the exchange of keys through some other means. Smart card logon verifies the identity of the user through a certificate and a PIN or password, referred to as two-factor authentication. EFS requires a certificate to verify the owner of a file and the encrypting keys. IP security requires encryption and the validation of the client and the server, which will require a certificate. Secure e-mail supports digital signatures and encrypted e-mail requires PKI.

3. A, C, D, E. Depending on the management or legal needs of the organization, you will need to design a CA hierarchy based on the organization (employee, contractors, partner), geography (USA, France, Asia), function (S/MIME, EFS, smart card), or department (Marketing, Finance, Accounting).

4. A. You would use a web enrollment page to request, renew, and manage certificates that are used in the organization.

5. A, C. Windows XP and Windows Server 2003 are the only two operating systems that support autoenrollment for certificates with a Windows Server 2003 enterprise CA server.

6. A, B, D. You can have three different roles for a CA in an organization: root, intermediate, and issuing. The root CA is responsible for signing all certificates issued in the PKI and is the most trusted CA. The intermediate CA is used to approve requests for enrollment and renewal of certificates. The issuing CA is responsible for issuing or deploying the certificate and CRL to the clients.

7. B. You would need to enable Success and Failure on the Audit Object Access setting to make it possible to audit file, Registry, or CA auditing. You then would set the audit property on the item you would like to audit.

8. A, D, F. You would need to issue new certificates if the CA or private key was compromised. If you retire the CA, you will need to revoke the old certificate and issue the new CA's certificate.

9. B, D, F, G. The CA Administrator can configure the CA server, manage permissions, and renew CA certificates. The Certificate Manager role can initiate a key recovery, manage certificate enrollment, and revoke certificates. The Backup Operator can back up and restore the CA databases. The Auditor can read the security log and configure auditing.

10. B. You distribute the administrative function of the CA servers among four different roles. This will minimize damage done to the CA hierarchy if one of the administrator accounts were infiltrated.

Case Study

You should give yourself 20 minutes to review this testlet and complete the questions.

Overview

Get Results Marketing is a global advertising and market research company based out of New York.

Physical Locations

The company has locations in Hong Kong, London, and New York. There are approximately 1,200 employees in New York, 400 in London, and 150 in Hong Kong. The IT staff is based out of the New York location.

Planned Changes

The company plans to upgrade all clients to Windows XP. It also plans to implement a wireless network and add smart card security to the network.

Infrastructure

Get Results Marketing has Active Directory installed and uses Exchange 2003 for e-mail. The company has upgraded its domain servers to Windows Server 2003.

Interviews

CIO   We plan to implement wireless networking at all three locations. We also suspect that some information about our accounts has been leaking to our competitors, so we want to install a two-factor authentication system.

We also need to come up with an audit plan for the servers.

Network Administrator   I am concerned about the security breaches. The network is not well organized and policies are not applied consistently across servers on the network, so I am unable to effectively track the problem.

CSO   We need to implement a PKI to issue digital certificates for two-factor and wireless authentication. The root CA must be secured. Additionally, we need dedicated servers to issue the required digital certificates. These certificates must be deployed by using the minimum amount of administrative effort. We are worried about legal requirements for certificates in some of the countries we operating in.

Security Policy

The company's security policy contains the following requirements:

- Accounts data must be accessed through the SQL Server 2000 database and shared folders on a file server. All access to account data should use certificate-based authentication.

- E-mail sent to partner companies must be signed.

- E-mail that is sent to partner companies and contains information that has been flagged as sensitive must be encrypted.

- Employees will not be allowed to use the wireless infrastructure until there is an appropriate infrastructure to validate them. This infrastructure should support certificate-based authentication.

Case Study Questions

1. You need to design a certificate solution for the internal users of Get Results Marketing. What should you do?

   A. Establish a website that users will use to request certificates.

   B. Give users Enrollment Agent rights on the system.

   C. Write a login script that determines the user and requests the appropriate certificate from the web server.

   D. Install some enrollment stations in the company and store client certificates on smart cards.

2. What type of technology should you recommend for securing and signing e-mail?

   A. SSL

   B. TLS

   C. S/MIME

   D. IPSec

3. You need to design an auditing policy for the PKI. What should you recommend for Get Results Marketing? Choose all that apply.

   A. Enable all of the settings for auditing on a CA.

   B. Enable object access auditing to track PKI server access.

   C. Enable success/failed login attempts.

   D. Enable file access auditing to track access to certificate files.

4. What type of PKI should you recommend for the issuing servers?

   A. Stand-alone

   B. Active Directory integrated

   C. SQL Server integrated

   D. Third party

5. What type of hierarchy should you recommend for Get Results Marketing?

   A. Functional

   B. Geographical

   C. Departmental

   D. Organizational

6. Where would you place the different types of servers in the organization? Drag and drop the proper server type to the proper location of the organization. Answers may be used more than once.

Location	Server type
Hong Kong	root CA
New York	intermediate CA
London	issuing CA

Answers to Case Study Questions

1. D. The company wants to implement two-factor authentication for increased security, which would involve using smart cards and a password or PIN to gain access to the system. You would need to create some enrollment stations for enabling a smart card for a user and distribute the smart card to the users. The administrators issuing the smart card certificates on behalf of users would need Enrollment Agent rights, but you would not need to issue these rights to users. The web server and login scripts do not provide for two-factor authentication but could be a means to issue certificates to computers or users without using smart cards.

2. C. S/MIME is a web standard technology that is used to sign and encrypt e-mail messages. It requires a PKI to manage the certificates that are necessary for the technology. Because Get Results Marketing will have a PKI, this would be the recommended approach. SSL, TLS, and IPSec are used to encrypt network traffic and verify computers. They are not appropriate for verifying individuals or encrypting individual messages and not others.

3. A, B, C. The network administrator expressed concerns about not being able to track information and various occurrences on the network. You will need to focus on the CA infrastructure and authentication on the network. You should plan to size the log file to accommodate the increased volume of logging.

4. B. Because the clients are Windows XP based, the company would benefit from an Active Directory–integrated issuing server because it can automatically issue machine certificates to computers based on domain credentials. This would minimize the effort of the network administrators in managing machine certificates.

5. B. Since the CSO states that they are worried about legal requirements for certificates and encryption in countries they operate, you should implement a hierarchy based on geography. This would give the individual regions control over the local CA servers, to make sure they comply with local laws. The organizational, departmental, and functional hierarchies would be more difficult to lay out in such a way to follow local laws because they focus on group servers by other requirements like a department or function in the organization.

6.

Hong Kong
intermediate CA
issuing CA
New York
root CA
intermediate CA
issuing CA
London
intermediate CA
issuing CA

You would want to keep the root secure at the company headquarters where the IT staff is based. You would then need to provide issuing and intermediate CAs to each geographical region the country is in to provide local control over how and what certificates are issued and renewed to comply with local laws.

Chapter 7

Designing Security for Internet Information Services

MICROSOFT EXAM OBJECTIVES COVERED IN THIS CHAPTER:

✓ **Design user authentication for Internet Information Services (IIS).**

- Design user authentication for a Web site by using certificates.
- Design user authentication for a Web site by using IIS authentication.
- Design user authentication for a Web site by using RADIUS for IIS authentication.

✓ **Design security for Internet Information Services (IIS).**

- Design security for Web sites that have different technical requirements by enabling only the minimum required services.
- Design a monitoring strategy for IIS.
- Design an IIS baseline that is based on business requirements.
- Design a content management strategy for updating an IIS server.

✓ **Design security for servers that have specific roles. Roles include domain controller, network infrastructure server, file server, IIS server, terminal server, and POP3 mail server.**

- Define a baseline security template for all systems.
- Create a plan to modify baseline security templates according to role.

Internet Information Server (IIS) is a group of services that host web communications. This includes the World Wide Web Publishing Service that uses the HyperText Transfer Protocol (HTTP), File Transfer Protocol (FTP), Simple Mail Transfer Protocol (SMTP), and Network News Transfer Protocol (NNTP), all of which allow you to communicate with clients or other servers that support these protocols. These services support many of the functions that we use daily to retrieve and send information through the Internet. Because these services are generally connected to the Internet or host important applications for businesses, they are the target of many types of attacks. These attacks include denial of service (DoS) attacks, defacement of websites, and the use of viruses and worms designed to take advantage of programming or administration mistakes in IIS. You should make sure you focus on IIS when designing security. In the following chapter we will look at securing IIS. We will explore the strategies used in creating security and monitoring policies for IIS. We will also discuss the authentication options when connecting to IIS. Finally, we will look at techniques that can be used when designing for a content management and update.

Securing domain controllers, network infrastructure servers, file servers, and POP3 mail servers is covered in Chapter 8, "Designing Security for Servers That Have Specific Roles." Securing Terminal Server is covered in Chapter 10, "Designing Secure Network Management Infrastructure."

Designing Security for Internet Information Server

When designing security, you will begin by finding out the business and security requirements with respect to the use of the Web by a company and its applications. You will use the information to determine the baseline of services, permissions, and applications to install on the various IIS servers in the organization. You will then decide what the minimum services required for each website hosted on the IIS server are and prohibit the services not required.

Designing an IIS Baseline Based on Business Requirements

Many organizations use the Internet to generate cost savings by expanding their applications to include partners or to make it easier for employees to work. They can see these cost savings wiped out by a security incident or two. Therefore, you will need to analyze your organization's business, application, and security requirements carefully. You will then need to establish a baseline for security.

Requirements can usually be determined by asking a series of questions. The following list includes some examples of the types of questions you should ask:

What is the organization's tolerance for lost data?   You will need to determine how much data the business can afford to lose versus the cost of backing up the data. You can obtain systems that do real-time backup if you cannot afford to lose any data, but these systems come at a cost. Some organizations may determine that their nightly backups are just fine and they can recreate the day's information in case of a loss at a cheaper cost, or that taking out an insurance policy would be cheaper.

How important is it that the data is kept private when it is sent across a WAN link?   You will need to discuss with the business whether the data contains sensitive or secret information. If this is the case, you will need to consider the network connection's vulnerability, which you can use to determine if you need encryption and the strength of encryption required.

What are the requirements for controlling access to the data?   You will need to consider what groups of users or applications should have access to the data and then what types of permissions they need. You will want to give them the minimum permissions required to accomplish the tasks for which they will use the data.

Are there groups of employees that require different levels of access to a website?   You will want to create groups for these employees and use either different virtual directories or URL authentication to control access to parts of the web application. You can secure virtual directories with NTFS permissions or through the web.config <authorization> section for ASP.NET applications.

What means will users use to update the content?   You will need to determine the requirements that the organization has for updating content on a website. This will require determining the security, application, and ease of use preferences that are in the organization.

What level of auditing will be required?   There are many things that could go wrong in relation to security. For example, someone can exploit a bug in your web server software or web application, or one of your server administrators could be stealing information and selling it to your competitors. You can determine whether or not a break-in occurred and what action was taken by using auditing.

Will the server be able to see the Windows domain controller or will another server be used for authentication?   You will need to analyze the network architecture to determine if the web server will be able to communicate with the domain if you need to authenticate users with your organization's domain. If you determine that this is not possible, then you will need to configure a solution that uses Remote Access Dial-in User Service (RADIUS), a separate domain, or the local Security Accounts Manager (SAM) database that redirects or contains only the accounts that need to authenticate against the web server.

Will the IIS server be located on the network, and if so, where?   You can place the IIS server in the perimeter network, internally, externally, or you can outsource hosting and not even install the server on your network. You will need to determine where it is located and take the proper security precautions to protect the server.

What services are required by the applications that the business runs? You will need to analyze the applications that the business runs and determine the minimum amount of services required on a given server to support the applications. This will minimize the number of services that can be attacked on the server.

Is the risk of enabling the service outweighed by the value of the application to the business? You will also need to look at the services that an application requires and determine if the risk associated with enabling the service outweighs the convenience, cost savings, or features of using the application.

What is the means to protect the server from viruses? You will need to install adequate virus protection on your servers to help guard against viruses, worms, or Trojans that may be uploaded to your servers.

How will software updates be installed? You can use a manual/custom mechanism or Microsoft's Software Update Service (SUS) to make sure that the services, applications, and operating systems that you are using are kept up-to-date to guard against vulnerabilities due to bugs in the software. You will learn more about keeping servers patched and up-to-date in Chapter 9, "Designing an Infrastructure for Updating Computers."

These are a few of the questions you should ask when evaluating the business and security requirements for IIS. After you have gathered requirements, you will generate a baseline for the IIS servers that are installed or will be installed in the organization. You will need to consider the following:

Set suitable access control lists (ACLs) on Web content. You should consider the minimum permissions with regard to content. You will need to pay attention to permissions on log files to prevent alteration or revealing too much information. If you enable Write permissions, you should enable disk quotas to prevent too much space from being used if there is a problem. You will need to make sure the scripts and executables have the necessary Execute permissions. You can make managing security on your web server easier by creating directories for common content and setting permissions on the directories. You should also define groups based on the roles or groupings that represent the various tasks that people need to do on the website. For example, if managers need access to content that regular users can't access, you would have a managers group and a users group. You would then apply the permissions to the groups.

Install only components that are being used by the IIS server. Software that is installed but not used is usually not maintained or set up properly. This makes it a great target for attacks. Having extra services running also increases the odds that you will be attacked through a bug in one of the components. Also, an attack can be difficult to track down because generally you are not logging information properly.

Enable only the services being used by a website. An IIS server may host more than one website. Some websites may require Web Distributed Authoring and Versioning (WebDAV), Active Server Pages (ASP), or common gateway interface (CGI) scripts to run, while others will not. You can disable application extensions on an individual website basis through the *Web Service Extensions* section of the IIS Manager. You should make sure only the extensions required by the website are enabled.

Evaluate the rights of accounts used by IIS and applications.   IIS uses many accounts to run applications, log on anonymous users, and run its own services. You will need to evaluate what permissions the following accounts have:

IUSR_*ComputerName*   This is the default account used by everyone with anonymous access to the server. Scrutinize the permissions on this account closely.

Network Service   This is a new account that was created for Windows Server 2003 to allow the services of IIS and other services to run under an account with the minimum rights granted. This allows you to avoid using the Local System account, which has administrative rights to the server.

ASPNET   ASP.NET applications run under the context of this account.

IWAM_*ComputerName*   This account is used by ASP and Internet Service API (ISAPI) applications that are running in isolated processes. You will need to evaluate this account if you are running in IIS 5 Isolation mode to support legacy applications that don't function properly under IIS 6.

You will also need to pay attention to accounts used to access services like databases and directories on the network. In addition, you should make sure that your services are not running in the security context of a domain account; if they are, it will be easier to obtain domain account passwords if the server is physically compromised. Make sure all accounts that are used have the minimum amount of rights and permissions necessary. It is usually easier to use Group Policy objects (GPOs) to apply the permissions consistently and repeatedly.

Use secure communication mechanisms where appropriate.   Determine what connections are vulnerable to eavesdropping and use appropriate encryption mechanisms over the connection. The most common mechanism for HTTP applications is Secure Sockets Layer (SSL). You should choose transport layer IP Security (IPSec) for encryption of protocols like FTP and NNTP. You can choose to use Transport Layer Security (TLS), which works like Secure Sockets Layer (SLL), to establish an encrypted SMTP session.

Decide what protocols you need and filter anything else.   You will need to evaluate the protocols you are using on the server. This means not only evaluating the application's protocols (like HTTP and SMTP), but also looking at the protocols used to manage the application and to update the content of the application. You will then apply TCP\IP packet filtering or, for more security, IPSec filters to deny access to the server for protocols that are not used. Filtering on the server should not take the place of a good firewall; it is an added precaution. You never know when something will be configured improperly or a bug will be discovered.

You should use IPSec filters to enhance the level of security on your vulnerable IIS servers, like those serving content to the Internet. In its *Windows Server 2003 Security Guide,* Microsoft recommends that you apply the following IPSec filters:

Service	Protocol	Source Port	Destination Port	Source Address	Destination Address	Action	Mirror
Terminal Services	TCP	Any	3389	Any	Me (localhost)	Allow	Yes
Domain Member	Any	Any	Any	ME	Domain Controller	Allow	Yes

Service	Protocol	Source Port	Destination Port	Source Address	Destination Address	Action	Mirror
HTTP Server	TCP	Any	80	Any	Me	Allow	Yes
HTTPS Server	TCP	Any	443	Any	Me	Allow	Yes
All Inbound Traffic	Any	Any	Any	Any	Me	Block	Yes

These settings act as a basic starting point for an IIS server hosting web pages. Depending on your administration requirements, application requirements, and content update strategy, you may need to apply additional filters. You may also want to tighten up the communication to domain controllers in this recommendation by only opening the appropriate ports for Active Directory, RPC, DNS, and other protocols running on the server.

Remove any samples or demonstration applications.   The sample applications are meant to show a developer how to solve some particular problem or use a certain technology. As a result, they are generally not secure and can be the source of attacks that are relatively easy to make on your infrastructure. They should be removed from production servers.

Enable logging on the server.   Logging is how you track what is happening on the server. You will be able to use logging information to report trends about usage and performance. It can also be used after a security incident to determine the damage done to the server or as evidence to prosecute the attacker. IIS supports protocol logging, HTTP.sys logging, Windows auditing, and monitoring with System Monitor.

Install and configure UrlScan.   You can install UrlScan 2.5 on a Windows Server 2003 service with IIS 6 installed. *UrlScan* is an ISAPI filter that screens and analyzes URLs and requests before IIS has a chance to process them. IIS 6 incorporates features that make UrlScan less necessary than with previous versions of IIS. You still need UrlScan if you want to do the following:

- Filter URLs based on their length
- Filter HTTP commands, which are called verbs (GET, POST, PUT, SEARCH, BPROP to name a few)
- Remove the server header to conceal the identity and version of the web server and operating system.

You can download UrlScan 2.5 from Microsoft's web site. They move it around from time to time so it is easiest just to search for UrlScan 2.5. Alternatively, you can install it from the Windows Security Update DVD in TechNet. Once installed, UrlScan will create a directory called `urlscan` that will include the `urlscan.ini` file with the settings of what you want to filter and what you want to allow. It will also contain the log files for UrlScan, which will have information about what was blocked by UrlScan and why it was blocked. You can use these log files to troubleshoot applications that are having trouble connecting to the server.

Install and configure Authorization Manager.   Managing permissions for applications at a granular level through New Technology Filesystem (NTFS) can be tedious and difficult. IIS 6 introduces the ability to provide authorization to URLs. This means that you can assign a group or user access to applications, or parts of applications, and not have to worry about the NTFS permissions. You can use *Authorization Manager* to provide for this role-based access control. You will be able to control access to your web application through URLs, instead of relying on NTFS permissions.

Create a plan to keep the server up-to-date.   Keeping up with security updates on a server with IIS is very important. You can use the automatic update service to directly connect to Microsoft and update the server, or if you need more control, you can install Software Update Service. Just make sure you have a plan to keep up with the critical security updates. For example, the patch for the Code Red worm came out a month before the worm struck, yet the worm was able to infect an estimated 250,000 servers.

See Chapter 9, "Designing an Infrastructure for Updating Computers," for more information.

Create a plan to back up all of the server content.   The successful implementation of a backup plan can help you recover the server quickly in the case of a security breach, like a website deface-ment. You will need to consider a plan for backing up the log files on a regular basis and determine how much information you will need to keep.

See Chapter 1, "Analyzing Security Policy, Procedures, and Requirements," for more information.

Create a plan for updating content on the server.   You will need to decide how new content will get moved to the server. Moving content can introduce security issues if it is not carefully considered. You should understand what protocols are available and what the network infra-structure will allow. We will discuss this in more detail later in the chapter in the section titled "Designing a Content Update and Management Strategy."

You must make sure that the IIS baseline does not have conflicting settings. For example, suppose you install UrlScan 2.5 and design rules to filter URLs that do not meet your applica-tion or business needs. You carefully analyze the applications used by the business and deter-mine a safe URL length. You also decide that FrontPage Server Extensions are dangerous and filter URLs that contain the letters *vti*, which are in URLs that are used by FrontPage Sever Extensions. If the business has decided to use Microsoft Visual InterDev to update its website based on ASP, then you will have broken its publishing mechanism. In this case, the security and business requirements may conflict. If the security requirements conflict with the business requirements, you will need to determine which is more important, typically by considering the potential costs of changing them. For example, you would compare the cost of upgrading soft-ware and training users with the cost of a potential security breakdown. This could be an easy decision if there was already a plan to update the tools or technology, say to Visual Studio .NET with ASP.NET, in which case you can make sure the tools support features that will work with your security plan.

You should take advantage of tools that Microsoft provides to aid in enforcing and verifying your baseline. You can use the Group Policy File System node to create a policy for the permissions you decide are appropriate for your website. The policies will be applied to the IIS servers. You can use the Microsoft Baseline Security Checker to verify that you are up-to-date with your patches on the server. You can use UrlScan to guard against attacks that use a URL by filtering based on the length and content of the URL. Just make sure that, if your business requirements change, you look at the implementation in your tools to determine if you need to change them.

In the Design Scenario "Designing a Baseline Based on Business Requirements," you will use the business requirements to determine the security baseline for an IIS server.

 Design Scenario

Designing a Baseline Based on Business Requirements

Background

Wonder, Inc. is a company that manufactures and sells electronics and electronic parts. Its corporate headquarters is located in Denver, Colorado. The company has retail outlets in many cities through the U.S. It also sells components to other companies. It either sells stock components or works with a company to manufacture and provide the component. Wonder, Inc. has a sales staff that handles this work. In addition, each of the retail stores sell stock electronic components to the public.

Interviews

Chief Information Officer   All content sent between the field and corporate is done over network connections that are not secure. This content can contain sensitive information, like sales projections or pricing formulas, and should be protected. We also need to track individual access to the applications.

Direct Sales Manager   We need to have access to portions of the sales and customer management application in the field. These applications are web applications that use the user's network logon to authenticate them.

VP Retail Sales   We need access to information about inventories in our store and other stores to locate parts a customer may request. We only need access to POS information for the store itself.

1. **Question:** What are the business requirements for the web server? **Answer:** You would need to authenticate users of the website to meet the requirements that they need to track access to applications and have access to the sales and customer management application. You would then be able to authorize users to have access only to the content or applications they are allowed to use. You would also need to enable logging on the server to meet the CIO's requirement to track individual access to the applications. You will also encrypt the communication over the WAN links to protect sensitive information.

Designing for Minimum Required Services for Websites

One of the reasons many servers are infiltrated is that they have services running that they do not require. These services may have been installed when they were needed or simply because someone was afraid that something would break if the service was not installed. Therefore, when you are designing for a secure IIS implementation, you should consider what services you will require on your website. You will need to decide what services and web server extensions (ISAPI applications or filters) must be installed or which ones will be allowed on the server.

For example, if have made a business decision to support the web portion of a line-of-business application written with Active Server Pages (ASPs), you will need to install and start the World Wide Web Service on the server and enable ASP to run on the server.

You can decide what services to include by analyzing the security baseline generated by your business requirements. You will first need to make sure that the minimum services are installed on Windows Server 2003. Then you can decide what services you will install for IIS. Finally, determine the minimum Web Service Extensions that your website will require.

Real World Scenario

Code Red Worm

The Code Red worm was the first big worm to attack IIS and has inspired many derivatives, such as the Nimda worm and Code Red 2. This virus took advantage of a buffer overflow error in the Index Server service. A buffer overflow attack attempts to exploit a program that does not validate a text value, like a URL, for length and allows a larger value to be placed in memory than the amount of space allocated. For example, the Code Red virus uses the following URL to exploit IIS:

```
/default.ida?NNNNNNNNNNNNNNNNNNNNNNNNNNNNNNNNNNNNNNNNNNNNNNNNNNNNNNNNNNNNNNNNN
NNNNNNNNNNNNNNNNNNNNNNNNNNNNNNNNNNNNNNNNNNNNNNNNNNNNNNNNNNNNNNNNNNNNNNNNNNNNNNNN
NNNNNNNNNNNNNNNNNNNNNNNNNNNNNNNNNNNNNNNNNNNNNNNNNNNNNNNNNNNNNNNNNNNNNNNNNNNN%u9
090%u6858%ucbd3%u7801%u9090%u6858%ucbd3%u7801%u9090%u6858%ucbd3%u7801%u9090%u909
0%u8190%u00c3%u0003%u8b00%u531b%u53ff%u0078%u0000%u00=a
```

The N in the URL is taking up space to overflow the string buffer (an array of characters with a finite length), and the %u represents binary commands that the sender wants to execute. Subsequently, the program will not allocate enough space in memory to store a text value, which means that the additional information will "break the stack" and insert the value starting at the %u9090 as the next command on the stack to execute. This value represents code that will run with the permissions of the service running the code (administrator equivalent).

As a result of the buffer overflow, the sender of the Code Red worm is allowed to execute arbitrary code with the Local System Account privileges. This is dangerous because it means that the attacker has complete control over the infiltrated system. If you have IIS 4 or IIS 5 servers that have Index Server installed they will be affected by this vulnerability unless they are patched. The Code Red exploit can occur even if the indexing server service is installed but stopped or disabled. You will need to make sure that you do not have the indexing service installed.

This is an example of why you need to make sure that you install only the products you are using. If you don't need it, don't install it. You can also avoid the Code Red worm by keeping your server up-to-date with security patches, which would be appropriate if you depend on index server. You can also help prevent worm type attacks by configuring IIS to only respond through host headers since most worms use the IP address of the IIS server, and not the host name.

Designing for Minimum Services on Windows Server 2003

When you're using IIS 6, your website is hosted on a Windows Server 2003 server. You will need to determine what services you will allow to be installed on the server to minimize security risks on your network. When you first install Windows Server 2003, there are services installed that you will not want on your IIS server in many situations. The services installed by default that you might consider disabling are listed in Table 7.1.

TABLE 7.1   List of Services Installed by Default on Windows Server 2003

Service Name	Description
Application Layer Gateway Service	This service allows third-party vendors to write plug-ins for Internet Connection Sharing (ICS)\Internet Connection Firewall (ICF) that support their protocols. Disabling this service will prevent the server from running ICS or ICF. Generally, these services are provided more securely through a dedicated firewall.
Application Management	This service is used in conjunction with Software Policies on a GPO to assign, publish, enumerate, and remove programs. Most environments do not use this on their servers and therefore it is not needed.
COM+ System Application	This service is responsible for tracking and configuring COM+ applications that are installed on the server. Many servers do not host COM+ applications, so this service can be disabled.
Distributed File System	This service creates a logical namespace that will integrate your file-sharing resources. It is not needed on IIS servers in general unless you use it to replicate your site content.

TABLE 7.1 List of Services Installed by Default on Windows Server 2003 *(continued)*

Service Name	Description
Distributed Link Tracking Client	This service acts as the client to Distributed Link Tracking service and will disseminate information about shortcuts and respond to change events from the server.
Distributed Link Track Server	This service will track files on an NTFS partition across a network or on a local computer and will automatically update shortcuts when the file is renamed or moved.
Distributed Transaction Coordinator	This service coordinates operations that occur between multiple computers on the network to make sure they were all successful or all unsuccessful. It is used against databases, message queues, and file systems. You will need to verify that the applications on the server are executing distributed transactions. Most servers are not.
Error Reporting Service	This service collects and reports errors in running applications to Microsoft, which is then used to improve the product. It is not needed on a production server.
File Replication	This service allows files to be automatically copied to other servers on the network. This is very useful on domain controllers, but may have limited use on an IIS server unless you are using DFS for replication.
Help and Support	This service allows the Help and Support application to run on the server. You generally will not need to use it on the server.
Logical Disk Manager	This service integrates with the Plug and Play events for new drives being added and sends the information about the new drive to the Logical Disk Manager Administrative Service. You generally don't dynamically add drives to your server, so it can be disabled.
Print Spooler	This service manages and prints to local and network print queues. You will not need to print from a server, so it can be disabled.
Remote Access Auto Connection Manager	This service will attempt to discover an unsuccessful authentication attempt to the remote access service and will automatically provide another means to connect if available. For example, if a program tries, but fails to connect to a remote network, this service will offer to try a dial-up connection if it is configured.

TABLE 7.1 List of Services Installed by Default on Windows Server 2003 *(continued)*

Service Name	Description
Remote Access Connection Manager	This service manages dial-up and VPN connections from the server to the remote network.
Remote Desktop Help Session Manager	This service launches and manages the Remote Assistance feature of the Help and Support application. This is needed only on client computers.
Remote Procedure Call (RPC) Locator	This service enables RPC clients to automatically locate RPC services using the RPC name service database. This is not required for RPC connectivity.
Removable Storage	This service identifies and catalogs removable media. It is used by Windows Backup, so don't disable it if you are using Windows Backup.
Secondary Logon	This service allows a user to launch a process with different security credentials than the user's current security context. This is usually used to launch administrative tools from a restricted account. This is generally not beneficial on a server because you are usually required to be an administrator or operator to log on to the server locally and there is potential for abuse.
Shell Hardware Detection	This service will perform the autoplay function on CD and DVD media.
Smart Card	This service reads smart cards. It is not needed if you do not have a smart card reader attached to your computer.
Special Administration Console Helper	This service allows you to remotely manage a server through an out-of-band method like a serial port. This is needed only if you have headless operation configured.
Task Scheduler	This service enables you to schedule executables to run based on time or CPU usage. It must be started if you are using Windows Backup to schedule backups of your server.
Telephony	This service provides a means to control telephony and voice over IP connections. It is generally not needed on an IIS server.

TABLE 7.1   List of Services Installed by Default on Windows Server 2003 *(continued)*

Service Name	Description
Upload Manager	This service is used to upload drive data to Microsoft, where it is used to help users find the proper device drivers for their computers. This is a synchronous or asynchronous file transfer service.
WinHTTP Web Proxy Auto-Discovery Service	This service uses the Web Proxy Auto-Discovery (WPAD) protocol to find and configure the web browser's proxy configuration.
Wireless Configuration	This service automatically configures IEEE 802.11 wireless adapters to connect to a wireless network.

You may decide that you need to use some of these services to satisfy business requirements. The services in Table 7.1 are just suggestions for a minimum set of services on most installed IIS servers.

In addition, the NTLM Security Support Provider is not installed by default, and you may need to install and enable it if you want to allow clients to authenticate with the NTLM protocol. Otherwise, the server supports only Kerberos v5 authentication. You will also need to make sure the HTTP SSL, IIS Admin, and World Wide Web Publishing services are enabled to host a web server. If you need to add additional services to the server, you can do this manually through the Add Or Remove Programs Control Panel applet or you can use the Configure Your Server Wizard or the Manage Your Server administration tool.

Remember that any service, application, or executable is a potential point of attack. You need to make sure that you take precautions to remove unused services, applications, or executables. If you cannot remove them, then you will need to figure out a way to disable them. This will greatly limit the attack footprint of your server.

Many security policies will not allow IIS to be installed with other services because of the security risks that IIS poses to the other services due to the many documented vulnerabilities. For example, the security policy might state that IIS is not to be installed on a domain controller because this will pose security risks to the domain accounts that are contained on the domain controller instead of just to the local accounts database on the IIS server itself.

Designing for Minimum Service on IIS

After an analysis of the services allowed on the Windows Server 2003 machine, you will need to determine what IIS services to install. By default, IIS is not installed on a Windows Server 2003 computer, so you will need to install it. During the installation you will have the option of installing many different services. Consult your baseline to determine the minimum services that you should install. You can install or uninstall services for IIS through the Windows Components Wizard's Internet Information Services dialog box, as shown in Figure 7.1.

FIGURE 7.1   Selecting the IIS services to install through Windows Component Wizard's Internet Information Services (IIS) dialog box

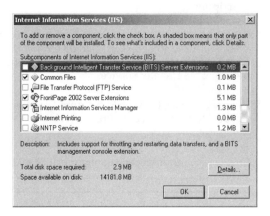

You can also use the Application Server dialog box through the Control Panel's Add and Remove Program and the Add\Remove Windows Components to install or uninstall the components of IIS that you require.

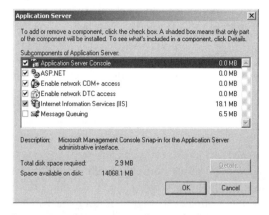

Table 7.2 describes the services that you can choose from.

TABLE 7.2   List of Services in the Application Server dialog box

Service	Description
ASP.NET	Enables ASP.NET applications to be run on the server.
Enable Distributed Transaction Coordinator (DTC)	Enables network access to the DTC.

TABLE 7.2   List of Services in the Application Server dialog box *(continued)*

Service	Description
Message Queuing	Installs guaranteed message delivery for applications.
Background Intelligent Transfer Service (BITS)	Enables support for throttling and restarting file transfers using the BITS. Software Update Service (SUS) and Automatic Update do not require this component to run; they use only the BITS client and do not require the service.
File Transfer Protocol (FTP)	Supports transferring files through the standard FTP protocol.
FrontPage 2002 Server Extensions	Installs support for the authoring of web pages through Microsoft FrontPage, Visual InterDev, or Visual Studio .NET.
Internet Printing	Allows printers to be managed and shared over the Internet.
Network News Transfer Protocol (NNTP)	Enables support for the Usenet news articles, including distribution and posting.
Simple Mail Transfer Protocol (SMTP)	Enables support for sending e-mail over the Internet.
World Wide Web Publishing Service (HTTP)	Enables support for the World Wide Web.

You will need to set the Enable Network COM+ Access setting to enable network access for COM+ applications; otherwise, they are limited to local access. This setting is required for FTP, HTTP, and BITS. You will also need it set for any custom COM+ application that you may be running on your server. You can set this setting in the Application Server dialog box.

These services should be disabled unless you need them. For example, if you enable the World Wide Web Service, you will need to enable network COM+ access.

The following components on the Internet Information Services (IIS) dialog box are generally recommended as a baseline to be installed for a server acting as a web server:

- World Wide Web Service

- Common Files

- Internet Information Services Manager

On the Application Server dialog box, the following components are recommended:

- Enable Network COM+ Access

- Internet Information Services

You will also want to consider configuring the rights on the server to prevent access to the Deny Access To This Computer From A Network setting and adding the following accounts to this group:

- Anonymous Logon

- Built-In Administrator

- Guest

- All Non-Operating System Service Accounts

The Deny Access To This Computer From A setting will deny access to the server from a network for most of the network protocols like Hypertext Transfer Protocol (HTTP), Server Message Block (SMB), NetBIOS, COM+, and FTP, to name a few. This will guard against someone using another logon to gain access to your server.

You can then decide to include additional components as required by your business. You will also be able to decide if Web Service Extensions are installed on the server through the World Wide Web Service dialog box in the Windows Component Wizard. You need to install the proper components if they are used by a website on your server. If you decide to install them, you will need to determine the Web Service Extensions each website will support on a per-site basis.

Designing for Web Service Extensions

Finally, you will need to determine the types of applications that your website will host. By default, a website only serves static HTML pages and images like GIF and JPEG files. If you would like to host Active Server Pages (ASPs), Active Server Pages .NET (ASP.NET), common gateway interface (CGI), or Web-based Distributed Authoring and Versioning (WebDAV) applications, you will need to enable these features for your website. Figure 7.2 shows where you can enable and disable the Web Service Extensions.

FIGURE 7.2 Prohibiting or Allowing Web Service Extensions.

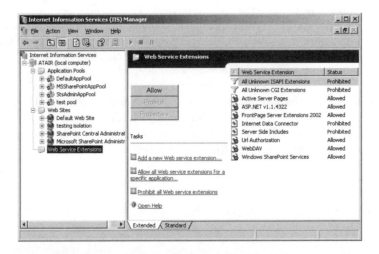

You can use this dialog box to allow or prohibit the application extensions that your website requires or to add custom ISAPI or CGI extensions that you require. The ISAPI or CGI applications that you add to the Web Service Extensions define the DLLs or EXEs that are required for the ISAPI applications and whether it is allowed or prohibited.

You will need to analyze the applications that you are running on the web server for the application extensions that are required. If there is poor documentation, you can look for file extensions on the server to determine if the application uses extensions like `.asp` or `.aspx`. You could also look at the WWW protocol log to determine what HTTP verbs or URLs are being used on your web server. This may aid in determining if the web application uses WebDAV or FrontPage Server Extensions. Table 7.3 illustrates signatures for various applications.

TABLE 7.3 Web Service Extensions and their Common Extensions.

Web Service Extension	Extension or Verb Signature
ASP.NET	`.aspx`
ASP	`.asp`
Server Side Includes	`.ssi, .inc`
Internet Data Connector	`.ida, .idc`
WebDAV	`SEARCH, BPROPS, PUT for example`; basically anything other than `GET` and `POST` (see RFC 2068 for a complete list)
FrontPage Server Extensions	Anything that refers to a directory, which contains .vti
CGI or Custom ISAPI Application	Anything the developer wants to create

Table 7.3 is generally the case for what files are processed by ISAPI extensions, but there may be a custom ISAPI application or CGI application installed, which could process requests for anything that the developer wants. You will need to consider this and add a Web Service Extension to process the custom ISAPI or CGI application.

In the Design Scenario "Designing for Minimum Services with IIS," you will design for minimum services on a Windows Server 2003 server running IIS 6.

Authenticating Users on a Website

Many applications that you build will need to identify the user connecting to the web server. This is necessary to protect the parts of the application and to find out who the user is for logging and authorization purposes. There are many ways of authenticating users with an IIS server, and each method has its strengths and weaknesses depending on the security level that you require.

Design Scenario

Designing for Minimum Services with IIS

You have installed an IIS server in the perimeter network of Wonder, Inc. It will host the company's e-commerce website and a sales application through which the direct sales staff in the field can verify customer orders and specifications. The e-commerce application is written in ASP and the direct sales application is written in ASP.NET. The CIO is concerned about security. The application is updated using FTP, which is started only when the application is updated. Content updates need to be secure. The server needs to support sending e-mail notifications.

1.   **Question:** What application server components should you install on the server? **Answer:** World Wide Web Publishing, File Transfer Protocol, Simple Mail Transfer Protocol, ASP.NET, IPSec.

2.   **Question:** What Web Service Extensions should you enable for the e-commerce website? **Answer:** ASP.

3.   **Question:** What Web Service Extensions should you enable for the sales support website? **Answer:** ASP.NET.

You will have the ability to let a Windows domain controller authenticate the user with basic, digest, anonymous, .NET Passport or integrated Windows authentication. You can also use certificate authentication or other servers to authenticate your users through ASP.NET forms-based authentication or RADIUS.

Using Internet Information Server Authentication

IIS supports five main authentication mechanisms for authenticating users coming to a website:

- Anonymous access
- Integrated Windows authentication
- Digest authentication for Windows domain servers
- Basic authentication
- .NET Passport authentication

All of these authentication methods can be set in the Authentication Methods dialog box, as see in Figure 7.3. To open this dialog box, open the website's Properties dialog box, click the Directory Security tab, and click the Edit button in the Authentication Methods section.

The default configuration is anonymous access and integrated Windows authentication.

FIGURE 7.3   Setting authentication mechanisms in the Authentication Methods dialog box

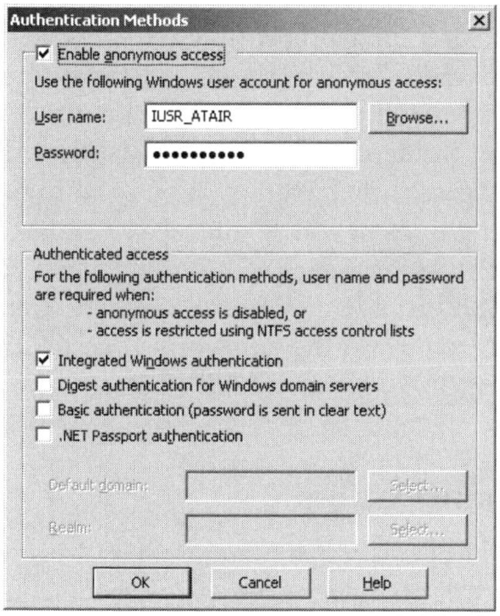

Using Anonymous Access

It can be a difficult problem to authenticate large numbers of users on the Internet. Many web applications don't require knowing who the user is because their purpose is to disseminate information and not differentiate between users. Even though these users don't "authenticate" with the web server, they still need to get access to resources on the server. Every user who connects to an IIS server must exist in some security context. When a user connects to IIS through *anonymous access,* they are authenticated as the IUSR_**ServerName** account by default, where **ServerName** is the name of your IIS server.

You will typically use anonymous access when you set up a web server to serve the public on the Internet. The Internet anonymous user is the default authentication for users, so if it is enabled, all of the other authentication mechanisms will be ignored unless you deny access to the anonymous user account (by default this account is IUSR_*computer name*).

You can configure the account and password that will be used for everyone that will connect to the web server via anonymous access.

Using Basic Authentication

Basic authentication allows clients to authenticate with the domain or local server using a username and password. The main problem with basic authentication is that it sends the passwords over the network in the clear text. This means that anyone with access to any network that the password crosses over will potentially be able to view the credentials. As you can see, an attacker could then use the captured credentials to impersonate you.

You would use basic authentication to provide a client authentication mechanism that supports the greatest number of browsers. You would need to use an encryption mechanism like SSL or IPSec to guard against password theft.

Using Digest Authentication for Windows Domain Servers

Digest authentication provides support for encrypting passwords, even over an unencrypted connection. Digest authentication hashes the user credentials using the Message Digest 5 (MD5) algorithm. This will prevent someone who intercepts the credentials from reading the password. IIS 6 supports advanced digest authentication, in which the password is pre-hashed and stored in Active Directory. This eliminates the need to store the passwords with reversible encryption in Active Directory when using digest authentication as you had to in the past.

You would use digest authentication in situations in which you need to authenticate users with a mechanism that supports most HTTP 1.1–compliant web browsers and you don't want to use an encryption mechanism like SSL (usually due to unacceptable overhead or expense). It provides a reasonably secure way to protect the password. Digest authentication requires Active Directory on Windows Server 2003 and is evaluated before basic authentication if you had both enabled.

Using Integrated Windows Authentication

Integrated Windows authentication uses the mechanism that Windows uses to authenticate computers and users in a domain. The client will not present the user with a logon dialog; it sends the logon credentials that it used when the user logged on to their Windows operating system. It will either use the NTLM protocol for authentication or Kerberos v5, depending on the client operating system. If you are using Windows 2000 or greater, Kerberos v5 will be used. Otherwise, the client will use NTLM authentication.

These protocols do not require encryption because they have mechanisms to guard against the credentials being captured. Integrated Windows authentication requires the use of Internet Explorer, so it tends to work best on intranets where the user won't need to log on to the server and will be using Internet Explorer. This mechanism will be evaluated before basic authentication.

Using Microsoft .NET Passport Authentication

Microsoft .NET Passport authentication is an authentication method that doesn't require the user to have their credential checked directly. The credentials are not sent to the IIS server; they are sent to a .NET Passport web service over SSL. If the credentials are correct, a cookie that contains a valid ticket will be written to the client. The server will check for a cookie that contains a Passport authentication ticket. If the cookie contains valid credentials, the server will authenticate the user. If the ticket is not valid, the client is redirected to the Passport Logon Service. Upon successful authentication, the client is redirected back to the original URL.

You would use .NET Passport authentication on sites that need to participate in a single logon for the Internet. This would allow the user to manage their information in a single place.

In the Design Scenario "Designing an Authentication Strategy with IIS Authentication," you will decide on an authentication strategy for IIS.

Design Scenario

Designing an Authentication Strategy with IIS Authentication

Wonder, Inc. has created a new web application that will be used in the corporate network to provide reports on the company's store activity and the effectiveness of the sales staff. Much of the information is confidential and the CIO wants to make sure that it is available only to authenticated users. All computers are running Windows XP and the employees use Internet Explorer.

1. **Question:** What should you do to configure the server? **Answer:** You should disable anonymous access and make sure that integrated Windows authentication is enabled. Also, apply the proper permissions on the directories and files in the web application.

Using Forms-Based Authentication

Web applications can also take advantage of *ASP.NET forms-based authentication* to provide for custom authentication of users. The developer would need to create a page to capture the profile information of the user and a page to capture the username and password. You would then need to configure the ASP.NET application to support forms-based authentication.

You specify the web page to redirect the user to if they have not successfully authenticated. This is handled in the web.config file that is located in the ASP.NET web application's directory. The web.config is an Extensible Markup Language (XML) file that is used to configure an ASP.NET application. The settings in the web.config file will override the settings configured in IIS for the application. This makes it easier for developers to deploy the application. There is a tag in the web.config file that is called <authorization>.

In order to use forms-based authentication, you will need to determine which parts or pages of the application will require authentication. You will use the <authorization> tag in the web.config file to deny or allow users to access parts of the application as follows:

```
<location path="AdminPage.aspx">
<system.web>
   <authorization>
      <deny users="?"/>
   </authorization>
</system.web>
</location>
```

This section taken from a web.config file is denying the anonymous user, represented by the question mark, access to the AdminPage.aspx page. This will force the user to authenticate when trying to access the AdminPage.aspx page. ASP.NET will look at the authentication tag to determine what method to use for authentication. You would set the authentication tag to the following to use forms-based authentication:

```
<system.web>
<authentication mode="Forms">
```

```
<forms name="MyAppAuth" loginUrl="login.aspx" protection="All" path="/"/>
</authentication>
</system.web>
```

This will set the authentication mode to Forms and then specify the page to handle the logon as login.aspx. The user will be redirected to the login.aspx page if they do not have a valid authentication token in the cookie. The developer would then provide the code to test the credentials and either redirect the user to the page they originally requested or redirect them back to the login.aspx page for another try.

Forms-based authentication provides the best integration into the look and feel of the website because its authentication and account maintenance are done through web pages that are part of the website. It also provides the greatest flexibility in the data sources against which the users are authenticated. The user accounts can be contained in anything from an XML file to a SQL Server or Oracle database to Active Directory. The problem is that a developer will need to write code that will authenticate the user against the data source, so this option is not readily available to administrators.

In the Design Scenario "Designing an Authentication Strategy with Forms-Based Authentication," you will decide on a forms-based authentication mechanism.

Using Certificate Authentication

Certificate authentication allows users to authenticate with the IIS server using a digital certificate. The certificate can be obtained from a third-party certificate vendor or from your own public key infrastructure (PKI). The client certificate validation is a feature of SSL. Just remember that certificate authentication can not be used if SSL is not enabled.

 Design Scenario

Designing an Authentication Strategy with Forms-Based Authentication

Wonder's developers have created a new application for the Internet site that will allow the user to register. This will allow the marketing department to collect information and suggestions from customers. The customer will also need to register on the site to purchase products. As a convenience to the user, you will allow them to log in and not have to reenter their information again.

1. **Question:** What authentication mechanism should you recommend that the developers use? **Answer:** Create a web page that allows the user to register their information, and then create a form to capture logon information. Next, configure the ASP.NET application to use forms-based authentication that uses this form. The developers would provide the code to store and authenticate the user with information in a SQL Server database.

Certificates are extremely difficult to forge and are appropriate for extranet applications or situations in which you require stronger security than just a user ID and password. You will need to configure the website to accept client certificates or require client certificates to be able to enable client certificates through the Secure Communications dialog box, shown in Figure 7.4.

You can access the Secure Communications dialog box by opening the Properties dialog box for the website and choosing the Directory Security tab. On the Directory Service tab, click the Edit button in the Secure Communications section. This option will be grayed out unless you have installed a server certificate on the web server.

See Chapter 6, "Designing a Public Key Infrastructure with Certificate Services," for more information on server certificates and SSL.

Client certificates can be mapped to user accounts to control access to resources based on certificates (technically, you control access through the account mapped to the certificate). You can use a one-to-one mapping, where you have one certificate mapped to one account. Or you can create a many-to-one mapping that is based on a rule that will match the certificate to a user account. This means that more than one certificate can be associated with a single user account or with a few. You can configure the account mappings through the Account Mappings dialog box shown in Figure 7.5 by clicking on the Edit button under the Enable Client Certificate Mappings check box on the Secure Communications dialog box.

You can also control which root certificate authority (CA) servers you trust. If the client certificates don't come from a trusted root CA, they will be rejected. This will allow you to trust only your company's and partner company's root CAs.

FIGURE 7.4   Requiring client certificates to access the website

FIGURE 7.5   Mapping your certification using the Account Mappings dialog box

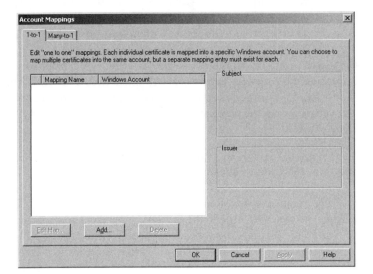

In the Design Scenario "Designing an Authentication Strategy with Certificate Authentication," you will design an authentication strategy using certificates.

Using RADIUS Authentication

You can control access to an IIS server from a remote connection through Remote Authentication Dial-in User Service (RADIUS). *RADIUS authentication* allows the RADIUS client to authenticate against a RADIUS server and has become the standard for integrating various vendors' products. RADIUS is typically used by Routing and Remote Access Services (RRAS) to authenticate, authorize, and audit logon requests in a standard way. Microsoft calls its RADIUS server Internet Authentication Service (IAS), and it can be configured either as an end point for the RADIUS client or to forward authentication, authorization, and accounting traffic to another RADIUS server.

 Design Scenario

Designing an Authentication Strategy with Certificate Authentication

Wonder, Inc. has ventured into a partnership with Elektronics R Us to produce a complicated component for a customer. It needs to coordinate communication and various other aspects of the project closely. The CIO wants a secure solution for use over the Internet. Wonder, Inc. has a PKI. Due to firewall issues, the protocol should work over HTTP or HTTPS.

1.   **Question:** What should you recommend for authenticating users? **Answer:** Certificate authentication with a one-to-many mapping to Windows user accounts would work over SSL and provide a great deal of security. This mechanism would work well because Wonder has a PKI.

IAS can act as an end point to authenticate and authorize requests from the RADIUS client against the Active Directory. The client will connect to the RRAS server and request that it authenticate. The RRAS server, configured as a RADIUS client, will forward the request to the IAS server. The IAS server is installed on a domain controller and will use the Active Directory to attempt to authenticate the user. If successful, it will notify the RADIUS client (RRAS server) and the account will be allowed on the network.

An IAS server configured to forward RADIUS traffic to another server is called IAS proxy. This is most useful when the RRAS and RADIUS infrastructures are maintained by different organizations or where the authentication database (Active Directory) is not directly accessible because the IAS server is located in a perimeter network. You create rules in the Connection Request Policies section of the IAS MMC snap-in. These rules control how the request will be processed and handled.

You can use RADIUS to manage the accounts of users that connect over a VPN through an RRAS server, so it is usually appropriate with partner organizations. Its main benefit is that it provides a standard way to authenticate, authorize, and audit logons, so both organizations don't need to be using the same vendors for their network infrastructure or operating systems. It also will ease management of duplicating accounts on IIS or in your organization because you can configure IAS to forward RADIUS traffic to the partner organization to verify the account.

In the Design Scenario "Designing an Authentication Strategy with RADIUS," you will determine the authentication strategy for Wonder, Inc.

Monitoring and Auditing IIS

You will need to track what the users are doing on the IIS server to be truly secure. You will use the information to verify that there are no security problems with the website and to build a case if you have been successfully attacked. You will then be able to determine the extent of the damage and may be able to recover more quickly. You can track what users do by configuring protocol logging and audit policies.

 Design Scenario

Designing an Authentication Strategy with RADIUS

Wonder, Inc. wants Elektronics R Us, its partner organization, to maintain the accounts of its own employees that will authenticate with the website. Wonder needs a mechanism to forward requests to authenticate to Elektronics R Us and receive validation as to whether the employee will have access to the content. The folks at Wonder are concerned about security and require that the solution support auditing.

1. **Question:** What technology should Wonder, Inc. implement? **Answer:** Wonder would use IAS, which is Microsoft's RADIUS. This will allow Wonder, Inc. to authenticate, authorize, and audit access by Elektronics R Us employees without having to maintain their accounts.

Configuring IIS Protocol Logging

You can track each request of the underlying protocol to the server by enabling *IIS protocol logging* on the service's virtual server. You can use this information to track the user's activities or to determine what an attack affected. You will need to make sure that this is secure to prevent an attacker from manipulating or deleting the files to cover their tracks.

You can enable logging by checking the Enable Logging check box on the Web Site tab of the website's Properties dialog box, as shown in Figure 7.6.

You have the option of choosing the following from the Active Log Format drop-down box:

- Microsoft IIS Log File Format
- NCSA Common Log File Format
- W3C Extended Log File Format
- ODBC Logging

You would choose the NCSA log file format to be compliant with engines that parse and report with this file format. The NCSA web server was the first successful web server, and its log file format was used as the basis for many reporting tools. The World Wide Web Consortium (W3C) extended the NCSA log file format to allow you to include additional information in the log file which is called the W3C extended log file format. This format is the more popular choice for local logging now. You can choose the items you want to log on the Advanced tab for the log format, as seen in Figure 7.7.

FIGURE 7.6   Enabling logging through the Web Site tab

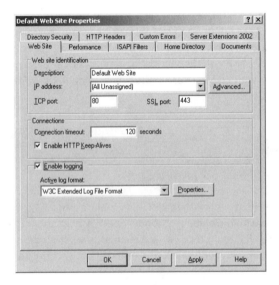

FIGURE 7.7   The Advanced tab of the Logging Properties dialog box is where you can configure additional information to log.

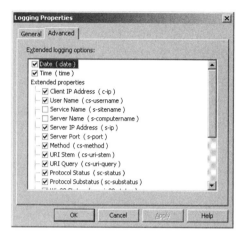

You should consider enabling logging of the following items when choosing the W3C Extended log file format:

- Client IP Address (c-ip)
- User Name (cs-username)
- Method (cs-method)
- URI Stem (cs-uri-stem)
- Protocol Status (sc-status)
- Win32 Status (sc-win32-status)
- User Agent (cs(user-agent))

The Win32 Status is useful for debugging security problems. An error code of 5 indicates that access is denied. You can run `helpmsg` *errNum* on the command line, where *errNum* is the error number in the Win32 Status field.

You should consider adding the following items in a multiserver environment to track what server the information came from because you will typically run scripts that will combine the log files into a single database to report on them:

- Server IP Address (s-ip)
- Server Port (s-port)

ODBC Logging allows you to log directly to an ODBC data source like SQL Server 2000. This can save you the step of moving the text-based log formats discussed earlier into a database server. You will log directly to the database at the cost of performance, which may be an issue if you host many websites or one busy site.

The Microsoft IIS Log File Format is a format that was introduced by Microsoft when they released IIS. It is not a popular log file format and few tools even support the log file format. You will only need to support this format if there is a reporting tool that requires it.

You can create a separate log for each website on your server. The logs will track what was viewed on the site, when it was viewed, and who viewed it. You could give website administrators access to their websites' log files. IIS log files are only available to individuals in the Local Administrators group. The owner of the log directory and files must be in the Local Administrators group or IIS will log an error to the system event log.

Some IIS servers may need to host hundreds of websites and logging can be degraded. You can improve performance by enabling centralized binary logging. All server activity is written to a single log file in a binary log file format. This will reduce the number of logs and, therefore, writes to the disk drive, increasing the performance. This makes logging feasible for large hosting sites. You can enable binary logging by setting the W3SVC/CentralBinaryLoggingEnabled metabase property to True and then restarting the web service.

HTTP.sys Logging

In addition to protocol logging, you can enable HTTP.sys logging. You may remember that HTTP.sys is the new kernel mode driver for IIS 6.0 and is responsible for parsing each incoming HTTP request to the IIS server and submitting it to the proper queue for the application. Since it sees every request for your web server, HTTP.sys is responsible for logging web traffic if you have enabled logging for your website. HTTP.sys only logs web traffic, not FTP, SMTP, NNTP, or other traffic, which is handled by the `inetinfo.exe` process. HTTP.sys logging guarantees that the request is logged if you are experiencing a denial of service attack, or if a malformed request (whether malicious or unintentional) is causing your web applications to fail. After all, if the application fails it may not log this information. But there are times when HTTP.sys has had a problem and the standard logging function will not work. It will then create a file called `httperr.log` in the `System32\logfiles` directory and log the requests. If your whole web server hung, you should inspect this file for malformed requests or other information that may help you determine the problem.

Configuring Audit Policies

When security professionals refer to a secure implementation of a server, they call it hardened, not secure. This is because you can never be sure that the server is totally secure; you have to assume that the security measures can be overcome. If the server is compromised, or even if someone is attempting to compromise it, you would like to know. You can track what users are failing to do or successfully doing with the server through audit policies and logging.

You will need to set up an *audit policy* to track security events like access to files or authentication attempts with the server. This information will be written to the Windows security log, which can be viewed with Event Viewer. You can use this information to determine what is going on with the server and where your security mechanisms may be breaking down. However, if you audit everything, you will be overwhelmed with information and will more than likely miss seeing patterns in the logs, not to mention the performance issues this will cause on the server or the security log filling up quickly. You will need to determine what you should audit.

You should configure an audit policy to track the logon and logoff of sensitive accounts like administrators and server operators, but this could also include individuals that have high levels of access to applications, like database administrators.

You should also enable the Audit Object Access policy so that you can track access to sensitive files and data or access to the Registry. In fact, you can use Audit Object Access to track access to any kind of object in Windows. For example, you can track the use or attempted use of files, folders, Registry keys, or printers. You will not cause any events to be audited by just turning on the Audit Object Access setting. You will need to enable auditing on the individual resource for events to be generated when the object access is successful or failed. The Success setting will generate an event whenever the object is successfully accessed. The Failure setting will generate an event whenever someone tries to access the object but fails due to the security settings. You would enable the Global Audit setting, and then on each resource, you would configure the information that you want to audit. You can set detailed events to control whether you want to audit just reads or writes to the resource.

For example, you can use the Write And Append Data Auditing on website files to track changes to the web pages. This could notify you that your site is being compromised.

You should also track changes to the audit policy, which could be an indication that someone is trying to cover their tracks.

You will need to use the business and security requirements to determine what the audit policy will be for your environment. You can set the audit policy by using the Audit Policy node in the Domain Security Policy MMC or in the Local Security Policy MMC if the server is not a member of the domain. You can generally choose to audit the success or failed use of a right or access to a resource. The Audit Policy settings are located in Security Settings\Local Policies\Audit Policy of the server, as seen in Figure 7.8.

In the Design Scenario "Designing a Monitoring and Auditing Strategy for IIS," you will design an auditing strategy for IIS.

FIGURE 7.8   Configuring the audit policy

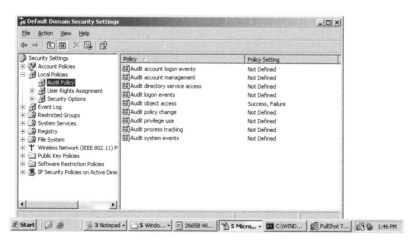

Design Scenario

Designing a Monitoring and Auditing Strategy for IIS

Wonder, Inc. has installed its web server to host its e-commerce site and is concerned about an attacker trying to gain access to its website. The folks at Wonder have taken measures to harden their server by configuring and verifying the NTFS permissions on the site, installing the minimum amount of services, and keeping the server up-to-date. They know that there may still be a security incident and are worried about how they will detect it.

1. **Question:** You need to come up with a strategy for detecting a security incident that will alleviate the CIO's concerns. What should you do to help detect a security incident?
   Answer: You should plan on creating an audit policy for the server that will track object access, user authentication, and changes to the audit policy itself. You should also enable protocol logging on the IIS protoccls that you are using.

Designing a Content Update and Management Strategy

Almost any web content will need to change at some point in its lifetime, whether you need to just update the look of the site or fix a bug in some of the ASP.NET code. Therefore, you will need to decide on a method to update the content on the website. The best method for updating content on your server will vary from website to website depending on the following:

- Applications used to create the website
- Firewall configuration
- Location of the web server on the network
- Security requirements of the company
- Ease-of-use requirements

You have basically four different options to choose from for updating your website's content when you devise a strategy:

- File share
- FTP
- WebDAV
- FrontPage 2002 Server Extensions

Using File Share

The file share option is probably the most familiar to Windows administrators and users alike. You would share the directory in which the content is located on the web server or a staging directory where the content will first be tested and then moved into production. This would allow users to map a drive to the share and is supported by any application that is running on Windows (all versions of Windows). You simply copy the new content to the share to update the server. The administrator can control who can update the server through share-level and NTFS permissions.

This option is appropriate when you do not understand the other methods and need a simple solution to update the server. You will generally limit your users to using Windows-based workstations to update the site; that way, you won't need to install complicated clients like SAMBA or File and Print Services for Macintosh. It also uses the Server Message Block (SMB) protocol on ports 138 and 139. This protocol is usually filtered by firewalls, so this option usually will not be available to IIS servers in perimeter networks.

Using FTP

File Transfer Protocol (FTP) is an Internet standard protocol for moving files between a server and client. It requires that the FTP service be installed on the server to accept requests from a client. It will then communicate with the server through port 21. You can choose to allow anonymous FTP, which means the user will not authenticate, or to authenticate the user through the underlying operating system. The credentials are generally passed as clear text. On Windows, you can use IIS permissions and NTFS permissions to control access to the underlying files.

FTP has widespread support because it is a standard. In fact, it is so popular for updating web content that you find an FTP client integrated in many web content authoring tools. If your tool does not contain an FTP client, you can find FTP clients for almost any platform in existence, so it will be easy for content to be updated from various platforms. Most FTP clients pass user credentials in the clear, so you will need to enable a form of encryption, like IPSec, to protect the confidential information. You will also need to consider whether the firewall allows FTP traffic; although it is allowed more often than SMB traffic, it is still often restricted.

Using WebDAV

WebDAV is a W3C standard for updating the contents of a web server. WebDAV extends HTTP by adding commands (verbs) that allow you retrieve, delete, list the properties of, search for, update, and keep a version history of content uploaded and changed on the web server. It supports a simple check-in and check-out strategy for allowing group development on a website. Because it is an extension of HTTP, it uses the exact same transport mechanisms (HTTP or HTTPS), making it much easier to route through firewalls. It is a standard protocol, so many tools support it for updating websites.

WebDAV is a good choice for updating the server. It uses the same authentication and encryption mechanism that you already have in place for the web server, so you can use basic, digest, certificate, or integrated Windows authentication. You can use SSL to provide encryption. Because it uses the same ports HTTP uses, it will generally pass through the firewall with ease, except for filtering firewalls, which may be searching HTTP headers for WebDAV requests and drop them.

Using FrontPage Server Extensions

FrontPage 2002 Server Extensions are proprietary mechanisms that Microsoft introduced with its FrontPage web authoring product. They allow for the administration of a website, including updating permissions, deleting web site content, and updating the website. They also allow for the authoring of web content much as WebDAV does, except they are not a standard. FrontPage 2002 Server Extensions are supported only by Microsoft products like Microsoft Visual InterDev, Microsoft FrontPage, and Microsoft Visual Studio .NET, so you are limited in your authoring tools if you choose to use them.

FrontPage 2002 Server Extensions use HTTP as the transport protocol, so they are firewall friendly. However, due to some major security issues with them early on, they are greatly mistrusted by administrators and they may be filtering them. You can use standard mechanisms, like SSL, to provide encryption for the content that is sent to the server.

In the Design Scenario "Designing a Content Update Strategy," you will design a strategy for updating the content of the IIS server.

 Design Scenario

Designing a Content Update Strategy

Wonder, Inc. needs a strategy to update its web server. Internal staff and the web design company need access to update the server. The web server has been installed in the perimeter network, and the firewall has been configured to allow users to access the web server from the Internet through only ports 80 and 443. Additionally, the internal staff uses FrontPage 2003 and the design company is using Dreamweaver MX.

1. **Question:** What content update strategy should you recommend and why?
   Answer: You should use WebDAV because it is supported by the software products being used. It can pass through the firewall because it operates on the same ports HTTP operates on. It can be secured by using SSL if security should be required. You should then make sure to authenticate the user through one of the authentication strategies discussed earlier.

Summary

You need to analyze business and security requirements to create a baseline for security on your IIS servers. You should consider the minimum services and account permissions needed to meet the requirements. You will use the information gathered to create a base IIS install. You should then try to automate this policy as much as possible through GPOs or scripts.

Next, you need to implement the minimum number of services required to meet the needs of your applications. This will include paying attention to what is installed on the IIS server and then determining what services each individual website will require. You also need to pay attention to the accounts used by the services.

The baseline will also help you determine how you will authenticate users on the website if you are required to do so. You will have a choice between basic, digest, integrated Windows, forms-based, certificate, anonymous, .NET Passport and RADIUS authentication. Each has their strengths and weaknesses. You will need to decide which authentication protocol would be best for your situations.

Security will also require that you track what the users are accessing on the site. This will allow you to identify security incidents or determine what damage was done by a security breach. You will need to devise a plan for logging information on the server.

Finally, you need to determine a strategy for updating content on the IIS server. Look at the security and business requirements to determine which protocol to use when updating the server. You can choose between WebDAV, FTP, FrontPage Server Extensions, or even a file share. You will also need to determine if encryption will be required when updating content, and you need to verify that permissions are correct for allowing users to update the content.

Exam Essentials

Understand how to identify the key issues for designing IIS security. Pay attention to the services required, the privacy requirements for the information (meaning what forms of encryption you should use), content update issues, and the authentication methods available. You will also want to pay attention to the location of the server on the network (internal, perimeter network) and how the firewall will affect your choices of content update and authentication methods.

Remember that client certificate authentication requires SSL. Before you can map certificates to user accounts, you need to enable SSL on your web server. You will need to then generate certificates for each user and map these certificates to the Windows user accounts.

Know when to use basic, digest, integrated Windows, and Microsoft .NET Passport authentication. Basic authentication passes the user's password as clear text, so it will require another means for encrypting the credential exchange. This method enjoys the most widespread support in browsers. Digest authentication requires Active Directory and is supported in most browsers that use HTTP 1.1. It will hash the password and send the hash over the network to be validated by the server. This option protects your password without requiring SSL or another means of encryption. Integrated Windows authentication is supported by Internet Explorer. It supports NTLM and Kerberos v5 as means of authentication. This will provide secure mechanisms for clients to authenticate within the domain. This option works best for intranets and maintains a single logon. Microsoft .NET Passport authentication provides a single logon for the Internet or between different networks. This would be appropriate for large sites on the Internet that want a single logon or to provide a single logon for multiple organizations.

Identify when you would use forms-based, certificate, or RADIUS authentication. Forms-based authentication is best used for web applications that require the use of a database, a third-party LDAP server, or even an XML file. This option provides the best integration into your website and gives you the most flexibility. Certificate authentication provides a mechanism for authenticating users that is extremely difficult to forge. Certificates are usually appropriate for partner authentication and extranets when you have a PKI in place. With RADIUS authentication, the web server allows IIS to authenticate clients against RADIUS servers. This provides for flexible sources of user accounts against which to authenticate the clients.

Understand the options for logging access to the server. You can enable protocol logging to gain the most information about traffic to the server. You may also enable auditing and use the event log to monitor resource access and exercising of rights.

Remember to install only the services that you need. You will need to determine what the applications require and install only the necessary services. You will also need to determine what extensions you will enable or prohibit for a website.

Identify what issues will occur when the content of the server is updated. You need to realize what the network infrastructure is around the web server and what effects this will have on updating content. You will need to identify requirements for security and applications.

Remember that IIS 6 supports URL authorization that will give you role-based control over resources. You can use Authentication Manager to authorize access to URLs on the website to groups or users. This is less granular than using NTFS to authorize user access to web content. This in essence supports role-based authentication to web applications.

Key Terms

Before you take the exam, be certain you are familiar with the following terms:

anonymous access	IIS Protocol Logging
ASP.NET forms-based authentication	integrated Windows authentication
audit policy	Microsoft .NET Passport authentication
Authorization Manager	RADIUS authentication
basic authentication	UrlScan
certificate authentication	Web Service Extensions
digest authentication	

Review Questions

1. Your company has the following requirement: All traffic sent over WAN links must be secure. What protocol would you enable for web content sent over the WAN? (Choose all that apply.)

    A. HTTP

    B. SSL

    C. IPSec

    D. MD5

2. What protocols are included as part of IIS? (Choose all that apply.)

    A. SMTP

    B. HTTP

    C. SMB

    D. NetBIOS

3. Your company has had some security issues with the WebDAV protocol due to improperly applied permissions. Your boss has decided that WebDAV does not need to be running on the IIS servers. You need to prohibit WebDAV. What should you do?

    A. Set the EnableWebDAV key in each website's portion of the metabase to False.

    B. Set the EnableWebDAV key in the IIS portion of the Registry to False.

    C. Install UrlScan 2.5 on the server. Configure UrlScan to filter WebDAV.

    D. Prohibit WebDAV in the Web Service Extensions section of the IIS Manager administration tool.

4. You need to authenticate a user with a domain controller running Active Directory. The client is using Internet Explorer 6 on Windows XP. You want to use the Kerberos protocol to authenticate your users. Which option should you choose for authentication?

    A. Basic authentication

    B. Digest authentication

    C. Integrated Windows authentication

    D. .NET Passport authentication

5. You need to enable authentication on your server, but you need to support any browser that the user chooses to use. You will also need to use a SQL Server 2000 database to store the credentials. What authentication method should you use?

    A. Forms-based authentication

    B. Basic authentication

    C. .NET Passport authentication

    D. Certificate authentication

6. You need to provide a secure authentication mechanism for an extranet with two partner sites. The partner sites will have approximately 200 users each. You want a secure but easy-to-manage authentication method. You do not require the identification of each individual user, just the organization. What should you do?

    A. Enable SSL on the extranet website. Generate a certificate and user account for each user in the partner company. Enable the one-to-one certificate mapping with the appropriate Windows user account. Set proper permissions based on the user account.

    B. Enable SSL on the extranet website. Generate a certificate and user account for each partner in the partner company. Enable the many-to-one certificate mapping with the appropriate Windows user account. Set proper permissions based on the user account.

    C. Enable .NET Passport authentication.

    D. Enable forms-based authentication. Assign each user a username and password. Have each user authenticate through the web page.

7. You need to authenticate a user with a domain controller running Active Directory. The client will use an HTTP 1.1–compliant browser, but it will not necessarily be Internet Explorer. You do not need encryption for all content and have chosen not to enable SSL. You need to provide for password security. Which option should you choose for authentication?

    A. Basic authentication

    B. Digest authentication

    C. Integrated Windows authentication

    D. .NET Passport authentication

8. One of your company's web applications keeps crashing. You suspect that an attacker is exploiting a bug in the server to cause it to crash, thereby creating a denial of service attack. You need to determine what web requests are causing the web server to crash. What type of logging should you enable on the server?

    A. Protocol logging

    B. Audit object access with Windows auditing

    C. ODBC logging

    D. Network Monitor logging

9. You need to log what users are downloading from the website. What should you do?

    A. Enable protocol logging for the website.

    B. Use Performance Monitor to monitor the Downloads\Content counter.

    C. Install Network Monitor to record all activity with the server.

    D. Enable auditing on the directories from which the content is hosted. Audit successful downloads of content.

10. You need to update the content on your web server. The content is sensitive and should remain private. Your server is on the other side of a firewall that allows only HTTP and HTTPS to pass through it. What should you do?

A. Use WebDAV to update the content of the server. You don't need to worry about encryption because WebDAV is secure.

B. Use WebDAV to update the content of the server. Enable SSL on the site to encrypt the content as it is being updated.

C. Install FTP on the web server. Configure FTP to update the virtual directory. Use FTP to upload the new content.

D. Install FTP on the web server. Configure FTP to update the virtual directory. Use FTP to upload the new content. Configure IPSec on the server and client to encrypt the traffic.

Answers to Review Questions

1. B, C. SSL and IPSec would both be correct with the information provided in the question. Both of these protocols allow you to establish a secure session with a server. HTTP does not provide encryption. MD5 is a signing algorithm, not an encryption protocol.

2. A, B. Simple Mail Transfer Protocol (SMTP) and Hypertext Transfer Protocol (HTTP) are part of IIS. Server Message Block (SMB) and NetBIOS are not, but they are part of Windows networking.

3. D. IIS 6 introduces the Web Service Extensions section of the IIS Manager. It allows you to enable or prohibit various ISAPI extensions installed on the server. This is the preferred way to disable WebDAV with IIS 6. You could install UrlScan and filter the WebDAV protocol, but it is no longer the preferred method. The metabase and Registry keys do not exist.

4. C. You would choose integrated Windows authentication, which supports either NT LAN Manager or Kerberos v5 for authentication. Basic authentication sends the credentials to the server in plain text but does not use Kerberos. Digest authentication will encrypt the password but does not use Kerberos. .NET Passport authentication uses a mechanism similar to Kerberos to authenticate users, but it is not Kerberos.

5. A. You should create a web page to request the information required to authenticate the user. This means a developer will need to write code to authenticate the credentials against a database in SQL Server 2000. If the credentials check out, then the user is directed to the requested URL. Basic, .NET Passport, and certificate authentication support many different clients but require the use of Active Directory.

6. B. You will want to enable a certificate mechanism to be most secure because the user needs a certificate to authenticate. .NET Passport authentication and forms-based authentication are not as secure and require more work in the form of custom programming for the website. Option A requires more work than necessary in setting up and maintaining all the user accounts, certificates, and mappings because the business requirements state that they are not interested in identifying individual users, just the partner organizations. You would map certificates to the partner organization based on a rule.

7. B. You would choose digest authentication because it will provide for encryption of the password and works with HTTP 1.1–compliant browsers. This option requires using Active Directory on Windows Server 2003. Basic authentication sends the password in clear text. Integrated Windows authentication only works with Internet Explorer. .NET Passport authentication does not use Active Directory.

8. A. Protocol logging logs the URLs and additional information for each request that comes to the server into a text file. This file can be a standard form that is readily parsed by a number of applications for reporting purposes. Audit object access with Windows auditing would only log access to files on the NTFS file system that the website was on. The hacker may be exploiting a bug that never touches a file on the file system, so this log may yield nothing useful. ODBC logging is just an option to store your protocol log, so it could capture the information, but it is a more complex form of logging and is not the simplest solution. Network Monitor would work in capturing the information if it is configured correctly, but it is not the simplest approach.

9. A. You would enable protocol logging for the website; protocol logging will record all requests sent to the server in a text file or in an ODBC-compliant database like SQL Server 2000. This is the easiest way to get this information. Network Monitor would record the information, but it would be more difficult to parse and read, so protocol logging is a better choice. You cannot use Performance Monitor or auditing to obtain the same information.

10. B. You will need to use WebDAV because the firewall will not pass FTP traffic. You will also need to use SSL to encrypt the content update because WebDAV has no built-in encryption mechanism.

Case Study

You should give yourself 20 minutes to review this testlet, review the table and exhibits, and complete the questions.

Overview

Thrilling Sporting Goods, Inc. is a purveyor of sporting goods worldwide. Along with carrying the standard equipment for team and individual sports, it specializes in equipment for adventure sports like rock climbing and kayaking. This area is a fast-growing area of the company's overall business. It has traditionally used a catalog and its five storefronts to sell its goods. The company would like to look at using the Internet as a vehicle to sell merchandise and support its sales staff.

Network Infrastructure

IIS servers that serve partners and the Internet are located on the perimeter network.

There is a server named SportWeb that is not a member of the domain located in the perimeter network. This server runs an ASP application that is used by the company's sales force to view inventory information.

Each office contains several servers, as the following table shows:

Server Name	Function	Location
SportWeb	Web server (IIS 6.0)	Perimeter network
SportISA1	Firewall server	Between internal and perimeter networks
SportISA2	Firewall server	Between perimeter network and the Internet
SportApp	Microsoft SQL Server 2000 server	Perimeter network
SportDC	Domain controller	Internal network
SportIntranet	Web server	Internal network

Interviews

Chief Information Officer   We have an initiative that all new applications must be web based. In addition, we are retrofitting legacy applications with web components. We need to track and report on what resources users and partners are using. This will help us keep the websites beneficial and secure. We have purchased a package that will produce reports from log data stored in SQL Server 2000.

IT Director   We manage our network with Group Policy objects (GPOs) to ease the burden of accessing each server and workstation.

Chief Security Officer   We need to make sure that we have a strong authentication mechanism for authenticating with the extranet. Partner companies often have weaker security policies and employees tend to write down user IDs and passwords. The ISA servers allow HTTP, HTTPS, IPSec, and FTP traffic. We do not allow the NetBIOS protocols through the firewalls.

Security Policy

IIS must not be installed on domain controllers or infrastructure servers.

ASP applications can be run only if they are installed on SportWeb or SportIntranet. Further application development will be done in ASP.NET and take advantage of the security of ASP.NET.

All users who access the website from the internal network must be authenticated by an Active Directory server. The user credentials must be protected while the user is authenticating.

The attack surface on any web server must be as minimal as possible.

All company data must be secured so internal and external users only have appropriate access.

All WAN communications must be encrypted.

All user access to the website must be tracked. The log must be stored in a SQL Server 2000 database for reporting purposes.

Case Study Exhibits

Partner Extranet

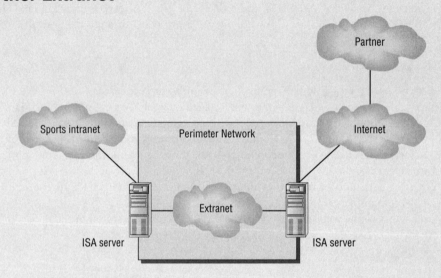

Perimeter Network

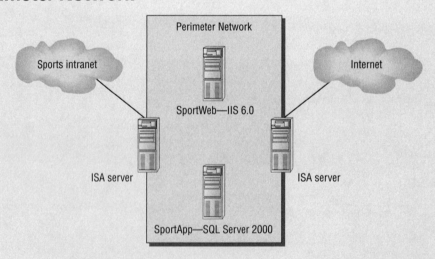

Case Study Questions

1. You need to design an authentication strategy that will allow only authorized users to access the SportWeb server from the extranet. What should you do?

   A. Configure the website to use SSL. Configure the website to require certificates. Enable and configure client certificate mappings to the website.

   B. Configure the website to use SSL. Disable anonymous access to the website. Configure the folder that represents the website with Read permissions for the groups of users allowed to view the content.

   C. Configure the web server to require IPSec traffic (Server Require). Configure the web server to communicate only with client computers whose IP addresses are located in the partners' IP address range. Disable anonymous access on the website. Configure the client computers to use IPSec (Client Respond).

   D. Configure the website to use digest authentication. Disable anonymous access. Configure the web server to communicate only with client computers whose IP addresses are located in the partners' IP address range.

2. You need to design an authentication strategy for internal users to the extranet. What should you do?

   A. Disable anonymous access to the website. Verify that Windows authentication is the only authentication method enabled.

   B. Create a Local group called ExtranetUsers. Create a Group Policy object (GPO) that will deploy a computer certificate to all client computers. Create a mapping for the certificate to the website. Apply Read permissions to the GPO for ExtranetUsers.

   C. Configure the website to use digest authentication. Disable anonymous access and integrated Windows authentication.

   D. Configure the website to use Microsoft .NET Passport authentication. Disable anonymous access and integrated Windows authentication.

3. Using the following exhibit, which of the following business and security requirements does the proposed solution meet? (Choose all the apply.)

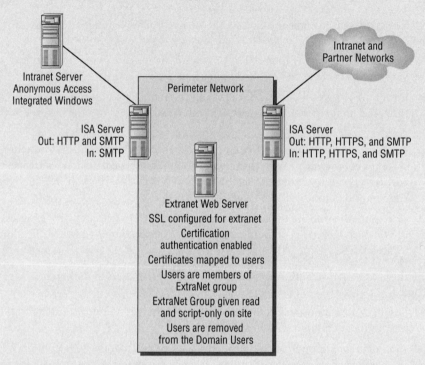

A. Traffic is encrypted between the partners' networks and the extranet.

B. Integrated Windows authentication with the intranet web servers to support a single logon.

C. Certificate authentication between the partners' networks and the extranet web server.

D. Partners can connect to only the web server that hosts the extranet application.

4. You need to design a way to update the content on the web server. Your solution must meet the business and security requirements contained in the scenario. What are two possible solutions? (Choose two.)

A. Use WebDAV over an SSL connection to connect to the web server to update content.

B. Install the FrontPage Server Extensions on the web server. Enable the FrontPage Server Extensions through Web Service Extensions. Use FrontPage or Visual Studio to update content.

C. Use FTP over IPSec connection to transfer content to the web server.

D. Share the folder that holds the contents of the website. Connect to the file share on the web server. Transfer content through the share.

5.   You need to design a strategy to log access to the company's web server. What should you do?

   A. Enable logging on the company's website and select the NCSA Common log file format as the log file format. Store the log files on a SQL Server computer.

   B. Use System Monitor to create a counter log that captures network traffic to the web server by using the Web Service object. Store the log files on a SQL Server computer.

   C. Run Network Monitor on the web server. Create a capture file. Store the captured information in SQL Server.

   D. Enable logging on the company website and select ODBC Logging. Configure the ODBC Logging options and use an account that is not an administrator to connect to the SQL Server machine.

Answers to Case Study Questions

1. A. The CSO has stated that they need a strong security mechanism to access the extranet servers. He doesn't think that a username and password scheme will be enough because the partner companies have weaker security policies that often allow users to write down passwords (or potentially have users giving out passwords over the phone). You can protect against these problems by using a two-part authentication mechanism that uses a certificate and username/password on the website. This will make it so that the cracker needs both items to log on to the server as a user. You will also need to enable SSL to support client certificates as it is part of the SSL protocol.

2. B. The CSO has stated that they need a strong security mechanism to access the extranet servers. This is enabled for the partner networks. You would then need to distribute certificates to your users who need to access the extranet. You can make this easier by using Active Directory Group Policy to distribute certificates for a group and then give the group appropriate access permissions to the site.

3. A, C, D. The solution allows encrypted web traffic to the extranet through the firewall and has enabled all the necessary features on the extranet server to allow for the use of certificate authentication. It also has removed users of the ExtraNet group from the Domain Users group so that they would not be able to authenticate on other servers. The internal ISA server will not pass any traffic except SMTP to prevent access from the outside world, including the extranet users.

4. A, C. The requirements state that the solution is secure and all WAN communications must be encrypted, which means that you will need to make sure that the users authenticate and the content is encrypted. You will need to look for protocols that are possible and a corresponding means to encrypt the content. In this case WebDAV with SSL, and FTP with IPSec will work because they provide a means of encryption. The other solutions do not provide encryption.

5. D. The requirements for logging state that the log needs to be kept in a SQL Server 2000 database. You will need to use ODBC logging to do this with the options we presented here. You could also move the information in the text-based log files to the database by using a script or third-party product. This would be done offline and would probably be a more scalable solution if the website had a high traffic volume.

Chapter 8

Designing Security for Servers with Specific Roles

MICROSOFT EXAM OBJECTIVES COVERED IN THIS CHAPTER

✓ **Design network infrastructure security.**

  ▪ Secure a DNS implementation.

✓ **Design security for servers that have specific roles. Roles include domain controller, network infrastructure server, file server, IIS server, terminal server, and POP3 mail server.**

  ▪ Define a baseline security template for all systems.

  ▪ Create a plan to modify baseline security templates according to role.

In order to maintain a secure network environment, your organization will need to specify the configuration settings for its hardware and software as well as the procedures that are in line with your organizational security policy. This configuration information is known as a *trusted computing base*. A trusted computing base is the total combination of protection mechanisms in a computer system. A secure baseline applies pieces of this trusted computing base to computers.

In this chapter, you will learn how to create and maintain a secure baseline for the various types of servers in your environment.

Securing Internet Information Services (IIS) was covered in Chapter 7, "Designing Security for Internet Information Services," and securing Terminal Server is covered in Chapter 10, "Designing Secure Network Management Infrastructure."

Implementing Security Baselines

One of the best techniques to secure your infrastructure is through the use of security templates. A *security template* will contain a definition of the security settings that are to be configured for a computer. The template can be used either to implement the configuration or to evaluate the differences between the settings in effect on the machine and those defined in the template. To better define the settings that should be configured in the templates for your organization, you will need to begin with a trusted computing base.

The *trusted computing base* is made of the following components:

- The detailed configuration and procedure of each component. Each option should have a required setting—for example, Enforce Password History should be 24 passwords remembered.

- Elaborate documentation. Each configuration step should documented.

- Change and configuration management. Procedures must be defined for applying changes, such as service packs and hotfixes.

- Procedural review. All procedures should be reviewed regularly to identify potential weaknesses.

A secure baseline is a detailed description of how to configure and administer a computer. The secure baseline will implement the components of the trusted computing base on an individual computer.

A secure baseline contains the following elements:

Service and application settings   You will specify the settings that need to be configured for each service that runs on a machine as well as the settings and business rules for each application. An example would be a business rule that specifies that only users in the human resources department can run the human resources application. You may also include for a service a rule that dictates that it should accept only connections coming from a specific machine or network segment.

Operating system component configuration   You will also want to specify the settings for the operating system components. For example, your organization might specify that IIS's home directory must be `systemvolume\IISApp\WebROOT`. Having a policy in place for the configuration of each of the operating system components should introduce a standard configuration and lower the total cost of ownership of the computers in your organization because you will know, based on the role of the machine, how it is configured.

 Changing the default directory that IIS uses as its home directory can alleviate some Internet worms that have the path of IIS hard-coded in their code.

Permissions and user rights assignments.   You should also create a policy that specifies the standards that your organization will follow as it relates to permissions and user rights assignments. Examples of this would be having a rule that states that only members of the Domain Administrators security group will be able to log on locally to the domain controllers. You would also want to have a written guideline for resource permissions—for example, only auditors can access client financial data for their clients remotely.

Administrative procedures   The business that your organization is in will determine the importance of administrative procedures. An example of a procedure that must be defined and carried out would be a rule stating that the password must be changed on all administrative accounts every 30 days.

Before you can define a template for the computers in your organization, you will need to audit your environment by completing the following steps:

Record all applications and services on a computer.   You must make an inventory of all of the hardware and software components on a system. Without this inventory, you might fail to properly secure an essential component or you might not notice a hardware change that will require a change to be made in the baseline.

Record the required security configuration for the operating system and its applications and services.   Each security-related setting and configuration task, including administrative procedures, must be documented clearly.

Automate the application of these settings for all computers.   Consider using Group Policy or some other automated technique to apply these settings to the computers in your environment. This will minimize errors, ensure consistent configuration settings, and save time.

Establish procedures to audit computers in order to detect changes to the baseline. Regular audits will detect changes in the computer settings in addition to changes in the baseline that haven't been applied.

In the following sections, you will learn how to define security baseline templates that can be automatically verified and or applied to computers within your organization. You will be introduced to the main types of servers that you will encounter and how they may require different types of baseline templates based on their role in the organization.

Defining a Secure Server Baseline Template

The secure member baseline provides common settings for all of the member servers in an organization. In this section, you will learn how to plan a secure baseline for your member servers. You will also learn about security templates and the ways to create, modify, and deploy them.

Windows Server 2003 can perform several different roles, that of domain controller, POP3 mail server, database server, web server, and so on. Because a server can assume a vast array of roles, you must take great care to remove the components and services that it doesn't need to perform its role. For example, if a computer is running as a database server, you do not need to include services such as IIS, DNS, or DHCP.

In most cases within an organization, the security settings for a specific role will be the same on multiple machines. For example, the security settings for one Microsoft SQL Server computer in your organization are likely to have the same configuration requirements as those of another Microsoft SQL Server computer running in your organization. That being said, you can create a template for all of the servers running Microsoft SQL Server and another for another computer role, such as Microsoft Exchange Server, and have different templates for each. You can utilize Group Policy to automate the assignment of the templates to the different computers. Group Policy will also automatically reapply the template settings should any of the settings be modified on a computer.

You will want to monitor the changes to the baseline using the Security Configuration And Analysis Microsoft Management Console (MMC) snap-in. The Security Configuration And Analysis snap-in is used to analyze and configure the security of the local machine. It will detect any conflicts that exist between the settings defined in a specified template file and those that are in effect on the computer. After it analyzes the two, it can be used to apply the templates settings to the computer.

The expression security template also refers to the name of the file that some of the Microsoft tools can utilize to examine and apply security settings to computers. Windows Server 2003 provides several predefined security templates that contain the Microsoft-recommended security settings for some of the more common configurations. Table 8.1 lists each of the predefined templates that come with Windows Server 2003.

Be sure you know which predefined template should be used for specific situations.

TABLE 8.1   Table 8.1 Predefined security templates

Name (filename)	Description
Default Security (`setup security.inf`)	Default security settings that are applied when the operating system is installed, including the file permissions for the root of the system volume.
Domain Controller Default Security (`DC security.inf`)	Default security settings on files, Registry keys, and services. This template is created when a server is promoted to a domain controller, and if reapplied to an existing DC, it may overwrite permissions on new files, Registry keys, and services that were created by other applications.
Compatible (`compatws.inf`)	Default settings for workstations and servers. Grants the typical permissions to three local groups: Administrators, Power Users, and Users. The Administrators group is granted the most privileges.
Secure (`securedc.inf` and `securews.inf`)	The secure templates for enhanced security with a low likelihood of conflicting with application compatibility. The secure templates limit the use of LAN Manager and NTLM authentication by configuring workstations to use NTLMv2 and servers to refuse LAN Manager; therefore, for this to work in your organization, all domain controllers must be running Windows NT 4 Service Pack 4 or higher. The securedc.inf file is used for Domain Controllers, while the securews.inf file would be used for workstations and member servers.
Highly Secure (`hisecdc.inf` and `hisecws.inf`)	A superset of the Secure templates. Even more secure configuration settings than those defined in the Secure templates. The highly secure templates will impose higher restrictions on LAN Manager authentication and the like. In order to apply the `hisecdc.inf` template on a DC, all of the DCs in all trusted or trusting domains must be running Windows 2000 or later. The hisecdc.inf file is used for Domain Controllers, while the hisecws.inf file would be used for workstations and member servers.
System Root Security (`rootsec.inf`)	Default root permissions for the OS partition. Applies the permissions and propagates them to child objects that are inheriting from the root.

You can use the MMC snap-in named Security Templates to create, view, and modify security templates. Figure 8.1 shows the snap-in within a custom MMC session.

As you can see, there is not a predefined template for a Microsoft SQL Server or any other application server role. Therefore, you will need to define them yourself. The templates that you create are referred to as *custom templates*, and it is usually a good idea to use a predefined template as a starting point for them.

FIGURE 8.1 Security Templates MMC snap-in

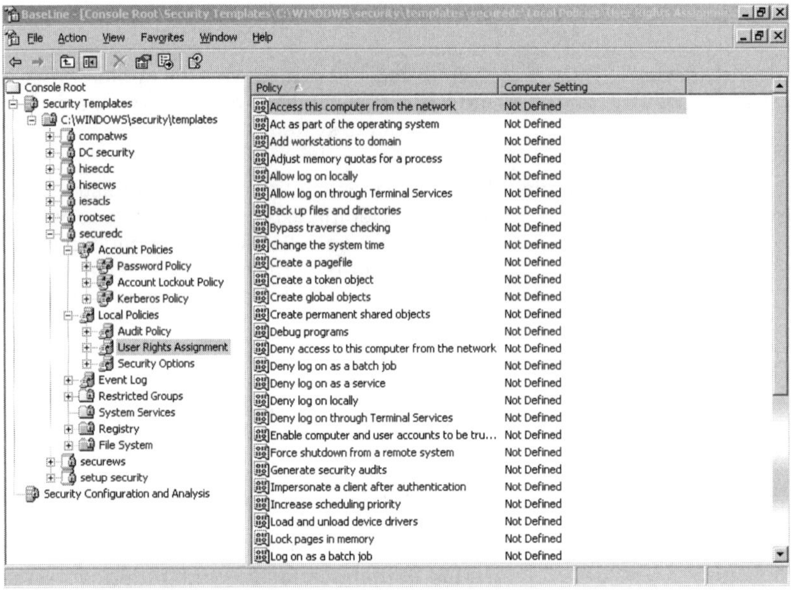

To create a new template, right-click the template directory in the Security Templates snap-in and choose New Template.

All computers running Windows Server 2003 store the security templates in the *SystemRoot\ security\templates* folder, and by default, authenticated users can read all of the settings within a GPO. You will want to make sure that your production baseline templates are secured such that only authorized administrators have the ability to view and modify them. It is also considered best practice to designate a single domain controller to hold the master copies of the templates; this diminishes versioning problems that can occur with multiple copies being modified at the same time.

There are three classifications that Microsoft defines based on security needs: a Legacy Client environment, an Enterprise Client environment, and a High Security environment. The following list will explain the differences in these environments:

Legacy Client environment The *Legacy Client environment* supports Windows 98, Windows NT 4 Workstation, Windows 2000 Professional, and Windows XP Professional as clients and supports only Windows 2000 or later domain controllers. Windows NT 4 member servers can exist. This environment only supports the predefined templates because they do not discriminate by operating system version. It's the least secure of the three environment classifications.

Enterprise Client environment The *Enterprise Client environment* supports Windows 2000 and Windows XP Professional as clients, and all domain controllers and member servers must run Windows 2000 or higher. This environment supports both predefined and custom templates. It is more secure than the Legacy Client environment yet less secure than the High Security environment.

High Security environment   The *High Security environment* has the same operating system support as the Enterprise Client environment: Windows 2000 and Windows XP Professional as clients and all servers running Windows 2000 or higher. This environment supports predefined as well as custom templates yet places more emphasis on security than on functionality and manageability. For example, terminal services are disabled on all computers and all administration must be performed locally at each machine.

You should customize the templates supplied for the classifications to further secure member servers in your domain. The template that you create will be referred to as the Member Server Baseline Policy (MSBP). You create this baseline template by modifying the predefined templates and manually making changes to the respective security templates. The manual modifications for the Audit Policy portion of the template are defined in the Microsoft *Windows Server 2003 Security Guide*. For the most part, you will be auditing the success and failure of the security-related tasks, such as logon events, privilege use, and so on. For Legacy, Enterprise, and High Security machines, you should manually configure the following User Rights assignments in your custom templates for the listed accounts:

- Deny Access To This Computer From The Network:
  - Built-In Administrator
  - Support 388945a0
  - Guest
  - All NON-Operating System service accounts
- Deny Log On As A Batch Job
  - Support_388945a0
  - Guest
- Deny Log On Through Terminal Services
  - Built-In Administrator
  - Guests
  - Support_388945a0
  - Guest
  - All NON-Operating System service accounts

 All NON-Operating System service accounts does not include LOCAL SYSTEM, LOCAL SERVICE, or the NETWORK SERVICE accounts, which are built-in accounts that the operating system uses. The Support_388945a0 account is used by Remote Assistance.

You will also disable all services that are not required by the server that you are configuring. You can examine the *Security Guide* for a complete list of the services that are typically installed and which ones should be disabled. The actual implementation is going to be specific for each individual server. Figure 8.2 shows the Properties window for the World Wide Web Publishing service from the Security Templates snap-in.

FIGURE 8.2   Security Templates World Wide Web Publishing Service properties

Using the environment classifications, you can make determinations as to what templates you can use and whether or not there may be compatibility issues.

In the "Determining the Security Environment" Design Scenario, you will evaluate a scenario and decide what environment you will use when choosing security templates.

You will also want to define IPSec filters that prevent networks that shouldn't be able to from accessing the server. Any service that is not to be consumed across the Internet should have a filter defined that prevents it from being accessed from the Internet or DMZ.

In the next section, you will learn about some of the modifications to these generic templates that you would make in order to secure servers that have specific roles.

Defining a Domain Controller Baseline Template

The domain controller role is the most important server role to secure in an Active Directory environment. Because these servers are so critical to the domain, you should make sure that they are physically stored in a secure location and are only accessible to qualified and authorized administrative staff. If you must store a domain controller in an unsecured location, such as a satellite office, there are several security settings that can be configured to minimize the potential damage resulting from physical threats.

Design Scenario

Determining the Security Environment

You are the security architect of a large corporation that manufactures and distributes office furniture. The corporate headquarters is located in Philadelphia and there are warehouses all across the country. All servers are physically located in the headquarters and are running the Windows Server 2003 operating system. There are workstations in each warehouse that run the mission-critical inventory application that communicates with the database server in Philadelphia. The workstations are running Windows 2000 and Windows XP Professional. The application must continue to operate regardless of security enhancements. The database server is running the Windows 2000 Server operating system and SQL Server 2000.

You decide to upgrade the database server's operating system to Windows Server 2003 in order to achieve better performance, stability, and scalability, as well as to increase the security supported.

1. **Question:** Which predefined security templates could be used to secure the database server? **Answer:** The server is not a domain controller, therefore the only templates that should be candidates for the database server are securews.inf and hisecws.inf.

2. **Question:** Which security environment classification should you use for security template decisions? **Answer:** Now that the server has been upgraded, there is no need to maintain the Legacy Client environment. You need to make sure that the inventory application continues to run unaffected by security policies, which means that functionality has a higher precedence than security for this application and you are limited to using the Enterprise Client environment.

Once the Domain Controllers Baseline Policy (DCBP) is created, you should link the policy to the Domain Controllers organizational unit (OU), and once linked, you should make sure that it takes precedence over the Default Domain Controllers Policy.

Linking an improperly configured GPO to the Domain Controllers OU could severely impact the operation of the domain.

Depending on the environment you are using, the DCBP will specify additional settings for the various sections of the template. One of the sections that provides a higher degree of security is the User Rights Assignment section under the Local Policy heading. It is in this portion that you can specify who is permitted to perform certain tasks.

The following is a partial list of the user rights assignments that are configurable:

Access This Computer From The Network   The Access This Computer From The Network user right permits the users granted it the ability to communicate with the server, and access shares and services over the network.

Add Workstations To Domain   The Add Workstations To Domain user right gives the user or group the ability to join the computer to the Active Directory Domain.

Change The System Time   This user right allows the user or group to change the time on the machine.

Log On Locally   The Log On Locally user right allows a user or group to log on interactively on the computer.

Log On As A Service   The Log On As A Service right grants a user or group the ability to register a process as a service.

Manage Auditing And Security Log   The Manage Auditing and Security Log right grants a user or group the ability to configure the audit and security log.

As you can see, securing these rights could be critical to the overall security of your server and environment. Figure 8.3 shows the User Rights Assignment portion of the Security Templates snap-in when the Access This Computer From The Network assignment is being configured.

FIGURE 8.3   User Rights Assignment

In addition to the predefined settings, you should manually add some configuration settings to the templates to further secure your domain controllers. You should use these advanced rights to make the domain controller as secure as possible. According to the *Windows Server 2003 Security Guide,* your domain controllers should have the following rights configured in the template:

- Deny Access To This Computer From The Network:
  - Built-In Administrator
  - Support_388945a0
  - Guest
  - All NON-Operating System service accounts
- Deny Log On As A Batch Job
  - Support_388945a0
  - Guest
- Deny Log On Through Terminal Services
  - Built-In Administrator
  - All NON-Operating System service accounts

When configuring the template for an Enterprise Client or High Security environment, you will want to enable the Network Security: Do Not Store LAN Manager Hash Value On Next Password Change setting. Figure 8.4 shows this setting being configured from the Security Templates MMC snap-in.

WARNING Some legacy operating systems and third-party applications may fail when this setting is enabled. See Chapter 5, "Designing an Access Control Strategy for Network Resources," for more information.

All classifications of domain controllers have the following services configured to start automatically in the System Services section of the predefined templates, including the Domain Controller Default template:

- Distributed File System (DFS)
- DNS
- File Replication (NTFrs)
- Intersite Messaging (IsmServ)
- Kerberos Key Distribution Center (KDC)
- Remote Procedure Call Locator (RpcLocator)

In addition to configuring the template, you will want to use Internet Protocol Security (IPSec) to increase the level of security for your servers. In a High Security environment, you would create IPSec traffic filters that allow traffic from any trusted source to reach the domain controller for these services:

- CIFS/SMB server
- RPC server
- NetBIOS server
- Terminal Services server
- Global Catalog
- DNS server
- Kerberos server
- LDAP server
- NTP server
- Predefined RPC range (ports 57901-57950)

FIGURE 8.4 Do Not Store LAN Manager Hash Value On Next Password Change Setting dialog

You would also create a filter that blocks all other protocols and ports not explicitly granted access from the preceding list.

 All traffic rules should be mirrored to allow for two-way communication.

Now that you have created a template for your organization's domain controllers, you will next focus on creating baseline templates for other specific server roles.

Defining an Infrastructure Server Baseline Template

In this section, we will explain the baseline template that will be used for infrastructure servers, which refers to servers providing Dynamic Host Configuration Protocol (DHCP) or Microsoft Windows Internet Name Service (WINS) functionality. We will demonstrate only the settings that have been modified from the Member Server Baseline Policy (MSBP) template you learned about earlier in this chapter.

If the server is a DHCP server, then you will want to modify the System Services settings such that the DHCP service is set to Automatic in all environment classifications. Likewise, if the server is a WINS server, you would configure the WINS service to be set to Automatic. You can configure these settings in the baseline template for the server role and make sure each setting persists by configuring a GPO that will maintain it.

Most of the settings for infrastructure servers are defined in the MSBP. However, separate templates should be created for servers with the infrastructure role to guarantee consistency.

You should also configure IPSec filters to allow the following services:

- Terminal Services
- WINS Resolution server (if a WINS server)
- WINS Replication client (to a WINS Replication partner only)
- WINS Replication server (to a WINS Replication partner only)
- All ports and protocols for domain member communication with domain controllers (to domain controllers only)

You would also create an additional filter that blocks all other inbound traffic from any of the services and protocols not listed in the preceding list. All traffic rules should be mirrored to allow for two-way communication.

In the next section, you will learn how to modify the MSBP for file servers.

Defining a File Server Baseline Template

In this section, we will explain the settings for the baseline template for file servers within your organization. We, again, will demonstrate only the settings that are different from those configured in the MSBP template defined earlier in the chapter.

A recurring theme throughout this book has been to minimize the attack surface of your organization generally and your servers specifically. One of the most effective techniques is to disable or remove any unneeded service or application from the server. You will make organization-specific determinations as to which services that will entail for the file server role.

The following services were enabled in the MSBP, but if you do not require them to be running on all file servers, you should modify the baseline template to disable them accordingly. These services, for example, should be disabled unless they are required to be enabled by all servers affected by the template:

- Distributed File System (DFS)
- File Replication Service (NTFRS)

You should also configure IPSec filters to allow the following services and their respective ports and protocols:

- CIFS server
- NetBIOS server
- Terminal Services
- All ports and protocols for domain member communication with domain controllers

You would also create an additional filter that blocks all other inbound traffic from any of the services and protocols not listed in the preceding lists. All traffic rules should be mirrored to allow for two-way communication.

Remember that the changes listed here for File Servers are to be made to the original member server baseline policy (MSBP) template and should be used as a baseline template for all of the file servers in your organization.

Next, you will learn about the security settings that need to be specified for a POP3 mail server.

Defining a POP3 Mail Server Baseline Template

As is the case with other server role templates, the MSBP will act as a starting point. The settings are specified here. If you are using the Microsoft POP3 service, you will need to modify the System Services portion of the template in order to allow the POP3SVC to start automatically. You should also configure IPSec filters to allow the following services and their respective protocols:

- POP3 server
- All ports and protocols for domain member communication with domain controllers (to domain controllers only)

You would also create an additional filter that blocks all other inbound traffic from any of the services and protocols not listed here. All traffic rules should be mirrored to allow for two-way communication.

In the "Defining custom templates for servers with specific roles" Design Scenario, you will determine what customizations must be made, if any, to the predefined templates for servers that have specific roles.

In the next section, you will learn how to deal with modifications to the baseline templates and what you can do to ensure a smooth application of their settings to your existing servers.

Modifying Baseline Templates

As changes occur in your organization, you may need to make changes to some of your baseline templates. Changing a template is simple using the various tools that Microsoft provides, one of which is the Security Templates snap-in. In addition, you can evaluate and apply the policy template, that you created or modified in the Security Templates snap-in, to a computer using the Security Configuration And Analysis MMC snap-in.

To use the Security Configuration And Analysis MMC snap-in to analyze and configure a machine, you would complete the following steps:

1. Start the Microsoft Management Console.

2. From the File menu, choose Add/Remove Snap-In.

3. Click the Add button in the Add/Remove Snap-In dialog box.

4. Select the Security Configuration And Analysis snap-in from the Add Standalone Snap-In dialog box and click Add. Then click Close.

5. Click OK in the Add/Remove Snap-In dialog box.

6. From the MMC, right-click the Security Configuration And Analysis snap-in and select Open Database (if a database does not already exist, type a name in the File Name text field of the Open Database dialog box) and select the database from the file system.

7. If prompted to import a template, choose the template that you would like to configure or apply to the current machine. If you are not prompted to import a template, follow these steps:

    ▪ From the MMC, right-click the Security Configuration And Analysis snap-in and select Import Template.

    ▪ From the Import Template dialog box, select the template that you would like to compare or apply to the current system; for example, `hisecws.inf`.

8. From the MMC, right-click the Security Configuration And Analysis snap-in and select Analyze Computer Now.

9. Enter the path and filename for the location of the error log and click OK to begin the analysis.

10. Expand the various settings to see if any conflicts exist between the template and the machine. The Database Setting column contains the settings defined in the template.

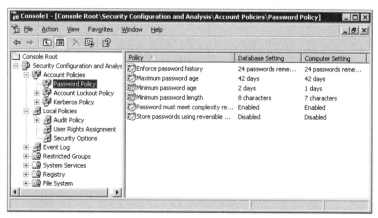

11. If you want to apply the configuration settings that are defined in the template to the machine, right-click the Security Configuration And Analysis snap-in and select Configure Computer Now.

You can take advantage of Active Directory Group Policy to assign the security settings to a container. Once you link the template settings to a GPO, the security settings will be refreshed automatically in the following conditions:

- Each time a computer is restarted
- Every 90 minutes for workstations (if a change has been made)
- Every 5 minutes for servers (if a change has been made)
- Every 16 hours regardless of whether or not a change was made
- When the `gpupdate` command-line utility has been manually executed (the `/refreshpolicy` switch of the `secedit` utility is no longer supported)

If there are conflicting settings defined by Group Policy objects, the following precedence is used to resolve the conflicting settings:

1. OU
2. Domain
3. Site
4. Local computer

For example, if an OU has a GPO linked to it that states that the maximum password age is 30 days and the site has a GPO that states 42 days for this policy, because the OU has a higher precedence than the site, the setting will be 30 days for all of the users and computers located within the OU.

As another example, if the DNS service is disabled in the domain policy GPO but enabled in the OU policy for the just-created DNS Servers OU, then all computers in the DNS Servers OU will have the DNS service enabled. In Figure 8.5 an OU named "DNS" was created in order to separate the policy application on the DNS Servers within that organizational unit. By creating a different OU for the DNS Servers, whose policies differ from those that are assigned at the parent OU. By having children OUs under the "Servers" OU, the GPO inheritance model becomes easier to maintain. Figure 8.5 shows that a GPO could be linked to the Servers OU that would apply to all computers in all children OUs. In addition, the DNS Server–specific policy settings would be stored in a GPO that would be applied to the DNS OU. Likewise, SQL Server database servers are placed in a separate OU, SQL Servers, that is also a child of the "Servers" OU. The figure is an example of how the policy application can drive the design of your OU model.

FIGURE 8.5   Sample OU design for Group Policy

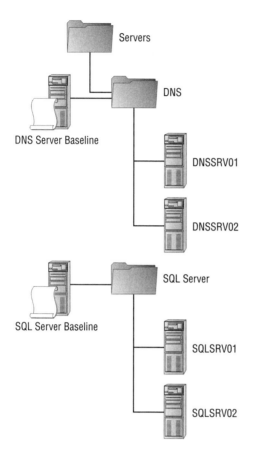

 Design Scenario

Defining Custom Templates for Servers with Specific Roles

Examine each of the following scenarios and choose the correct template for the server's baseline.

Scenario 1

You need to design a technique in which all of the member servers in your organization meet the requirements set forth in the written policies of your company. The solution must be implemented with the least amount of administrative effort.

1.   **Question:** What should you do? **Answer:** You should create and apply a custom security template that contains the security settings that are defined in your company's security policy.

Scenario 2

You have been told that the security settings have been modified on one of your member servers and it is no longer in compliance with the security policy. You have created a custom template that holds the settings that should be configured on the server.

1.   **Question:** What should you do to evaluate the compliance of the server; the solution should use the least amount of administrative effort? **Answer:** You should use the Security Configuration And Analysis utility to compare the settings that are current on the server with those that are defined in the template.

Securing DNS Servers

Earlier in this chapter, you learned about the general principles that you can apply to secure your infrastructure servers, including DNS servers. In this section, you will learn the different techniques within the DNS service itself that can be configured to increase the level of security for your organization.

Probably the single most important service running in support of Active Directory is the DNS service. If an attacker can gain control of your DNS infrastructure, there are several ways that your organization's security can be compromised. One of the simplest exploits occurs when insecure zone transfers are allowed. Insecure *zone transfers* would allow an attacker to request your entire DNS zone, thereby giving the attacker all of the names and TCP/IP addresses of the hosts in your network. In addition to the names and addresses of the hosts, the attacker would know which servers are running which services.

In Figure 8.6, you can see that having an entire zone returned to a server that you don't control would allow an attacker to view, among other things, the SRV record for the Global Catalog server, the Kerberos server, and so on.

Once the attacker has this information, they would know enough to direct attacks at the servers that host the services that they want to hijack. The attacker could spoof or poison the DNS data so that a DNS query would return their server's address when a request is made for a trusted server.

If zone transfers must be allowed, you should prevent an attacker from retrieving the entire zone. You accomplish this by specifying which servers are allowed to receive the zone data. The most secure setting is to supply the IP addresses of the authorized DNS servers, setting it to Only To Servers Listed On The Name Servers Tab. This setting requires a DNS lookup to determine whether or not the requesting server is allowed to receive the zone transfer. This would be susceptible to DNS spoofing. To alleviate the potential for DNS spoofing to affect your DNS security, you should select the Only To The Following Servers option and manually add the IP addresses of the appropriate servers, which eliminates the need for a DNS lookup. These settings can be modified in the Zone Transfers tab of the DNS server Properties window, shown in Figure 8.7, from the DNS Management MMC snap-in.

FIGURE 8.6   DNS zone SRV records

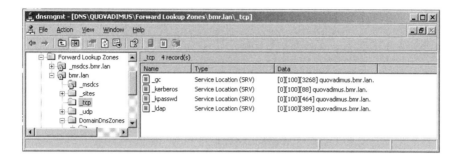

    By default, zone transfers are disabled.

The next DNS-specific vulnerability that can be exploited is the dynamic update feature. The most secure solution is to simply disable dynamic updates; however, this would require much more administrative tasks. To disable dynamic updates completely, you would set the Dynamic Updates drop-down list on the General tab to None, as seen in Figure 8.8.

FIGURE 8.7   Zone Transfers tab

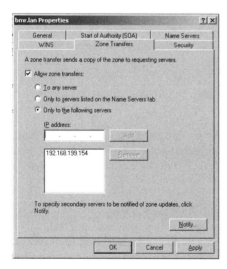

FIGURE 8.8   Dynamic updates via the General tab

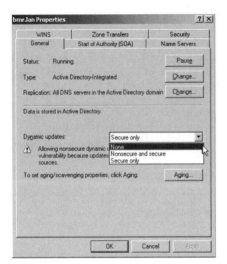

If you decide to support dynamic updates, you will want to make sure that only secure updates are allowed, which prevents unauthenticated users from creating entries. If you allow insecure updates, anyone could create a record in your DNS zone that points to the server of their choice. To support secure updates, the zone must be Active Directory–integrated to provide discretionary access control lists (DACLs) on the DNS data.

You should have a separate DNS infrastructure for your public or Internet presence and your internal network. The internal DNS servers could support dynamic updates, while the public DNS servers would not. Also, by default the DNS service will listen on all interfaces on the computer. If the DNS service is running on a multihomed computer, you should specify which interfaces it should be listening and responding to.

The last major attack to DNS is accomplished by poisoning the DNS cache. An attack of this sort is very difficult to prevent if you control the master server for the zone and nearly impossible if you do not control the master server. Poisoning, in this scenario, refers to changing the data in the cache on the downstream DNS servers such that they are pointing to bogus or malicious addresses instead of the proper address. This can occur because of a malicious or invalid update to the master server that gets propagated to a downstream DNS server where it is considered to be valid until the cache expires. Figure 8.9 shows the correct process of DNS caching.

FIGURE 8.9   Proper DNS caching process

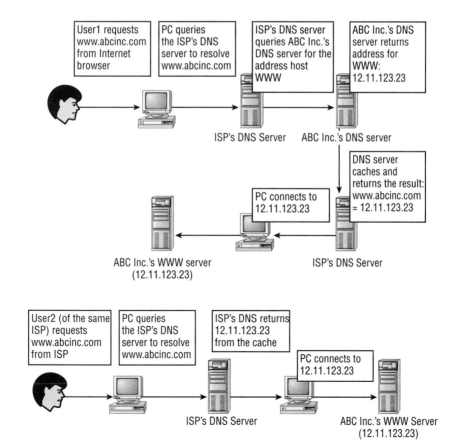

If a hacker can modify the cache on the ISP's DNS server, any requests for that cached data will be serving the malicious information. In Figure 8.10 it is an attacker's IP address.

You can minimize the poisoning of the DNS cache to a certain extent by selecting the Secure Cache Against Pollution option (the default setting) on the Advanced tab in the DNS server Properties dialog box (see Figure 8.11).

FIGURE 8.10   Compromised process

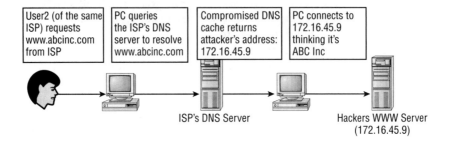

FIGURE 8.11   DNS server properties

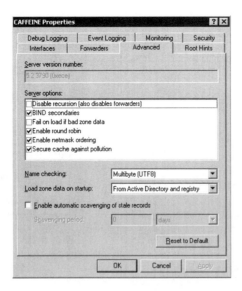

In the "Securing the DNS infrastructure" Design Scenario, you will evaluate the scenario and make the appropriate security-driven decisions to secure the DNS infrastructure.

Windows 2003 DNSSEC Support (RFC 2535)

The security extensions that were added to DNS, named DNSSEC, describe the services that perform data origin authentication and integrity checking. Windows Server 2003 DNS does not fully support the features specified in DNSSEC. Windows Server 2003 DNS provides, as stated by Microsoft, "basic support" of the DNS security extensions, which means that Windows Server 2003 DNS servers can be secondary servers to an existing DNSSEC-compliant secure zone. Windows Server 2003 is not capable of signing zones and resource records or validating the SIG resource records. The DNSSEC resource records are SIG, KEY, and NXT. For more information, examine RFC 2535.

 Design Scenario

Securing the DNS Infrastructure

You are the security architect of a large company that will be using a Windows Server 2003 Active Directory domain. You will have an Internet presence in which your organization will be maintaining its own DNS records for the Internet-accessible servers. You also need to support dynamic DNS for your internal network. Currently, you have two DNS servers, one for the Internet hosts (your ISP will maintain a secondary DNS server for your Internet domain) and the other for the internal hostname resolution. The IT budget will allow for the purchase of just one more server to maintain the internal DNS infrastructure.

1. **Question:** You need to make sure that you prevent an attacker from the Internet from making unauthorized changes to the DNS servers while minimizing the administrative requirements of maintaining these servers. What should you do? **Answer:** You should first make sure that the Internet-accessible DNS servers do not allow dynamic updates. You should also configure an IPSec policy that prevents the internal DNS servers from being accessed by any computers outside of the local network segment. In addition, you should configure the internal DNS server to accept only secure updates and to allow zone transfers to the new backup DNS server by IP address only.

Summary

In this chapter, you learned how to define baseline security templates for different roles. You learned how to use the predefined security templates in different environments and which ones are more appropriate for different types of servers.

Next we showed you what types of customizations you would make for the various servers: domain controllers, infrastructure servers, and other application roles such as database and mail servers.

You learned what modifications you should make to the templates using Group Policy as well as how to compare the current settings with those defined in a template using the Security Configuration And Analysis snap-in.

Finally, you learned the different exploits that can plague your DNS infrastructure and the steps that you can take to minimize or prevent the servers from being targeted for attack.

Exam Essentials

Make sure you know which tools are used for each of the common security tasks.   Know that the Security Configuration And Analysis snap-in is used to compare the settings of a machine with those defined in a template as well as it can apply the settings defined in the template to the machine. The Security Templates snap-in is used to create and modify security templates.

Know the major types of settings that can be applied with security policies.   You should be aware of how the security policies are applied and how they will resolve conflicts when different settings are assigned at different locations within the Active Directory organization.

Make sure you know which environment applies to your infrastructure.   This will help you to determine what, if any, custom templates need to be created or which predefined template you will use.

Know how to secure your organization's DNS servers.   Separate the name resolution role for the internal network and the external network. This will allow you to permit updates, securely, on the internal DNS servers while preventing updates to the DNS servers accessible from the Internet. Make sure you restrict zone transfers, if they need to be supported, to a predefined list of IP addresses.

Key Terms

Before you take the exam, be certain you are familiar with the following terms:

custom templates	security template
Enterprise Client environment	trusted computing base
High Security environment	zone transfers
Legacy Client environment	

Review Questions

1. You are the administrator for a small company and you need to apply security settings to the domain controller. You don't have the time to create a custom security template and you need to make sure that there is as little an impact on the installed applications as possible. Which of the following predefined templates should you apply to the company's domain controller?

   A. DC security.inf

   B. securedc.inf

   C. hisecdc.inf

   D. compatdc.inf

2. You need to secure your DNS infrastructure and make sure that unauthorized Internet users cannot modify the records on your DNS servers. You currently have separate DNS servers for internal and external hostname resolution. What task should you complete to secure your DNS servers from this type of attack? (Choose the best answer.)

   A. Disable dynamic updates on the external DNS server and put the internal DNS server behind a firewall.

   B. Disable insecure updates on the internal and external DNS servers.

   C. Configure your Internet firewall to prevent the DNS service port from coming through to your Internet DNS server.

   D. Implement DNSSEC on your DNS servers.

3. Which server operating systems are supported in a High Security environment for security templates? (Choose two.)

   A. Windows NT 4

   B. Windows 2000 Server

   C. Windows NT 3.51

   D. Windows Server 2003

4. Your network currently supports clients running Windows 98 and Windows 2000 Professional. You need to secure the workstations and the servers, which are all running Windows Server 2003. Which security environment should be used when selecting pre-defined security templates?

   A. Legacy Client environment

   B. Enterprise Client environment

   C. High Security environment

   D. Secure Server environment

5. You have created a custom template for file servers that has been applied to your server. You have decided to install the WINS service on this server. You have already configured IPSec filters for the file server. What two tasks must you complete before users on your network are able to use the WINS service that you have installed? (Choose two.)

   A. Configure an IPSec filter for the WINS service.

   B. Configure a DNSSEC filter for the DHCP service.

   C. Create a new security template that sets the WINS service to autostart and sets the other settings specific to this server role.

   D. Create a new security template that allows the FTP server port to run on the server.

6. You are the administrator for a small company that needs to apply security settings to the main file server. You need to implement the highest security possible even if it causes some applications to fail. Which of the following predefined templates should you apply to the company's domain controller?

   A. `securews.inf`

   B. `securedc.inf`

   C. `hisecdc.inf`

   D. `hisecws.inf`

7. You need to reduce the potential for DNS spoofing to exploit and force your servers into transferring the zone records to an unknown server. What is the best way to reduce the occurrence of this type of attack?

   A. Configure the DNS server to transfer zone information to a specified list of servers by their fully qualified domain names only.

   B. Enable the Prevent Full Zone Transfer option.

   C. Configure the DNS server to transfer zone information to a specified list of servers by their IP addresses only.

   D. Configure the DNSSEC policy according to the standard.

8. You are concerned that changes have been made to the domain controller of your network and they conflict with the policies defined in its baseline template. Which tool can you use to determine if the template's settings are current on the server?

   A. Security Templates snap-in

   B. Group Policy Editor

   C. Active Directory Users And Computers snap-in

   D. Security Configuration And Analysis snap-in

9. You are going to be developing a security template that will be used to maintain your organization's security baseline based on server function. Which of the following settings can be configured using a security template? (Choose all that apply.)

   A. Account Policies

   B. System Services behavior

   C. User Rights Assignment

   D. IPSec Filters

   E. Security Group Membership

   F. Audit Policy

10. You are the security administrator for your organization and are charged with the implementation of your organization's security policies. Your boss has asked you to evaluate your organization's risk for DNS zone information to be transferred to insecure servers. You are asked to make sure you disable zone transfers entirely when you install the new DNS servers. After you install the new DNS servers with the default options, what additional task must you complete in order to meet this requirement?

   A. Uncheck the Allow Zone Transfers check box in the DNS server's Properties dialog box.

   B. Disable the DNS service.

   C. Nothing.

   D. Configure the server to allow secure zone transfers by specified IP addresses only.

Answers to Review Questions

1. B. The `securedc.inf` template provides enhanced security with a low likelihood of conflicting with application compatibility. The `DC security.inf` template is the one created when the server is promoted to a domain controller and has the default security settings for domain controllers stored in it. The `hisecdc.inf` template is more secure than the `securedc.inf` template, mostly because it puts a higher priority on security than application compatibility or functionality. There is no predefined template named `compatdc.inf`.

2. A. The best way to prevent malicious updates from the Internet is to not allow Internet-accessible DNS servers to accept updates. Therefore, option A is better than option B. If you prevent the Internet DNS Server from being accessed through the DNS server port, Internet users will not be able to resolve the name of your Internet servers. Windows Server 2003 does not fully support DNSSEC and cannot be used for security or authorization with only Windows Server 2003 DNS servers.

3. B, D. Windows NT 4 and Windows NT 3.51 are not supported server operating systems for the High Security environment. Windows 2000 Server and higher are the supported server operating systems.

4. A. The Enterprise Client and High Security environments support only clients running Windows 2000 Professional and Windows XP Professional. There is no predefined security environment named Secure Server environment.

5. A, C. You must configure IPSec so that WINS requests and responses will be processed to and from the server. DNSSEC is not supported fully on Windows Server 2003 and doesn't have any filtering attributes to its functionality, nor is it relevant to the operation of a WINS server. You will need to configure a template that includes the automatic startup behavior for the WINS service. This is not an FTP server and therefore the FTP port doesn't need to be open on the server.

6. D. The `hisecws.inf` has the highest level of security in a predefined template that could be applied to a file server. The `securedc.inf` and the `hisecdc.inf` are to be applied to domain controllers, not file servers. Therefore, options B and C are incorrect. The `securews.inf` file is not as secure as the `hisecws.inf` file. Therefore, option A is incorrect.

7. C. Both options A and C would work. However, option A is susceptible to DNS spoofing because it relies on name resolution for the allowed server list, whereas specifying the IP addresses of the machines that are allowed to receive the zone information does not depend on any name resolution feature, so a DNS spoof attack will not compromise the zone transfers. Therefore, option C is correct and option A is not. Option B is incorrect because there is no Prevent Full Zone Transfer option. Option D is incorrect because Windows Server 2003 does not fully support the DNSSEC standard, not that it would aid you in this scenario if it were supported.

8. D. The only utility that provides the functionality to analyze the differences between the effective settings on a machine and those that are defined in a template is the Security Configuration And Analysis snap-in. The Security Templates snap-in is used for creating and modifying templates, the Group Policy editor is used to modify Group Policy settings; and the Active Directory Users And Computers snap-in is used for, among other things, to create containers and objects in the Active Directory.

9. A, B, C, F. You can define Account Policies and Local Policies settings, including Auditing and User Rights Assignment settings —as well as the behavior of System Services from within security templates. Therefore options A, B, C, and F are correct. Options D and E are incorrect because they cannot be configured using security templates. IPSec filters are configured from within the network connection settings, and security group membership is usually managed using Active Directory Users And Computers.

10. C. Zone transfers are disabled by default. Therefore, there is no need to change any setting or configuration option. Options A, B, and D are incorrect.

Case Study

You should give yourself 20 minutes to review this testlet and complete the questions.

Background

Minneapolis Concrete Sawing and Drilling (MCSD) plans and completes custom concrete sawing and drilling in the greater Minneapolis area for several different industries.

The company's main office is located in Minneapolis, Minnesota. The company has branch offices in Rochester, Minnesota, and Wilmington, Delaware.

MCSD is entering into a partnership with Custom Blades Inc. to supply all of the blades for the specialized saws. MCSD needs to be able to have encrypted communications with Custom Blades Inc.

Existing Environment

Users in the sales department require access to the sales data by using a custom ASP.NET application hosted on a server running IIS 6.

Sales and product information is stored on Microsoft SQL Server 2000 running in the Minneapolis office. There is an intranet web application that is used to access this data.

Each location has a file server with a sales and customer share that is to be accessible to only authorized users.

The following table lists the servers on the network with their location, role, and operating system version:

Server Name	Location	Operating System	Role
Server1	Minneapolis	Windows Server 2003	Microsoft SQL Server 2000
Server2	Minneapolis	Windows Server 2003	File, print, and DHCP server
Server3	Minneapolis	Windows Server 2003	File and Global Catalog server
Server4	Minneapolis	Windows Server 2003	Microsoft Exchange Server 2003
SrvWeb01	Minneapolis	Windows Server 2003	ASP.NET web server running IIS 6
Server83	Minneapolis	Windows Server 2003	Domain controller, web server running IIS 6
Server5	Minneapolis	Windows Server 2003	ASP.NET web server running IIS 6
Server51	Minneapolis	Windows Server 2003	File and primary DNS server
Server54	Rochester	Windows Server 2003	Global Catalog server
Server6	Rochester	Windows Server 2003	File, print, and DHCP server

Server Name	Location	Operating System	Role
Server6b	Rochester	Windows Server 2003	File and secondary DNS server
Server76	Wilmington	Windows Server 2003	Domain controller
Server7	Wilmington	Windows Server 2003	File, print, and DHCP server
Server7a	Wilmington	Windows Server 2003	File and secondary DNS server

Firewalls are configured to allow web traffic originating from the Internet to only SrvWeb01.

The Custom Blades network consists of a Windows NT 4 domain in which all client computers are running Windows 2000 Professional.

The following problems must be evaluated:

- Administrators need to manually apply policies on individual servers and workstations using the Local Policy MMC snap-in on each computer.
- Configuration changes that cause the security to be relaxed are occasionally made to computers.

Interviews

Chief Executive Officer   It is important to maintain a high level of collaboration with Custom Blades; however, we need to make sure that we are not allowing them to see too much information regarding our business plans. Custom Blades does business with several of our competitors.

Chief Information Officer   The information that is being shared with Custom Blades needs to be secured and must be kept confidential.

The security policies need to be maintained, and as servers are moved or have their roles modified, the security policies need to be dynamically modified. The security architect has guaranteed that the security of our resources will be kept as our number one priority when it comes to our systems. With the exception of our web servers, we will even sacrifice functionality if it is for better security.

Security Architect   We need to make sure the security infrastructure is kept at a higher priority than compatibility and interoperability.

Business Requirements

The following security requirements must be evaluated:

- Application functionality must not interfere with security.
- DNS records are not allowed to be transferred to external sources.
- The DNS cache should be as secure as possible.
- Security updates must be automatic.
- Security changes to the web servers should have a minimal effect, if any, on the functionality of our applications or services that are accessed from them.

Case Study Questions

1. You need to design a security solution for the application servers in your organization. The solution must meet the business requirements. Which of the following tasks should you complete in order to create a custom server baseline?

    A. Use the Microsoft Baseline Security Analyzer (MBSA) to generate the custom template and apply it to the servers.

    B. Use the Security Configuration And Analysis MMC snap-in to customize the High Security template.

    C. Use the Security Templates MMC snap-in to customize the High Security template.

    D. Use Notepad to modify the DNSSEC template.

2. You need to design a method to standardize and deploy a baseline security configuration for your Microsoft SQL Server machines. Your solution must meet business requirements. What should you do?

    A. Create a script that installs the `hisecdc.inf` security template.

    B. Use a Group Policy object (GPO) to distribute and apply the `hisec.inf` security template.

    C. Use the System Policy Editor to configure each server's security settings.

    D. Use a Group Policy object (GPO) to distribute and apply a custom security template.

3. You need to design the configuration of DNS to meet business requirements. What should you do? (Choose all that apply.)

    A. Disable recursion for the DNS service.

    B. Configure the DNS server to prevent cache pollution.

    C. Configure dynamic DNS to allow only secure updates for the internal DNS servers and disable updates for the Internet DNS servers.

    D. Restrict zone transfers on all DNS servers to specific internal DNS IP addresses.

    E. Configure DNSSEC on all DNS servers.

4. You need to use a template to secure Server3 using the Security Configuration And Analysis snap-in. Which template would you use?

    A. `securews.inf`

    B. `securedc.inf`

    C. `hisecdc.inf`

    D. `hisecws.inf`

5. Match each predefined template to the server it should be applied to. You might not need to use all templates.

Server	Template
Server1	`setup security.inf`
Server3	`compatws.inf`
Server2	`DC security.inf`
Server4	`securedc.inf`
SrvWeb01	`securews.inf`
Server51	`hisecdc.inf`
Server6b	`hisecws.inf`
Server83	`rootsec.inf`
Server54	
Server76	
Server6b	

Answers to Case Study Questions

1. C. The Security Templates MMC snap-in is the tool that you will use to customize or create security templates. The Microsoft Baseline Security Analyzer (MBSA)—covered in Chapter 9, "Designing an Infrastructure for Updating Computers"—is used to detect which, if any, insecure settings are configured or security patches have not been applied. The Security Configuration And Analysis MMC snap-in is used to compare the current settings with those defined in a template. There is no predefined template named DNSSEC; DNSSEC is a security standard that is not fully supported by the Windows Server 2003 DNS service.

2. D. A custom security template needs to be created and deployed using Group Policy as stated in option D. The `hisecdc.inf` security template is not sufficient for the Microsoft SQL Server machines because it is a predefined template and will not have settings defining SQL Server–specific configurations. There is no predefined template named `hisec.inf`. There is a `hisecdc.inf` and a `highsecws.inf` template for servers and workstations, respectively. Therefore, option B is incorrect. Using the System Policy Editor on each server would not minimize administrative overhead, so it would not meet the business requirements.

3. B, C, D. The business requirements specify that only authorized users should be able to update the local DNS servers. Therefore, you must enable secure dynamic updates. To secure zone transfers from being used against your organization, you should allow them to be sent to predefined DNS servers by address only. The business requirements state that the DNS cache should be as secure as possible, which includes trying to prevent the poisoning or pollution of the DNS cache, therefore answer B is correct. Disabling recursion for the DNS service will not meet the specified business requirements. Windows Server 2003 does not fully support the DNSSEC standard.

4. D. The `hisecws.inf` has the highest level of security in a predefined template that could be applied to a file server. The `securews.inf` file is not as secure as the `hisecws.inf` file; therefore option A is incorrect because it is not the best answer. The `securedc.inf` and the `hisecdc.inf` are to be applied to domain controllers, not file servers, so options B and C are incorrect.

5.

Server1
`hisecws.inf`
Server3
`hisecdc.inf`
Server2
`hisecws.inf`
Server4
`hisecws.inf`
SrvWeb01
`securews.inf`
Server51
`hisecws.inf`
Server6b
`hisecws.inf`
Server83
`securedc.inf`
Server54
`hisecdc.inf`
Server76
`hisecws.inf`
Server6b
`hisecdc.inf`

The business requirements state that all security changes to web servers should have a minimal effect on them. Therefore, all web servers (SrvWeb01 and Server83) are not able to use the `hisecws.inf` or `hisecdc.inf` templates. Server83 is a web server and a domain controller. Therefore, the only template the meets the requirements is the `securedc.inf`, not the `hisecdc.inf`.

The CIO stated that security takes a higher priority than functionality, with the exception of the web servers. Therefore, all other servers should be using the `securews.inf` or `securedc.inf` templates. Server3, and Server54 are domain controllers and thus the `hisecdc.inf` template should be applied. All other servers should have the `hisecws.inf` template applied.

Chapter

9

Designing an Infrastructure for Updating Computers

MICROSOFT EXAM OBJECTIVES COVERED IN THIS CHAPTER:

✓ **Design a security update infrastructure.**

- Design a Software Update Services (SUS) infrastructure.
- Design Group Policy to deploy software updates.
- Design a strategy for identifying computers that are not at the current patch level.

✓ **Design a strategy for securing client computers. Considerations include desktop and portable computers.**

- Design a strategy for hardening client operating systems.
- Design a strategy for restricting user access to operating system features.

Every application and service that is running within your network could be used as the launching pad for an attack. It is for this reason that you will want to make sure that you can control the applications and services that can be installed on the machines in the network. Once you are able to prevent your users from installing, intentionally or otherwise, applications that you haven't approved, you must update and patch the applications and operating system services that are running as new fixes are released from their vendors. You will want to make sure that the only applications that are installed on your network are those that have been tested and approved by the IT department.

In this chapter, we will show you how to secure the client computers in your organization by hardening the operating system and restricting users from accessing specific operating system features. Once you have learned how to secure your client infrastructure, we'll explain how to update the software and services that are running inside your organization. It is here that you will be introduced to the variety of methods that are available for this purpose, such as Software Update Services (SUS) to distribute updates to the Windows operating system and its core services. The last part of this chapter will discuss hardening the client operating system by restricting different portions from the users as well as using software restriction policies to prevent specific applications from being installed and run.

Securing Client Computers

In Chapter 8, "Designing Security for Servers with Specific Roles," we showed you how to secure servers based on the roles they play in your network. You will apply similar techniques when you need to secure the clients in your network. You need to make sure that the client computers in your environment are as secure as possible. There are several steps in securing the client computers in your infrastructure.

In the following sections, you will learn how to harden the security configuration of the computers in your organization.

Hardening Security on Client Computers

You will be following many of the same principles when you secure the client computers as you did when you were securing your server infrastructure. The first step is to segregate your clients based on their roles.

First, you will separate the clients based on their functional nature. Are they desktop workstations or are they portable computers such as laptops that will travel outside of the physical security infrastructure in place in your company? You should harden the clients differently, or more so, if they will be "in the wild" as opposed to under the direct control of your IT department at all times. In addition to separating the clients based on roles, you will want to separate them based on the operating system that they are running because different operating systems expose different services and thereby have different risks associated with them. You will use this information within your Active Directory design to build organizational units (OUs) that will accommodate this concept.

In the following section, you will learn the best techniques that you can employ when designing your OUs in this manner. This will be especially important as you use this model for Group Policy and other hardening techniques that you will learn later in this chapter.

Designing an OU Model for Client Computers

You will be creating an OU structure to facilitate the application of Group Policy to the various computers based on their membership in one container versus another. You will want to separate the computers based on how you will utilize Group Policy on them. You can organize the OUs based on computer role. Group Policy objects (GPOs), and OUs, in order to apply policies on the computer designations such as laptops, desktops, kiosks, are only useful if the client computers in question participate in a Windows Server 2003 or a Windows 2000 domain.

When you are designing the Group Policy infrastructure for the client computers in your organization, it is best to consider how you will be applying GPOs. If, for example, you have a specific GPO that needs to be applied to all laptop computers, it is easiest to put all of those computers in a single OU and link the respective GPO to it. If you are trying to build a Group Policy and OU infrastructure where ease of administration is the goal, you should design the OUs so that you don't need any special filters on the way that Group Policy will propagate down. Figure 9.1 shows an example hierarchy that would make for an easier Group Policy deployment with the assumption that the client operating system will have specific policy settings that will be applied and that should cascade down to laptops as well as desktops.

FIGURE 9.1   Example OU hierarchy for application of Group Policy based on operating system

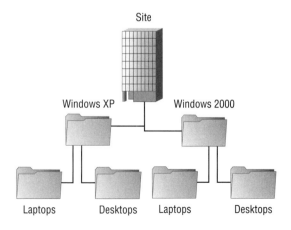

In a similar fashion, should you want a policy to start at the type and cascade to the operating system, you would configure the OU model as shown in Figure 9.2.

In both of these cases, it makes sense to have separate OUs for the operating system version and the role of the computer because each computer type or operating system version will likely require the application of different policies. For example, Windows XP Professional has different services and options compared to Windows 2000 Professional, and by separating the different operating systems into different OUs, each operating system can have its own policy defined. The best technique to implement is to create a GPO for each policy and link it to the appropriate organizational unit.

If, however, you will be applying Group Policy based on the departmental role that the computer falls within, you can filter the application of Group Policy based on the operating system or role of the computer.

It is an important concept to understand that you will need to build an OU design that allows for the easy application of policies for different operating systems and roles. Different operating systems are capable of running different services and have different utilities that need to be configured differently. Obviously, this applies to the different uses of client computers as well. Laptops would be better candidates for configuring the encrypting file system (EFS) than the typical desktop. A support professional's workstation may need to have policies that are different than the policies for other desktops in the department so they can support different clients. To facilitate this, computers should be members of specific security groups created for the application and filtering of Group Policy. Figure 9.3 shows how you may design an OU structure by department assuming that you are using security groups to segregate the operating systems.

FIGURE 9.2 Example OU hierarchy for application of Group Policy based on computer type

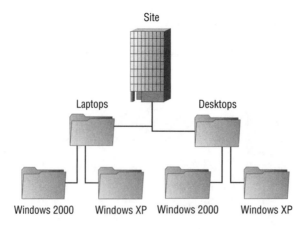

FIGURE 9.3 OU Model with security groups for computer function.

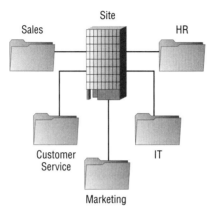

Group Policy objects can be linked to the OUs that represent the business unit, and you can configure computer group membership to further filter the application of the policies on the different types of computers. Figure 9.4 shows a computer's Properties dialog box with the Member Of tab selected to display the groups that the computer—in this example, Computer1—belongs to. The group membership can then be used to filter Group Policy. This type of scenario is more difficult to design and implement, but it does offer great flexibility.

FIGURE 9.4 Computer Properties dialog box

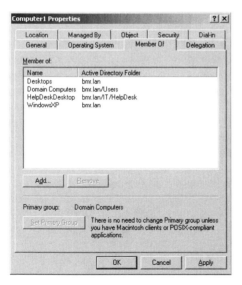

There are various ways that you can configure your OU structure to facilitate a secure client computer system; the best rule of thumb is that you should design the OU structure around your Group Policy plans. If you know that all laptops must have a specific policy applied to them, it would be a good idea to create a Laptops OU and link the GPO or GPOs to it.

In the "Designing an OU Model" Design Scenario, you will be presented with a basic scenario for which you will try to choose the best OU design based on the requirements.

Design Scenario

Designing an OU Model

You are the engineer in charge of designing the OU model for a large accounting conglomerate. You must design an infrastructure that facilitates the distribution of the line-of-business applications for the various departments throughout the company. You need to make sure that the accounts receivable department has access to the AR application, that accounts payable has access to the AP application, and that the accounting managers have access to both. In addition, all accountants will have access to the Accounting General application.

You also need to make sure that if any AR or AP users are using laptops, the encrypting file system is configured appropriately. Desktop computers do not require EFS, but you also need to be able to update antivirus software on them on a regular schedule.

You need to design an OU model that will facilitate, with the least administrative effort, the application assignment and the security requirements stated.

1. **Question:** What should you do? **Answer:** Your proposed solution should look like the following:

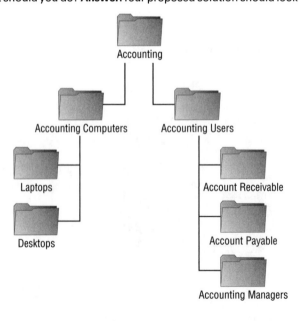

Because all accountants need access to the Accounting General application, you would want to create an OU at the top of the user hierarchy for this department that will hold, either directly or indirectly, all of the accounting users. In the diagram, this is named Accounting Users. You would assign the Accounting General application to this OU in Group Policy. Also in the scenario, you were told that there was an AR application for the accounts receivable users and an AP application for the accounts payable users. This would lead you to create an OU for each group of accountants to assign the software that they will require. Because the AR and AP users are also accounting users, these new OUs should be children OUs of the Accounting Users OU. The accounting managers would also require their own OU because they require that both the AR and the AP applications be assigned to them. As membership changes, a user object could simply be moved from one OU to another in order to have the new applications assigned to them, thus minimizing administration. That covers the user objects and the policies that will apply to them. However, there is also a requirement based on the type of computer that is being used regardless of the user that is using it. As a result, separate OUs should be created for each type of computer, in this case desktop computers and laptop computers.

Please note that the solution given is one possible answer and that many scenarios could be correct in this situation.

Now that you have learned how to evaluate client computer needs as they pertain to the design of the OU hierarchy, you will look at exploiting this design to harden the client operating systems. In order to harden the client computers, you will use security templates, as you learned in Chapter 8, and apply the templates using Group Policy based on the role to which the client computer belongs.

Designing Security Templates for Client Computers

You learned how to use security templates in Chapter 8. You will use them here in the same manner for the hardening of client computers based on their roles. You will want to start with an extremely locked down baseline template and apply a custom template for the particular role of the computer that you wish to harden. In Chapter 8, we used the *Windows Server 2003 Security Guide* as a good reference for the security recommendations; here we will suggest the *Windows XP Security Guide* as the resource to refer to regarding best practices on configuration of the templates. It also includes templates for laptop and desktop computers for both an enterprise and a high-security environment.

You can download the *Windows XP Security Guide* from Microsoft's website at www.microsoft.com/downloads/details.aspx?FamilyID=2d3e25bc-f434-4cc6-a5a7-09a8a229f118&DisplayLang=en.

Whether or not you choose to use the templates that are provided with the *Windows XP Security Guide*, you should create a secure baseline template and customize it for use for a client computer with a specific role. When creating such a template, consider the user rights that need to be restricted in the template, the audit policies, security options, and the system services' behavior. Next, we will briefly provide some best practices for configuring each of these segments of the overall security template.

Auditing is always a beneficial process and should be utilized on client computers in addition to servers. If you are able to determine which computer in your organization was used to launch an attack, you can evaluate its audited history and determine what happened. You can evaluate the *Windows XP Security Guide* to see what the Microsoft recommendation is as far as auditing is concerned.

In addition to configuring the audit policy, you should specify other security settings, ideally within the base template that you will apply. The following are some of the more important settings that you should consider applying:

User Rights Assignment There are a couple of important security-related policies that are assigned within the User Rights Assignment portion of the local policy or the template that you are creating:

> **Deny Logon Through Terminal Services** Once this setting is enabled, you can add user accounts or security groups that will be prevented from logging on using Terminal Services. This is especially important for clients running Windows XP Professional.

> **Deny Access To This Computer From The Network** The users or groups that you add to this policy will be prevented from accessing the client computer via the network. Adding the local administrator account can be useful on laptops that will be attached to other networks, public or otherwise.

Security Options In terms of security, there are also some important computer policy configuration settings within the Security Options portion of the local policy or the template that you are creating:

> **Interactive Logon: Number Of Previous Logons To Cache** The settings that you configure here will determine how many credentials are cached on the local machine and are then available if a domain controller cannot be reached. Setting this option to 0 will prevent anyone from logging onto the computer unless the domain controller can be reached. For preventing a highly secure workstation from being accessed without a domain controller performing the authentication may certainly be desirable, but it would not be plausible for a laptop computer that travels outside of the corporate network. Should the laptop computer also need to be secured tightly, you may consider setting this option to 1.

> **Recovery Console: Allow Floppy Copy And Access To All Drives And Folders** You can disable this setting to prevent someone from using the Recovery Console to copy secure files or other data, such as the Security Accounts Manager (SAM) database, to an insecure location.

Event Log The various settings within the Event Log portion of the policy allow you to use policies to configure the behavior for all of the event log data. You can specify how long to retain the logs as well as whether the local guests group is able to access the predefined logs (application, security, and system). When configuring a high-security client computer, it may become important to make sure that all security-related information is kept. You can configure the retention method for a specific log, such as the security log, by selecting the Do Not Overwrite Events (Clear Log Manually) option. This prevents log entries from being overwritten automatically. If you configure this option (to not overwrite existing entries), make sure that the log is cleared out periodically or it can become full and prevent new entries from being recorded.

Restricted Groups   You can use the Restricted Groups portion of the policy or template to use policies to manage membership within the group. The main feature here is that if the Administrators local group were listed in this policy and a local administrator grants someone membership, that membership would last only until the next policy refresh because it is within the policy itself that the membership is defined. Consider restricting the following groups:

- Administrators
- Power Users
- Remote Desktop Users

System Services   To minimize the attack surface, just as we did for servers in Chapter 8, you will want to disable any nonessential services. Consider disabling the following services, unless you have business reasons for allowing them to run:

- Background Intelligent Transfer Service
- Computer Browser
- Fax Service
- FTP Publishing Service
- IIS Admin Service
- Messenger
- Net Meeting Remote Desktop Sharing
- Network DDE
- Network DDE DSDM
- Remote Registry Service
- Simple Mail Transfer Protocol
- Universal Plug and Play Device Host
- Wireless Zero Configuration
- Telnet
- World Wide Web Publishing service

Registry and File System   In most cases, the settings specified in the *Windows XP Security Guide* are more than adequate for securing common client computers. In some highly secure situations, however, you may need to change the settings for the file system and the Registry. Make sure that you test your changes comprehensively to assure that there will be no unexpected side effects.

It is extremely important that you make sure that critical operating system functions and services are appropriately locked down. Even a well-meaning user could inadvertently expose the entire network to security problems by enabling a service or some other part of the operating system that shouldn't have been available to them.

Similarly, you will also need to prevent the users from your organization from installing software that hasn't been approved by the IT department. This concept of restricting the software that a user can run can be significantly important because it alone can prevent certain Trojan horse applications from being installed in the network.

Designing Software Restriction Policies

Software restriction policies provide administrators with the ability to specify software that is not allowed to execute. Software restriction policies will harden the operating system by giving the administrator the ability to prohibit viruses, Trojan horse applications, and other programs from executing. The policies can then be applied to a Group Policy object (GPO) and then managed as such.

Next you will learn the individual options that you are presented with when configuring software restriction policies.

Configuring Policy-Wide Software Restriction Settings

Be default, software restriction policies allow all software to run, requiring you to define a policy to prevent individual applications from running. This is certainly not the most secure default behavior that could be configured. You will determine the default behavior in Group Policy by configuring the security level in the software restriction policy.

There are two options when configuring the security level of the software restriction policy:

Unrestricted   The access rights for software will be determined based on the access rights of the user who is trying to execute it. Unrestricted is, as mentioned, the default behavior in Group Policy.

Disallowed   Software will not run, regardless of the access rights of the user who is trying to execute it.

You configure this setting in the Group Policy Object Editor or the Group Policy Management Editor, which can be downloaded from the Microsoft web site. To configure the setting, complete the following steps:

1. Open the Group Policy Object Editor (`gpedit.msc`) for the Group Policy object that you are modifying.

2. Select Windows Settings ➤ Security Settings ➤ Software Restriction Policies.

3. Click the `Security Levels` folder.

4. Right-click the Disallowed option and select Set As Default, as shown in Figure 9.5.

WARNING   It is more secure to disallow all applications and define exceptions than to allow all applications and define applications that are not allowed to run.

Before you begin defining individual application policies, you will need to make decisions as to the enforcement of the policies. Figure 9.6 shows the Enforcement Properties dialog box.

FIGURE 9.5   Setting the default security level

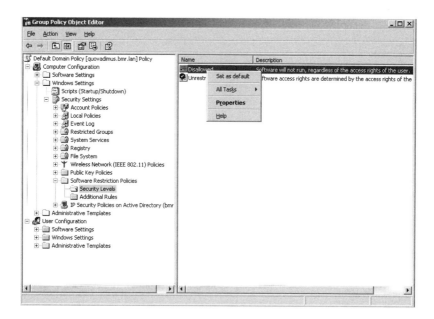

FIGURE 9.6   The Enforcement Properties dialog box

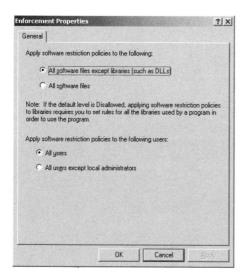

The first decision is to determine the types of files that will fall under the control of the software restriction policy. There are two options:

- All Software Files Except Libraries (Such As DLLs)
- All Software Files

In many situations, it is appropriate to secure all of the files except the libraries because there are numerous library files in use by many applications. If you select the All Software Files option, which is certainly the more secure option, you will be required to explicitly allow each library file, or DLL, that is used by each application. Choosing All Software Files Except Libraries allows you to define a policy for the application without being required to deal with the granularity of granting the library files permission to run within the policy.

The next enforcement option that you need to select is whether or not you want the policy to apply to local administrators or not.

Now you must select what file types will be considered to be executable as far as the policies are considered. There are several file types that are already defined in the policy, such as .bat, .cmd, .com, to name a few. If there are additional file types that become available, you can add them using the Designated File Types Properties dialog box, shown in Figure 9.7.

The last option before you define policies for individual applications is determining who can select a publisher to be trusted: end users, local computer administrators, or enterprise administrators. Typically, you should not leave this option to the end users, but rather configure it to either local or enterprise administrators. Figure 9.8 shows the Trusted Publishers Properties dialog box.

FIGURE 9.7 The Designated File Types Properties dialog box

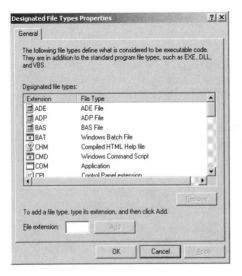

FIGURE 9.8   The Trusted Publishers Properties dialog box

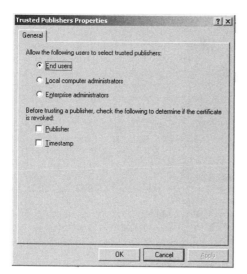

Once the policy itself is designed, the rules that will govern the individual applications will be configured. If the security level is set to Unrestricted, you will define rules that explicitly prevent software from running. If the security level was changed to Disallowed, you will define rules that explicitly allow individual applications to run.

Defining Software Policy Rules

There are four types of software restriction rules that can be defined within the policy:

Certificate rules   *Certificate rules* will grant or deny access to software by evaluating the software's signature and determining if it is signed by a trusted publisher. Certificate software restriction rules can not be used unless the security option System Settings: Use Certificate Rules On Windows Executables For Software Restriction Policies is enabled. If the signature is determined to be valid and the publisher has been approved, the software will run as determined by the security level configured in the rule.

Hash rules   *Hash rules* will create a hash of the specified executable file. When an attempt is made to run an executable, it too is hashed and then the hash is compared with the restricted hashes defined in the rules. In the event of a match, the executable will be granted or denied based on the security level defined in the rules. The importance of this type of rule is that the hash is independent of the filename, the path, and so on. If, however, the software gets updated, the hash will no longer match what is stored in the policy and will need to be redefined in order to be allowed to or prevented from running. Figure 9.9 shows the New Hash Rule dialog box after `Notepad.exe` was selected for hashing.

Internet Zone rules   *Internet Zone rules* will grant or prevent a Windows installer package from running based on the Internet zone from which it is downloaded. This rule type applies only to Windows installer packages and not to any other file type.

FIGURE 9.9   The New Hash Rule dialog box

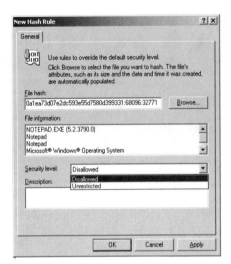

Path rules   *Path rules* will identify an executable based on its file path. Obviously, this would need to be modified if you move an application from its original executing directory. The paths that you specify can include environment variables such as %userprofile%, %windir%, %programfiles%, and so on. Make sure that you use great care when using path rules; all a user would have to do in order to circumvent the policy is copy the executable to another directory from which it is allowed to execute.

If you need to be certain that unauthorized software cannot run on client computers, the best use of the software restriction policy is to set the security level of the policy to Disallowed. This prevents all software from running, except those executables that have an explicit rule defined for them.

In the "Designing Software Restriction Policies" Design Scenario, you will be presented with two scenarios. Determine what the most appropriate use of software restriction policies is for each scenario.

In the next section, you will learn how you can restrict users' access to specific operating systems features and services.

Restricting User Access to the Operating System

It is very common to give users the ability to make certain changes to the operating system that they use on a daily basis. The changes may range from installing certain hardware (such as a printer) to installing an application (such as Microsoft PowerPoint). There are several predefined Windows groups that you can use to give a restrained set of abilities to the various types of users that you will need to support. The following list displays the different security groups and their typical permissions:

- Backup Operators have the ability to override the security restrictions for the exclusive purpose of backing up or restoring files.

- Network Configuration Operators can manage some of the network configuration settings.

- Power Users are given rights similar to local administrators. This group is given the ability to run most legacy applications as a result of the extra permissions granted them.

- Print Operators are able to manage printers. Managing printers includes the ability to create, share, and delete printers as well as manage a printer and its respective queue.

- Remote Desktop Users can log on to the machine using the RDP client protocol.

 Design Scenario

Designing Software Restriction Policies

Scenario 1

You are the security architect for a laboratory that works closely with dangerous chemicals. The hazardous materials are stored in a vault that is secured using a Windows-network-aware application. You need to make sure that under no circumstances is any software run on your network other than applications that have been tested and approved as secure by a government security auditor. There are several physical security mechanisms in place that prevent users from bringing laptop computers and media into the organization. However, sometimes a user is able to sneak a floppy disk or CD into work. No portable computers are allowed in and no computers are allowed to leave the secure environment.

You need to define a policy that will prevent users from running an application that hasn't been approved.

1. **Question:** How should you design the software restriction policy in this scenario with the main focus on security? **Answer:** You should configure a domain-level policy that is set to Disallowed and delete the default path rules. You would then create custom rules to allow the applications that have been tested and verified to run. To make sure that no one can attempt to fool the policy, the exception rules should specify a hash or certificate for verification of the application instead of using path or zone rules, which are less secure.

Scenario 2

You need to design a solution that will prevent users from running virus-infected programs on their computers after the virus has been detected and the program file moved to the quarantine folder by your organization's antivirus software. The solution that you employ cannot prevent users from installing applications that are approved by your organization.

1. **Question:** What should you do? **Answer:** You should create a software restriction policy path rule in the Default Domain Policy Group policy object in your domain that will set the security level on the quarantine folder to Disallowed. To prevent users from copying the file from the quarantine folder to a path that they are allowed to execute from, you would change the Default Domain Policy Group policy object to Disallowed for all software and use a custom hash rule for each approved application and its installer. You would also need to delete the default path rules because they allow unrestricted execution of applications from specific paths.

You should use these predefined groups if your users need to have the rights that are associated with them to perform their work-related tasks. Make sure that you keep the Principle of Least Privilege (PoLP) in mind. For example, if a user needs the ability to manage only a single printer and not all of the printers defined on a machine, they should not be added to the Print Operators group. You should create a new group that has been given only the permission to manage the one specific printer in this example and add the appropriate users to this newly created group. Thus, the users are not given the permissions to do anything that they are not explicitly required to do.

In the "Using Groups to Restrict Access to the Operating System" Design Scenario, you will evaluate the scenario and either choose the appropriate predefined group or create a new group to allow for the required permissions.

 Design Scenario

Using Groups to Restrict Access to the Operating System

You need to provide Joel, the office manager at the remote Miami office, with the appropriate permissions to back up the files on the server. The Miami server is a member server in the Tandyman.lan domain and Joel needs to be able to manually back up and restore all of the files on the server.

1.   **Question:** What group would you add Joel's user account to, if any, in order to allow him to execute his job without hindrance (you need to make sure that Joel is not given any permissions that he doesn't require)? **Answer:** Joel should be added to the Backup Operators local group of the Miami server, which is a predefined group that grants the ability to back up and restore files on the Miami server only.

You can configure hundreds of specific options in the Administrative Templates (.ADM files) portion of a Group Policy object. Figure 9.10 shows the Group Policy Editor with some of the administrative templates viewable.

 You can add or remove templates using the Group Policy Editor snap-in. Just right click the Administrative Templates folder and choose Add/Remove Templates.

As you can see, there are more options than would warrant being listed here. To see the specific information for any one of the settings, right-click the setting you want to learn about and choose Properties. Then select the Explain tab. Figure 9.11 shows the Explain tab for the Remove File Menu Setting of the Windows Explorer Administrative template.

FIGURE 9.10   Administrative templates

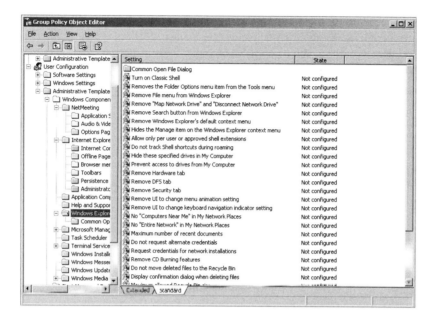

FIGURE 9.11   The Explain tab for the Remove File Menu From Windows Explorer Properties dialog box

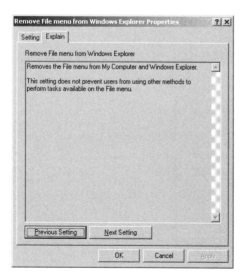

You should examine the many different options here so that when you are given a policy directive, you will know which template you would use to implement it. For example, if a manager were to specify that Windows Messenger should not be allowed to run on Windows XP computers, you should know how to achieve this using the Windows Messenger template and enabling the Do Not Allow Windows Messenger To Be Run setting, as shown in Figure 9.12.

The administrative templates that are installed by default are shown in Table 9.1.

TABLE 9.1 Default Administrative Templates

Template	Example Setting
Windows Components	Remove Security Tab From Windows Explorer
Start Menu And Taskbar	Lock The Taskbar
Desktop	Remove Properties From The My Computer Context Menu
Control Panel	Prohibit Access To The Control Panel
Shared Folders	Allow Shared Folders To Be Published
Network	Prohibit TCP/IP Advanced Configuration
System	Turn Off Autoplay

FIGURE 9.12 The Do Not Allow Windows Messenger To Be Run Properties dialog box

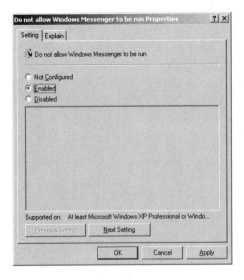

In the "Selecting the Appropriate Template Setting" Design Scenario, you will be presented with a business rule that must be implemented using the administrative templates in Group Policy.

Design Scenario

Selecting the Appropriate Template Setting

You have gotten word that several viruses have been propagating across the Windows Messenger application. You need to make sure that users in the Customer Support OU are not able to run the Windows Messenger service. You also need to make sure that, for all users of the domain, the Windows Messenger application does not start automatically.

1. **Question:** How should you implement this business rule? **Answer:** You should create a Group Policy object that enables the Do Not Automatically Start Windows Messenger Initially setting and link it to the Domain OU. You should create another GPO that enables the Do Not Allow Windows Messenger To Be Run setting and link it to the Customer Support OU.

In the next section, you will be introduced to designing a security update infrastructure. You will learn about secure configurations and security hotfixes and patches as well as how to configure them using the assorted tools that Microsoft has provided.

Designing a Security Update Infrastructure

There is much more to updating the security of your infrastructure than just applying new patches. In addition to applying security-related patches, you should make configuration changes as new information and attacks are known or as new services or applications are installed. In this section, we will show you the different tools that you can use to solve your security update woes as well as the benefits and drawbacks of each potential solution.

To create a security update infrastructure, you obviously must be able to determine what needs to be updated and how it will be accomplished. Unfortunately, as far as security updates go, there is no panacea; no single solution solves all of the problems that plague your network infrastructure. It is for this reason that there are several methods for updating the security of computers that, when used in concert, can help you achieve a complete security update infrastructure.

Table 9.2 lists the different methods of updating in a Windows network, including the operating system that the method supports, and whether or not it supports software patches or configuration changes or both.

TABLE 9.2 Security Update Methods

Method	Operating Systems	Supports
Microsoft Windows Update	Windows 98 and higher	Software patches
Software Update Services (SUS)	Windows 2000 and higher	Software patches
SMS with SUS feature pack	Windows 98 and NT 4 and higher	Software patches and configuration changes
Security Configuration And Analysis	Windows 2000 and higher	configuration
Group Policy	Windows 2000 and higher	Software patches and configuration changes

Each method listed in Table 9.2 is explained in the following list:

Microsoft Windows Update The *Microsoft Windows Update* website (located at `http://v4.windowsupdate.microsoft.com/en/default.asp`) is a wonderful utility for individual computers and small businesses to allow the users to update their own systems. It doesn't support modifying the configuration of any of the software on the running machine. It also does not provide specific information as to how the patch that is being applied will affect other applications on the computer.

Microsoft Software Update Services (SUS) *Microsoft Software Update Services (SUS)* gives an administrator the ability to deploy critical and security-related updates and services packs to servers running Windows 2000 or Windows Server 2003 and clients running Windows 2000 and XP Professional. The updates can be synchronized from the Microsoft Windows Update website and saved to a SUS server where an administrator can test the update to see if it is compatible with the configuration and applications that are currently running in the network environment. When the administrator determines that there are no conflicts, they will approve the updates to be distributed by the SUS server. The client computers, running the Automatic Updates component, will download the approved updates from the SUS server and apply them.

Microsoft Systems Management Server 2003 (SMS 2003) *Microsoft Systems Management Server 2003* is a comprehensive change management and configuration solution. It is capable of deploying applications, managing security and software patches, managing assets, and more to clients ranging from Windows NT 4 and Windows 98 up to current computers running Windows XP and Windows Server 2003. Unlike SUS, SMS 2003 is not free and requires a SQL Server database for its datastore.

Security Configuration And Analysis As you learned in Chapter 8, the Security Configuration And Analysis MMC snap-in is used to evaluate the configuration of systems and optionally apply a template to adjust the configuration of the target computer based on the settings defined in the template. It cannot be used to install software patches, only for configuration. It is also not a great solution alone to deploy the configuration changes across the network. It can create templates that are deployed by means of Group Policy for multiple computers.

Group Policy   Group Policy, in the context of software updates and security configuration, can be used to install patches and, when used with administrative templates, can deploy broad-based configuration settings. It requires that Microsoft Active Directory services be configured for the network and that all target computers will be Active Directory clients. It also requires that a specific policy be defined for each update as it comes out.

When you must decide which security update method to apply, you should consider how many client computers need to be updated. The Microsoft Windows Update site is useful when only a small number of computer systems require updating because it typically requires an inter-action with the Web interface. With supported client computers, however, Windows Update can be configured to automatically download and apply updates. But there is no check to see how it will affect other installed applications or services.

A Microsoft Software Update Services (SUS) server can update a relatively small number of client computers as well as several hundred. Configuring SUS hierarchy, which is covered later in this chapter, will allow for the update of even more client computers.

Microsoft SMS 2003 can be used to update a practically limitless number of client comput-ers. It is usually reserved for the larger enterprise organizations because it is expensive and requires its own administrative staff to configure, deploy, and manage its own infrastructure.

In most cases, a configuration made up of both SUS and Group Policy will solve all of the issues that need to be addressed, from scalability to client support.

 You can evaluate the differences between Windows Update, SUS, and SMS 2003 at www.microsoft.com/windowsserversystem/sus/suschoosing.mspx.

In the following sections you will learn some of the factors that will be considered when designing your SUS infrastructure. In addition you will find out how to use the Microsoft Base-line Security Analyzer (MBSA) utility to identify those computers that are not at the appropriate patch level.

Design a Software Update Services infrastructure

SUS is a customized solution for medium-sized organizations that follows the lead of the Microsoft Windows Update website to provide software updates and security patches to com-puters. The purpose of SUS is to distribute critical updates to computers in your organization with as little difficulty as possible.

SUS offers the following benefits:

Behind the corporate firewall   The SUS server located behind the corporate firewall, which allows you to define a single point inside your organization that will synchronize with the Microsoft Windows Update site whenever new updates are made available for Windows 2000, Windows Server 2003, or Windows XP.

Administrator-approved updates   The administrator can now test the updates from the public Microsoft Windows Update site prior to deploying them to the computers within their organization. The administrator can also determine the schedule upon which the updates will be delivered to the target computers. There can be several servers within a network running the SUS, and in that event, the administrator can, through Group Policy or Registry modifications, configure the target computers with the SUS server that they will use.

Administrator-configured synchronization with the Windows Update site   The administrator can design SUS infrastructure that is made up of several servers running the SUS. In addition, the administrator can define one of the SUS servers to download the updates from the Microsoft Windows Update site and make the new patches and fixes available to the other servers within the SUS infrastructure. This minimizes the Internet bandwidth required because only a single server must retrieve patches from the Windows Update site.

Staged deployment for test to production   Your administrative team can configure in a test environment a server that will publish updates to client computers within the test environment first. If there are no compatibility or other problems with the deployment of the security update, you can publish the updates to the rest of your organization by approving the other SUS servers, those configured for the production computers, to deliver the update to the production computers.

SUS notification e-mail list   The administrator can subscribe to a Microsoft-maintained e-mail distribution list that will send notification when a patch is added or updated to the Microsoft database.

There are two parts to the SUS solution:

- The server (or servers) that is running SUS and downloads updates from the Microsoft Windows Update servers or from other internal SUS servers.

- The Automatic Updates client that downloads the updates from either the Microsoft Windows Update site or a SUS server in your network. Before applying the updates, SUS will check the digital signature to make sure that it bears Microsoft's signature. If the update package is not signed, it will not be applied.

Now that you've learned the concepts of SUS you will now learn how to configure the settings of the SUS servers in your organization.

Configuring SUS Servers

SUS runs on Windows 2000 Server, Service Pack 2 or higher, and on the Windows Server 2003 family of operating systems. SUS must be installed on an NTFS partition and the system partition of the server must also be on an NTFS volume.

   SUS Service Pack 1 can be installed on domain controllers, unlike SUS 1.

You can download the installer for SUS by navigating to `http://go.microsoft.com/fwlink/?LinkId=6930`.

Once you install SUS, you configure and administer it using the web application that is installed on the SUS server in the `SUSAdmin` virtual directory, as you can see in Figure 9.13.

If you decide that you do not want to use the default website on the server, you must either disable or delete it. SUS will always install into the default website if the website exists on the server. In addition, should you decide that you would like the website that hosts the SUSAdmin application to use a different port, you could change that setting from the Default Web Site Properties dialog box in the Internet Information Services (IIS) Manager MMC snap-in, as you can see in Figure 9.14.

It is by using this administrative website that you will configure the SUS service to meet your specific needs. You configure the service to automatically download new patches and updates on a defined schedule, or you can specify that it will update them only when you, the administrator, manually initiate the synchronization process. Figure 9.15 shows the Synchronize Server administration page. You should make sure that new patches and updates are synchronized regularly, ideally every day. Each SUS server can handle updating about 15,000 client computers; you should add additional SUS servers as needed. You can still make sure that only one of the SUS servers in your hierarchy retrieves the updates from Microsoft and then configure the other SUS servers to download the updates from the SUS server that receives the updates directly from Microsoft.

FIGURE 9.13   Software Update Services administrative website

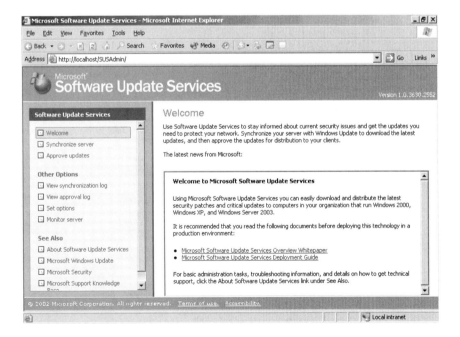

FIGURE 9.14 The Default Web Site Properties dialog box

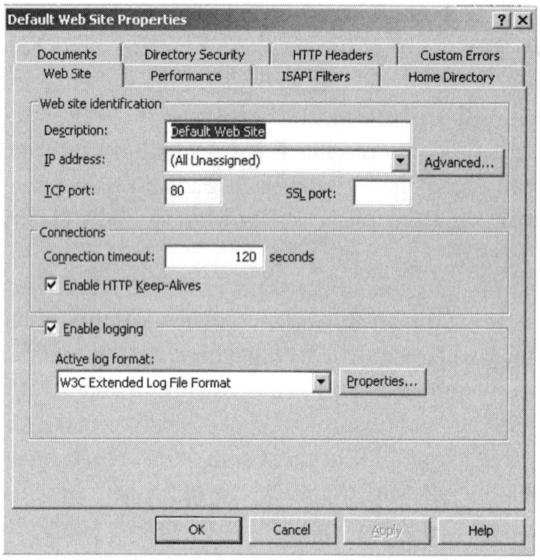

FIGURE 9.15 The Synchronize Server page

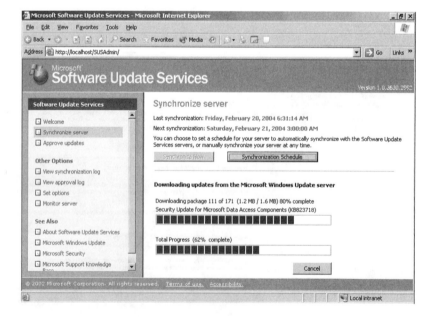

Once the updates are downloaded, you will be able to choose which updates to approve and distribute from the Approve Updates page. Figure 9.16 shows the Approve Updates page from the SUSAdmin web application.

You should consider having a different SUS hierarchy that will be responsible for each group of computers based on how updates are going to be approved. In this case, you may have two types of workstations that you need to have patched: normal desktops and mission-critical desktops. You could configure the normal desktops to use one SUS server in which most patches are approved rapidly by its administrator and the mission-critical desktops to use a separate SUS server that requires more meticulous and rigorous testing before a patch can be approved for the mission critical workstations.

When you have decided that an update will be delivered to the SUS clients, you select it from the Approve Updates page and click the Approve button.

Configuring SUS Clients

Now that you have installed and configured your SUS server(s) to download and maintain the updates that are being released from Microsoft on a regular basis, you will need to configure the computers in your organization to look to their respective SUS server, if you have more than one, to retrieve and apply the updates.

In the following sections, we will look at the different techniques that you can use to configure a computer to use your SUS infrastructure.

FIGURE 9.16   SUSAdmin Approve Updates page

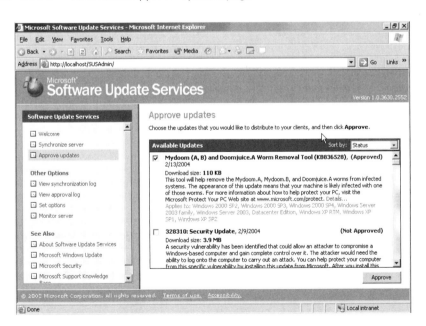

Using Group Policy Objects to Configure SUS Clients

The recommended method of configuring SUS clients is to use Active Directory's Group Policy. As is the case with any other configuration options being set in a GPO, Group Policy allows an administrator to configure a policy once and have it be applied consistently throughout the directory.

To define a GPO to configure the SUS client, first navigate to the appropriate section of the GPO:

1. Launch the Group Policy Object Editor (GPEDIT.msc).

2. Expand Computer Configuration ➤ Administrative Templates ➤ Windows Components.

3. Select Windows Update. (If you do not have the Windows Update section under the Windows Components container, right-click Administrative Templates and select Add/Remove Templates and add wuau.adm.)

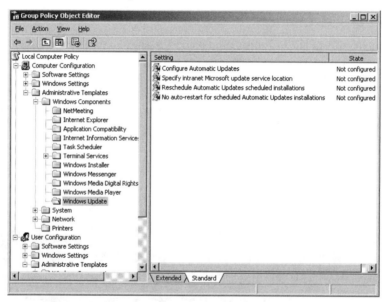

There are four settings for the Windows Update policies that can be configured and set:

Configure Automatic Updates   This setting allows you to define the behavior of the automatic updates. Once this setting is enabled, you must choose the method of automatic updating as seen in Figure 9.17:

Notify For Download And Notify For Install   The user of the computer is prompted to both download and install the updates.

Auto Download And Notify For Install   The update is automatically downloaded from the Update server and the user of the machine is prompted to apply the update.

Auto Download And Schedule The Install   The update is automatically downloaded from the Update server and automatically installed based on the schedule defined in this setting. If this option is selected, the scheduled install day and scheduled install time will apply.

Specify Intranet Microsoft Update Service Location   This setting, once enabled, gives you the opportunity to specify the address of your SUS server so the client can download the updates from it. To use this setting, you must define the server from which the Automatic Updates client will detect and download updates as well as the server to which updated workstations upload statistics. As seen in Figure 9.18 both values can point to the same intranet server.

FIGURE 9.17   The Configure Automatic Updates Properties dialog box

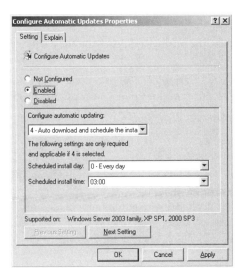

FIGURE 9.18   Specify Intranet Microsoft Update Service Location

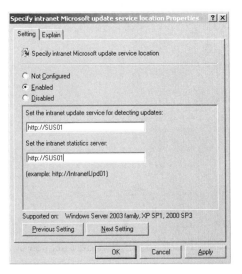

Reschedule Automatic Updates Scheduled Installations   This setting specifies the amount of time that the Automatic Updates service will wait after the computer starts up before beginning a scheduled installation that it had previously missed (typically because the computer was powered off when the schedule dictated installation should occur).

No Auto-Restart For Scheduled Automatic Updates Installations   If enabled, this option prevents the computer from automatically restarting itself after an update is installed. The update will not be complete until the interactive user of the computer manually restarts the computer.

Manually Configuring SUS Clients

In addition to using a GPO, you can configure the settings manually on the client using any one of the following techniques:

- Use the Local Security Policy on each workstation. The steps are identical to when configuring a GPO, but this is applied only to the computer that you configure it on.

- Use the Automatic Updates tab of the System Properties Control Panel applet, as seen in Figure 9.19.

- Manually modify the Registry on each client.

As you can see, the only realistic option is to use a GPO when there is a moderate quantity of client computers involved. You will want to make sure that your OU structure is designed in such a way that software updates and patches can be deployed with a minimum of administrative effort.

In the Designing a Patch Management Solution" Design Scenario, you will evaluate the provided scenario and decide the best way to design a patch management solution from the possible answers.

FIGURE 9.19   The Automatic Updates tab

Design Scenario

Designing a Patch Management Solution

You are the security architect of Kellum Enterprises, a worldwide bicycle manufacturing company. You currently support over 25,000 computers that are made up of Windows NT, Windows 2000, and Windows Server 2003 operating systems. Your network is divided into four major sites: North America, South America, Asia, and Europe. Each site is connected to the Internet, and they connect to each other using VPN connections. You need to design a patch management solution for this enterprise that can handle all of the clients and doesn't put any unnecessary burden on any one server. Administrators for each site will approve the patches to be deployed to computers in their site. There are approximately 6,500 computers in each site.

1. **Question:** How should you configure a security patch management solution? (Choose the best answer.)

   A. Install a single SUS server in the North America site to retrieve the updates from the Microsoft Windows Update site. Install secondary SUS servers in each of the other sites and configure them to retrieve the updates from the North America SUS server. Create a GPO for each site that configures the clients to use the SUS server in the same site.

   B. Install a SUS server in each site and configure it to retrieve the updates from the Windows Update site. Create a GPO for each site that configures the clients to use the SUS server in the same site.

   C. Install a SUS server in the North America and the Europe sites to retrieve the updates from the Microsoft Windows Update site. Install secondary SUS servers in South America and Asia. The South America SUS server will retrieve its updates from the North America SUS server; the Asia SUS server will retrieve its updates from the Europe SUS server. Create an OU for each site and create a GPO for each one that identifies the appropriate SUS server for clients in the OU to use.

   D. Create a single GPO that configures the client computers to retrieve the updates directly from the Microsoft Windows Update Internet site. Link the GPO to the domain.

   Answer: B

   Because the administrator at each site needs the ability to approve its patches and fixes, each site should have a primary SUS server. Option A is incorrect because it puts an undue burden, when compared to answer B, on the North America SUS server; it would have to distribute the updates to the other sites. It also would prohibit patches that North America doesn't approve from being downloaded to other SUS servers. Option C is incorrect because it creates new OUs for the sites, which is unnecessary because GPOs can be linked to a site. In addition, an undue burden is placed on the North America and Europe SUS servers by making Asia and South America download the updates from them. Also, the South America and Asia SUS servers would be able to download only the approved updates from North America and Europe, respectively. Option D is incorrect because it doesn't allow for each site's administrator to approve the patches that will be applied.

Identifying Computers That Are Not at the Current Patch Level

Now that you have designed an infrastructure that supports the process updating the computers in your organization, you will want to define a technique to verify that it is working. In other words, you will need to audit the patches of the machines on your network to make sure that the correct patches are applied. Microsoft has created a utility to accomplish this task: *Microsoft Baseline Security Analyzer (MBSA)*.

MBSA is used for two different tasks: analyzing the configuration of a computer and generating a report of the security vulnerabilities and determining if there are patches that are available for the operating system or services on a machine that have not been applied.

You can use MBSA to analyze a single computer, a range of addresses, or an entire Windows domain. The current version of the MBSA utility (version 1.2) can analyze the following operating systems and services:

- Windows NT SP4, 2000, XP, and Server 2003
- Internet Information Services (IIS) 4–6
- Microsoft SQL Server 7.0 and 2000
- Internet Explorer 5.01 and higher
- Office 2000 and higher

The MBSA utility can be configured to compare the target computer with the patches that have been approved by a SUS server.

 SUS version 1 does not currently support Microsoft SQL Server or Office applications.

You can use the MBSA user interactive interface when you want to manually analyze a computer or group of computers. Figure 9.20 shows an example of the interactive MBSA utility.

In order to truly exploit the power of the MBSA on an enterprise scale, you will use it in scripts that include the command-line version of the MBSA utility. You can evaluate all of the command-line options by executing mbsacli /? from the MBSA installation directory. It can be scheduled to scan a group of computers and store the report to be viewed at a later time. For example, the following command line will scan a domain named myDomain.com, store the results in the c:\results\scanresult.txt file, and use the SUS server London for a list of approved updates:

```
Mbsacli /d myDomain.com /f "c:\results\scanresult.txt" /SUS
  ➥"http://London"
```

Once the scan has completed, you should evaluate the contents of the scanresult.txt file, which would be similar to the following:

```
Computer Name, IP Address, Assessment, Report Name
------------------------------------------------------
NWTRADERS\LONDON, 192.168.247.8, Severe Risk, NWTRADERS - LONDON
  (2-20-2004 11-19 AM)
```

There would be an entry for each computer in the domain. You would use this information and evaluate the details of each computer using the report viewer in the MBSA GUI client. Figure 9.21 shows what a completed MBSA security report might look like.

FIGURE 9.20 MBSA manual scan interface

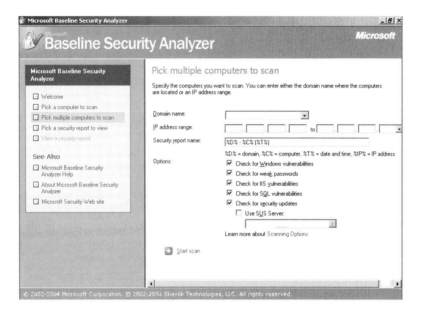

FIGURE 9.21 MBSA security report

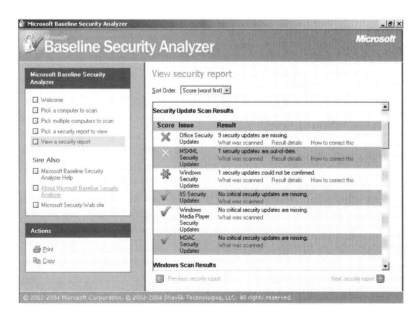

Using this information, you would either apply the appropriate patches to the specified computers or begin troubleshooting to find out why they weren't applied in the first place. As with any good solution, you must verify it over time to make sure that it continues to work. No patch management solution is complete without a patch auditing solution to verify that the patches are being applied.

In the "Auditing Your Security Patch Solution" Design Scenario, you will determine the best way to determine whether or not a critical patch has been applied.

 Design Scenario

Auditing Your Security Patch Solution

You are using a combination of SMS 2003 and SUS to patch all of the appropriate applications to the current level. You have several Windows, IIS, and SQL Server servers that must be updated with the latest updates available, and you must constantly verify the patch level.

1.   **Question:** How would you configure MBSA to audit the patches that are being applied to these servers? What resource should they use to determine which patches are available? **Answer:** You should use a script to automate the MBSACLI command-line utility and specify that it should get the update information from the Internet instead of from the SUS server. SUS doesn't support SQL Server patches in its current version.

Summary

In this chapter, you learned how to apply many of the same principles for securing clients that you used in Chapter 8 for securing servers. You saw that you will have to apply different policies based on how a client computer will be used. A properly designed Active Directory OU model is priceless when it comes to securing computers and accounts based on the roles that they play in the network.

In accordance with Chapter 8, we revisited the concept of creating security templates and applying them in concert with Group Policy. You will want to design a different security template for each type of computer—for example, laptops and desktops. There are also additional templates that can be obtained from Microsoft as part of the *Windows XP Security Guide*.

We then explained the benefit of defining software restriction policies that you can use to make sure that you have control over the software that is running on the computers in your charge. You saw the difference between configuring the default behavior to be unrestricted with rules denying specific applications or paths and configuring the default behavior to be disallowed with rules explicitly allowing applications or executable paths. Disallowing the default behavior is more secure, while the Unrestricted option interferes less with the user of the computer. There are pros and cons for each rule type—certificate, hash, path, and Internet zone—depending on the details of the situation and the level of administrative burden you are willing to endure.

Next you learned how to prevent users from accessing certain sections of the Windows operating system itself. You can use built-in groups to assign specific rights to users when it is appropriate. You can also use administrative templates in a GPO that grants or denies access to a feature of the operating system.

Finally, you were introduced to security patch management, namely with Software Update Services (SUS) and Group Policy. You learned the basics of configuring a SUS server as well as SUS clients. We showed you the different implementations of SUS and some basic guidelines that you should try to follow. You learned that, with SUS, you can choose which updates to deploy to your client computers rather than configuring all of the computers to use the Microsoft Windows Update site as the authority on which patches and fixes to apply.

To verify your patch management, and for that matter to secure configurations, you learned how to use the Microsoft Baseline Security Analyzer to audit one or more computers under your control. You saw that it can be invoked manually or automated in a script using its command-line version.

Exam Essentials

Know how to define and configure a software restriction policy.   Make sure that you can identify the difference between the Unrestricted and Disallowed options for configuring the default behavior of software. Know which circumstances will drive the different type of software restriction rules: path, hash, certificate, or Internet zone.

Understand how Group Policy can be used to manage client software and configuration. You will want to make sure that you understand the environment so that you can recommend an appropriate Group Policy strategy. If you are dealing with an OU model, you need to determine the best technique for creating and linking GPOs to the various containers: sites, domains, and OUs.

Recognize the various administrative templates and how they can be used.   Make sure that you know when it would be appropriate to use administrative templates in a GPO to remove access to specific operating system or application services or functionality.

Consider all options when designing a patch management solution.   Be able to compare the varied options that are available, and based on the requirements in your scenario, you will be directed to the appropriate solution. Know that for a small number of clients, it is appropriate to use the Microsoft Windows Update site directly. To control which updates are deployed to the clients, you will need to use SUS. Along similar lines, you should also decide which server or servers will be responsible for downloading the updates from Microsoft and on what schedule.

Remember that you can use the Microsoft Baseline Security Analyzer (MBSA) to audit the security patches and configuration of computers.   Make sure you know when to run the MBSA interactively by using the command-line version and launching it via script or schedule.

Key Terms

Before you take the exam, be certain you are familiar with the following terms:

certificate rules

hash rules

Internet zone rules

Microsoft Baseline Security Analyzer (MBSA)

Microsoft Software Update Services

Microsoft Systems Management Server 2003

Microsoft Windows Update

path rules

software restriction policies

Review Questions

1. You are the lead Active Directory architect for a large-scale network. You need to define a strategy that prevents computers from launching applications that are explicitly prohibited by the corporate policy. You need to prevent users from moving or renaming files in order to bypass the defined policy. What should you do? (Choose all that apply.)

    A. Define a software restriction policy and leave the security level as Unrestricted.

    B. Create a path rule for each application that you want to allow.

    C. Create a hash rule for each application that you want to prevent.

    D. Create a path rule for each application that you want to prevent.

    E. Create a hash rule for each application that you want to allow.

    F. Define a software restriction policy and change the security level to Disallowed.

2. You are the administrator of medium-sized network and you need to prevent users from changing the configuration of their computers. Which of the following can be used to accomplish this? (Choose all that apply.)

    A. Administrative Templates settings in Group Policy

    B. Microsoft Baseline Security Analyzer

    C. Software Update Services

    D. Removing users from local Administrators or Power Users groups on their computers

    E. Software restriction policy

3. You are the network architect of a large electronics manufacturer that has just opened a new sales office in Alaska. The main office is located in Miami, Florida; both offices have a direct connection to the Internet. There is a complete SUS infrastructure that is already designed in the Miami office and that handles over 5,000 computers and servers. There are 10 client computers and 2 servers in the Alaska site. You need to make sure that, because the new office is so remote from the main office, updates are installed often and automatically. No approval is necessary because there is no custom software running in the Alaska office that could conflict with any portion of the operating system. You need to make sure that all of the computers in the Alaska office get all of the updates that Microsoft releases with the least amount of administrative effort. The Alaskan office needs to be able to retrieve updates even if it cannot connect to the Miami office. What should you do?

    A. Install SUS on one of the servers in the Alaska site and configure the other computers to use it.

    B. Configure all of the computers in the Alaska site to use the SUS infrastructure already configured in Miami.

    C. Configure all of the computers to use the Microsoft Windows Update site.

    D. Manually download and install the patches and service packs as they become available.

4. You need to audit your security patch strategy to verify its effectiveness. You want this auditing to occur on a semi-regular basis, with the least amount of administrative effort. What utility should you use for this functionality?

    A. On a regular basis launch the Microsoft Baseline Security Analyzer (MBSA) and evaluate the resulting report.

    B. Use the intranet administration web application for Software Update Services, SUSAdmin, to generate and schedule its reporting features.

    C. Create and schedule a script that uses the Microsoft Baseline Security Analyzer command-line utility (MBSACLI.EXE).

    D. Define and enable a patch policy in a Group Policy object (GPO) and link it to the domain container.

5. You are the administrator for a medium-sized organization that manufacturers transparent aluminum. The CIO tells you that the HR managers need to be able to manage one of the printers that is located on the HR server, which is a member server in the TranAlum.LAN domain. You need to grant the HR managers, who are all members of the HR Managers global group, this ability without giving them more rights than they require, and you should do this with the least amount of administrative effort. What should you do?

    A. Add the HR Managers group to the Administrators local group on the HR server.

    B. Add the HR Managers group to the Print Operators group of the HR server.

    C. Add the HR Managers group to the Power Users group of the HR server.

    D. Create a custom local group on the HR server, grant it the ability to manage the HR printer, and add the HR Managers global group to the newly created local group.

6. You are the administrator responsible for updating the workstations and servers for your company. You need to be able to apply software patches and adjust the configuration of the computers to make them more secure. You need to select a solution that meets both these requirements. Which of the following methods can be used to deploy patches as well as modify the configuration of the computer? (Choose all that apply.)

    A. Microsoft Windows Update site

    B. Software Update Services (SUS) version 1

    C. Systems Management Server with SUS feature pack

    D. Security Configuration And Analysis MMC snap-in

    E. Group Policy

7. You are the administrator responsible for updating all 8,000 client computers in the Philadelphia region. The computers are running Windows NT 4, Windows 2000, and Windows XP Professional and are configured as members of a large Windows Server 2003 Active Directory domain. What software patch distribution solution should you choose?

    A. Software Update Services (SUS) version 1

    B. Systems Management Server 2003 with SUS feature pack

    C. Group Policy

    D. Microsoft Baseline Security Analyzer (MBSA)

8. You have just installed and configured a SUS server in your organization and created a schedule to download updates from the Internet. You now need to configure the 2,500 workstations and servers in your environment. You need to make sure that all of the clients are updated to use the SUS server to download the updates. Which of the following techniques can be used to configure the SUS clients? (Choose all that apply.)

   A. Modify the Registry of each computer to point it to the newly installed SUS server.

   B. Create a custom script on each computer that runs the `MBSACLI.EXE` utility to configure the SUS information.

   C. Create a GPO that configures the SUS information on each computer and link it to the appropriate container.

   D. Use the Security Configuration And Analysis MMC snap-in and apply its template to all of the computers that need to be updated with the SUS server information.

9. You are the security architect of a multinational exporter with offices across the U.S. and Europe. The two main offices are New York and Paris. All U.S. sites connect to the Internet through the New York site, and all European offices connect to the Internet through Paris. Each office in the U.S. connects to New York with a dedicated 256k line and each office in Europe connects to Paris with a dedicated 256k line. You need to design a patch management solution that distributes and applies security patches to workstations and servers on both continents. Your solution must minimize WAN bandwidth. What should you do?

   A. In each office, use one new SUS server that will download all of the security patches. Configure the computers in each office to use their respective SUS server.

   B. Use one new SUS server in New York and one in Paris to download all security patches. Configure the U.S. offices to use the SUS server in New York and the European offices to use the SUS server in Paris.

   C. Use one new SUS server in New York and one in Paris to download all security patches. In the U.S., configure a SUS server in each office to synchronize the content from the SUS server in New York. In Europe, configure a server in each office to synchronize the content from the SUS server in Paris. Configure the clients in each office to use the SUS server in their respective office.

   D. Configure all clients to download the patches from the Microsoft Windows Update site.

10. You are the security architect of a large law firm, and consultants sometimes temporarily have access to certain network resources. The attorneys often store confidential client-related data on their workstations, and you need to make sure that only attorneys can access the data over the network. Which of the following security techniques should you use to prevent the consultants from accessing the attorney's workstations?

   A. Security templates

   B. Software restriction policies

   C. Administrative templates

   D. MBSA script

Answers to Review Questions

1. **A, C.** In this question, only the software that is explicitly stated in the corporate policy as being prevented should be kept from executing. Therefore, you should enable software restriction and leave the security level set to Unrestricted. Thus, option F is incorrect. Because an Unrestricted security level allows all software not explicitly defined in a rule to execute, you do not specify rules for applications to be allowed, so options B and E are incorrect. A path rule can be bypassed, which is why option D is incorrect. Creating a hash rule for the applications that are to explicitly be denied from executing is the best answer in this situation, which is why options A and C are correct.

2. **A, D.** To prevent a user from making configuration changes to the operating system of their workstation, you can use Administrative Templates settings in a Group Policy object (GPO), you can manually edit the Windows Registry, you can use custom scripts or third-party applications, or you can simply remove the users from the Power Users or Administrators group on the workstation. The Microsoft Baseline Security Analyzer (MBSA) is used to audit the security patches and configuration on a computer or group of computers. Therefore, option B is incorrect. Software Update Services (SUS) is used to apply patches and service packs, not restrict operating system features, which is why option C is incorrect. Option E is incorrect because a software restriction policy is used to define which applications can or can't be executed; it is not able to prevent a user from making changes to operating system functionality.

3. **C.** Option A is incorrect because it requires that updates be approved in order to be distributed to the computers in Alaska. Option B is incorrect because it requires that the Alaskan office communicate with the Miami server, and allows only the approved updates, as defined in Miami, to be deployed to the computers in Alaska. Option D is incorrect because it requires a significant amount of administrative effort, which would be decreased by configuring the computers to get the information directly from Microsoft. Answer C is correct because it requires the least amount of administrative effort by not requiring any administrator to approve updates.

4. **C.** The MBSA command-line interface can and should be scheduled in a script to facilitate the requirements defined in the question. Therefore, option C is correct. The Microsoft Baseline Security Analyzer (MBSA) is the utility that produces the desired functionality; however, the interactive version cannot be scheduled, which is why option A is incorrect. Software Update Services does not include a reporting element. Therefore, option B is incorrect. There is no such thing as a patch policy. Therefore, option D is incorrect.

5. **D.** The only solution that doesn't give the HR managers more rights than they require is D. Adding the HR Managers group to the Administrators local group on the HR member server will allow them do to almost anything on the server, which is significantly more rights than they require. Therefore option A is incorrect. Adding the HR managers to the Print Operators group will give them the ability to manage the printer on the HR member server; however, it will also give them the right to manage all of the printers on the server, not just the one printer that they need to manage. Therefore, option B is incorrect. Adding the HR managers to the Power Users local group would also allow them to manage all of the printers, which is too many rights based on the requirements stated in the question. Therefore, option C is incorrect.

6. C, E. Both SMS 2003 with the SUS feature pack and Group Policy can be used to deploy patches as well as make configuration changes. Therefore, options C and E are correct. Both the Microsoft Windows Update site and Software Update Services version 1 can be used only to deploy software patches, not make configuration changes. Therefore, options A and B are incorrect. The Security Configuration And Analysis MMC snap-in can only make configuration changes, not deploy software patches, which is why option D is incorrect.

7. B. Only Systems Management Server (SMS) 2003 with SUS feature pack can deploy patches to Windows NT 4 clients. SUS version 1 and Group Policy require Windows 2000 and higher; they do not support Windows NT 4 clients. Therefore, options A and C are incorrect. The MBSA tool is used to audit the security of a computer or group of computers. It will not distribute software patches, which is why option D is incorrect.

8. A, C. You can configure the computers by using a GPO or by manually editing the Registry of each computer, which is why options A and C are correct. The MBSACLI.EXE utility is the command-line interface of the Microsoft Baseline Security Analyzer utility that is used to audit and report on the security configuration and applied patches of computers; it will not configure a computer to use a specific SUS server. Therefore, option B is incorrect. The Security Configuration And Analysis MMC snap-in can be used to apply security templates to computers; however, it will not configure the computers to use a specific SUS server. Therefore, option D is incorrect.

9. C. Option C is correct because it is the only solution that allows for all of the computers to receive the updates and minimizes WAN traffic. Option A is incorrect because it causes too much WAN traffic by having each office download updates from the Internet. Option B is incorrect because there would be, from each workstation and server retrieving the updates, too much traffic across the U.S. going to the N.Y. SUS server and too much traffic in Europe going to the Paris SUS server. Option D causes each client to generate too much WAN traffic by downloading the updates directly from the Microsoft Windows Update site.

10. A. You would define a security template that enables Deny Access To This Computer From The Network for the users not in the Attorneys group. Software restriction policies are used to prevent a user from running software, not from accessing network resources. Therefore, option B is incorrect. Administrative templates are used to restrict a user's access to the operating system of the computer that they are logged on to, not accessing remotely. Therefore, option C is incorrect. The MBSA is used for auditing and reporting on security configuration; it doesn't change the configuration. Therefore, option D is incorrect.

Case Study

You should give yourself 20 minutes to review this testlet, review the table, and complete the questions.

Background

T&C Incorporated manufactures and markets sporting goods across the U.S. The company has four offices. The main office is in Philadelphia, PA, and it has branch offices in Wilmington, DE, Minneapolis, MN, and Los Angeles, CA. The company's employees and departments are distributed as shown in the following table:

Location	Employees	Departments
Philadelphia	1,000	Executive and Information Technology (IT)
Wilmington	75	Sales and Marketing
Minneapolis	5,000	Manufacturing
Los Angeles	30	Customer Support

Existing Environment

The IT staff in the Philadelphia office uses client computers to remotely administer all of the T&C servers, including domain controllers. Employees use the corporate workstations to access the sales material and marketing data as well as domain controllers. Most of the corporate information is hosted on an internal website that is running Internet Information Services (IIS) 6.

T&C's network is contained within a single Active Directory domain named tandc.com. All of the servers are running Windows Server 2003, Enterprise Edition. Administration of the Active Directory is centralized in Philadelphia. Wilmington and Los Angeles user and computer accounts are located in child OUs for their location.

All client computers are running Windows XP Professional. All sites are connected using VPNs across the Internet. Wilmington is connected directly to the Philadelphia office with a dedicated T1 line.

The following business problem must be considered: Executives connect to network resources using laptops that need to be secured differently than the desktop computers in the executive's office.

Interviews

Chief Information Officer   Security is a major concern here at T&C. We must make the security much stronger on client computers, servers, and especially domain controllers.

System Administrator   Different departments will require different security patches. We will need to evaluate the patches before we deploy them to the computers. After the patches are tested, they need to be deployed to the servers in each department. You need to use as little network bandwidth as possible for deploying security patches.

Chief Security Officer   We need to verify that the appropriate security patches are applied to the computers in our organization.

Business Requirements

A standard set of written security settings must be defined and configured from a central location and deployed to all servers and client computers in the marketing and customer support departments. The IIS and SQL Server machines must be routinely evaluated for missing patches. Internet traffic must be kept to a minimum.

Case Study Questions

1. You need to design a patch management solution that distributes and applies security patches. Your solution must meet business and security requirements. What should you do?

   A. Use one new SUS server in each of the four offices to download all security patches. Test the security patches. Use SUS to deploy the security patches to computers in each office.

   B. Use one new SUS server in Philadelphia and one in Los Angeles to download all security patches. Use a GPO that is based on user configuration for each domain to deploy security patches to servers in each geographic location.

   C. Use a new SUS server in Philadelphia, Los Angeles, and Minneapolis to download all security patches. Use SUS to deploy security patches to computers in their respective offices. Configure the Wilmington computers to use the SUS server in Philadelphia.

   D. Use one new SUS server in Philadelphia and one in Los Angeles to download all security patches. Test the security patches. Deploy security patches to servers in each geographic region.

2. You need to design the configuration of IIS and SQL Server machines to meet the requirements in the written security policy. What should you do?

   A. Log on to a domain controller and use MBSA to scan all servers for Windows vulnerabilities.

   B. Create a startup script in a GPO and link it to the SQL Server machines and Web Servers OU and GPO that runs MBSA when the computer starts up.

   C. Create a script that runs the MBSA against the SQL Server and IIS servers and schedule it to run weekly.

   D. Log on to each SQL Server machine and each IIS machine and use MBSA to scan each server locally.

3. You need to make sure that the executives' laptops are secured and that the configuration that secures them is different than the configuration used to secure the desktops that they use. All client computer accounts are in the ClientComputers OU. What should you do to ease the application of the configuration information in a GPO to the laptops without causing the same settings to be applied to the desktops?

   A. Create an OU for laptops and move all of the laptop objects into it.

   B. Create a software restriction policy that prevents laptop computers from executing software that isn't allowed.

   C. Use the Security Configuration And Analysis tool and set the -portable switch so that it will apply only to laptop computers.

   D. Use the MBSA utility and set the -portable switch so that it will apply only to laptop computers.

4. You need to deploy patches to the computers in each department, and you need to make sure that your solution meets with the approval of the system administrator. What should you do?

   A. Create a single SUS server to approve patches for the enterprise.

   B. Create a single SUS server for each department to approve patches.

   C. Create a single SUS server for each site to approve patches.

   D. Create a single SUS server for each office to approve patches.

5. Due to an acquisition, a new office has been added to your infrastructure in Phoenix. The Phoenix site has a high-speed link directly to the Los Angeles office. You need to redesign the Software Update Services (SUS) infrastructure for the company. You will need to decide whether or not each of the new SUS servers will be receiving new updates directly from Microsoft servers on the Internet or from another SUS server within the company. Your solution must use the fewest number of SUS servers that retrieve their updates from the Internet while still preserving Internet bandwidth. What should you do?

To answer place the appropriate SUS server with the appropriate site. Some options may be used more than once, others may not be used at all.

Site	SUS Server Options
Philadelphia	SUS server that retrieves updates from the Internet.
Wilmington	SUS server that retrieves updates from Philadelphia.
Minneapolis	SUS server that retrieves updates from Wilmington.
Los Angeles	SUS server that retrieves updates from Minneapolis.
Phoenix	SUS server that retrieves updates from Los Angeles.
	No SUS server.

Answers to Case Study Questions

1. C. To minimize Internet traffic, each site should connect to the Microsoft Windows Update site and download the patches that they require independently of one another. Because the Wilmington office has a high-speed connection to the Philadelphia office, there is no need for it to get the updates from the Internet, nor does it need to maintain its own SUS server. Option A is incorrect because Wilmington doesn't need to access the Internet or be running a SUS server. Options B and D are incorrect because the link between Los Angeles and Minneapolis is over the Internet and there would be a significant increase in Internet traffic if all patches were deployed across the site link.

2. C. Option C allows each of the required servers to be scanned on a regular basis, which is why it is correct. Option A is incorrect because all of the servers are scanned, not just the SQL Server and IIS servers, as stated in the security requirements. Option B evaluates the servers only when they start up, which should not happen very frequently, and therefore it is incorrect. Option D puts too much of a burden on the administrator to manually run the MBSA utility.

3. A. Moving the laptop computers into their own container, or OU, is the best solution for applying the GPO only to them. Software restriction policies will not affect the security configuration on the computers. The Security Configuration And Analysis tool can be used to analyze only one computer at a time, whereas a template can be used to analyze multiple computers. The MBSA utility is used only for auditing and reporting and will not make configuration changes to any of the computers.

4. B. According to the system administrator, each department needs the ability to approve different security patches; therefore, each department needs its own SUS server. Only option B allows a set of patches to be approved for each department. Option A is incorrect because it only allows one set of updates to be approved for all computers in the enterprise. Options C and D are also incorrect because they don't allow different patches per department.

5.

Site	SUS Server
Philadelphia	SUS server that retrieves updates from the Internet.
Wilmington	SUS server that retrieves updates from Philadelphia.
Minneapolis	SUS server that retrieves updates from the Internet.
Los Angeles	SUS server that retrieves updates from the Internet.
Phoenix	SUS server that retrieves updates from Los Angeles.

Wilmington and Phoenix, because of their high-speed link to a main site, do not require a SUS server that retrieves the updates from the Internet. The Wilmington SUS server will retrieve its updates from the Philadelphia SUS server, and the Phoenix SUS server will retrieve its updates from the Los Angeles SUS server. Each site requires its own SUS server for patch approval. Philadelphia, Minneapolis, and Los Angeles will retrieve their downloads from the Microsoft Internet site.

Designing Secure Network Management Infrastructure

MICROSOFT EXAM OBJECTIVES COVERED IN THIS CHAPTER:

✓ **Design security for network management.**

- Manage the risk of managing networks.
- Design the administration of servers by using common administration tools. Tools include Microsoft Management Console (MMC), Terminal Server, Remote Desktop for Administration, Remote Assistance, and Telnet.
- Design security for Emergency Management Services.
- Design security for servers that have specific roles. Roles include domain controller, network infrastructure server, file server, IIS server, terminal server, and POP3 mail server.

A network will need constant maintenance and administration to keep running successfully. You will need to use tools to manage the network, but these tools can put your network at risk for attack. You will be able to locally manage a server by sitting down at the console and keyboard and logging in to the server. But there will be times when this is inconvenient or impossible. For example, you may not have access to the server room where the equipment is housed; you may be required to have access to the system seven days a week, twenty-four hours a day; or your computers may be hosted by a remote company like an ISP or an offsite data center for disaster recovery purposes. You will need to decide whether you will allow remote administration of server and the extent to which you will need to remotely manage the network before you deploy your Windows 2003 Server machines.

In this chapter, you will learn how to decide if you can afford the security risks associated with managing the network and how to manage these risks. You will then need to decide what tools you will use to manage the network and what the risks are with each of these tools. Finally, you will need to consider the need for headless network management through a new feature in Windows 2003 Server called Emergency Management Services, which will let you manage your server even when it is locked up and not responding to normal management tools.

Securing IIS was covered in Chapter 7, "Designing Security for Internet Information Services." Securing domain controllers, network infrastructure servers, file servers, and POP3 mail servers was covered in Chapter 8, "Designing Security for Servers that have Specific Roles."

Analyzing and Managing the Risks of Administering Networks

The most secure way to manage your network is by allowing only local administration of servers. This would mean that you would have to sit down at the keyboard attached to the server and log on as an administrator to manage the server. This is impractical for many organizations, and if this is the case in your organization, you will need to manage your servers remotely. But before you begin to do so, you will need to develop a remote management plan.

A *remote management plan* ensures that the proper tools and configuration you choose for managing your servers are in line with your security policy and infrastructure. Your remote management plan will help you understand what type of management each server needs, whether they need to be managed locally or remotely, the location of the servers in your organization, who will administer them, and what the requirements for security are on the servers. You should use the following steps to develop the remote management plan:

- Evaluate remote management needs.

- Determine the tools and hardware needed to meet your remote management needs.

- Design the hardware and software configuration.

- Configure the network infrastructure to accommodate remote management.

- Plan remote management deployment.

Evaluating Remote Management Needs

When developing your remote management plan, the first thing you need to do is determine which servers you will manage remotely. Then you can consider what the cost, convenience, and availability requirements should be for managing the servers on your network. Your company's security policy might include requirements that would make it more costly to administer a server remotely than the inconvenience or increase in staffing to maintain availability would warrant.

For example, suppose your company's security policy requires that data on sensitive database servers be protected by an expensive authentication and data encryption system if the servers are to be remotely accessed. The system might contain per-server and yearly subscription fees that make remote administration more expensive than just using local administration of the server as the only administrative option.

Remote administration provides convenience by allowing you to manage the network from a location other than the server console. You need to decide whether you will allow remote administration from the internal network only or from an external network and internally. You can allow remote administration from the internal network of your company. This will allow server administrators a gain in productivity by avoiding frequent trips to the server room or another location.

You could also allow remote administration through a VPN, HTTP, or dial-up connection. This will allow server administrators to check on the status of servers from home or other locations through an Internet or dial-up connection. This is convenient for administrators who are on call or for someone with more expertise who is helping out in an emergency situation.

Remote administration can help increase the availability of your network without increasing the staffing cost of the organization. Administrators can access the network from their desktop at work or from home to resolve problems and maintain servers instead of having to drive to the branch office or company to resolve the problems. This will mean server problems can be resolved and servers made available more quickly. You could gain the same availability on a locally managed network by increasing staff to provide an administrator around the clock.

Of course, each of these items will impact the others. If you reduce cost by allowing only local administration, you decrease convenience, and perhaps decrease availability of the server (unless you increase staff). For example, suppose you require that a database server is only administered locally for security reasons. This server also has an availability requirement that states it can be down for no longer than 30 minutes and needs to be available 24/7 except for scheduled maintenance. You could have a staff member carry a pager and manage the server from home to resolve most problems if you allow remote management. Without remote management additional staffing will be required to meet the 24/7 onsite management or require the employees on page duty to be within 15 minutes of work. Either way, maintaining this security requirement is certain to affect your staffing costs. You need to look at costs to determine which approach is the best for this server.

Benefits and Threats of Remote Management

Remote management introduces new threats to your servers. When you remotely manage a server, you need to consider additional security measures. Remotely managing computers will allow potentially sensitive information to be transmitted across the network. You must ensure that the management tool provides the necessary means to prevent eavesdropping on the data it sends or you must provide this service yourself (through VPN, IPSec or SSL usually). This would not be a necessary consideration if you just used local management. Remote management will also increase your exposure to attacks using management tools.

You will need to make sure that the management tool you use can be used by only a select group of individuals and that the necessary password protections are enforced. Out-of-band remote management can be threatened because there is no logical security on the serial connections used to manage the server. You need to determine which servers can benefit or be threatened by remote management.

Remote management provides the following benefits:

- Reduced total cost of ownership
- Increased availability of servers
- Increased convenience and productivity of administrators

There are some threats associated with remote management:

- Increased attack surface because attackers can use the tools
- Security holes in remote administration tool or service that are not patched or kept up-to-date
- Sensitive data sent across the network
- No logical security on serial connections for out-of-band communications

In the "Evaluating Remote Management Needs" Design Scenario, you will determine which servers in the organization can benefit from remote management and which should be managed locally.

Determining the Tools and Hardware Needs

Remote management tools in Windows Server 2003 make it possible to perform any management action on the server remotely except for hardware installation. You can take advantage of in-band and out-of-band remote management tools. *In-band remote management tools* are the traditional tools that you use to manage your server, such as Terminal Services For Remote Administration or Active Directory Users And Computers. These tools work if the server is functioning correctly and can communicate with the network.

Design Scenario

Evaluating Remote Management Needs

Expo, Inc. is a corporation that provides party and convention planning services in North America. It has offices in 17 major cities throughout the United States. Currently, each office has its own IT administrative staff. Expo would like to consolidate their IT staff in their corporate headquarters in Los Angeles. Expo, Inc. will need to implement remote management to be able to successfully manage remote servers. Management is concerned about security issues that remote management presents.

1. **Question:** What are the security threats to remote management? **Answer:**

    - Eavesdropping, both intentional and accidental, on the remote management tool's network communications

    - Weak passwords or password technology to authenticate the remote management session

    - Servers that are not patched regularly and might have a known security hole in the remote management service

The main in-band remote management tools in Windows Server 2003 are listed here:

Microsoft Management Console (MMC)   MMC is a framework for hosting administrative tools called snap-ins. You can customize MMC to meet your administrative needs by adding or removing snap-ins. Each snap-in can be made up of tools, web pages, folders, and other items that are used to administer applications and services.

Windows Script Host   Windows Script Host allows you to write scripts that are used to automate administrative tasks. You can choose to write a script in any common script language, including Microsoft Visual Basic Scripting Edition (VBScript) and ECMA Script (known as JScript or JavaScript). You will want to make sure that the extensions (.vbs, .js, .vbe, .jse, .wmf) of script files are not mapped to the Windows Scripting Host executables (wscript.exe or cscript.exe). This will prevent them from executing without typing **cscript.exe** *ScriptName* at a command prompt, increasing security against accidental execution of scripts. You will also want to make sure that only administrative accounts have execute access to the wscript and cscript executables.

Remote Desktop for Administration   This will allow an administrator to manage a network computer from any computer on the network. You use Remote Desktop for Administration to log onto a remote server and you will see the remote server's desktop. This tool was known as Teminal Services for Remote Administration in Windows 2000. You will be able to interact with the remote server as if you were managing it locally. You will log on to the remote server with your own account, so if someone is already logged on to the server, they will not see what you are doing, nor will you compete for the mouse pointer. They have added a new feature to Remote Desktop for Administration that allows you to connect to the console session, so you can run programs remotely that require console access, like Microsoft SQL Server hotfixes. This is one of the favorite management tools on Windows Server 2003.

Web Interface for Remote Administration This is a web-based application that allows you to administer a server using a web browser and the HTTP protocol. This tool is particularly useful for managing a web server, and you can perform the following configuration tasks: create websites, delete websites, configure websites, configure network settings, restart the web server, and manage local user accounts.

Remote Assistance Remote Assistance will allow you to remotely manage another computer much as you can with Remote Desktop for Administration except that you must be given permission to manage the server or workstation by the current user. You will then take over the mouse and keyboard functionality as if you were local. Remote Assistance allows administrators or help desk personnel to aid users in new or difficult tasks. Remote Assistance also allows you to chat in real time with the user.

Command-line administration tools These are tools like Telnet and SSH, which can be used to have a remote command line on the server. The commands that you type in the Telnet window will run on the server that you are connected to. It is sometimes more convenient to use command line tools over a slow network connection or from other operating systems.

Designing security for in-band management tools, except for Windows Scripting Host because it was discussed above, will be discussed in detail in the section entitled "Designing a Secure Administrative Strategy for Server Management Tools."

Out-of-band remote management tools are used if the server is not responding to standard network communications. This could be because the server is hung up or the network device has stopped functioning. Using out-of-band management tools combined with the appropriate hardware, you will need to locally manage a server only for hardware upgrades and maintenance. Out-of-band services are provided by the Emergency Management Services (EMS) on Windows Server 2003. To effectively use EMS, you may need to purchase additional hardware and you'll need to weigh the cost of additional hardware with the benefit of the service. Out-of-band connections usually involve using the serial port on the server to administer the server. This connection can be established remotely through specialized hardware or a dial-up connection.

You will learn more about out-of-band communication later in this chapter in the section entitled "Designing for Emergency Management Services."

Designing the Hardware and Software Configuration

It's important to design for securing the hardware and configuring the security of the software used for remote management. You will need to consider the type of remote management you'll use and secure it against intentional attacks or even accidents. With in-band remote management, you must pay attention to requirements of how the administrators will authenticate to the server and mechanisms for encrypting communications with the server. You will also need to consider the impact of in-band remote management on your firewall configuration. Out-of-band communication has no logical security, so you will need to plan for the physical security of the serial connections required. You will also need to design the appropriate rights and folder permissions to protect the remote management tools so that only the appropriate administrators can access them.

In general, your security strategy for remote management should consider the following:

- User authentication—The server should allow remote management from only the appropriate administrator.

- Machine authentication—The server should allow remote management from only the appropriate machine.

- Physical security—The hardware should be physically secure, especially in the case of out-of-band remote management.

- Encryption—Information sent over the network because of remote management needs to be confidential.

- Auditing—All access due to remote administration should be logged in a secure fashion.

In the follow sections we will consider how each of these points affect your remote management security strategy.

User Authentication

Most remote management tools require that you authenticate with the server before you can manage the server. The tool may take advantage of the underlying operating system for authentication or require a separate username and password. You will need to consider the authentication mechanisms available in the management tool when you design for remote management security because they may not be strong enough for your security policy.

For example, your policy may state that all network authentication use Kerberos for centralized management and the strong protections that would be afforded. If the management tool does not support Kerberos, you may not be able to use it remotely. In general, consider the authentication mechanisms available in the tool and whether they are appropriate for protecting the server you are managing.

Strong authentication mechanisms on Windows Server 2003 include Kerberos and smart card authentication. You should consider also having a separate password policy that requires administrators to have longer and more difficult passwords than regular users have. You may even consider using smart cards for remote administration, even if you don't use them for regular users. These can be enforced through Group Policy and Active Directory. You will also want to make sure that you audit the accounts that have been given remote management access.

Medium authentication mechanisms on Windows Server 2003 would allow for using NT LAN Manager (NTLM) security for authentication. You would also want to enforce the strong password policies on administrative accounts, as well as audit access by these accounts to the servers. It is not recommended that you use less security than this for remote access.

After you have decided on the authentication mechanism you are going to use, you will need to decide which administrators will perform which administrative tasks. You will design security groups and assign administrators user accounts to each group. You will want to assign to each administrator the minimum security level they need to perform their remote management tasks. Generally, you will use three mechanisms to control the remote management tasks you can perform:

User rights   User rights define what administrative tasks can be performed on the server, such as logging on locally or setting up new hardware.

Shared folder permissions   Shared folder permissions allow you to control which users or groups can access a share over the network. Many administrative tools use shared folders to log access, launch the administrative tools, access administrative shares over the network (for example, C$), or log onto computers remotely using terminal emulation programs.

NTFS permissions   NTFS permissions allow you to control who can launch various programs, including remote administrative tools.

 These settings were discussed in Chapter 8, "Designing Security for Servers with Specific Roles."

Machine Authentication

You will want to establish which computers you'll use to perform remote management. You will use machine authentication in conjunction with the authentication of the user account to provide additional security. There are two main mechanisms that you can use to verify the computer:

IP address filtering   IP address filtering is used to decide which IP addresses are allowed to connect to the server. You would configure the server to allow the remote management workstations to connect. IP address filtering is a static process that is appropriate only to statically assigned IP addresses. It is also susceptible to IP address spoofing, so you shouldn't rely on it solely. It is one more mechanism in your security toolkit to harden your servers. A stronger mechanism is to use computer certificates.

Computer certificates   Computer certificates uniquely identify each computer on the network. Since computer certificates are next to impossible to forge, their use is a strong security mechanism, especially if combined with a strong authentication mechanism like smart cards. An attacker would need the computer certificate and an administrator account credentials to attack the machine through the remote administration tools. IP address filtering can be made stronger when used in conjunction with computer certificates to provide for even stronger security if feasible.

Physical Security

You should always include physical security in your security design for your servers. But servers that use out-of-band management need special consideration. The serial connections between servers and out-of-band management hardware need to be protected physically because there is no authentication available. You should lock server rooms that contain the out-of-band management components and servers. Use a physical identification mechanism to determine who is entering and leaving the server room. Try to contain all the serial connections and equipment to the locked server room.

Encryption

You need to consider how you will protect the data that the remote management tools transmit over a network. Does the tool itself provide encryption options, or if you will need to provide encryption, what mechanism is appropriate? Chances are your security policy will state the acceptable encryption strength for sensitive data in your organization and even the technologies that are preferred.

Regardless of whether the tool supports its own encryption mechanism, you may decide to encrypt access to the servers in a more general and manageable fashion. There are two main mechanisms for encrypting data on Windows Server 2003 for remote management:

IP Security (IPSec)   IPSec is generally the mechanism used for mitigating the security vulnerability of unencrypted or weakly encrypted data in the remote management tool. Configure the server and the remote management computer to require IPSec for a connection. This will work with an IP-based management product.

Secure Sockets Layer (SSL)   SSL is used to secure the communication of tools that use HTTP to communicate with the server.

Auditing

You must make sure that you devise a means for securely auditing the use of remote management tools. Your audit logs should track who used the tool, from what machine they used it, when it was used, and what was done during the administrative session.

You can use the built-in auditing in Windows to track who logged into the server and the machine that they used. You will need to investigate the logging capabilities of the management tool to gain a more detailed log of a specific remote management tool. This will allow you to track detailed information like what the administrator did. Design a plan for securing the audit logs from attackers or administrators that may want to change them to cover up misdeeds. It would also be wise to have a separate auditor that would read the logs or reports from the logs about activity for remote management to detect unauthorized use.

You can use the follow tools to configure Windows auditing:

- Domain Security Policy's Audit Policy

- Domain Controller Security Policy's Audit Policy

- Local Security Policy's Audit Policy

- Group Policy Management

- NTFS or Registry Property dialog boxes.

You can then view the audit log using the Event Viewer's security log. You will need to investigate if the particular application has additional settings and tools for handling auditing.

Secondary Network

In addition to authenticating users and machines, securing the physical structure, encrypting network traffic, and auditing, you can establish a secondary network specifically designed for remote management traffic to add extra security to the remote administration. A secondary network can increase the performance, security, and availability of your remote management solution by separating the traffic for remote management to its own network, accessed using a secure router. You would be allowed to remotely administer boxes only if you had access to this network, along with having the correct user and machine credentials and user rights.

🌐 Real World Scenario

Designing for Remote Access

We have two offices for our company, the corporate headquarters located in Wilmington, Delaware, and a branch office located in Philadelphia, Pennsylvania. Most of the servers are located at our corporate headquarters and are used to provide support for business applications, our website, and e-mail. Our branch location in Philadelphia contains servers that provide some backup for important systems and support that location. We also have routers, wireless access points, and phone systems at each location that need to be managed.

Our IT staff is very limited, so the convenience and productivity gains of remote management are very important to our company. This easily outweighs the security risks associated with remote management in our situation. We just could not afford to hire the people necessary for local administration, nor do we feel like going into the office on Sunday afternoon to fix an e-mail server that is not responding. We need to be able to manage the servers and devices from home or from either of the two locations. We are concerned about security because, when there is a security incident, it usually involves time to resolve and we want to keep customer information private.

We use strong passwords for administrators, strong password protocols like Kerberos and certificate-based authentication of machines, and encrypt the communications to perform remote management. We installed Windows Server 2003 on some of our key servers for out-of-band support, so if a server locks up, we can fix it remotely or provide access to the routers through the serial port with terminal emulation. We also use secure HTTP with client certificates to manage some of our devices and the services we provide. We have a patching process in place so that the servers are kept up-to-date with any security fixes that Microsoft posts.

If you decide to use remote management tools, you will need to decide what means you will use to secure them as the next Design Scenario explores.

Configuring the Network Infrastructure to Accommodate Remote Management

Configuration changes must be made to the network infrastructure to support remote administration. There are a few things to consider:

- Types of connection
- Changes that will need to be made to firewall configurations
- Changes to IP packet filtering settings to support remote management

The type of connection you use will depend on which type of connection will support the remote management tool you are using. Beyond that, the type of connection you choose will

Design Scenario

Evaluating Remote Management Security Needs

Expo, Inc. is a corporation that provides party and convention planning services in North America. It has offices in 17 major cities throughout the United States. Currently, each office has its own IT administrative staff. Expo would like to consolidate their IT staff in their corporate headquarters in Los Angeles. Expo, Inc. will need to implement remote management to be able to successfully manage remote servers. Management is concerned about security issues that remote management presents.

1. **Question:** What suggestions would you make to lessen threats with remote management?
   Answer:

   - Require encryption, like using a VPN, when using remote management tools.

   - Require a strong password policy for remote administrators.

   - Use smart cards or other means of two-factor authentication.

   - Keep the remote management tools and servers up-to-date with patching.

   - Physically secure any devices and their connections that will communicate with the serial port.

determine whether you need additional security in terms of establishing a VPN connection first to encrypt the traffic that passes over the connection. Certain types of connections may also pass through a firewall.

If you need to manage a server through a firewall, you should verify the firewall settings to determine if the management tool can work through the firewall. If it will not, you must determine the port numbers used by the management tool. You will also need to analyze the ports required for the remote management tool and decide whether the risk of opening the ports is worth the benefits of using the management tool through the firewall. You may determine it is not, in which case you should look for an alternative tool to manage the server. You will also need to consider any IP packet filtering you may be doing on the firewall, routers, or servers.

IP packet filtering allows you to control which packets can pass through a network device. This is useful for controlling the applications that can communicate with the server or through a router or firewall. You might need to reconfigure these settings for the remote management tool to work properly.

Planning Remote Management Deployment

After you have designed security for remote management, you should test the design in a lab setting that simulates your production environment. You will need to verify that your configuration is secure and meets the organization's needs for remote management. You should also verify network connectivity, hardware and software configurations, and the security settings of your servers for remote administration.

You will need to verify that you can connect to network resources for the required remote management tools. The following is a list of some of the things you should configure and test according to your design:

- Configure and test a secondary network for remote management if your design calls for it for availability or security purposes.

- Configure and test the dial-up settings over a VPN connection if you plan to support secure remote management through dial-up.

- Configure and test the firewall settings if you will use remote management tools through the firewall.

- Configure and test the IP packet filter settings if you have configured the servers or routers to filter for specific applications.

- Configure and test the IPSec and SSL settings to the servers if you plan to use IPSec or SSL to encrypt remote management traffic. Verify that the traffic is encrypted through a network monitoring utility.

Verify the hardware and software configurations in your design, particularly your out-of-band hardware configuration and your auditing settings. The following is a list of some of the items that you will need to do:

- Verify out-of-band remote management configuration and hardware settings.

- Install and test Emergency Management Services.

- Configure auditing and verify that it collects the information that you need.

- Verify any additional software or hardware settings that your design calls for.

- Verify that you can accomplish your remote management needs through the chosen tools.

You will need to verify the security settings that you have configured for remote administration. You should verify the following settings for your remote management configuration if they are applicable:

- Verify the authentication protocols used to access the server remotely.

- Verify that physical security is adequate for the servers and out-of-band remote management components.

- Verify that the proper encryption protocols are being used with your design.

- Verify any Group Policy settings that you are using to manage the security settings of your servers, including control of remote management.

- Verify that the security groups and user rights assigned to perform administration of servers only perform the proper remote management tasks.

- Verify the shared folder and NTFS permissions for your remote management plan.

In the next Design Scenario, you will decide what remote management tool would be beneficial and what risks it poses for the network.

Design Scenario

Risks of Managing Networks

Expo, Inc. is a corporation that provides party and convention planning services. It has offices in 17 major cities throughout the United States. Currently, administration staff is at each location to manage the servers located there.

Expo, Inc. would like to save money by centralizing most of the administrative functions at its corporate headquarters in Los Angeles. The company wants to be able to use local contractors on an as-needed basis to manage the hardware locally. Contractors can take up to 24 hours to respond to a unscheduled incident based on the contract, so the company is looking for a solution that will minimize the unscheduled use of contractors.

Expo, Inc. will be using the Internet as the network between its locations. There is concern about using the Internet to manage the servers and devices at its other locations without local access to the servers.

1. **Question:** What remote management options would work best for Expo, Inc.? **Answer:** Expo would want to provide an in-band management option like Remote Desktop for Administration to manage the remote networks. The in-band remote management option should include the ability to encrypt the communication with the server and should support strong authentication mechanisms for remote administrators. Expo would also want to provide an out-of-band remote administration option to reduce the dependence on contractors when the server is not responding to in-band remote management tools, such as when it is hung. That way, it will only need to use contractors to install and maintain the server hardware.

Designing a Secure Administrative Strategy for Server Management Tools

The most secure way to manage a server is through local access to the server, but this is not always practical for most organizations. Business requirements for availability or concerns about employee productivity may necessitate remote management tools. After all, who wants to trek to the server room every time you need to change something on the server?

There are two methods for remotely managing your servers: in-band and out-of-band. In-band remote management is the standard method you use to manage your server over a network. It involves the use of tools that you are familiar with for managing networks, like the Microsoft Management Console or Telnet. Out-of-band remote management is also known as headless management; it allows you to manage your network without a keyboard, monitor, or working network card, or even if the computer is hung, in some cases. Headless management is known as Emergency Management Services (EMS) in Windows 2003 Server and additional hardware and software may be required to enable the feature.

We will discuss EMS in the section "Designing for Emergency Management Services" later in this chapter.

When evaluating tools for administering your servers, you will need to determine what security capabilities each has, changes to security infrastructure like firewalls and routers, authentication, and means for securing network traffic from the tool. We will first look at designing for security with the in-band management tools.

Using Microsoft Management Console

The *Microsoft Management Console (MMC)* is the standard administrative tool in Windows Server 2003. The MMC is really a framework to host various management tools. It provides administrators with a standard environment from which they can manage their servers and network.

The tools that are added to the MMC are called MMC snap-ins, and you can create custom combinations of the console by adding the snap-ins that you need to administer your servers. The MMC console can be executed through the mmc.exe program, which will bring up a blank console that can be populated with various administrative snap-ins as shown in Figure 10.1. MMC can be used to manage a local server or a remote server.

Once you have a blank console, you can add management snap-ins to it by clicking the Console menu and choosing Add/Remove Snap-in from the Console menu. Each snap-in is different, so you will need to read the documentation on each one, which can usually be found under the Help menu. You will need to verify the remote management capabilities and the security features of the snap-in you want to use for remote management.

FIGURE 10.1 The MMC console

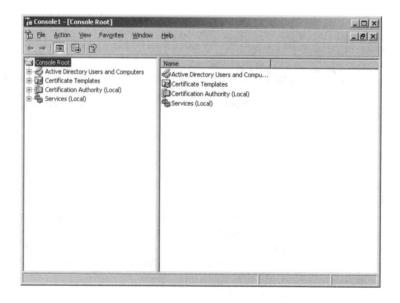

Snap-ins are essentially independent management tools that integrate into the MMC, so the security provided can vary greatly from one snap-in to another. The MMC uses a technology called the Component Object Model (COM), which provides standard interfaces for the developer to create an administrative snap-in for the server or application. Since each snap-in is different, you will need to refer to the documentation for the snap-in you want to use to determine when it will be appropriate or inappropriate for securely managing your server. For example, you should see if there are options for encrypting the transmission of data and passwords or whether you need to provide your own through an IPSec session with the server or other means. You will need to determine whether the snap-in supports the following security options:

Encryption capabilities   Does the snap-in support encryption internally and what strength is the encryption? If it does not support encryption, you need to determine how to encrypt its network traffic or not use it for network management.

Authentication capabilities   Are passwords encrypted or passed as clear text, what authentication protocols can be used, does the snap-in support integration with Windows authentication or do you have to manage a separate password database and policies for the application, and does the management tool support two-factor authentication, like smart card authentication?

Network communications technology   What protocols does the snap-in support for network communication? Since most snap-ins will support TCP\IP, you should determine the ports that it uses for communication in case you will need to manage a server through a secured router or firewall. Some common ports for management tools include 3389 for the Remote Desktop Protocol (RDP), 135 RPC for DCOM–based applications like many MMC snap-ins, 23 for Telnet, 22 for Secure Shell (SSH), 80 for HTTP, and 43 for HTTPS.

Based on the information you discover about the snap-in, you will then determine if it is the best tool to use to manage the server.

For example, many snap-ins use the network version of COM, which is called Distributed Component Object Model (DCOM). DCOM uses remote procedure calls (RPCs) to communicate between the client and server. DCOM supports encryption by using the Packet Privacy option in the dcomcnfg tool used to configure DCOM. This encryption supports the RC4 public key encryption algorithm with a symmetric key strength of up to 128 bits. DCOM also supports the use of other algorithms implemented through the cryptoAPIs of Windows. DCOM authentication is integrated into Windows and supports NTLM and Kerberos authentication. Because it uses RPCs, it can support various network protocols, but generally you will be using TCP/IP. The TCP port 135 and UDP port 135 used for RPCs would need to be opened on the firewall if you will be using the tool through a firewall. Due to the danger to the security of your network of these ports being opened (all RPC traffic uses these ports, so it would be difficult to differentiate between programs), your security administrator may not allow you to use the tool directly through the firewall. You could use the tool over a VPN connection to avoid this issue. The protocol used could provide features for security; for example, a snap-in that uses HTTP as a protocol could use SSL and be set up to navigate firewalls without a VPN.

You can install many of the MMC snap-ins that you use to manage Windows Server 2003 in the adminpak.msi file located in the Windows\system32 directory. You can also use this file to install the tools on a client like Windows XP Professional or Windows 2000 Professional.

Real World Scenario

Using MMC to Manage Windows Server 2003

We have Windows Server 2003, Exchange Server 2003, and SQL Server 2000 installed to support various applications on the network. We could support these applications by walking to the server room every time we need to reset a password, create a user, manage the database, or create a mailbox.

We have decided to support convenience and provide access to the servers inside our company by installing the proper MMC snap-ins on client workstations in the organization. This will allow more than two administrators to connect to a server at a time. Our security policy does not require the encryption of connections internally in our organization, but we require strong password authentication for our administrator accounts.

In following Design Scenario, you will design for secure server management with MMC.

Design Scenario

Designing for Secure Server Management with MMC

Expo, Inc. wants to manage its servers using various MMC snap-ins to create user accounts and manage the Exchange e-mail servers, Microsoft SQL Server machine, DHCP, and DNS. The administrators will need to manage servers that are in various cities. They also will need to traverse firewalls that exist between branch offices and the corporate office.

1. **Question:** What would you need to determine if a particular snap-in would work for Expo, Inc.? **Answer:** You would need to consider the port numbers for allowing traffic to pass through the firewall, the encryption capabilities, authentication capabilities of the snap-in, and the versions of Windows that the snap-ins will run on.

Using Remote Desktop for Administration

Remote Desktop for Administration (Remote Desktop for short) provides a graphical user interface to remote computers over a local area network (LAN) and wide area networks (WANs). All application processing happens on the server; just the display, keyboard commands, and mouse motions are sent over the network to and from the client. The Remote Desktop does all of this through the *Remote Desktop Protocol (RDP)*.

 Remote Desktop for Administration was known as Terminal Services in Windows 2000.

Using Remote Desktop has become one of the most popular ways to remotely manage Windows servers on a network. Remote Desktop provides the following features for administering Windows Server 2003 and Windows 2000 servers:

- Remote reboots of servers
- Encryption of up to 128 bits in strength
- Support for low-bandwidth connections
- Support for two remote administrators sharing remote sessions for collaboration
- Access to session 0 on Windows Server 2003, which is the session that you would interact with if you were sitting at the local console
- Local printing, clipboard mapping, and serial device redirection
- Support for smart card redirection (Only supported in Windows 2003)
- Roaming disconnect support, which means that if your connection is disconnected, programs will continue to run, which will prevent interrupted installs or long running tasks.

Remote Desktop for Administration is installed on a Windows Server 2003 machine by default, but don't worry about it being a security risk because it is disabled by default. To enable it, follow these steps:

1. Open the System Properties dialog box through the Control Panel.
2. Click the Remote tab to show the settings for Remote Desktop and Remote Assistance.
3. Check the Allow Users To Connect Remotely To This Computer check box to enable Remote Desktop for Administration, as shown in Figure 10.2.

FIGURE 10.2   Enabling Remote Desktop for Administration

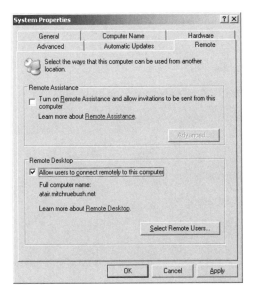

FIGURE 10.3   Warning about users without a password

When you enable Remote Desktop, you will be warned that any accounts that do not have a password will not be able to create a Remote Desktop session with the server, as shown in Figure 10.3.

You will have the option of connecting through the Remote Desktop client in Windows or through the web version of the Remote Desktop, which provides an ActiveX control that will allow you to connect over an HTTP connection. You would need to install Internet Information Services (IIS) on each server that you want to support Web-based Remote Desktop connections. You will then need to take precautions for securing IIS, which were discussed in Chapter 7, "Designing Security for Internet Information Services."

By default, Remote Desktop for Administration requires 128-bit encryption for the connection. This is supported by the Remote Desktop client in Windows XP and Windows Server 2003. If you have an older version of the terminal service client, you will not be able to connect to a Windows Server 2003 machine with the default settings for RDP. You can configure RDP by navigating to Administrative Tools and clicking the Terminal Services Configuration utility. Expand the Connections folder and then right-click the RDP-Tcp protocol and select Properties. On the General tab, select the Client Compatible option to support clients that do not support 128-bit encryption, as shown in Figure 10.4.

FIGURE 10.4   Setting the encryption level for the RDP protocol

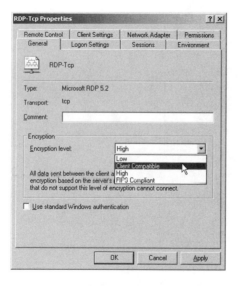

We have many servers in our environment and connect to them from various Windows operating systems and locations. We need the flexibility to remotely manage the servers from Windows 98 or greater operating systems or from different locations. We don't want to mess with having to install the proper tools on the client for the problem to be fixed. We also require that all remote administration traffic be secure.

We choose to use Remote Desktop for Administration because it provides for secure access to servers by authenticating the administrators and encrypting the traffic between the client and the server. It also simplifies access to the management tools because we do not have to worry about installing them or compatibility issues with the operating system we happen to be using.

It is recommended that you use the highest possible encryption for remote management tools, so you should leave the RDP protocol setting set to High and upgrade the client tools if possible. Only change this option if it is necessary to support an older client that cannot be updated. For example, you may have a Remote Desktop client that runs on a Linux workstation or a Windows CE device that does not support 128-bit encryption and cannot be upgraded.

You will need to also consider allowing administrators to connect to the console session of the Windows Server 2003 machine. Using the console session is the same as if you were physically sitting in front of the server. You can connect to the console session by launching the `mstsc.exe` (Remote Desktop client) with the `/console` switch or launch the Remote Desktop MMC snap-in and choose to connect to the console. This means that you can view all messages and use applications that only work with the console session. Whenever you connect to the console session, the physical console will lock for security so that nobody can watch what the remote administrator is doing by physically sitting at the console.

You can connect up to two simultaneous remote administrators with Remote Desktop for Administration. You will need to coordinate administrative efforts or you may risk damaging something. You can configure the RDP protocol if you do not have mechanisms in place to prevent competing administrators. You can verify if there are other administrators connected by using the Terminal Services Manager tool in the `Administrative Tools` folder. You will want to coordinate the efforts of the administrators to ensure that they do not cause damage to the server by trying to run a tool like Disk Management at the same time. Because only two simultaneous remote administration connections are allowed, administrators may find that they are unable to establish a remote connection to the server if two different administrator accounts are connected or have disconnected from the server but not logged out. You will need to address these concerns in your security designs.

In the following Design Scenario, you will design for security in situation in which Remote Desktop for Administration is used.

Design Scenario

Designing for Secure Server Management with Remote Desktop for Administration

Expo, Inc. would like to save money by centralizing most of the administrative functions at its corporate headquarters in Los Angeles. The company wants to be able to use local contractors on an as-needed basis to manage the hardware locally.

During the design phase, you spoke to the CSO and the network administrator:

CSO   Remote administration traffic must be secure. We don't have time to evaluate each administration tool individually for its security features.

Network Administrator   We use different OSes through the day and we don't want to have to install the administrative tools on the clients before we can use them; besides, the snap-ins are not supported on the Pocket PC 2003 devices that the current administrators have.

1.   **Question:** What tool would you recommend for performing remote management in Expo, Inc. and why? **Answer:** You would use Remote Desktop for Administration because it supports strong authentication and encryption. It also will encrypt all communications for any tool because the tool runs locally on the server but sends only screen, mouse, and keyboard information in encrypted RDP packets. This would meet the CSO's requirements.

You only need to use the Remote Desktop client to communicate with the server and use any tools installed on the server. This means you won't have to install utilities and you won't have compatibility problems with the OS. This meets the network administrator's requirements.

Using Remote Assistance

Remote Assistance uses the same technology as Remote Desktop, but it was designed to allow someone to connect to a Windows computer to provide assistance. When a Remote Assistance session is established, both users will see the same screen and can chat with each other through the Remote Assistance chat program. You can even allow the remote user to take control of your computer, with your permission of course. This differs from Remote Desktop, where only one user can be logged in at a time. Remote Desktop is primarily used to manage the computer by administrators, where Remote Assistance is used by help desk staff to help users solve their problems. Remote Assistance does not use the RDP protocol, like Remote Desktop, but is based on the technologies and protocols of Microsoft Netmeeting.

Remote Assistance is installed on Windows XP and 2003 servers and clients by default but is disabled by default.

To enable Remote Assistance, follow these steps:

1.   Open the System Properties dialog box through the Control Panel.

2.   Click the Remote tab to show the settings for Remote Desktop and Remote Assistance.

3.   Check the Turn On Remote Assistance And Allow Invitations To Be Sent From This Computer option, as shown in Figure 10.5.

FIGURE 10.5 The Remote tab of the System Properties dialog box

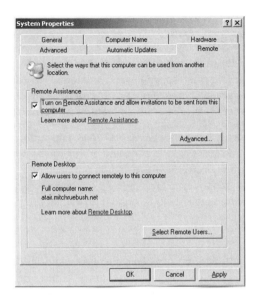

Once you select this option, you will be able to click the Advanced button to reveal the Remote Assistance Settings dialog box, shown in Figure 10.6.

You will then be able to choose to allow your computer to be controlled remotely. If you do not want to allow remote control, you can turn off this setting but still chat with the user and allow them to see the desktop of your computer. You will also be able to control how long an invitation for remote assistance will remain open. By default, it is set to 30 days. You may want to shorten it for security reasons.

Remote Assistance is generally used in organizations to provide a means for the help desk to support a user without needing to send someone to the user's workstation. This can help increase the productivity of the support staff. The utilization of this service can present some security issues that you will need to include in your security design.

FIGURE 10.6 The Remote Assistance Settings dialog box

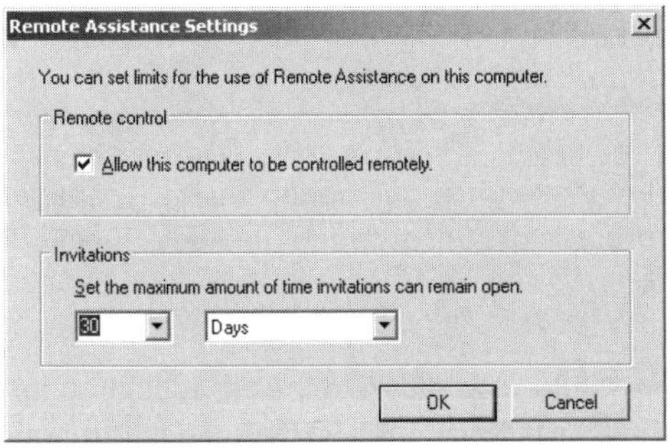

Real World Scenario

Using Remote Assistance to Support Users

We have users we need to support in two locations but a very small help desk staff. The help desk staff needs to be as productive as possible when solving users' problems. They also don't have time to travel between locations extensively. Many of our users' problems are due to misconfigured applications or lack of the proper skills to use certain features of a program.

The Remote Assistance feature of Windows XP or Windows Server 2003 helps immensely in maximizing the help desk's time. They spend less time traveling and more time helping users, meaning we can operate well with the staff we currently have and do not need new hires to keep up with a growing workload. Remote Assistance allows the help desk staff to guide users through difficult procedures instead of trying to talk them through it on the phone or sending someone to their desktop.

The first of the security issues is that you will need to determine if you should change your firewall configuration to support Remote Assistance. Remote Assistance requires that TCP port 3389 be opened on a firewall to pass through it. You will also need to determine if you will allow Remote Assistance by enabling it on the clients that you want to support it. This can be done by navigating to Start ➢ Control Panel ➢ System and clicking on the Remote tab as shown above. You can enable Remote Assistance by using Group Policy if you want to enable it for a large number of clients in your organization.

You should also set up a password that the user would need to enter to connect to a Remote Assistance session. You will need to communicate the password to the person assisting you through some means, such as an e-mail (you can use S/MIME to encrypt the email), before they will be able to connect. You should make sure the password you choose is strong, especially if the invitation will be left open for a long period of time. You should set a short invitation period for Remote Assistance and use a password that is at least eight characters long and is a mixture of symbols, numbers, and letters.

In the next Design Scenario, you will look at making design decisions for the secure use of Remote Assistance.

Design Scenario

Designing for Secure Remote Assistance

Expo, Inc. wants to be able to use local contractors on an as-needed basis to manage the hardware locally. The company is also in the process of consolidating help desk functionality.

During the design phase, you spoke to the CSO and the help desk manager:

CIO We need to save money wherever possible. In addition to the consolidation for network administration, we are consolidating the help desk functions of different departments into one location at our central office.

Help Desk Manager Most of our calls for assistance involve working with users that are having trouble with an application or have a configuration problem. We usually end up getting frustrated with talking them through steps on the phone and send someone to their desktop. This will no longer be an option because we will be using contractors who will be billing the company. We need a mechanism to help the user visually and verify that the problem is really a hardware problem before we send someone to the aid of the user.

1. **Question:** What should you recommend for the help desk at Expo, Inc. and why? **Answer:** You should use Remote Assistance because the company needs a solution that will allow help desk employees to assist users remotely with having to send personnel to them. This is what Remote Assistant is designed to accomplish.

Using Command Line Remote Management Tools

Command line management tools are not the most convenient way to manage Windows Server 2003 most of the time, but there are situations where they can be effective remote management tools. The first is when you have very little bandwidth to communicate with the server over. Command line management tools are very lightweight in terms of bandwidth usage and can help you quickly accomplish the task. The second reason would be to support the maximum number of clients. Command line tools tend to be supported by many different platforms, so they are a good means to manage Windows Server 2003 from another operating system if no other options exist. We will discuss two command line tools: Telnet and Secure Shell (SSH).

Using Telnet

Telnet is a program that runs a command console on the client computer much like the command console in Windows Server 2003. The one difference is that the commands that you execute do not run on the client but on the server you are connected to. This is similar to the capability provided by Remote Desktop for Administration except it is command line only. Telnet provides a basic option for remote management from any operating system that supports TCP\IP. The capability that Telnet provides is called terminal emulation.

You can run Telnet by clicking Start ➤ Run and typing **telnet** to launch the client. You would then type **open** *server_name* to connect to the remote server running Telnet. You can then issue commands that run on the server, as shown in Figure 10.7.

Telnet is not considered secure in and of itself and should not be used alone on a network, especially over a WAN. It requires that you log on using a username and password, but they are passed in clear text over the network. Authentication is limited to passing the username and password in clear text without support for smart cards or other forms of authentication. Also, all commands and data are sent over the network without any forms of encryption. You will need to consider using another means of encryption, like establishing a VPN using L2TP and IPSec for providing a stronger means of authentication and encryption of network traffic or using an alternative to Telnet called Secure Shell (SSH).

FIGURE 10.7   Telnet to a Windows Server 2003 machine

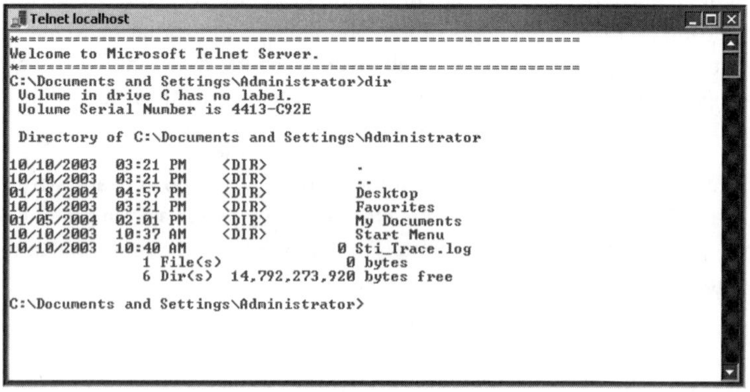

Secure Shell

Secure Shell (SSH) is a technology that was developed by SSH Communications Security, Ltd. to provide for secure authentication and communications for remote shells and file transfers. SSH provides for strong authentication mechanisms, including the capability to use certificate-based authentication like smart cards. SSH guards against eavesdropping on packets and IP redirection by encrypting the communications between the server and client. If available, SSH is preferred over Telnet for providing remote administration through the command line.

Designing for Emergency Management Services

Emergency Management Services (EMS) is a collection of out-of-band management tools that enable the ability to manage Windows Server 2003 machine when it is no longer responding to in-band management tools. You can access the EMS through a terminal emulator, like Hyper-Terminal, that connects to a serial port on the server.

EMS is made up of standard Windows Server 2003 components that have been modified to redirect their output to the out-of-band communication port in addition to the video card. The following Windows components support out-of-band communication:

- Recovery Console
- Remote Installation Services (RIS)
- Text mode setup
- Setup loader

In addition to the standard Windows components, EMS includes two new remote management consoles: *Special Administration Console (SAC)* and *!Special Administration Console (!SAC).*

Using the Special Administration Console is the most common way to access the EMS services on Windows Server 2003. SAC provides you with a command-line environment to manage the server when it is locked up, as shown in Figure 10.8.

The SAC will be available as long as the kernel of Windows Server 2003 is running. This means you can issue commands early in the boot process because as soon as the kernel is running, you can have access to the SAC, if it is enabled on your server. You can issue commands to the SAC that will support the following administration features:

- Restarting the server

- Shutting down the server

- Displaying the list of running processes

- Killing a process

- Configuring the IP address on the server

- Starting a command prompt in the operating system if possible

- Generating a stop error so the server dumps memory

The SAC provides user mode access through the cmd command. This will launch a command shell that you can then use to launch a command-line in-band management tool like Telnet to make managing the server easier. SAC also provides for viewing the setup logs generated during the setup process to check on the progress of the setup or to diagnose problems with the setup. You can press Esc+Tab to switch to the SAC and view the setup logs during the GUI portion of the setup.

FIGURE 10.8   Special Administration Console

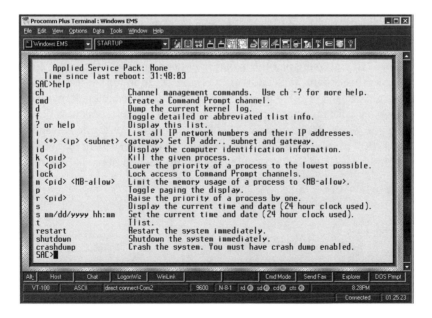

The !SAC is the failsafe special management console that will load if the SAC fails to start for some reason. This is an automatic process. The !SAC does not provide all of the same functionality the SAC provides. In fact, it only provides two functions:

- Restarting the server
- Redirecting stop error messages

You can utilize the EMS services that are built into Windows Server 2003 to provide management of the server if the kernel is running or during loading. If you purchase additional hardware like a service processor or if you have a firmware console, you can manage the server even if the kernel is not working.

You will need to decide how you will connect to the server to support EMS. Generally, you are going to connect to a serial connection on the server. Serial connections have no logical security, so you will want to make sure that you have strong physical security for the serial connection. This will mean keeping the computers and devices that connect to the serial connection in the secure server room and keeping the connection itself secured. You can lay out different designs for supporting EMS. There is additional hardware you can purchase to add network support for EMS. There are four basic designs for laying out your EMS infrastructure: direct serial connection, modem serial connection, terminal concentrator, and intelligent Uninteruptable Power Supply (UPS).

Using a Direct Serial Connection

A *direct serial connection* is the simplest of the out-of-band connections to a server. You can establish the connection by using a null modem cable between the management computer and the server running EMS. The management computer is a computer that is running some kind of terminal emulation software. The easiest software to use is HyperTerminal because it comes with any Windows operating system, but almost any type of terminal emulation software will work.

You will need to make sure that the management computer and the server are physically secure to protect this design. You can set up a remote solution for a direct serial connection by setting up a management computer in the server room and enabling Remote Desktop for Administration on it. Set up HyperTerminal to connect to the serial port with the connection to the computer you would like to manage. This can provide secure remote management, but it's really only practical for a single computer or very few. The main benefit of direct serial connections is that they are easy to set up because they require no additional hardware.

FIGURE 10.9   Direct serial connection

Server   Management Computer

The direct serial connection has a number of disadvantages:

- Computers need to be close to each other for physical security.

- It has the most limited functionality.

- It's difficult to manage more than a few boxes using a direct serial connection.

Figure 10.9 shows an example of a direct serial connection.

The direct serial connection is a great way to quickly connect a laptop computer to diagnose a server problem, like a hung server.

Using Modem Serial Connection

A *modem serial connection* is similar to a direct serial connection except it involves putting a modem between the management computer and the servers. You would then dial into the modem and use a terminal emulation program. You have two connections to secure: the connection between the management computer and the modem and the connection between the modem and the server. Security on the connection between the management computer and the modem is based on security features found in the modem. For example, you could enable call-back features in the modem to allow only connections from known numbers. Security on the serial connection between the modem and the server will need to be physically maintained.

Figure 10.10 shows how a modem setup would look.

The benefits of using a modem for out-of-band communications are as follows:

- It's easy to set up and configure for use because there are no complicated devices to purchase and configure.

- The management computer can remotely connect to the server.

There are some disadvantages:

- Security features in a modem are limited.

- It's difficult to manage more than a few computers using a modem.

FIGURE 10.10   Remote EMS through a modem

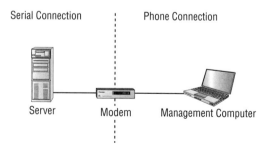

Serial Connection   Phone Connection

Server   Modem   Management Computer

Using a Terminal Concentrator

There are two problems with the direct serial or the modem serial connection to the server. The first problem is that the management computer is limited to two to four serial ports and therefore you can have only two to four EMS connections to your servers. The second problem is that the management computer needs to be physically secured to prevent access to the SAC. There is no logical security for the connection. You can manage a larger number of servers and remove the necessity of physically securing the management computer by setting up a *terminal concentrator* to support a larger number of connections.

The terminal concentrator contains a larger number of serial ports than a server contains and can support a connection to a server for each port it contains. The terminal concentrator can then be connected to a network or a modem to provide terminal access to the servers it is connected to. This makes it easier to provide out-of-band communication to a larger amount of servers. A terminal concentrator also makes it easier to secure out-of-band communications.

You will need to physically secure the terminal concentrator's connection to the servers, just as you would any other serial connection. You should include the terminal concentrator in the server room with the servers that you will manage through it. The main difference is that the management computer and user can be logically authenticated.

You usually connect to a terminal concentrator using a command-line terminal emulator like Telnet. Better yet, many support SSH, which can provide many options for authentication, including smart card and Public Key Infrastructure (PKI). SSH also encrypts the traffic between the terminal concentrator and the management computer, further protecting the data from eavesdropping and manipulating. You should look for a terminal concentrator that supports SSH as a connection option. If your terminal concentrator does not support SSH, then attackers could sniff packets to obtain administrative information. You should consider using a secondary network for remote management only if this is the case.

Figure 10.11 illustrates what a network with a terminal concentrator would look like.

The following are benefits of using a terminal concentrator:

- It supports logical authentication mechanisms.
- It can support encryption.
- It supports a larger number of servers for out-of-band management.
- It can support features in firmware like powering on and off the servers.

The main disadvantage is that you need to purchase additional hardware in the form of terminal concentrators.

Using an Intelligent UPS

You may already have devices that can act as terminal concentrators in the form of an *intelligent UPS*. The intelligent UPS can provide the same features a terminal concentrator provides. An intelligent UPS can form two connections to the server for use by EMS. It can connect using the standard serial connection and it can connect to the server through the AC power line. This means that not only can you manage the servers, but you can remotely control the power to the servers.

FIGURE 10.11 Using a terminal concentrator

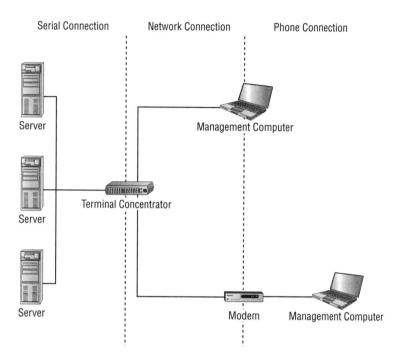

You would need to manage and secure intelligent UPSes in the same way you treat terminal concentrators. Physically secure the device in the server room with the servers and then use logical security to secure the network connection to the UPS. Having one device that does two functions may save you the costs of purchasing separate terminal concentrators.

 Real World Scenario

Using EMS to Manage Servers

We use Exchange Server 2003 for e-mail in our organization. The server has been giving us some problems lately, just locking up with no explanation. We suspect it is a hardware problem, but we needed to keep the server running until we could get replacement hardware. The server would lock up and nobody could get to e-mail without the server being rebooted. The server would tend to lock up at inconvenient times, such as on weekends and at night.

We decided to install EMS on the server and set up a serial connection to another server called ServerA. Whenever the Exchange server locks up, we can then connect to the server and launch HyperTerminal to connect to the e-mail server through the out-of-band communication channels. We can then issue a reboot command to the server to fix the problem.

FIGURE 10.12   Intelligent UPS setup

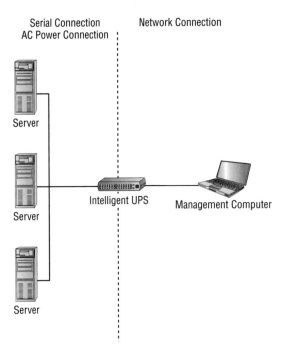

Figure 10.12 shows what a configuration using an intelligent UPS would look like. The following are benefits of using an intelligent UPS:

- It supports logical authentication mechanisms.

- It can support encryption.

- It supports a larger number of servers for out-of-band management.

- It can support features in firmware like powering on and off the servers

The main disadvantage is that if you don't own an intelligent UPS, you need to purchase additional hardware.

In the following Design Scenario, you will look at designing a security infrastructure for EMS.

 Design Scenario

Designing for Emergency Management Services

Expo, Inc. wants to be able to use local contractors on an as-needed basis to manage the hardware locally.

During the design phase, you spoke to the CSO and the network administrator:

CSO   All remote management must be secure.

Network Administrator   We are having problems with some of our critical servers hanging from time to time. This usually happens at night or on weekends. Whoever is on pager duty must then go into the office to reset the server so it will be available for our clients. We need a means to remotely manage these servers, even if they have hung, to determine what the problem may be and to resolve the problem through a reboot. We would like to apply the solution to all 26 of our servers. They are all running Windows Server 2003.

1.   **Question:** What should Expo, Inc. do solve this problem? **Answer:** The company should purchase a terminal concentrator that supports SSH. The terminal concentrator will scale to support all 26 servers, where the direct serial connection and modem connection will not accommodate this. Using intelligent UPSes could also work, except you would have the added cost of purchasing the UPSes. The terminal concentrator solution would be more cost effective. Administrators should install this in the server room where it can be kept physically safe and connected to the servers via serial cables. The administrators can then connect to the server through SSH and perform actions like rebooting the server, even if user mode is hung.

Summary

There are benefits and risks to remotely managing a network. The first thing you will need to decide is whether to allow remote management of servers on your network. In addition to the risks associated with providing access to the server remotely, somebody might eavesdrop on the data that is being sent over the network and authentication capabilities of the management tool could be too weak. Once you've decided to allow remote management, you should decide how and if you will mitigate remote management risks on your network. You will also need to look at the features in the management tools.

Remote management tools are provided by Windows Server 2003. These tools provide different mechanisms for managing your servers. You use the Microsoft Management Console to host various management tools called snap-ins. The snap-ins can vary with regard to capabilities and security features. The most popular means of remote management is to use Remote Desktop for Administration. This tool allows you to manage a computer remotely as if you were sitting at the server itself. Remote Assistance is another tool that provides access to the desktop of a remote user to provide assistance when they are having a problem. You can also provide a command-line remote interface through Telnet and SSH. All together, these tools are known as in-band management tools because they use the standard network connections for management. Windows Server 2003 provides for out-of-band management also.

Emergency Management Services (EMS) is used to access the server through a serial interface usually. This means that you may be able to administer the server remotely even if the server is not responding to in-band tools. You can use the Special Administration Console (SAC) to restart the computer or try to troubleshoot the problems.

Key Terms

Before you take the exam, be certain you are familiar with the following terms:

!Special Administration Console (!SAC)	Remote Assistance
Direct serial connection	Remote Desktop for Administration
Emergency Management Services (EMS)	Remote Desktop Protocol (RDP)
In-band remote management tools	Remote management plan
Intelligent UPS	Secure Shell (SSH)
Microsoft Management Console (MMC)	Special Administration Console (SAC)
Modem serial connection	Telnet
Out-of-band remote management tools	Terminal concentrator

Exam Essentials

Remember that remote administration is vulnerable to eavesdropping. You should evaluate the encryption capabilities of the remote management tools. If the tools do not support encryption, you will need to come up with a method to encrypt the data being sent to and from the server with management tools. This is especially important if you are managing the server over the Internet.

Know that MMC is not a management tool in itself. MMC is a shell or framework that provides a common environment for management tools called snap-ins. Snap-ins can vary greatly in the features they support, so you will want to verify their security features, such as encryption, authentication, and remote management capability.

Understand what Remote Desktop for Administration does. Remote Desktop for Administration provides a graphical user interface for managing a server. It also provides for encrypting network traffic through the RDP configuration.

Remember that Remote Assistance and Remote Desktop are built upon the same technology but provide different functions. You use Remote Assistance to provide assistance to users on the network without having to visit the desktop.

Understand that Telnet provides command-line remote administration but it contains no security mechanisms. You will need to either provide encryption externally to the tool or use the secure form of a remote shell called Secure Shell (SSH).

Know that EMS allows you to perform out-of-band management of your servers. This means that you will have the ability to manage your server even if it is not responding to in-band management tools.

Review Questions

1. You are evaluating remote management options for your company. Your network administration staff and CSO are worried about spoofing attacks, eavesdropping, sniffing, and manipulation of data in packets sent through the remote management tools. What technology would you use to alleviate these concerns?

   A. Local administration only

   B. Strong encryption

   C. Strong authentication protocol

   D. Patch management policy

2. You need to provide security for your remote management tools. Unfortunately, not all of the tools support strong authentication mechanisms and/or encryption. You have unsuccessfully searched for alternative tools. You need to perform remote management of these applications but also require security. What can you do to alleviate this problem?

   A. Install a secondary network for performing remote management only. The administrators would need to authenticate with the router to gain access to this network. This private network would alleviate many of the security risks associated with management over the normal network.

   B. Perform all management locally. This would ensure that nobody can infiltrate the remote management data.

   C. To prevent eavesdropping, create a policy that sets forth strict penalties for any employee sniffing the network.

   D. Use a Windows client to connect to the server you need to manage because it will automatically secure the connection.

3. You currently use an MMC snap-in to manage your Windows Server 2003 Active Directory infrastructure. The communication from this snap-in needs to pass through a firewall that separates you from a branch office so you can manage a domain controller that is there. The management application uses RPC and LDAP (389) to communicate with the server. What ports would you need to open on the firewall for RPC?

   A. 110

   B. 135

   C. 23

   D. 3336

4. Ann needs to set up remote management with a server. She does not want to worry about install-ing the proper management tools on the clients. She discovers that not all clients will support the management tools for the applications she and her fellow administrators use. She is also con-cerned about eavesdropping on network management data. What remote management tool should she use?

   A. Microsoft Management Console

   B. Remote Assistance

   C. Remote Desktop for Administrators

   D. Telnet

5. What is the main purpose for using Remote Assistance to remotely manage networks?

   A. Remote Assistance provides administrators with a graphical user interface to manage a server as if they were sitting at the local console.

   B. Remote Assistance provides administrators with a command-line interface that is com-patible with many servers and devices.

   C. Remote Assistance provides administrators with the ability to remotely assist end users with problems on their computers.

   D. Remote Assistance provides administrators with the ability to manage a server even after it has locked up in many cases.

6. What are the security issues with using Telnet to perform remote management of servers or devices on the network?

   A. Telnet does not have a graphical user interface.

   B. Telnet is not supported by all devices or Windows by default.

   C. Telnet does not provide for encryption or strong authentication.

   D. Telnet only works over a serial connection.

7. Which of the following can you perform using out-of-band management tools?

   A. Restart the server.

   B. Configure the IP address of the server.

   C. List the running processes on the server.

   D. Kill a process.

   E. Start a command prompt.

   F. Generate a stop error.

   G. All of the above.

8. What is the main purpose of using Emergency Management Services (EMS) to remotely manage networks?

   A. EMS provides administrators with a graphical user interface to manage a server as if they were sitting at the local console.

   B. EMS provides administrators with a command-line interface that is compatible with many servers and devices.

   C. EMS provides administrators with the ability to remotely assist end users with problems on their computers.

   D. EMS provides administrators with the ability to manage a server even after it has locked up in many cases.

9. What is the most effective way of handling serial connections to many servers and the most secure way to set up EMS for out-of-band remote management?

   A. Purchase a terminal concentrator that supports SSH. Connect the terminal concentrator to the servers through the network using SSH. Connect to the terminal concentrator from the management computer through a null serial connection. Physically secure the terminal concentrator in the server room with the servers.

   B. Purchase a terminal concentrator that supports Telnet. Connect the terminal concentrator to the servers through the network using Telnet. Connect to the terminal concentrator from the management computer through a null serial connection. Physically secure the terminal concentrator in the server room with the servers.

   C. Purchase a terminal concentrator that supports Telnet. Connect the terminal concentrator to the servers with null serial cables. Connect to the terminal concentrator from the management computer through Telnet. Physically secure the terminal concentrator in the server room with the servers.

   D. Purchase a terminal concentrator that supports SSH. Connect the terminal concentrator to the servers with null serial cables. Connect to the terminal concentrator from the management computer through SSH. Physically secure the terminal concentrator in the server room with the servers.

10. What is the main purpose for using Remote Desktop to remotely manage networks?

   A. Remote Desktop provides administrators with a graphical user interface to manage a server as if they were sitting at the local console.

   B. Remote Desktop provides administrators with a command-line interface that is compatible with many servers and devices.

   C. Remote Desktop provides administrators with the ability to remotely assist end users with problems on their computers.

   D. Remote Desktop provides administrators with the ability to manage a server even after it has locked up in many cases.

Answers to Review Questions

1. B. Strong encryption like RC4 128-bit encryption will prevent many of the most damaging attacks against remote management. You should consider encryption for all remote management tools that support it. If they don't support it, you should consider implementing a VPN or other means of encrypting the remote management traffic.

2. A. You would use a secondary, remote management–only network to keep the remote management traffic off the network on which it would be a greater risk. This is not as good as encrypting the information because administrators who have access to the network could view the information.

3. B. Microsoft uses port 135 for DCOM RPCs that are supported by many snap-ins for the MMC. Port 110 is used for POP3, 23 is used for Telnet, and 3336 is just a random port.

4. C. Remote Desktop for Administrators provides a remote interface that will let you interact with the server as if you were sitting at the server locally. This alleviates the need for Ann to distribute the proper management tools to the clients. The Remote Desktop client is supported by many different operating systems, but MMC snap-ins can sometimes be incompatible with the underlying operating system. Remote Desktop supports 128-bit RC4 encryption to prevent eavesdropping. It also provides for strong, integrated authentication with Windows. Remote Assistance is used to support users and generally not for Remote Management. Telnet does not provide any encryption and passwords are sent over the wire in clear text.

5. C. Remote assistance is used to remotely provide assistance for a computer user. You can ask the user to allow you to see what they see and even chat with the user or take over their session and do a task for them while they watch.

6. C. Telnet does not encrypt the authentication or administration traffic and is susceptible to eavesdropping. This is particularly troublesome when the tool is being used to remotely manage servers and devices because administrator passwords can be compromised or sensitive data could be captured. You would need to address security issues for using Telnet, which could involve using a secondary network for remote management, using a VPN to secure the traffic, or switching to SSH if supported. The question was about security, so the fact the Telnet does not have a graphical user interface or that it is not supported by all devices are not relevant. Telnet supports network connections and does not need a serial connection.

7. G. All of these commands can be executed from the Special Administration Console to administer the server when connections through in-band means will not work.

8. D. EMS is one of the out-of-band management tools provided with Windows Server 2003. These services let you connect, diagnose, and resolve server issues without having network access or even user mode access to the server. This means that you could connect to a locked-up server and reboot or diagnose the problem as long as kernel mode is still running.

9. D. You would need to set up a terminal concentrator to more readily support many servers for out-of-band communication. When purchasing a terminal concentrator, you would want to look for one that supports SSH to provide logical security for the network connections.

10. A. Remote Desktop for Administration is a popular way of providing remote in-band management to Windows Server 2003. It provides a graphical user interface that shows what is happening on the server, and all keyboard and mouse movements in the Remote Desktop window are sent to and handled on the server. With Remote Desktop, it's as if you were sitting at the local server, but you still gain the productivity and convenience of remote administration.

Case Study

You should give yourself 20 minutes to review this testlet, review the exhibit, and complete the questions.

Overview

Starlight Industries is a manufacturer and distributor of novelty gifts with locations in six cities in the United States. The company uses several custom-built client server applications to manage its business. In addition, it has two web applications that allow resellers and the general public to purchase goods and manage their accounts through their website.

Physical Locations

The company headquarters is located in Omaha, Nebraska, and contains about 500 employees. The management offices and website are located there.

   The company has locations that contain warehousing and sales functions in the following cities (each city has approximately 125 employees):

- Los Angeles, California
- Boise, Idaho
- Philadelphia, Pennsylvania
- Boca Raton, Florida
- Phoenix, Arizona

Planned Changes

Starlight Industries wants to cut costs by consolidating its network administration to its headquarters in Omaha. The plan is to have all network and server administration and help desk function take place from this location.

   All clients will be upgraded to Windows XP.

Active Directory

The Active Directory environment consists of a single forest with one domain running in Windows 2000 Forest Functional Level.

Network Infrastructure

The client's existing network infrastructure is shown in the exhibit. See the case study for the exhibit.

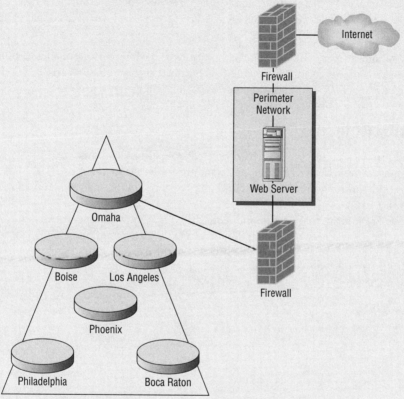

Client computers currently run a mixture of Windows XP and Windows 98.

Each location contains a domain controller running Windows 2000 Server that acts a file and print server also. The perimeter network in Omaha contains a web server running Windows Server 2003. Omaha also contains a Windows Server 2003 machine that is running SQL Server 2000, which supports the client server applications used to run the business.

The company runs a custom client server application located on a Windows Server 2003 computer at each of its warehouse sites. It provides a command-line administrative interface and a custom-built GUI administrative interface.

Problem Statements

Administrative costs need to be reduced by centralizing all administrative and help desk functions.

Unauthorized users should not be able to perform administrative functions.

All administrative traffic must be secured.

Interviews

Chief Information Officer   The costs for maintaining separate administrators and help desk functionality at each site have continued to soar over the years. We must cut costs by centralizing these functions. The business units fear a loss of service, so we need to make this as functional as possible.

Network Administrator   We have DSL connections to the Internet from each location and will need to use the Internet for management. This means that the communications will need to be secure and we are concerned about the potential abuse in the system.

Security Policies

All updates to the web servers must be protected from eavesdropping.

All management activities must be protected from eavesdropping.

The website must require a valid user ID and password before allowing a user access to account information.

All customer information sent to and from the website must be encrypted.

Users will need to know if the help desk is watching their computer.

Network administrators must be able to manage the network from any location.

Case Study Questions

1. The help desk currently visits the desktop of each user who needs assistance to help step them through processes or look at what is going on the screen. What technology should Starlight Industries use to replace this function when they centralize the help desk?

    A. Remote Assistance

    B. MMC

    C. SSH

    D. Telnet

2. The security for certain users needs to be updated for the custom client/server applications used at the warehouses by Starlight Industries. Which of the following remote administration tools should the administrator use to manage the application?

    A. Remote Assistance

    B. Remote Desktop for Administration

    C. Microsoft Management Console

    D. Telnet

3. Match the administration technology with the appropriate device on the network (administration technologies may be used more than once).

Administration Technology	Network Devices
Remote Assistance	Local server administration
Remote Desktop for Administration	Remote server administration
Secure Shell (SSH)	Remote router and switch administration
Microsoft Management Console (MMC)	Workstation administration
	Workstation user assistance

Answers to Case Study Questions

1. A. Remote Assistance is the technology located in Windows XP and Windows Server 2003 to allow a remote person to assist a user through a process. This can involve seeing what the user sees, sharing applications, or taking over the mouse to show them how it is done. MMC, SSH, and Telnet will not allow for this and will not replace this functionality. Remote Assistance also supports encryption which is important to Starlight Industries.

2. B. You should choose Remote Desktop for Administration because it provides secure communication between the client and the server by default and can be used to manage any application as if you were sitting at the local console. This is useful because the warehouse application supports a custom management GUI. There is no MMC for the custom warehouse application, so that is not a solution. There is a command-line interface to the warehouse application, but Telnet does not provide a secure connection. Remote assistance is best used to help a user, not for remote management of servers.

3.

Local server administration
Microsoft Management Console (MMC)
Remote server administration
Remote Desktop for Administration
Remote router and switch administration
Secure Shell (SSH)
Workstation administration
Remote Desktop for Administration
Workstation user assistance
Remote Assistance

Local server administration On the server itself you will use the proper MMC based management tools for the application, like Active Directory Users and Computers to create users in Active Directory, to manage the services and applications on your server.

Remote server administration Remotely, you will need to use something that can cross the firewalls and does not require installation of additional software. Windows XP and Windows Server 2003 have Remote Desktop built in, so you will not have to install additional software to support remote administration.

Remote router and switch administration Generally all routers and switches support Telnet, or if you are lucky, you will be able to use ssh to administer them.

Workstation administration You can use Remote Desktop for Administration to manage workstations running Windows XP, in addition to Windows Server 2003.

Workstation user assistance Remote Assistance was designed to help users with their problems. It supports application sharing, chatting, white boarding, and so forth, as tools that can be useful in aiding the user.

Glossary

!Special Administration Console (!SAC)   The !SAC is the special management console that will automatically load if the SAC fails to start. The !SAC will only restart the server, and redirect stop error messages.

802.11a   A wireless network protocol that can transmit data at speeds as fast as 54Mbps but at a shorter range than the other more popular standards. It also uses a different part of the electromagnetic spectrum and so is not compatible with either 802.11b or 802.11g. Its short range and nonoverlapping 12 channels makes it a specification that is more appropriate for densely populated areas.

802.11b   A wireless network protocol that is currently the most popular specification for wireless networking. It supports speeds up to 11Mbps over a longer range than 802.11a supports. Devices that support 802.11b tend to be less expensive, hence the popularity.

802.11g   A wireless network protocol that supports speeds up to 54Mbps and is compatible with 802.11b because they both use the same part of the radio spectrum. It does have a shorter range than 802.11b to get the full 54Mbps speed.

A

access control entry (ACE)   An entry in an object's discretionary access control list (DACL) that grants or denies permissions to an identity. An ACE is also an entry in an object's system access control list (SACL) that specifies the security events to be audited for a identity.

access control list (ACL)   A list of security rights that apply to an object as a whole, a set of the object's properties, or an individual property of an object. There are two types of access control lists: discretionary (DACL) and system (SACL).

access point (AP)   An access point transmits and receives wireless network communications. It acts as a bridge between the wireless network and the hardwired network.

access token   A token that contains the security information for a logon session. The system creates an access token when a user logs on, and every process executed on behalf of the user has a copy of the token. The token identifies the user, the user's groups, and the user's privileges and passes the information to the object to determine access.

ad hoc mode   A peer-to-peer communication mode in which clients communicate directly with each other. Clients can be configured to allow incoming connections and support ad hoc mode.

anonymous access   Typically used when you need to authenticate large numbers of users on the Internet, and there is no need to differentiate between users. When a user connects to IIS through anonymous access, they are authenticated as the IUSR_*ServerName* account by default, where *ServerName* is the name of your IIS server.

ASP.NET forms-based authentication   Authentication in which a standard HTML form is used to provide for custom authentication of users. The developer creates a page to capture the profile information of the user and a page to capture the username and password. You would then need to configure the ASP.NET application to support forms-based authentication.

asset Anything of value in a company. An asset is an item that it worth securing.

audit policy A policy used to track security events like access to files or attempts to authenticate with the server. This information will be written to the Windows security log, which can be viewed with Event Viewer. You can use this information to determine what is going on with the server and where your security mechanisms may be breaking down.

authentication The process of determining an identity (for example, a user).

authorization The process of determining the resources an identity can access once it's authenticated.

Authorization Manager A program used to enable a role-based access control on a website. You can assign a group or user access to applications, or parts of applications (based on URLs), and not have to worry about the NTFS permissions.

B

back-to-back configuration Configuration in which the screened subnet is placed between two firewalls. The screened subnet is connected through a firewall to the Internet on one end and connected through another firewall to the internal network on the opposite end.

basic authentication Authentication scheme that allows clients to authenticate with the domain or local server using a username and password. The main problem with basic authentication is that it sends the passwords over the network in the clear text.

bastion host A type of firewall that is configured such that all traffic destined for an external network, such as the Internet, must pass through it. It is typically a multihomed computer with one internal and one external network interface.

C

CA Administrator This role is associated with the Manage CA permission on the CA server. It will allow the account to configure the CA server, manage permissions, and renew CA certificates.

certificate authentication Authentication scheme that allows users to authenticate with the IIS server using a digital certificate. The certificate can be obtained from a third-party certificate vender or from your own public key infrastructure (PKI). The client certificate validation is a feature of SSL. Just remember that certificate authentication can not be used if SSL is not enabled.

certificate authority (CA) A trusted and recognized entity that can be either internal or commercial that issues and manages security credentials and public keys for message encryption.

Certificate Manager This role is associated with the Issue And Manage Certificates permission. It will allow the account to initiate a key recovery, manage certificate enrollment, and revoke certificates.

certificate rule A rule within a software restriction policy that will grant or deny access to software by evaluating its signature and determining if it is signed by a trusted publisher.

certificate templates Templates used by Windows Server 2003 for generating certificates for various applications. They provide the fields necessary for the application that uses the certificate. An example would be secure e-mail certificates.

Challenge Handshake Authentication Protocol (CHAP) The industry standard protocol for performing Point-to-Point Protocol (PPP) authentication. Popular among Internet Service Providers (ISPs), this protocol uses the challenge-and-response mechanism for validating the user.

cross-certification Allows two organizations to trust each other and rely on each other's certificates and keys as if they were issued from their own certificate authorities.

custom template These are templates that you create. It is recommended that you base them on predefined templates.

D

delegation Assigning specific tasks to the appropriate user or group without giving them any more rights than are required in order to perform the tasks you have delegated to them.

delegation of control Assigning the responsibility of managing Active Directory objects to another user, group, or organization. By delegating control, you negate the need to have several high-level administrative accounts because any user or group can be delegated to control an object without it being added to an administrator group.

department CA hierarchy Hierarchy in which a CA for each department in the organization is installed so each department can control the deployment of their certificates.

digest authentication Authentication that provides support for encrypting passwords, even over an unencrypted connection. Digest authentication hashes the user credentials using the Message Digest 5 (MD5) algorithm. This will prevent someone that intercepts the credentials from reading the password.

direct serial connection The simplest of the out-of-band connections to a server. You can establish the connection by using a null modem cable between the management computer and the server running Emergency Management Services (EMS).

discretionary access control list (DACL) The part of the security descriptor that grants or denies specific users and groups access to an object.

domain trust A trust relationship between Windows domains. It can be between domains within the same tree, in separate trees, or in separate forests.

E

Emergency Management Services (EMS) A collection of out-of-band management tools that enable the ability to manage a Windows Server 2003 machine when it is no longer responding to in-band management tools. You can access the EMS through a terminal emulator, like HyperTerminal, that connects to a serial port on the server.

enrollment strategy The process of requesting and installing the certificates for the user, computers, or services that participate in the PKI.

enterprise CA This takes advantage of Active Directory to control the enrollment process. This means that you can use Group Policy to manage and distribute client certificates. You can also use the certificate templates to create a certificate.

extended rights Rights used for special operations that apply to specific types of Active Directory objects.

Extensible Authentication Protocol (EAP) A standard way of adding additional authentication protocols to Point-to-Point Protocol (PPP). EAP provides support for certificate-based authentication, smart cards, and other protocols like RSA's SecurID. It allows third-party companies to provide even stronger authentication protocols to meet your company's security needs.

external threats Threats that represent the potential for an attack to be initiated from outside of your organization, such as threats originating from the Internet.

external trust A nontransitive trust between an Active Directory domain and an external Windows domain, such as an NT 4 domain or a domain that is in a separate forest and doesn't have a forest trust with the source domain.

F

foot printing The systematic probing of a system to gather information about it.

forest trust A transitive trust that is between separate forests and can be either one or two way.

function CA hierarchy Hierarchy in which a CA based on the types of certificates that you wish to issue is installed, which allows you to have a separate issuing CA for each certificate type or application that requires PKI.

G

geographic CA hierarchy Hierarchy in which issuing CAs are installed at each geographic location in your company. Factors that would influence using this hierarchy would be legal requirements, such as a requirement that all PKI activity must be maintained within country boundaries, or availability requirements.

Group Policy   This allows administrators to define configurations for computers by defining local policies that will be applied to each computer. For computers that are part of an Active Directory domain, an administrator can use Group Policy to set policies that apply across a given site, domain, or range of organizational units (OUs).

H

hash rule   A rule within a software restriction policy that will create a hash of the specified executable file and specify whether the executable is allowed to run or not. When an attempt is made to run an executable, it too is hashed and then the hash is compared with the restricted hashes defined in the rules.

I

IIS protocol logging   Feature that, when enabled, logs every request received by the virtual server. You can use this information to track the user's activities or to determine what an attack affected.

In-band remote management tools   The traditional tools that you use to manage your server, such as Terminal Services For Remote Administration or Active Directory Users And Computers.

infrastructure mode   Mode in which the wireless clients are required to use an access point to access the network and not use ad hoc connections to other clients.

integrated Windows authentication   Authentication method that uses the mechanism that Windows uses to authenticate computers and users in a domain. Either the NT LAN Manager (NTLM) protocol or Kerberos v5 will be used for authentication, depending on the client operating system. If you are using Windows 2000 or greater, Kerberos v5 will be used. Otherwise, the client will use NTLM authentication.

intelligent UPS (uninterruptable power supply)   This can form two connections to the server for use by EMS. It can connect using the standard serial connection and it can connect to the server through the AC power line. This means that not only can you manage the servers, you can remotely control the power to the servers.

intermediate CA   Also known as a policy CA, this is the CA that approves client requests for certificates, which are known as enrollment requests.

internal threats   Potential attacks that would be initiated from within the organization.

Internet zone rule   A rule within a software restriction policy that will grant or deny access to software by evaluating its origin in relation to the Internet zones specified in Windows.

interoperability constraints   Restrictions brought on when two applications cannot communicate with each other and therefore cannot support the security protocols used to authenticate users on a network.

IP address filtering   This involves filtering traffic based on the IP address of the client computer. You have two options to enable IP filtering: you can enable all traffic except traffic from the IP addresses listed, or you can exclude all IP addresses and allow only the IP addresses listed.

IP packet filtering   Filtering that prevents specific packets from reaching their destined ports on the server. This can be effective in guarding against packets for specific services that would not represent legitimate traffic to the server.

IP Security (IPSec)   A set of standards that will verify, authenticate, and encrypt data at the IP packet level. IPSec accomplishes this by authenticating the client and the server and exchanging keys that are used to encrypt and sign data.

Issuing CA   This is a CA that enrolls, deploys, and renews the certificates. The issuing CA is the CA that will communicate with the client applications and computers. It is the server that needs to be available all of the time for proper CA functionality.

K

Kerberos v5   The default authentication protocol for computers running Windows 2000 or higher that are in Active Directory domains.

L

LAN Manager   Authentication protocol used by older Microsoft operating systems such as MS-DOS and Windows 95. This protocol is the least secure method supported in Windows 2000 and Windows Server 2003.

M

Microsoft .NET Passport authentication   An authentication method that uses web services to authenticate users with a single logon on the Internet. If the credentials are correct, a cookie that contains a valid ticket will be written to the client. The server will check for a cookie that contains a Passport authentication ticket.

Microsoft Baseline Security Analyzer (MBSA) v.1.2   A utility that can perform local or remote scans of Windows systems. MBSA runs on Windows 2000, Windows XP, and Windows Server 2003 systems and will scan for common system misconfigurations in the following products: Windows NT 4, Windows 2000, Windows XP, Windows Server 2003, Internet Information Server (IIS), SQL Server, Internet Explorer, and Microsoft Office. MBSA 1.2 will also scan for missing security updates for the following products: Windows NT 4, Windows 2000, Windows XP, Windows Server 2003, IIS, SQL Server, IE, Exchange Server, Windows Media Player,

Microsoft Data Access Components (MDAC), MSXML, Microsoft Virtual Machine, Commerce Server, Content Management Server, BizTalk Server, Host Integration Server, and Microsoft Office. MBSA comes with a graphical version of the utility (MBSA.EXE) and a command-line interface (MBSACLI.EXE) version.

Microsoft Challenge Handshake Authentication Protocol (MS-CHAP)   Microsoft's version of CHAP. It uses the MD4 algorithm for the hash and the Data Encryption Standard (DES) encryption algorithm to generate the hash. It also provides a mechanism for changing passwords and reporting errors with the authentication process.

Microsoft Challenge Handshake Authentication Protocol Version 2 (MS-CHAPv2)   The protocol released by Microsoft in response to security issues discovered in the MS-CHAP protocol. This is the strongest password protocol supported by Windows Server 2003 for remote access and should be used when smart cards or certificates are not an option.

Microsoft Management Console (MMC)   The standard administrative tool in Windows Server 2003. The MMC is really a framework to host various management tools. It provides administrators with a standard environment from which they can manage their servers and network.

Microsoft Software Update Services (SUS)   A security update method that provides the ability for an administrator to deploy critical and security-related updates and service packs to servers running Windows 2000 or Windows Server 2003 and clients running Windows 2000 and XP Professional.

Microsoft Systems Management Server 2003 (SMS 2003)   A server product used to address change and configuration management. It is capable of application deployment, asset management, security patch management, mobile computer configuration, and Windows Management Services Integration.

Microsoft Windows Update   A web application that helps you to keep your computer up-to-date with patches, drivers, service packs, and other utilities for Windows.

modem serial connection   Similar to a direct serial connection except it involves putting a modem between the management computer and the servers. You then dial into the modem and use a terminal emulation program.

N

NT LAN Manager (NTLM)   A challenge-response authentication protocol based on the LAN Manager (LM) authentication protocol used as the authentication method for Windows 3.1, Windows for Workgroups 3.11, and Windows 95. NTLM is the default authentication protocol in Windows NT.

NT LAN Manager v2 (NTLMv2)   An enhanced version of NTLM that has better security and is supported by Windows NT 4 Service Pack 4 and later operating systems.

O

organizational CA hierarchy   Hierarchy in which the CAs are organized based on the classifications of employees in an organization. You would use an organizational CA hierarchy if you need to use different policies for issuing certificates to employees, contractors, administrators, partners, and various other classifications of users.

out-of-band remote management tools   Tools used to access the server by using something other than a network connection, like the serial port. This is helpful if the server is not responding to standard network communications, usually because the server is hung up or the network device has stopped functioning. Out-of-band services are provided by the Emergency Management Services (EMS) on Windows Server 2003.

P

parent/child trust   Parent/child trusts are by default created automatically when a new child domain is added to a preexisting domain tree. The trust between a parent and a child is two-way and transitive.

Password Authentication Protocol (PAP)   An authentication protocol where the user ID and password are transmitted in clear text to the server, where they are compared to the server's version of the same information. This is not a secure means of authenticating a user and should be avoided in most environments.

Password Extensible Authentication Protocol (PEAP)   A protocol that uses the EAP protocol with MS-CHAPv2 to authenticate users. PEAP allows the client to use a password to authenticate the user on the wireless network.

path rule   A rule within a software restriction policy that will grant or deny access to software by evaluating its file path.

permission   The part of a security right that determines what a user can do to a securable object.

Point-to-Point Tunneling Protocol (PPTP)   Developed and standardized by Microsoft to provide a simple mechanism to create a virtual private network (VPN) with Windows NT 4 and Windows 9*x* clients.

Principle of Least Privilege (PoLP)   This principle states that all users and processes should be operating using the fewest permissions necessary to complete the job. This minimizes the potential for damage should the user or process be used improperly.

property set   A group of interrelated attributes to which permissions can be granted rather than granting permissions to each individual attribute.

public key encryption (PKE)   An encryption scheme based on the Diffie-Hellman algorithm, which was first released in 1976. It allows users to share encryption keys without the need for a secure channel.

Q

qualitative analysis   A form of analysis that involves ranking the risks on a scale that reflects a resource's importance to an organization.

quantitative analysis   A form of analysis that involves estimating the actual value of an asset or what it would cost if the asset was unavailable for a period of time or if it was lost. This kind of analysis is easier to use for the availability and integrity aspects of risk analysis.

R

RADIUS authentication   A form of authentication that allows the RADIUS client to authenticate against a RADIUS server and that has become the standard for integrating various vendors' products. RADIUS is typically used by Routing and Remote Access Services (RRAS) to authenticate, authorize, and audit logon requests in a standard way. Microsoft calls its RADIUS server Internet Authentication Service (IAS), and it can be configured either as an end point for the RADIUS client or to forward authentication, authorization, and accounting traffic to another RADIUS server.

realm trust   A trust between a Windows Server 2003 domain and a non-Windows Kerberos realm. A realm trust can be either transitive or nontransitive and can go in one or both directions.

recommended security policies   Policies that may be necessary for only part of an organization. A division or department may choose to implement an optional security practice if they find it cost effective or determine that it applies to their assets.

Remote Assistance   This the same technology as Remote Desktop for Administration, but it was designed to allow someone to connect to a Windows computer to provide assistance. When a Remote Assistance session is established, both users will see the same screen and can chat with each other through the Remote Assistance chat program.

Remote Desktop for Administration   Remote Desktop for short, this provides a graphical user interface to remote computers over a local area network (LAN) and wide area networks (WANs).

Remote Desktop Protocol (RDP)   The protocol used by Terminal Services and the Remote Desktop Client.

remote management plan   The plan used to decide how to manage a network remotely, what tools should be used, and what servers should be managed.

root CA   This is the ultimate CA in an organization. It is responsible for signing all other subordinate CA certificates. The root CA is the only server role that trusts itself by signing its own certificate and issuing this root certificate to itself.

S

screened subnet   A protected area, typically a separate segment, on the network that is used to run services that are shared outside of the organization.

Secure Shell (SSH)   A technology that was developed by SSH Communications Security, Ltd. to provide for secure authentication and communications for remote shells and file transfers.

Secure Sockets Layer (SSL)   Protocol used to provide session encryption and integrity for packets sent from one computer to another. This could be client-to-server or server-to-server network traffic. It also provides a means for the verification of the server to the client and the client to the server through X.509 certificates (digital certificates).

securing data   A term that refers to controlling access to data.

security baseline   A tool that details the configuration procedures for each server, device, or application on your network.

Security Configuration And Analysis   An MMC snap-in used to evaluate the configuration of systems and optionally apply a template adjusting the configuration of the target computer based on the settings defined in the template.

security descriptor   Attributes attached to an object which identify a securable object's owner and primary group. It can also contain a DACL that controls access to the object and a SACL that controls the auditing of attempted access to the object.

security policies   Policies that explain what assets an organization secures, how they are secured, and what to do if the security is compromised. A security policy helps you make decisions about what type of security to implement by defining an organization's security goals.

security risk analysis   The process of reviewing an asset that needs to be protected and comparing the cost of protecting the asset and the likelihood that the asset will be attacked.

security threat   Anything that will prevent the availability, undermine the integrity, or breach the confidentiality of an asset.

Server Message Block (SMB) signing   An option that adds a keyed hash to each SMB packet. This allows you to guard your network against man-in-the-middle, replay, and session hijacking attacks.

Service Set Identifier (SSID)   A unique identification for a wireless network. The first security mechanism that the 802.11 standards use is the SSID. The SSID is used as a means of preventing clients from connecting. Only clients that have been configured with the same SSID as each other or the access point can connect.

Shiva Password Authentication Protocol (SPAP)   Developed for the ShivaLAN Rover product, this protocol transmits the password in a reversible encryption format. This means that this protocol is subject to replay and server impersonation attacks.

smart cards   Devices that are used to provide security solutions for authentication, e-mail, and data encryption. Smart cards store certificates and the corresponding private key in a secure manner.

software restriction policy   Policy that provides administrators with identification of the software running in their domain and that can be used to control whether or not software is allowed to execute.

Special Administration Console (SAC)   A command-line environment that provides the most common way to access Emergency Management Services (EMS) on Windows Server 2003. Used to manage the server when it is locked up or not responding to in-band communications.

stand-alone CA   Certificate authority (CA) that does not take advantage of Active Directory. When you use a stand-alone CA, you will not be able to use Group Policy to manage certificates and will be limited to a web-based or command-line utility enrollment.

standard security policies   Policies that are implemented organization-wide and represent a baseline of security in an organization. All users must comply with them, and hardware or software can be used to make sure they are enforced and to ease the burden of the security policies on the user.

system access control list (SACL)   Part of the security descriptor used for auditing securable objects.

T

Telnet   A program that runs a command console on the client computer much like the command console in Windows Server 2003.

terminal concentrator   A piece of equipment which contains a large number of serial ports that can support a connection to a server. The terminal concentrator can be connected to a network or a modem to provide terminal access to the servers it is connected to. This makes it easier to provide out-of-band communication to a larger amount of servers. A terminal concentrator also makes it easier to secure out-of-band communications.

threat modeling   A process used to describe the threats to a system and the harm they could to do to the system if it has a vulnerability.

three-pronged configuration   Configuration in which a firewall system has a minimum of three network adapters. One adapter will be connected to the internal network, one to the external or public network, and the third to a screened subnet. This configuration allows for hosts from the public and internal networks to access the available resources in the screened subnet while continuing to isolate the internal network from the wild.

Transport Layer Security (TLS)   This type of security is used to provide session encryption and integrity for packets sent from one computer to another. This could be client-to-server or server-to-server network traffic. It also provides a means for the verification of the server to the client and the client to the server through X.509 certificates (digital certificates).

tree-root trust   A trust between the tree-root domains of each tree. It is created automatically when a new tree is created in an existing forest.

trust model   A model representing the configuration of the trusts between an Active Directory domain or forest and another environment.

trusted computing base   A trusted computing base is the total combination of protection mechanisms in a computer system.

two-factor authentication   Using this authentication method, you have some additional means of authentication in addition to a password. For example, you can use the physical smart card or biometrics in addition to a valid PIN to authenticate on the network or digitally sign an e-mail message.

U

Universal group   Active Directory security groups that can have members from any domain in the forest. Universal groups can be granted permissions in any domain, including in domains in other forests with which a trust relationship exists.

UrlScan   An Internet Service API (ISAPI) filter that screens and analyzes URLs and requests before IIS has a chance to process them.

V

validated write   A permission similar to the typical Write permission, except that it evaluates the content of the write and determines if the value supplied conforms with the specified semantics.

virtual private network (VPN)   A type of networking which establishes a secure connection over a public network like the Internet.

W

Web Service Extensions   A section of the IIS Manager that allows you to disable application extensions on an individual website.

Wi-Fi   The name given to wireless networks.

Wireless Equivalent Privacy (WEP)   This uses the RC4 symmetric key encryption to authenticate clients and provide for the encryption of transmitted data. WEP uses a symmetric key, which means that the client and the access point require the same shared secret key.

X

X.509 digital certificates   Also known as digital certificates or just certificates, these are electronic documents that contain information about their owner, the public key of the owner, and the signature of the CA that certified the information in the certificate.

Index

Note to the reader: Throughout this index **boldfaced** page numbers indicate primary discussions of a topic. *Italicized* page numbers indicate illustrations.

D

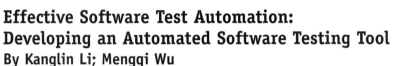

TELL US WHAT YOU THINK!

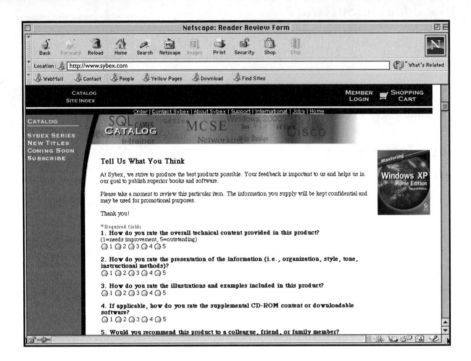

Your feedback is critical to our efforts to provide you with the best books and software on the market. Tell us what you think about the products you've purchased. It's simple:

1. Go to the Sybex website.
2. Find your book by typing the ISBN or title into the Search field.
3. Click on the book title when it appears.
4. Click **Submit a Review.**
5. Fill out the questionnaire and comments.
6. Click **Submit.**

With your feedback, we can continue to publish the highest quality computer books and software products that today's busy IT professionals deserve.

www.sybex.com

SYBEX Inc. • 1151 Marina Village Parkway, Alameda, CA 94501 • 510-523-8233